The New Santri

The **ISEAS – Yusof Ishak Institute** (formerly Institute of Southeast Asian Studies) is an autonomous organization established in 1968. It is a regional centre dedicated to the study of socio-political, security, and economic trends and developments in Southeast Asia and its wider geostrategic and economic environment. The Institute's research programmes are grouped under Regional Economic Studies (RES), Regional Strategic and Political Studies (RSPS), and Regional Social and Cultural Studies (RSCS). The Institute is also home to the ASEAN Studies Centre (ASC), the Singapore APEC Study Centre, and the Temasek History Research Centre (THRC).

ISEAS Publishing, an established academic press, has issued more than 2,000 books and journals. It is the largest scholarly publisher of research about Southeast Asia from within the region. ISEAS Publishing works with many other academic and trade publishers and distributors to disseminate important research and analyses from and about Southeast Asia to the rest of the world.

The New Santri

Challenges to Traditional Religious Authority in Indonesia

EDITED BY
NORSHAHRIL SAAT
AHMAD NAJIB BURHANI

First published in Singapore in 2020 by
ISEAS Publishing
30 Heng Mui Keng Terrace
Singapore 119614

E-mail: publish@iseas.edu.sg
Website: <http://bookshop.iseas.edu.sg>

All rights reserved. No part of this publication may be reproduced, stored in a retrieval system, or transmitted in any form or by any means, electronic, mechanical, photocopying, recording or otherwise, without the prior permission of the ISEAS – Yusof Ishak Institute.

© 2020 ISEAS – Yusof Ishak Institute, Singapore

The responsibility for facts and opinions in this publication rests exclusively with the authors and their interpretations do not necessarily reflect the views or the policy of the publisher or its supporters.

ISEAS Library Cataloguing-in-Publication Data

Name(s): Norshahril Saat, editor. | Burhani, Ahmad Najib, 1976-, editor.
Title: The new Santri : challenges to traditional religious authority in Indonesia / edited by Norshahril Saat and Ahmad Najib Burhani.
Description: Singapore : ISEAS – Yusof Ishak Institute, 2020. | Includes bibliographical references and index.
Identifiers: ISBN 978-981-4881-47-0 (paperback) | ISBN 978-981-4881-48-7 (PDF)
Subjects: LCSH: Authority—Religious aspects—Islam. | Islamic religious education—Indonesia. | Islamic preaching—Indonesia. | Islam—Indonesia—21st century.
Classification: LCC BP165.7 N53

Cover illustration: Febrian Doni
Typeset by International Typesetters Pte Ltd

CONTENTS

About the Contributors viii

1. Introduction 1
   Norshahril Saat and Ahmad Najib Burhani

   ## PART I: CHALLENGING TRADITIONAL AUTHORITY

2. Religious Authority in Indonesian Islam: Mainstream Organizations under Threat? 13
   M. Amin Abdullah

3. "Being Authoritative But No Authority?" Muslim Religious Intellectuals in Shaping Indonesian Islam Discourse 28
   Azhar Ibrahim

4. New Contestation in Interpreting Religious Texts: *Fatwa, Tafsir,* and Shariah 48
   Syafiq Hasyim

5. Aceh's Shariah Office: Bureaucratic Religious Authority and Social Development in Aceh 64
   Arskal Salim and Marzi Afriko

6. Muslim Female Authorities in Indonesia: Conservatism and Legal Notion of Women Preachers on Familial Issues 83
   Euis Nurlaelawati

7. Mobilizing on Morality: Conservative Islamic Movements and Policy Impact in Contemporary Indonesia — 105
Eunsook Jung

PART II: TRANSNATIONAL TRANSMISSION OF ISLAMIC KNOWLEDGE

8. Salafism, Knowledge Production, and Religious Education in Indonesia — 131
Noorhaidi Hasan

9. Opposing Wahhabism: The Emergence of Ultra-Traditionalism in Contemporary Indonesia — 151
Syamsul Rijal

10. Nurturing Religious Authority among Tablighi Jamaat in Indonesia: Going Out for *Khuruj* and Becoming Preacher — 177
Muhammad Adlin Sila

11. Religious Education, Sufi Brotherhood, and Religious Authority: A Case Study of the Sulaimaniyah — 196
Firdaus Wajdi

PART III: THE NEW *SANTRI*

12. Pop and "True" Islam in Urban *Pengajian*: The Making of Religious Authority — 213
Yanwar Pribadi

13. The Rise of Cool Ustadz: Preaching, Subcultures, and the *Pemuda Hijrah* Movement — 239
Wahyudi Akmaliah

14. New Religious Preacher in the Changing Religious Authority: The Offline and Online Preacher of Ustadz Abdul Somad — 258
Hamdani

15. *Santri*, Cinema and the Exploratory Form of Authority in Traditionalist Muslim Indonesia   278
    Ahmad Nuril Huda

16. The Politics of Religious and Cultural Authority: Contestation and Co-existence of Sultanate and Islamic Movements in the Post-Suharto Yogyakarta and Ternate   296
    M. Najib Azca and Moh Zaki Arrobi

17. Jihad Against the *Ghazwul Fikri*: Actors and Mobilization Strategies of the Islamic Underground Movement   317
    Hikmawan Saefullah

Index   351

ABOUT THE CONTRIBUTORS

M. Amin Abdullah is Professor of Islamic Philosophy, State Islamic University (UIN) Sunan Kalijaga, Yogyakarta. Currently he is the Head of Cultural Commission, Indonesian Academy of Sciences (AIPI).

Marzi Afriko (M. Hum) is Research Assistant of Contending Modernity Aceh (CMA) Study.

Wahyudi Akmaliah is Researcher at the Research Center for Society and Culture, Indonesian Institute of Sciences (PMB-LIPI). His study focuses on new media, Islam, and pop culture in Indonesia. Some of his works are published in the *Journal of Indonesian Social Sciences and Humanities*, *Indonesian Journal of Islam and Muslim Societies*, *Al Jami'ah: Journal in Islamic Studies*, and *Studia Islamika*.

Moh Zaki Arrobi is currently a PhD student at the Department of Cultural Anthropology, Utrecht University.

M. Najib Azca (PhD) is Senior Lecturer at the Department of Sociology, Universitas Gadjah Mada (UGM), Yogyakarta, Indonesia. He is currently the Head of the Centre for Security and Peace Studies (CSPS) at UGM.

Azhar Ibrahim (PhD) is Lecturer at the Department of Malay Studies, National University Singapore (NUS).

Ahmad Najib Burhani (PhD) is Senior Researcher at the Indonesian Institute of Sciences (LIPI), Jakarta.

About the Contributors

Hamdani (PhD) is Lecturer at the Graduate Programme of the Universitas Nahdlatul Ulama Indonesia (UNUSIA), Jakarta and Faculty of Social and Political Science (FISIP), Syarif Hidayatullah State Islamic University (UIN) Jakarta.

Noorhaidi Hasan is Professor of Islam and Politics at the State Islamic University (UIN) Sunan Kalijaga, Yogyakarta, where he also directs the Post-Graduate Studies Programme.

Syafiq Hasyim (PhD) is Director of Library and Culture of Indonesian International Islamic University (UIII). He is also Lecturer at the Faculty of Social and Political Sciences, UIN Syarif Hidayatullah Jakarta.

Eunsook Jung (PhD) is Assistant Dean in the College of Letters and Science at the University of Wisconsin-Madison (UW-Madison). She is affiliated with the Center for Southeast Asian Studies at UW-Madison.

Norshahril Saat (PhD) is Senior Fellow at the ISEAS – Yusof Ishak Institute, Singapore. He is Co-coordinator of the Indonesia Studies Programme and member of the Malaysia Studies Programme.

Ahmad Nuril Huda is currently finishing his PhD thesis on "The Cinematic Santri", at the Institute of Cultural Anthropology, Leiden University. He is also a lecturer in the Department of Religious Studies, State Islamic University (UIN) of Raden Intan Lampung, Indonesia.

Euis Nurlaelawati is Professor of Islamic (Family) Law in Universitas Islam Negeri (State Islamic University), Sunan Kalijaga, Yogyakarta and a member of the editorial board of *Al Jami'ah: Journal in Islamic Studies*.

Yanwar Pribadi (PhD) is Assistant Professor at the State Islamic University (UIN) Sultan Maulana Hasanuddin Banten, Indonesia. He is the author of *Islam, State and Society in Indonesia: Local Politics in Madura* (2018).

Syamsul Rijal (PhD) is Lecturer at the Faculty of Da'wa & Communication, Syarif Hidayatullah State Islamic University (UIN) Jakarta. His academic interests include Islamic studies, Islamic movements, Hadhrami-Arab diaspora, piety and popular culture, and Muslim youths in contemporary Indonesia.

Hikmawan Saefullah is a PhD candidate in Politics at the Asia Research Centre, Murdoch University. He is a lecturer at the Department of International Relations, Faculty of Social and Political Sciences, Universitas Padjadjaran.

Arskal Salim is Professor of Islamic Law at the Syarif Hidayatullah State Islamic University (UIN) Jakarta. Currently he is Director of Islamic Higher Education at the Ministry of Religious Affairs, Indonesia.

Muhammad Adlin Sila (PhD) is Research Professor at Research and Development Agency, Ministry of Religious Affairs, Indonesia. He is also a lecturer at the Department of Sociology, Faculty of Social and Political Sciences, Syarif Hidayatullah State Islamic University (UIN) Jakarta.

Firdaus Wajdi (PhD) is Assistant Professor of Islamic Education at the Universitas Negeri Jakarta. He is Coordinator of the Islamic Education Programme and board member of the Indonesian Islamic Education Lecturers Association (ADPISI), Jakarta.

ACKNOWLEDGEMENTS

This publication would not have been possible without the help from the ISEAS – Yusof Ishak Institute (ISEAS) and the Indonesian Institute of Sciences (LIPI). We wish to thank Mr Choi Shing Kwok (Director of ISEAS), Dr Laksana Tri Handoko (Director of LIPI), Mr Tan Chin Tiong (Senior Advisor of ISEAS), Prof. Tri Nuke Pudjiastuti (LIPI), and Dr Sri Sunarti Purwaningsih (LIPI) for their support. We also like to express our gratitude to Ms Aninda Dewayanti and Muhammad Suhail from ISEAS for their research assistance. Special thanks also go to ISEAS Publishing, namely Mr Ng Kok Kiong and Sheryl Sin Bing Peng for the hard work in reading, editing, and making the whole publication process smooth.

1

INTRODUCTION

Norshahril Saat and Ahmad Najib Burhani

Mills (1956, pp. 2–3) defines the power elite as "men whose positions enable them to transcend the ordinary environments of ordinary men and women; they are in positions to make decisions having major consequences." This definition applies to religious authority as well, but with divine and legal dimensions added, as Marc Gaborieau (2010, p. 1) defines, is "the right to impose rules which are deemed to be in consonance with the will of God". Authority here is certainly different from sheer power, or the use of force or violence, but the art of persuasion. A person with the said authority will be listened to, followed, and obeyed, not because of intimidation, money, or servitude, but because of shared values. People submit to a certain religious authority willingly and voluntarily because they believe he is the guardian of God's law, if not the voice of God on earth.

In Christianity, the institutions of authority that determine religious matters are councils or synods. Sunni Islam does not recognize such authoritative body because the gatekeepers of religion vary from one group or sect to another. Religious authority can refer to an individual *ulama* (*ustadz*) or Islamic organizations. Some of these *ustadz* serve as bureaucrats and received their appointments from the state, thus they can be referred to as "official *ulama*" (Norshahril 2018). In the case of Indonesia, the personalities can be learned individuals such as the late Haji Abdul Malik Karim Amrullah (Quranic exegete and novelist), Professor Quraish Shihab (an exegete of the Quran), the late Nurcholish Madjid (professor of Islamic studies) or Abdurrahman Wahid (former Indonesian President); or organizations such as Muhammadiyah, Nahdlatul Ulama (NU), and the Council of Indonesian Ulama (MUI). Religious authority, in different Muslim communities, can also refer to the *habaib* (descendants of the Prophet), *imam* or *marja'* (in Shia Muslim), and caliph (in Ahmadiyya). Traditionally, religious authority can be acquired and exercised by knowledgeable and devout Muslims. The construction of religious authority, as explained by Peter Mandaville (2007, p. 101), is conventionally based on "the interaction between text, discursive method and personified knowledge, with constructions of the authoritative in Islam seen as combining these ingredients to varying degrees and in diverse configurations".

In Islam, religious authority has never been monolithic, and in Sunni Islam, it has always been decentralized and contested (Feillard 2010; Mandaville 2007; Norshahril 2018). The fragmentation, pluralization, and contestation of religious authority has become a feature of Islam throughout its history. In this modern day and age, the intensity of the contestations among the different religious elites is likely to grow. In Indonesia, at least three factors have significantly influenced recent contestations within the Islamic religious arena: globalization, post-*reformasi* democratization (since 1998), and the growing number of private television stations and social media usage (Facebook, Twitter, Instagram, and YouTube). These three factors have a strong impact in shaping and animating the construction, contestation, fragmentation, and pluralization of religious authority in contemporary Indonesia.

Transnational movements, like the Hizbut Tahrir (HT), for instance, have ridden on globalization and geopolitical issues as devices to frame religious discourse, sense of unity, identity, loyalty among their followers, and construct their authority. The democratization of Indonesia after the *reformasi* in 1998 has made possible the emergence and establishment of religious organizations such as the FPI (Front Pembela Islam), MMI (Majelis Mujahidin Indonesia), and FUI (Forum Umat Islam). Some organizations that had been working underground, restricted or banned, are now actively promoting their vision of Islam in the public sphere. Some of these organizations are JI (Jemaah Islamiyah), DDII (Dewan

Dakwah Islamiyah Indonesia), LPPI (Lembaga Penelitian dan Pengkajian Islam), and HTI (Hizbut Tahrir Indonesia). These organizations have continuously challenged the authority of mainstream organizations like Muhammadiyah and NU.

The proliferation and establishment of private television channels and new modes of communication technologies have facilitated the rise of new preachers such as Abdullah Gymnastiar, Arifin Ilham, Yusuf Mansur, Abdul Somad, Mamah Dedeh, and Felix Siauw. These new media have transformed lay Muslims with limited religious qualifications—unlike the personalities mentioned above—into new religious authorities. These preachers are part of what we call in this book as a new *santri*. Still, television channels are beginning to be a thing of the past now, with preachers using alternative mediums to challenge traditional authority of the *ulama* class. Some ride on popular culture, while others on subculture and even counter-culture symbols.

For scholars on Indonesia or those who live in Southeast Asia, the term *santri* is often used to mean a religious or pious individual. The term is also used to refer to a person or groups trained in the religious sciences. In Morocco, the equivalent term with *santri* is *taleb*. Clifford Geertz (1964) has popularized this when he mentions *santri* as one of the trichotomy in the classification of Indonesian society, namely: *santri*, *abangan*, and *priyayi*. For Geertz (1964, p. 6), *santri* refers to those who adopted Islamic values as their way of life, whereas *abangan* are those who religiously stressed "on the animistic aspects of the overall Javanese syncretism". The inclusion of the last category, *priyayi*, in this classification on Indonesian people has been heavily criticized, mainly because it is a social class, and not a religious category (Burhani 2017). *Priyayi* could have *santri* religious values, i.e. *santri-priyayi*, and also an *abangan* way of life or *abangan-priyayi*.

Geertz is in fact not the first person to introduce the dichotomy of *santri-abangan*. Two Dutch missionaries and scholars S.E. Harthoorn and Carel Poensen (1836–1919) have also pointed out the categorization of Javanese or Indonesian society in the 1850s and 1880s. They wrote that the Javanese people divided themselves into two categories: the *bangsa putihan* and the *bangsa abangan* (whites and reds). The former refers to a group of people who considered Islam as their way of life inwardly and outwardly, while the latter refers to those who accepted Islam as their formal religion, but their ideas and practices were still guided by another "religion" called Javanism (Poensen 1886). In short, what is commonly called as a *santri* is the one who adopts Islam as his or her religion and makes Islamic values central to his or her life. Whereas *abangan* refers to a person who adopts Islam as his or her religion, but he or she does not make Islamic teaching central to his or her life.

In some Western scholarships, the term *santri-abangan* connotes *practising* and *non-practising* Muslims. In West Sumatra, the terms that refer to this kind of dichotomy are *kaum padri* and *kaum adat*. A few years ago, the terms commonly used by some Indonesian preachers to his dichotomy were *Islam kaffah* and *Islam KTP* (complete Muslim and Muslim only ID card). Although *santri* has been referred to as a religious category, it is actually not a single entity, and more importantly, it is an external imposition towards local indigenous communities. Previously, as Clifford Geertz mentioned in the 1960s, there were only two categories: *santri kolot* and *santri moderen*. The former refers to members of NU, commonly known as the traditionalist group of Islam, while the latter refers to members of Muhammadiyah, a modernist Muslim movement. With the development of Islam in Indonesia since the 1960s, these two categories can no longer cater to the dynamics and trajectory of *santri*. Besides the classic one, there are at least four additional groups of *santri*: neo-modernist, neo-revivalist, radicalist, and liberal (Burhani 2017, p. 345). During the 2019 Indonesian elections, one additional category of *santri* was introduced by the leaders of Prosperous Justice Party (PKS), namely: *santri post-islamism* (post-Islamism *santri*), which refers to persons like Sandiaga Uno, vice presidential candidate of Prabowo Subianto, who has a strong commitment to Islam although he is of no clear *santri* pedigree.

Some may ask, why do we use the word *santri* rather than *ulama* for the title of this edited volume? In the past, religious authority belongs solely in the realm of the learned *ulama* class, and we feel that this remains the ideal. The word *santri* is broader as it encompasses both *ulama* and religious preachers (*da'i*) in Indonesian setting, or even individuals who portray a pious image and have a wide following though not necessarily trained in religious sciences. With these new categories of *santri*, the religious authority in Indonesian Islam has become more contested. The high-brow *ulama* (those who have strong background in Islamic studies) have been contested by the low-brow (those with minimalist knowledge on Islam) but populist *ulama* and preachers. In terms of organization, previously, Muhammadiyah and

NU were often considered as the authoritative body of Islam and the main representations of Indonesian Islam. Now, one doubts if Muhammadiyah and NU remain the sole authorities in the religious sphere in this modern day and age. With contrasting *fatwās* available at their fingertips and in the world, youths can simply ask Google to get religious ideas and no longer need to rely solely on traditional clerics or big Islamic organizations.

The series of *Aksi Bela Islam* protests towards then Jakarta governor Basuki Tjahaja Purnama at the end of 2016 provided a clear example of the rise of an alternative religious authority. The authority of Muhammadiyah and NU, previously regarded as mainstream Islamic organizations in Indonesia, was challenged. The act of ridiculing, mocking, and disrespecting traditionalist *kiais* and high-brow *ulama*, such as Ahmad Mustofa Bisri, Quraish Shihab, and Ahmad Syafi'i Maarif, has become more evident in recent years. This has resulted in the undermining of *pesantren* and UIN or IAIN (State Islamic University) as the traditional system for producing *ulama* and Islamic scholars. On the other hand, new preachers and *habaib* (descendants of the Prophet Muhammad) have emerged to gain significant standing among Muslims apart from the traditional clergy.

The current phenomenon of contestation of religious authority can be seen, positively, as part of the democratization of religious authority. This can provide various Muslim communities access to religious authority and provide alternatives to the hegemony of Muhammadiyah and NU. On the other hand, religion could also be easily reshaped to cater to the demands of the market and capitalism, or prone to be manipulated to support certain political interests.

In 2010, ISEAS published a book entitled *Varieties of Religious Authority: Changes and Challenges in 20th Century Indonesian Islam*. This book focuses on *ulama*, *fatwa*, Islamic education or *madrasah*, and sufism and *tarekat* (sufi order). The book does not talk about the role of new media in constructing and deconstructing religious authority. It also briefly touches on the role of the transnational Islamic movements in the development and dynamics of religious authority in Indonesia.

This book tackles issues drawn from recent episodes. The background of this book mostly comes from the recent dynamics of religiosity in Indonesian Islam: the transformation of Habib Rizieq Shihab from, using his own term, *"pembasmi hama"* (pest eradicator) into *"imam besar umat Islam"* (highest religious authority in Indonesia Islam), the seemingly declining influence of Muhammadiyah and NU, the coming of transnational movements such as Hizbut Tahrir and Tablighi Jamaat, the rise of low-brow but populist preachers, the emergence of new *santri*, the humiliations of high-brow *ulama* like Quraish Shihab, Ahmad Syafi'i Maarif, and Ahmad Mustofa Bisri by laymen or ordinary people.

This book discusses and analyses the construction, contestation, pluralization, fragmentation, and segmentation of religious authority in Indonesian Islam. How this authority was traditionally constructed and now re-constructed? Which religious groups currently have strong influence in Indonesia? Who are the new actors who can shape the public discourse? How do these actors apply new media outlets such as Facebook, Twitter and Instagram? These are some of the questions, among others, addressed in this book.

The first part of the book discusses the general concept of religious authority and the current contestation of authority. In Chapter 2, Amin Abdullah appraises the current state of mainstream Islamic organizations in Indonesia, namely Muhammadiyah (a modernist organization formed in 1912) and NU (a traditionalist organization formed in 1926). He introduced the term "oppositional Islam" to characterize challenges to these organizations, which he referred to as official Islam. As opposed to mainstream organizations, which have shaped the country's moderate practices, oppositional Islam's message is divisive, as demonstrated during the 212 campaign against Jakarta Governor Basuki Tjahaja Purnama. Despite these challenges, Abdullah argues that official Islam's legitimacy remains strong. In Chapter 3, Azhar Ibrahim examines another group of scholars who are trained in the religious sciences but do not have religious authority. Although religious intellectuals, such as Nurcholish Madjid, Gus Dur (Abdurrahman Wahid), Amin Rais, and Ahmad Syafi'i Maarif are prominent figures in their respective fields, they are not seen as authoritative. Some even consider their views constituting blasphemy as liberal. Still, Azhar argues that their contributions and achievements must not be overlooked. Syafiq Hasyim (Chapter 4) provides a different perspective regarding traditional authority by looking at the various contestations among several Islamic groups in the field of Islamic interpretation. He posits that Islamic texts and traditions do not only undergo interpretation, but also re(interpretation) of views of classical Islamic scholars. Comparing to the authoritarian period under the Suharto New Order, where ironically the religious discursive space promoted progressive ideas, the current post-reform period resulted in conservative and exclusivist versions of Islam. Arskal Salim and Marzi Afriko (Chapter 5) provide a local example (in Aceh) of how religious authority can be weakened without proper thinking and planning, as well as lack of vision of the drafters of bureaucratic regulations. They highlighted the problems facing Dinas Syariat Islam (Department of Islamic Shariah [The DSI]) because of this lack of planning. In Chapter 6, Euis Nurlaelawati focuses on how female preachers tackle issues concerning family laws. On the one hand, women's role as religious authority is widely acknowledged in public; on the other hand, the discourse does not necessarily benefit women. Applying the theory of social movements, Eunsook Jung in Chapter 7 observes how conservative movements shape policies in contemporary Indonesia, which are no longer dominated by traditional Islamic organizations. Conservative groups are now pushing the state to adopt their Islamic worldview and competing with existing Islamic organizations that have all the while been promoting moderate Islam.

The second part discusses transnational Islamic movements and their role in the transmission of Islamic knowledge and the dynamics of religious authority in Indonesia. In Chapter 8, Noorhaidi Hasan discusses the Salafi influence which originated from Saudi Arabia's plan to spread Wahhabism to the global Muslim community. Returning graduates from the Middle East helped spread the movement of these ideas to Indonesia and organized themselves into small reading circles. Yet, the Salafi group in Indonesia is not homogeneous, and has to be distinguished from jihadist and quietists, thus not all Salafis can be considered as promoting radicalism and terrorism. In Chapter 9, Syamsul Rijal highlighted how certain groups that claimed to defend Sunnism Islam against Wahhabism ended up promoting an exclusivist, anti-liberal, and chauvinist understanding of the religion. Apart from the traditional NU, which is regarded as the gatekeeper of Sunnism, the author looks at new groups such as *sarkub* (scholars of the grave) and *habaib* that have gained popularity in the country. These groups contribute to a fair share of problems as well as gains for the whole Islamic discourse in the country. In Chapter 10, Muhammad Adlin Sila provides a new interpretation of *khuruj*, a method of preaching among Jamaat Tablighis. Based on an ethnographic study in Kebon Jeruk mosque, Jakarta, in 2010 and 2016, he argues that the practice of preaching during *khuruj* challenges the conventional conception of a religious preacher, including those from Muhammadiyah and NU or even to MUI. The *khuruj* is a way for Tablighis to obtain legitimacy even without having to obtain formal religious education. This does not bode well with the government, and some segments of society, who prefer a more centralized body to determine who can speak about Islam. In Chapter 11, Firdaus Wajdi examines the role of the Sulaymaniyah, a movement originated from Turkey. Indonesian students began to enrol in such schools not only because they can learn about religion and later become religious authorities, but are also attracted to the prospect of studying in luxurious dormitories and travelling to Turkey to complete the fourth and final year of their studies. The Sulaymanis are also sophisticated in their approach in order to gain acceptance among the students by changing their schools' name to *pesantren* (the name of Islamic boarding schools in Indonesia) and respecting the authority of the Indonesian religious ministry.

The third part of this book discusses recent issues, such as politization of religious authority and the role of new media in the fragmentation of religious authority. In Chapter 12, Yanwar Pribadi explores the complex entanglement between communal piety, religious commodification, Islamic populism, and Islamism, in urban religious congregations, known as *pengajian*. It also examines the making of religious authority in the increasingly democratized and Islamized Indonesia. He argues that the making of religious authority in Indonesia's urban areas has been frequently marked by the complexities of interactions between local expressions of Islam and foreign influences, mostly Salafism originated from Saudi Arabia and Egypt, in complex and fluctuated relationships. In the context of Islamic populism and Islamism, the members of *pengajian* groups appear to follow populist ideas in socio-political issues such as, among other things, identifying and condemning a collective enemy. In terms of ideology, middle-class Muslim groups tend to follow populist ideas on social and political issues. In Chapter 13, Wahyudi Akmaliah examines celebrity preacher Ustadz Hanan Attaki (UHA) and his movement *Pemuda Hijrah*, particularly on how online platforms such as Instagram and YouTube were used as means of Islamic preaching to reach out to young Indonesian Muslims. In contrast with established practices of Islamic teaching, this chapter argues that the key success of UHA lies in his new methods of preaching. Following the subculture's lifestyle and its symbol, he adjusted his fashion style and appearances as well as the approach's rhetoric in order to attract massive young audiences within the logic of pop culture. This, however, invited drawbacks from the subculture community, and thwarted Indonesia's moderate Islamic discourse. In Chapter 14, Denny Hamdani discusses about Ustadz Abdul Somad (UAS), currently a megastar preacher, whose way of preaching has opened the eyes of Muslims concerning a new method and proclivity of transmission of religious knowledge in the middle of old fashion Islamic preaching. The emergence of UAS in the era of new media does not only signify the changing patterns of religious authority, from traditional to a more intertwined trend of religiosity, but it has also demonstrated a successful experiment of new media as the tool of *dakwah* (propagation).

In Chapter 15, Ahmad Nuril Huda talks about the rise of cinematic *santri* in present day Indonesia that reflects the contestation and fragmentation of religious authority in the traditionalist Muslim Indonesia. He examines the extent to which the current rise of cinematic practices among the *santri* communities in present day Indonesia resonates with the projects of exploratory discourse and practices that inform the construction and fragmentation of religious authority in modern Islam. Among the *santri* communities, the role of textuality, discursive methods and personified knowledge remain central; yet this chapter shows that a turn to visual images has allowed the cinematic *santri* to explore the possibilities of using film technologies for Islamic purposes. This challenges the traditional construction of authority in their communities, which have been solidly institutionalized and dominated over centuries by and through textual tradition.

In Chapter 16, M. Najib Azca and Moh Zaki Arrobi explain the construction of cultural, religious, and political authority in the Sultanate of Yogyakarta and the Sultanate of Ternate. The narratives from these two sultanates have revealed that authority is a product of political struggle. The Sultanate of Yogyakarta has successfully reclaimed its political authority by demonstrating exceptional leadership during *reformasi*, including in maintaining peace and order and more importantly in gaining victory in the political struggle on the issue of *Keistimewaan* Yogyakarta in 2012. In Ternate, the repeated failure of the Sultanate of Ternate in reclaiming political authority during communal conflicts as well as during power struggle in the making of North Moluccas province has led to the collapse of its authority.

The issue of underground Muslim youth cultural groups is discussed by Hikmawan Saefullah in Chapter 17. He shows that unlike their predecessors who tended to regard religiosity as a private matter, some participants of "underground youths" (*pemuda underground*) display religious piety as a necessity and use right-wing Islamism as a political ideology. Overlooked by scholars of Indonesian Islam, this stream of underground movement played an important role in disseminating conservative and even "radical" narratives of Islam to marginalized youths through ways that were never carried out by mainstream Islamic organizations. The post-authoritarian Indonesia has paved the way for ideological prominence of right-wing Islamism in some underground music scenes, as manifested in the formation of religious youth collectives and communities such as the Liberation Youth, Punk Muslim, Underground Tauhid and One Finger Movement.

REFERENCES

Burhani, Ahmad Najib. 2017. "Geertz's Trichotomy of Abangan, Santri, and Priyayi: Controversy and Continuity". *Journal of Indonesian Islam* 11, no. 2: 329–50.

Feillard, Andree. 2010. "From Handling Water in a Glass to Coping with an Ocean: Shifts in Religious Authority in Indonesia". In *Varieties of Religious Authority: Changes and Challenges in 20th Century Indonesian Islam*, edited by Azyumardi Azra, Kees van Dijk, and Nico J.G. Kaptein. Singapore: Institute of Southeast Asian Studies, pp. 157–76.

Gaborieau, Marc. 2010. "The Redefinition of Religious Authority among South Asian Muslims from 1919 to 1956". In *Varieties of Religious Authority: Changes and Challenges in 20th Century Indonesian Islam*, edited by Azyumardi Azra, Kees van Dijk, and Nico J.G. Kaptein. Singapore: Institute of Southeast Asian Studies, pp. 1–16.

Geertz, Clifford. 1964. *The Religion of Java*. Glencoe, Ill.: Free Press.

Mandaville, Peter. 2007. "Globalization and the Politics of Religious Knowledge: Pluralizing Authority in the Muslim World". *Theory, Culture & Society* 24, no. 2: 101–15.

Mills, C. Wright. 1956. *The Power Elite: New Edition*. New York: Oxford University Press.

Norshahril Saat. 2018. *The State, Ulama and Islam in Malaysia and Indonesia*. Amsterdam: Amsterdam University Press.

Poensen, Carel. 1977 [1886]. "Letters about Islam from the Country Areas of Java, 1886". In *Indonesia: Selected Documents on Colonialism and Nationalism, 1830–1942*, edited and translated by Christian Lambert Maria Penders. St. Lucia, Queensland: University of Queensland Press, pp. 241–47.

PART I:

Challenging Traditional Authority

2

RELIGIOUS AUTHORITY IN INDONESIAN ISLAM: MAINSTREAM ORGANIZATIONS UNDER THREAT?

M. Amin Abdullah

Since the fall of the Suharto government (New Order) in 1998, Indonesia has transitioned towards a democratic and decentralized government. This has given Indonesians greater freedom to express their religious identity. This has also given rise to a variety of Islamic orientation embedded into political parties, civil society organizations, cultural movements, lifestyles, and entertainment (Rakhmani 2016). For the last twenty years, Indonesian Islam is not exclusively represented by the two largest Islamic organizations, Muhammadiyah and Nahdlatul Ulama (NU). Since the 2000s, the Internet and other forms of information and communication technology (ICT) have created new forms of "public sphere" through the cyberspace (Lim 2003). With the Internet, global religious fundamentalist ideology reaches out to Indonesians too. It played a significant role facilitating communications among Muslim fundamentalists, allowing them to disseminate information through their mailing lists and websites, which eventually led to a resurgence of Islamic fundamentalism in the country (Lim 2004).

Indonesian Islam transformed significantly with the end of authoritarian regime and the expansion of the use of digital technology. With the rapid growth of Internet access and extensive usage of social media platforms among Indonesians, these enable the Muslim community to express their religiosity openly, offering Quranic exegesis (*tafsir*), and starting conversations on Islamic matters. Social media platforms and private chat groups, such as WhatsApp and Telegram, also inevitably provide supporters of extremist groups such as the Islamic State of Iraq and Syria (ISIS) the space to propagate their messages (Nuraniyah 2017). Are the conservatives, the "jihadists", or the oppositional Islam (to be discussed shortly) threatening the authority of established state religious institutions, particularly Muhammadiyah and NU?

This chapter examines the current dynamics among Islamic-based groups in shaping the Indonesian Muslim identity. The first section defines "official" Islam and "oppositional" Islam and shows their distinctive characteristics. The next section addresses the problematic moves of recent oppositional Islam, using the 2017 Jakarta gubernatorial election as an example. The last section discusses existing challenges and internal reform that official Islam followers need to take so that they could lead the identity formation of Indonesian Islam that identifies with the universal values of inclusiveness, peace, and humanity.

"Official" Islam and "Oppositional" Islam

In 2002, Ian Markham and Ibrahim M. Abu-Rabi' published a book that offers a comprehensive analysis about 9/11 from a religious point of view. Citing 'Abd al-Madjid al-Charfi from Tunisia, they underlined the importance of differentiating Islam from Islamic thought. They stated that Islam can be seen from multiple lenses such as ideological, theological, and textual and anthropological perspectives (Markham and Abu-Rabi' 2002, pp. 29–30). Utilizing the ideological approach as explained by Markham and Abu-Rabi', this section defines what constitutes "mainstream" in mainstream Islam and mainstream organizations. There are two categories for the ideological approach: mainstream or "official" Islam on the one hand, and "oppositional" Islam (at times also known as Islamism) on the other hand. Mainstream or official

Islam is the way the elites understand Islam. Conversely, oppositional Islam is how non-elites understand the religion, which includes popular appreciation of the faith.

> ... Islamism, as opposed to the religious authorities allied with the state, articulate a vigorous interpretation of Islamic doctrine which finds resonance with the youth and the masses. In this case, Islamism is a major competitor of the "official" interpretation of Islam. The creative reworking of Islamic doctrine is not confined to abstract theological and philosophical discussion as much as it dwells on the problems and the concerns of the contemporary Muslim *ummah* (Abu-Rabi' 2010, pp. xvii–xviii).

It is important to note that oppositional Islam aims to change what official Islam seeks to maintain. Their understanding of Islam can be transformed into revolutionary acts. Here, Islam can no longer be perceived solely in terms of Muslims' passive acceptance of revelation. Jasser Auda (2008, p. 196) stressed that, "Fiqh and section of a prophetic tradition are shifted from being expression of the 'revealed' to being expression of 'human cognition of the revealed'". In other words, the understanding and interpretation of Muslims from various social backgrounds would determine their worldview and influence the role of Islam in their everyday life. For instance, in mainstream Islam, the elites use Islamic teachings to lead the public discourse on tolerance and religious diversity. Meanwhile, oppositional Islam uses Islamic teachings to justify their divisive messages during electoral political campaigning. In essence, the actual portrayal of Islam is more than a sacred core, as it can always be understood and interpreted differently, and even used as means to an end that suits specific interest (Markham and Abu-Rabi' 2002, p. 30).

Unlike Malaysia, Pakistan, Saudi Arabia, and Iran, Indonesia is not an Islamic state. Indonesia is a Muslim-majority country, and in its declaration of independence in 1945, there was no mention of Islam as the official religion in the constitution. However, religion or Islam is considered to be an integral element shaping its national identity. The nationalists have worked together with Muhammadiyah (formed in 1912) and NU (formed in 1926) to formulate the 1945 Constitution. The two organizations have played their roles in society, in the fields of education, economy, and cultural movement. Although the two organizations are not political parties, the founding fathers of Indonesia acknowledged their contribution in civil society, and regarded them as shapers of the Indonesian nationhood. When Christian representatives from Eastern Indonesia demanded to withdraw the phrase "... obligation to exercise Islamic teachings for Muslims" in the 1945 Constitution, key Muhammadiyah and NU leaders agreed to fulfill that request (Hefner 2018, p. 212; Latif 2017, p. 9). This particular historical moment showed that inter-religious solidarity was rooted in the formation of Indonesian national identity. The early involvement of Muhammadiyah and NU in the process of nation-building relates to how this chapter perceives them as mainstream or official Islam. Their roles as civil organizations remain the same today. They are non-state actors that work together with the government to foster peace and harmony in a religiously diverse Indonesia.

Muhammadiyah and NU elites have also participated in consultative boards to the government. When their opinions are needed in response to particular circumstances, their voices are deemed as valuable to the government's decision-making process. It goes without saying that Muhammadiyah and NU will more likely share the same stance with the government on various issues. The close relationship results in active support from Muhammadiyah and NU to state-related agenda including to defend Pancasila as the basis of Indonesian national ideology (Moesa 2007, p. 125; Syukrianto 2017, pp. 116–17).

Since the declaration of independence in Indonesia, there have been notable attempts by certain segments to rebel against the state. One example is from the DI (Darul Islam)/TII (Islamic Armed Forces) of Indonesia which sought to establish an Islamic state in the 1950s. Despite its failure, it was seen not only as a serious threat to the state's legitimacy, but also to mainstream organizations such as Muhammadiyah and NU. Today, the threats come from other ways. Undeniably, Indonesia has the world's largest Muslim population that is tolerant, living and co-existing peacefully with other communities. Islamist movements in the country are also not identical with that of the Middle East. However, they share similar spirit of revivalism that is to institutionalize Islamic law in the form of *khilafah* or *al-daulah al-Islamiyyah* as opposed to nation-state and "non-Islamic" developments, such as global capitalism, Western secularism, and modern democracy. The next section will discuss the characteristics of populist-oppositional Islam in post-authoritarian Indonesia and how they challenge the religious authority of Muhammadiyah and NU.

The Populist-Oppositional Islam

After the fall of the New Order, Indonesia entered the reformation (*reformasi*) period, ushering democratization at various levels. Other than reducing the military's role in the government agencies, one of the most significant reforms was decentralization (Hefner 2018, pp. 17–18). Ratified in 1999, and implemented since 2001, decentralization aims to bring autonomy to provinces and sub-provinces, enabling local governments to have greater control in managing resources and passing regulations. This move eventually led to the emergence of Islamic laws being passed and executed in many regions; one good example is the establishment of sharia laws in Aceh, Sumatra in 2003. The decentralization policy came together with press freedom, multiple political party system (compared to the three-party system under Suharto regime), and the ability to exercise one's constitutional rights to freedom of expression and freedom of assembly and association. These major changes provided space to previously marginal voices of oppositional Islam which were repressed by Suharto. Oppositional Islamic organizations then mobilized the masses, spreading their version of Islam through different organizations, such as Majelis Mujahidin Indonesia (MMI), Hizbut Tahrir Indonesia (HTI), Front Pembela Islam (FPI), Laskar Jihad, Jemaah Islamiyah (JI), and Forum Umat Islam (FUI) (Hasan 2006, pp. 5–6; van Bruinessen 2013, pp. 37–38, 40; George 2017, pp. 150–56; Kersten 2015, p. 281).

Several oppositional Islamic organizations are linked to Islamist organizations which proclaimed themselves to be "jihadists". They echoed sentiments that are against modern democracy, Western secularism, and Pancasila. Their interpretation of Islam is highly influenced by transnational Islamist groups, such as Ikhwanul Muslimin (Muslim Brotherhood), JI, and Salafi-Wahhabi (purist ideology) that equated modern state apparatus as *thagut* (an oppressive or unjust ruler who does not rule according to God's revelation). These ideological references relate to the background of terrorist attacks which happened from time to time since the Bali bombing in 2002, that was carried out by Al-Qaeda-linked "jihadists". Martin van Bruinessen (2013) coined the term "conservative turn" to refer to the rise of terrorist acts conducted by hardline militants after Indonesia's transition to democracy.

The term oppositional Islam here does not exclusively refer to "jihadist" movements responsible for deadly terrorist attacks in

Indonesia. More recently, oppositional Islam emerges in common public spaces: in mosques, Quranic study and recital groups (*pengajian, majelis taklim, daurah*), *rohis* clubs in high schools, and also the social media. These mediums are often utilized by oppositional Islam to promote their ideology. For example, in 2016, they mobilized the masses to pressure the government to imprison then-governor DKI Jakarta Basuki Tjahaja Purnama (Ahok) in 2016 over his allegedly blasphemous reference to Quranic verse 51 of the al-Ma'idah chapter. Oppositional Islam movements used the religious blasphemy law to pressure the government to accept their agenda (Bagir 2018, pp. 288–90; Hefner 2018, pp. 215–16). Although they were not officially registered as a political party or political civil organization, these Islam-based groups entered the political arena and openly opposed the government, riding on economic inequality and social injustice to serve their ideological interests.

To discuss the recent oppositional Islam movement in Indonesia, it is important to understand the use of the populist approach. Below are some of the essential characteristics of populism as explained by Jan-Werner Muller (2016, pp. 139–40):

- Populism is neither the authentic part of modern democratic politics nor a kind of pathology caused by irrational citizens. It is the permanent shadow of representative politics. There is always the possibility for an actor to speak in the name of the "real people" as a way of contesting currently powerful elites. There was no populism in ancient Athens; demagoguery perhaps, but no populism, since the latter exists only in representative systems. Populists are not against the principle of political representation; they just insist that only they themselves are legitimate representatives.
- Not everyone who criticizes elites is a populist. In addition to being anti-elitist, populists are anti-pluralist. They claim that they and they alone represent the people. All other political competitors are essentially illegitimate, and anyone who does not support them is not.
- It can often seem that populists claim to represent the common good as willed by the people. On closer inspection, it turns out that what matters for populists is less the product of a genuine process of will-formation or a common good that anyone with

common sense can glean than a symbolic representation of the "real people" from which the correct policy is then deduced. This renders the political position of a populist immune to empirical refutation. Populists can always play off the "real people" or "silent majority" against elected representatives and the official outcome of a vote.

Recent forms of oppositional Islam in Indonesia have these general features, specifically in the case of reactionary response to Ahok's candidacy in the 2017 Jakarta gubernatorial election. They repeatedly claimed to be the legitimate representative of the "true" Indonesian Muslim. They justify their anti-Christian rhetoric in the name of literal interpretation of Quranic verse 51 of the al-Ma'idah chapter: "O ye who believe! take not the Jews and the Christians for your friends and protectors: They are but friends and protectors to each other. And he amongst you that turns to them (for friendship) is of them. Verily Allah guide not a people unjust" (Ali 1934, pp. 155–56). The "real Muslims" versus "unreal Muslims" card was played "effectively" that it influenced several mosques in Jakarta to call on all Muslims not to perform funeral prayers for any deceased Muslim supporters of Ahok. Nowadays, the typical hostile images of Islam are easily found offline (banners, flyers) and online (status updates on social media, broadcast messages via Whatsapp, LINE, Blackberry Messenger, article posts on websites).

Oppositional Islam's divisive message is an antidote to the inclusivity approach championed by Muhammadiyah and NU. As mainstream organizations, they have been continuously working hard to build and preserve religious tolerance and strive towards peaceful co-existence among different communities. The two organizations have come a long way in promoting a compassionate Indonesian Islam narrative through *Islam Berkemajuan* (Progressive Islam) and *Islam Nusantara* (Archipelagic Islam) respectively. Both concepts generally represent the idea of Indonesian Muslims embracing multidimensionality in Islam and value plurality in Indonesia's diverse society. People who belong to communities nurtured by Muhammadiyah and NU generally believe firmly that the national slogan *Bhinneka Tunggal Ika* (many and varied, but one) is a fundamental building block that is not in conflict with Islam in any way. Despite all the hard work, Indonesia is now facing oppositional Islam, which has been gaining sympathy for its understanding and interpretation of Islam that leans towards conservatism and, to a greater extent, justifies the use of both real and symbolic violence. Moreover, sympathy and support for less moderate, inclusive religious points of view also come from Muhammadiyah and NU members (Burhani 2013, pp. 118–19), who joined activities organized by the Tarbiyah groups (Syechbubakr 2018).

Are Muhammadiyah's *Islam Berkemajuan* and NU's *Islam Nusantara* powerful enough to counter the populist rhetoric of oppositional Islam? And if the recent oppositional Islam has been seen as a serious threat to religious authority of the official Islam, how should mainstream organizations respond to the resurgence of homegrown Islamist militancy and the emergence of populist oppositional Islam? The next section elaborates on the existing challenges faced by mainstream organizations in reinforcing progressive Indonesian Islam in the future.

Conclusion: Securing the Future of Indonesian Islam

Previous studies on the "conservative turn" in Indonesia show that one of the notable factors contributing to the rise of hardline Islamist movements is the recruitment of economically marginalized people to be their devout members (van Bruinessen 2013, p. 2; Huda 2017, p. 110). Oppositional Islam targeted support from the urban poor too, including those left behind in today's global capitalistic development. Key preachers (*ustad, ustadzah*) utilize the slogan *al-Islam huwa al-hallu* (Islam is the only solution) to convince marginalized groups that the monolithic interpretation of Islam will be the ultimate saviour and hope. By delivering emotional content that resonate with their targeted audiences, oppositional Islam activists are getting new "members" that can be mobilized swiftly. On the other hand, Muhammadiyah and NU have been paying less attention to *wong cilik* (the marginalized, ordinary people) than their previous social works in the pre-reformasi era (Mulkhan 2016, pp. 26–27; Huda 2017, p. 140). The contemporary image of Muhammadiyah is one of an established organization occupied with the bureaucracy and business administration of its hospitals and schools. Meanwhile, NU leaders are busy with political affairs associated with the National Awakening Party (PKB) or United Development Party (PPP).

The absence of key Muhammadiyah and NU leaders at the grassroots level benefits oppositional Islam's reach and influence to low-income communities in urban and suburban areas. Oppositional Islam has managed to accommodate their disappointment towards the lack of economic opportunities promised by government officials, and exploit it to demand for a unitary state based on Islamic law. Their argument is that through the implementation of such laws, social injustice will end, and the government can deliver prosperity to everyone. Moreover, oppositional Islam thinks that official Islam fails to combat *al-nahyu'an al-munkar* or *haram* (sinful and forbidden) practices in society, such as gambling, the sale of alcoholic beverages, and prostitution, despite encouraging Muslims to do good deeds or *al-amru bi al-ma'ruf* (Huda 2017, p. 112). The FPI, for example, is infamous for "sweeping" (self-vigilante) public places carrying out *haram* practices (Huda 2017, p. 115; Burhani 2013, p. 136).

The rise of support for oppositional Islam can also be found within the middle- and high-income communities. Since the fall of the New Order, oppositional Islamic organizations have been able to publish books and other reading materials promoting their version of Islam. They circulate these materials in mosques, Quran reading groups, *rohis* clubs in public and private schools to gain access to the middle and upper classes. The religious-themed readings published by oppositional Islamic organizations, such as *Jihadi, Tarbawi, Ikhwani, Tahriri*, and Salafi groups are mostly consumed by young people because of their youth-friendly contents (Hasan 2018, pp. 267–80). Previously, the Ministry of Religious Affairs (*Kemenag*), Ministry of Education and Culture (*Kemendikbud*), and Ministry of Research, Technology and Higher Education (*Kemenristekdikti*) provide textbooks for religious education in state-based educational institutions. Muhammadiyah and NU also publish their own materials for teaching, such as *Kemuhammadiyahan* (foundational lesson about Muhammadiyah) and *Islam and Keaswajaan* (foundational lesson about NU) in their institutions. In addition, Lembaga Studi Agama dan Filsafat (LSAF), Lembaga Kajian Islam dan Sosial (LKiS), Maarif Institute, and the Wahid Institute are some of the leading research and publishing institutions that provide materials for general readers (van Bruinessen 2013, pp. 43, 44, 47). Given the changing contemporary Islamic literary sources that in one way or another contributes to the rise of support for oppositional Islam groups across all economic levels, I suggest that mainstream organizations should win back support for their version of Indonesian Islam by starting with the formal education institutions.

Since the 1980s, prominent scholars on Islam have pointed out that Indonesia should actively shape the face of the Islamic world through promoting its constructive Islamic education. Previously, Fazlur Rahman stated:

> I regard it as likely that, given time, opportunities, and facilities, Indonesian Islam, although currently and understandably heavily dependent on al-Azhar, *will develop a meaningful indigenous Islamic tradition that will be genuinely Islamic and creative*. Although the present state of affairs obviously needs much improvement, there are signs of hope for the future: *the feverish educational and intellectual activity*, although recent, appears to be heading in the right direction (Rahman 1982, p. 129, italics mine).

Published in *Frankfurter Allgemeine Zeitung*, Tibi (1995) also shared similar hope:

> ... since the Arab core countries of Islamic civilization have neither such a cultural-ethnical and religious foundation for inner peace nor—despite their oil-based prosperity—can neither offer economical successful development model the question comes up whether it is Southeast Asia—that is Indonesia, that will become center of Islamic civilization while moving into the 21st century because of its model capabilities.

These hopeful stance is the source of aspiration formulated in the concept of *wasatiyyah Islam* (middle path of Islam) through Muhammadiyah's *Islam Berkemajuan* and NU's *Islam Nusantara*, circulated via informal forums and Quran study sessions (*pengajian*). However, in educational institutions, the materialization of these concepts remains flawed due to a lack of social and humanities studies that discusses the complex nature of society.

Social sciences and the humanities are critical approaches that can prevent narrow-minded interpretation of Islam. They equip teachers, academics, and students with different layers of perspectives regarding the relationship between Muslims and non-Muslims, the power dynamics between Islam and the West, the fundamental values of democracy, human rights issues, and gender inequality. The failure to incorporate social sciences and the humanities also makes Islamic knowledge ('*Ulum al-din*) dull (Markham and Abu-Rabi' 2002, p. 29; Hasan 2018, pp. 272–73). Markham and Abu-Rabi' stated that:

> *The core of the field revolves around the Shari'ah and Fiqh studies that have been, very often, emptied of any critical or political content, or relevance to*

the present situation. A clear-cut distinction has been made between the "Theological" and the "political" or the "Theological" and the "social," with the former being understood as rites, symbols, and historical text only. Furthermore, *the perspective of the social sciences or critical philosophy is regrettably absent. The field of modern Shari'ah studies in the Muslim world has remained closed off to the most advanced human contributions in critical philosophy and social sciences* (Markham and Abu-Rabi' 2002, pp. 333–34, italics mine).

In addition, at the higher education and advanced studies level, Khaled Abou El Fadl also explained that:

… to become truly modernized, according to the puritans, means to regress back in time and recreate the golden age of Islam. This, however, does not mean that they want to abolish technology and scientific advancement. Rather, their program is deceptively simple [...] Muslim should learn the technology and science invented by the West, but in order to resist Western culture. *Muslim should not seek to study the social sciences or humanities. This is the reason that a large number of puritans come to the West to study, but invariably focus their studies on the physical sciences, including computer science, and entirely ignore the social sciences and humanities.* Armed with modern science and technology, puritans believe that they will be better positioned to recreate the golden age of Islam by creating a society modeled after the prophet's city-state in Medina and Mecca (Abou El Fadl 2005, p. 171, italics mine).

Recently, the National Counterterrorism Agency (BNPT) also reported similar observations, stating that "Islamic radicalization" activities are found in science and medical courses in universities.

Following Markham and Abu-Rabi (2002), Abou El Fadl (2005) and Rahman (1982, pp. 151–62), I believe that it is time for Muhammadiyah and NU to evaluate their religious education curricula and bring multi-discipline, inter-discipline and trans-discipline approaches (or also known as general education) into their educational institutions (Abdullah 2017b, pp. 53–89; al-Mestiry 2014, pp. 17, 28, 29). This will create a comprehensive learning system that provides students and teachers with analytical tools and empathy-based social skills, so that they would always keep an open mind when faced with the complexity of everyday life. Specifically, this aims to help students and teachers navigate their religious worldviews in non-reactive behaviours such that, as a Muslim and a global citizen, they would be able to manage social and cultural differences by encouraging compassionate dialogues.

In 2014, the Indonesian government declared a ban on ISIS. The key persons from the Ministry of Religious Affairs, Ministry of Education and Culture, and Ministry of Research, Technology and Higher Education denounced "radical" activities found in their institutions. They are aware that the breeding of conservative, puritan interpretations of Islam has taken place in public and private schools, as shown in the studies conducted by PPIM UIN Jakarta and Convey Indonesia (2017), Wahid Foundation (2016), Maarif Institute (2017), and Infid (2016). Referring to these findings, it is not an understatement to suggest that moderate Islam as maintained by the state, Muhammadiyah and NU is under threat at the level of discourse.

However, I believe that this does not de-legitimize the religious authority of official Islam in Indonesia. At the infrastructure level, moderate Islam in Indonesia has a strong basis in the universities, especially those at the state or national Islamic universities under the auspices of the Ministry of Religious Affairs (MORA) (Feener 2007, p. 225; Hefner 2018, p. 17; van Bruinessen 2013, p. 229; Kersten 2015, p. 288). Moreover, Islam in Indonesia has always been compromising, by re-approaching different spirituality and worldviews from the Hindu, Buddhist and the Javanese local culture and beliefs through *sinkretisme* (mystic synthesis) or the intricate convergence of *abangan* and *santri* in Javanese rural areas. These encounters barely find cultural resemblance in other Islamic communities (Ricklefs 2012, p. 10; Hefner 2018, p. 9; Lindsey 2018, p. 228; Hasan 2018, p. 255). Furthermore, unlike in the Middle East, Indonesian Muslims have had established a modern nation state and overcame ideological and political tensions that prevented them from getting defeated and de-legitimized by the transnational Islamist movements or similar oppositional Islam (*cf.* Markham and Abu-Rabi' 2010, p. xx). However, official Islamic organizations should be present at the grassroots level, deliver comprehensive religious education to all schools, colleges and universities and lead the public discourse on progressive Indonesian Islam.

REFERENCES

Abdullah, M. Amin. 2017a. "Islam as a Cultural Capital in Indonesia and Malay World: A Convergence of Islamic Studies, Social Sciences and Humanities". *Journal of Indonesian Islam* 11, no. 2: 307–27.

———. 2017b. "Multidisiplin, Interdisiplin dan Transdisiplin: Ilmu Pengetahuan dan Riset pada Pendidikan Tinggi Masa Depan". In *Era Disrupsi: Tantangan dan Peluang Perguruan Tinggi Indonesia*, edited by Mayling Oey-Gardiner. Jakarta: Akademi Ilmu Pengetahuan Indonesia.
Abou El Fadl, Khaled M. 2005. *The Great Theft: Wrestling Islam from the Extremist*. New York: HarperCollins.
Abu-Rabi', Ibrahim M., eds. 2010. *The Contemporary Arab Reader on Political Islam*. New York: Pluto Press.
Ali, Allama Abdullah Yusuf. 1934. *The Holy Qur'an*. New Delhi: Kutub Khana Ishayat-ul-Islam.
al-Mestiry, Muhammad. 2014. *Jadalu al- Ta'sil wa al-Mu'asarah fi al-Fikr al-Islamiy*. Tunesia: al-Magharibiyyah li al-Tiba'ah wa isyhar al-kitab.
Auda, Jasser. 2008. *Maqasid al-Shari'ah as Philosophy of Islamic Law: A Systems Approach*. London, Washington: The International Institute of Islamic Thought.
Bagir, Zaenal Abidin. 2018. "The Politics and Law of Religious Governance". In *Routledge Handbook of Contemporary Indonesia*, edited by Robert W. Hefner. London and New York: Routledge.
Bano, Masooda and Keiko Sakurai, eds. 2015. *Shaping Global Islamic Discourses: The Role of al-Azhar, al-Medina and al-Mustafa*. Edinburgh: Edinburgh University Press in association with the Aga Khan University.
Burhani, Ahmad Najib. 2013. "Liberal and Conservative Discourses in the Muhammadiyah: The Struggle for the Face of Reformist Islam in Indonesia". In *Contemporary Developments in Indonesian Islam: Explaining the "Conservative Turn"*, edited by Martin van Bruinessen. Singapore: Institute of Southeast Asian Studies.
Farquhar, Mike. 2015. "The Islamic University of Medina since 1961: The Politics of Religious Mission and the Making of a Modern Salafi Pedagogy". In *Shaping Global Islamic Discourses: The Role of al-Azhar, al-Medina and al-Mustafa*, edited by Masooda Bano and Keiko Sakurai. Edinburgh: Edinburgh University Press in association with the Aga Khan University.
Feener, R. Michael. 2007. *Muslim Legal Thought in Modern Indonesia*. Cambridge: Cambridge University Press.
George, Cherian. 2017. *Pelintiran Kebencian: Rekayasa Ketersinggungan Agama dan Ancamannya bagi Demokrasi*. Jakarta: Pusat Studi Agama dan Demokrasi (PUSAD), Yayasan Paramadina.
Hasan, Noorhaidi. 2006. *Laskar Jihad: Islam, Militancy, and the Quest for Identity in Post-New Order Indonesia*. Ithaca: Cornell Southeast Asia Program.
———. 2018. "Salafism in Indonesia: Transnational Islam, Violent Activism and Cultural Resistance". In *Routledge Handbook of Contemporary Indonesia*, edited by Robert W. Hefner. London and New York: Routledge.
———. eds. 2018. *Literatur Keislaman Generasi Milenial: Transmisi, Apropriasi, dan Kontestasi*. Yogyakarta: Pascasarjana UIN Sunan Kalijaga Press.

Hefner, Robert W. 2018. "The Religious Field: Plural Legacies and Contemporary Contestation". In *Routledge Handbook of Contemporary Indonesia*, edited by Robert W. Hefner. London and New York: Routledge.

Huda, Sholihul. 2017. *The Clash of Ideology Muhammadiyah: Pertarungan Ideologi "Moderat versus Radikal"*. Yogyakarta: Semesta Ilmu.

Ichwan, Much Nur. 2013. "Towards a Puritanical Moderate Islam: The Majelis Ulama Indonesia and the Politics of Religious Orthodoxy". In *Contemporary Developments in Indonesian Islam: Explaining the "Conservative Turn"*, edited by Martin van Bruinessen. Singapore: Institute of Southeast Asian Studies.

———. 2016. "MUI, Gerakan Islamis dan Umat Mengambang". *Maarif* 11, no. 2: 87–104.

Infid, Studi Tentang Toleransi dan Radikalisme di Indonesia. 2016. *Pembelajaran dari 4 Daerah: Tasikmalaya*. Yogyakarta: Bojonegoro dan Kupang.

Kersten, Carool. 2015. *Islam in Indonesia: The Contest for Society, Ideas and Values*. London: Hurst & Company.

Latif, Yudi. 2017. "Pancasila: Idealitas dan Realitas". Keynote address, inauguration ceremony of Indonesian Academy of Science (AIPI), Jakarta, 24 July 2017.

Lim, Merlyna. 2003. "From Real to Virtual (and back again): Civil Society, Public Sphere, and Internet in Indonesia". In *Asia.com: Asia Encounters the Internet*, edited by K.C. Ho, Randolph Kluver, and Kenneth C.C. Yang. London: Routledge.

———. 2004. "The Polarization of Identity through the Internet and the Struggle for Democracy in Indonesia". *The Electronic Journal of Communication* 14, nos. 3–4. http://www.cios.org/EJCPUBLIC/014/3/01437.html#Lim200 (accessed 25 May 2018)

Lindsey, Tim. 2018. "Islamization, Law, and the Indonesian Court. The More Things Change …". In *Routledge Handbook of Contemporary Indonesia*, edited by Robert W. Hefner. London and New York: Routledge.

Maarif Institute, Menolak Radikalisme dalam Pendidikan. 2017. *Menciptakan Sekolah Inklusif-Kebinekaan*.

Majelis Pendidikan Kader PP Muhammadiyah. 2017. *Negara Pancasila: Darul 'Ahdi Wasy-Syahadah: Perspektif Teologis dan Ideologis*. Yogyakarta: Penerbit Majelis Kader PPM.

Markham, Ian and Ibrahim M. Abu-Rabi', eds. 2002. *11 September: Religious Perspectives on the Causes and Consequences*. Oxford: Oneworld Publications.

Moesa, Ali Maschan. 2007. *Nasionalisme Kiai: Konstruksi Sosial Berbasis Agama. Pemikiran KH Ahmad Siddiq*. Yogyakarta: LKiS.

Mulkhan, Munir. 2016. "Asas PKO: Pendidikan Muhammadiyah Bagi Semua". *Warta PTM* (March–April): 24–27.

Muller, Jan-Werner. 2016. *What is Populism?* Philadelphia: University of Pennsylvania Press.

Nuraniyah, Nava. 2017. "Online Extremism: The Advent of Encrypted Private Chat Groups". In *Digital Indonesia: Connectivity and Divergence*, edited by Edwin Jurriens and Ross Tapsell. Singapore: ISEAS – Yusof Ishak Institute.

PPIM UIN Jakarta and Convey Indonesia. 2017. *Api Dalam Sekam: Keberagaman Muslim Gen-Z. Survey Nasional tentang Keberagamaan di Sekolah dan Universitas di Indonesia*.

Rahman, Fazlur. 1982. *Islam & Modernity: Transformation of an Intellectual Tradition*. Chicago: The University of Chicago Press.

Rakhmani, Inaya. 2016. *Mainstreaming Islam in Indonesia: Television, Identity and the Middle Class*. New York: Palgrave Macmillan.

Ricklefs, Merle C. 2012. *Islamisation and Its Opponents in Java: c. 1930 to the Present*. Singapore: NUS Press.

Syukrianto, AR. 2017. *Biografi Pak AR: K.H. Abdur Rozaq Fachruddin (Ketua Umum Pimpinan Pusat Muhammadiyah 1968–1990)*. Yogyakarta: Suara Muhammadiyah.

Tibi, B. 1995. "Indonesia: A Model for the Islamic Civilization in Transition to the 21st Century". Translated from *Fankfurter Allgemeine Zeitung*. 27 October 1995.

van Bruinessen, Martin, eds. 2013. *Contemporary Development in Indonesian Islam: Explaining the "Conservative Turn"*. Singapore: Institute of Southeast Asian Studies.

Wahid Foundation. 2016. *Potensi Intoleransi dan Radikalisme Sosial Keagamaan di Kalangan Muslim Indonesia*.

ONLINE SOURCE

Syechbubakr, Ahmad Syarif. 2018. "Nahdlatul Ulama and Muhammadiyah Struggle with Internal Divisions in the post-Soeharto era". *Indonesia at Melbourne*, 28 May 2018. http://indonesiaatmelbourne.unimelb.edu.au/nahdlatul-ulama-and-muhammadiyah-struggle-with-internal-divisions-in-the-post-soeharto-era/ (accessed 28 May 2018).

3

"BEING AUTHORITATIVE BUT NO AUTHORITY?" MUSLIM RELIGIOUS INTELLECTUALS IN SHAPING INDONESIAN ISLAM DISCOURSE*

Azhar Ibrahim

> When a society—or significant segments of a society—lacks the sort of atmosphere that values thought, that cherishes reflection, it becomes very difficult for a reform group to play its role as articulator and disseminator of ideas.
>
> Chandra Muzaffar

The rise of Indonesian religious intellectuals in the post-war period is an interesting sociological phenomenon. For the first time in history, religious intellectuals, be those trained abroad or locally, or those from mainstream education or Islamic ones, are providing leadership in the Muslim religious, cultural and intellectual discourse. Earlier, with the rise of reformist circles at the turn of the twentieth century, the traditional *ulama* (religious elites) could no longer claim to be the sole guardian and interpreter of Islam. Their authority was challenged by reformist groups, which saw religious traditionalism as a hindrance to the progress of the Muslims. In any intellectual history, inevitably the authority of one group is continuously challenged by another, be it subtle or overt. Indonesian intellectual history, especially in the domain of religious leadership, demonstrates a similar trait. The expansion of the middle class and the increase religiosity of Indonesian society lead to the expansion of Islamic education, including those at the higher level. It is within this socio cultural milieu that religious intellectuals emerged, which is separate from the traditional *ulama* hierarchy who are still the dominant elite grouping in Indonesian society.

The Indonesian intellectual discourse, like in other Third World countries, is still developing in breadth and depth. The challenge from the religious rightists—including neo-liberal market hegemony—is becoming more intensified and complex. Today there is an ongoing struggle between the various strands of Islamic orientation in Indonesia. This chapter attempts to discuss and evaluate the presence and contributions of Indonesian Muslim religious intellectuals whose position can be made distinct from the *ulama/kyai*, *ustaz*, *tuan guru* and *da'i*. To what extent can these critical voices make further inroads in challenging, or at least mitigating, and responding to, the rightist's assertions? Would intellectual responses suffice? Why is the presence of such ideas important? Underestimating them would be allowing the absence of critical ideas in the public sphere. Hence the task becomes imperative to nurture and encourage active engagement of ideas, at least in projecting itself as equally authoritative, in the midst of competing ideas. Insights into such intellectual discourse, or its feasibility, could remind us the urgency of propping a viable authoritative circle of ideas against the authoritarian postures and tendencies.

In contemporary Islamic scholarship, religious intellectuals are often associated as part of, or articulating, religious modernism. The latter, according to one writer,

> is advocated by individuals who are committed to religion, but who do not necessarily belong to the religious establishment. They are aware of science and the socio-cultural problems resulting from economic change. Their major concern is to prove that what they judge to be true religion is not irrelevant to the modern changing world (Jahanbakhsh 2001, p. 51).

In the discussions on religious intellectuals, we are essentially evaluating the role of intellectuals in society, whose presence need to be fully appreciated sociologically. As pointed out by Soroush:

> Let us not forget that intellectual activity is an offspring of modernity and that there was no specific group of people known as intellectuals in classical pre-modern society. The modern era gave birth to the intellectuals, because it was a period of rupture and transition ... in the Third World, where societies are moulting and moving from the classical or traditional age to the age of modernity, an intellectual plays a very important role which cannot be abandoned on the basis of hollow and even honourable excuses ... an intellectual's role is lasting and historical. On the basis of his theoretical innovations, the intellectual has the task of taking his society by the hand and guiding it from one state of being to another (Jameah 1999, p. 10).

These religious intellectuals are critical in opening up Indonesian Islam discourse, and introducing critical ideas and insights from the West and the Islamic world. Their intellectual interest brought about the appropriation of critical concepts into the Indonesian Islam discourse, alongside the translation of those works. For instance, it is not uncommon when perspectives from the Latin liberation theology could be traced, or thinkers like Erich Fromm and Paulo Freire are frequently quoted (many of Fromm's and Freire's work are today available in Indonesian translations) alongside their familiarity with critical Islamic scholarship that had been generated in other parts of the Islamic world, such as by Ali Syariati, Fazlur Rahman, Hassan Hanafi, Mohammed Arkoun, Jaber al-Jaberi, Abdullahi an-Naim, Asghar Ali Engineer, Fatima Mernissi, Amina Wadud, Khaled Abou El-Fadl, Farid Esack, Bassam Tibi, Adonis, Muhammad al-Ashmawy, Muhammad Sharur, Tariq Ramadan, Nasr Hamid Abu Zaid, and many more.

Defining Religious Intellectuals

Soroush's definition of religious intellectual is useful in the context of our discussion. It refers to a group of intellectuals who are "non-clerics, that is academics and people who studied the modern sciences and happen to be religious" (Jameah 1999, p. 21). At the core is an intellectual who, in Syed Hussein Alatas' (1977) terms "leadership in the realm of thinking", and the ability to explain the problems of society and find solutions to them. There are, of course, some clerics that could be considered as religious intellectuals, provided that they fulfil the attributes of being "insightful, critical, resistant strugglers, bold, familiar with multitude of sources, acquainted with modern ideas, and innovative and creative thinkers. Based on this definition, some clerics can be religious intellectuals and some academics are not" (Jameah 1999, p. 21). In other words they are theoretical innovators and critics of society and tradition.

Religious intellectuals, adds Soroush, are independent in the sense that they do not earn their livelihood from religion. Most importantly, they "are committed to religion as see it as a respected, accepted and traditional notion. And they try to explore the relationship between this notion and modern knowledge and rationality, which belong to modernity, and to build a bridge between them based on a critique of tradition and theoretical innovation" (Jameah 1999, p. 23). While religious intellectuals are inevitably challenged by clerics, few would acknowledge that their public roles have positive effects upon the clergy, a point observed by Soroush, which he saw as its revitalizing effects on the clerics:

> Religious intellectuals perform their own duty and do not do anything specifically for the clergy, but they can open their eyes to new sources and fields of knowledge and strive to mend their ways; they can warn them against transforming religion and religious thinking into an ideology; they can criticise and ameliorate their activities in their capacity as perceptive and critical observes; and they can serve as an independent group that acts alongside the clergy or facing it as a rival, thus making the clergy react and move. These are all intentional or incidental consequences of religious intellectualism, all of which can be seen as blessings for and beneficial to the clerical community (Jameah 1999, p. 24).

The Emergence of Indonesian Religious Intellectuals

Unlike the traditional *ulama*, the concerns and priorities of the religious intellectuals differed markedly, and these were demonstrated in their writings, although their tone and posture were nowhere challenging or dismissing the traditional *ulama*. Generally, the latter see the emergence of religious intellectuals not so much as an ideological threat, in comparison to the younger conservative activists in the later decades, who would see the religious intellectuals as a group deemed as sell-out or "liberals". Religious intellectuals need to be distinguished from those who have been identified as *ulama* (clerics) or traditional religious scholars. Post-independent Indonesia saw figures like A. Mukti Ali, Harun Nasution, Hazairin, M. Rasyidi, Faisal Ismail, and Alfian; these scholars were recognized as *cendekiawan Muslim*, a term to be distinguished from the traditional *ulama* and Western-trained scholars who have no or little Islamic affiliation (Rahardjo 1996). Illustrious Indonesian leaders like Haji Agus Salim, Mohammad Natsir, Syafruddin Prawiranegara and Mohammad Roem set the tone of the standing and place for religious intellectuals within the Muslim public sphere. Hadji Omar Said Cokroaminoto (in the early twentieth century) could be deemed to be the first Indonesian Muslim religious intellectual who provided leadership in Indonesian society, with a marked concern in dealing with the global, national and specific Muslim issues in Indonesia.

During the New Order (1966–98), Nurcholish Madjid, Gus Dur (Abdurrahman Wahid), Amien Rais, and Ahmad Syafi'i Maarif were among the emblematic religious intellectuals who had been at the forefront in the promotion of Islamic discourse, ranging from various fields of interests. In chapter 3 of his monograph, Bahtiar Effendy (2003) demonstrated that they also showed leadership for student activists. Today, the younger cohorts of religious intellectuals are expanding, mostly residing in academic vocation, locally and abroad, and their writings can be easily found in the local book market, apart from their active engagement in the public sphere. Amongst them are intellectual brokers, who become the interlocutor for the thinkers whose works and ideas are translated and introduced to the Indonesian Islam discourse.

The establishment of universities, think-tanks and a robust publication industry meant that there are avenues in which these religious intellectuals can write and publish. The most important marker of the religious intellectuals' contribution is raising critical and problematic issues in the public sphere. Their writings generally demonstrate an educational and engagement slant, differing from the traditional religious leaders whose works are primarily instructional and devotional; and among the resurgent *dakwah* circles, whose works are characterized by exclusive pronouncement for an "authentic" Islamic identity, free from secular and Western elements.

Trained mostly in Western or public universities, religious intellectuals like Nurcholish Madjid, Mansour Fakih, Moeslim Abdurrahman, Kuntowijoyo, Ahmad Syafi'i Maarif, Dawam Rahardjo, Jalaluddin

Rakhmat, Azyumardi Azra, Djohan Effendi, Haidar Bagir and a few others, were productive in generating critical discourse on Islam and society, which in the latter decades gave rise to younger cohorts of Indonesian intelligentsias who assumed and developed the discourse further. While their works demonstrate consistent and fair diagnosis of the problems and challenges of Indonesian society, their critical views on the current Islamic thought made them clash with resurgent Islamist groups.

If we extend the term religious intellectuals to include some clerics (defined by their training and social position as *ulama*), we can include names like Quraish Shihab, KH Aqil Siradj, KH Hussein, Gus Mus, Masud Masudi, and Nasaruddin Umar. These clerics (acknowledged as *kyai* or *ulama*), known for their Islamic scholarship and piety, in several ways shared many of the critical perspectives propagated by the religious intellectuals, although they are much closer to their *jamaah* or congregation. Today, clerics like Quraish Shihab (Jurnal Ahmad 2011) and Aqil Siradj (Ahmad Muntahal 2016; A. Ahmad Hizbullah 2011) are subjected to much criticism by their Islamist opponents, often questioning their religious standing and credibility.

Discursive Themes and Concerns

This group can be seen as responsible for developing Indonesian Islamic discourse where their contribution lies in four areas, namely in: (a) discursive themes beyond the conventional, theological, legal and faith-affirmation pronouncement, (b) introducing critical social sciences perspectives into the religious discourse, as well as (c) drawing modernist and reformist Muslim-world scholarship, which in turn brought an interest in the (d) translation of the above-mentioned works. All these bring Indonesian Islam into another level, alongside the bourgeoning middle class in the urban centres, including the *santrinization* of the middle class.

The ideas or themes taken up by the religious intellectuals include democracy and social justice; pluralism and civil society; legal reforms and interpretive methodologies; history and culture; educational reform and human rights; and accommodation for tradition and modernity. These are remarkable features of contemporary Indonesian Islam especially when we compare it to its peers in the neighbouring countries where the religious discourse is still predominantly formal traditionalistic and revivalist in content and style. Moreover the religious intellectuals' discourse generally demonstrated familiarity, if not mastery of the *turath*, in comparison with their resurgents' peers whose interests on the classical *turath* seems to be lacking, since their agenda is the return of the authentic scriptural sources. The interests in inter-faith and intra-faith dialogues have been part of their intellectual and community engagement.

But most importantly, the works of religious intellectuals are read and followed by many intelligentsia, students, activists in campuses and urban centres, especially those who have not received formal or extensive religious education. Works written by these religious intellectuals, sold and distributed in major bookstores, almost become the staple references on Islam, on issues dealing with theology, law, mysticism, history and literature. As Soroush once put it, "the religious community is heavily indebted to religious intellectuals" (Jameah 1999, p. 24) and this is obviously in the case of Indonesia. It will be interesting to note that these religious intellectuals have contributed to the development of Indonesian Islam, writing books and articles on various themes affecting the life of Indonesian Muslims, including responding to exogenous scholarship on Indonesia. Their academic training shaped their writings in terms of the range of themes, approaches and styles they adopted. Many amongst them affirmed or affiliated to reformist or reconstructionist frame of mind, which inevitably projected them as the dissenting voices against the traditionalist and resurgent camps. While the latter group performs primarily in providing religious instructions and spiritual leadership, the religious intellectuals' contributions can be seen in various fronts. Amongst others:

(a) Introducing reformist thought with the emphasis on human reason as the source of enlightenment and liberation;
(b) Contextualizing the discourse with historical and sociological discernment;
(c) Engaging in current issues and challenges, with the focus of resolving or mitigating them;
(d) Developing an Indonesian Islam discourse; affirming the universality of Islam within the particular contexts and needs of Indonesia; and
(e) Appropriating critical perspectives from social sciences and humanities, including those critical scholarships from the Islamic world, in developing Indonesian Islam discourse.

The presence of critical Islamic discourse in Indonesia today is the outcome of the intellectual leadership provided by the religious intellectuals. Their regular public engagements and publications are vital in the dissemination of critical ideas among the Indonesian Muslim public. These intellectuals were at the forefront speaking up for minorities, such as the ethnic Chinese and the Ahmadiyah community, especially when their rights and security were being challenged by the religious hardliners in Indonesia.

Although these religious intellectuals may not be recognized as *ulama*, their function as educative and discursive agents is something to be reckoned with. Their writings, often with critical depth and proper research, is a discursive terrain, that many in the traditionalist and resurgent camps have little interest and capability to commit. In the mood of *dakwah* resurgence and the growing religious rightists, their voices are not only relegated but also being subjected to criticisms and even venturing into character assassination. Such responses reminded the public of the danger of ideas of those Muslim intellectuals deemed as dangerous, aberrant and threat to the Islamic *ummah*. Today these religious intellectuals include female scholars like Siti Musdah Mulia and Siti Ruhaini Dzuhayatin, would need to justify their presence in Islamic discourse in an especially male-dominated realm (Nor Ismah 2016).

Understanding Authority

We live in an era where the authoritarian imposed their authority at will inasmuch as the non-authoritative type rose to prominence to become the authority. Fromm (2002, p. 37) distinguished two kinds of authority: the rational authority that is "based on competence, and it helps the person who leans on it to grow. Irrational authority is based on power and serves to exploit the person subjected to it". On a similar note, Freire spoke of two kinds of authority: one which is "authentic" and "true", helping to create possibilities for freedom and, in turn, is affirmed by the freedom it engenders. The second type is "authoritarianism" which is erroneous and inauthentic, often supported by an existing authoritarian power.

Authority as a form of power relation is always contested. It is challenged by virtue of one's religious credentials, and one's affiliation to some personalities and organizations. Every form of authority has never been final nor unchallenged. Possessing authority does not necessarily equate to the attainment of an authoritative status. The latter could well exists in a person, even if he has no authority in the official capacity nor acknowledged by some opposing quarters. The study of the dynamics of authority in society is useful as part of our understanding on how authority is constructed and challenged in Indonesia.

Generally Islamic religious authority in Indonesia, like in most Sunni Muslim countries, is not centralized like in the Shia and Catholic context, nor highly bureaucratized in the cases of Malaysia and Brunei. Instead we see several players, deemed as authority, spanning from the Majelis Ulama Indonesia (MUI or Council of Indonesian Ulama), in Muslim mass organizations, such as Nahdlatul Ulama (NU) and Muhammadiyah, and other religious groupings and personalities, be it clerics (*ulama*), intellectuals, teachers (*ustaz*) and preachers (*da'i*).

Sensing Authority and Authoritative

Overall, we need to deliberate why the progressive religious discourse initiated by these Muslim religious intellectuals could not make much inroads into the mainstream religious discourse. It is not uncommon that their intellectual and critical repertoires are deemed to be too high-brow, foreign-inspired or funded, and containing the agenda to undermine Islam in Indonesia.

These intellectuals are prominent figures in their respective fields, but they have never been or hardly accorded as the *authoritative* reference for Islamic thought. They consistently published, and their works are even read by segments of Muslim public, including those in the academia, but their ideas remained largely in the margin. Their academic and popular works often attract interests, and their writings are very much in circulation especially during the *reformasi* era. While they are shaping the discursive scene, and inspiring some activists and progressive circles, they also faced strong criticisms from the conservative groups, especially in the recent turn of rightist Islamic groups in the public sphere. In the urban areas, where Muslims organizations and intellectual circles have sprung, there are vocal criticisms launched against them. The diatribe against "Islam Liberal" is a case in point.

It is not uncommon that due to their ideas, the religious intellectuals are seen as "blasphemous" too (Hartono 2005), particularly relating to their positions on religious, ethnic and sexual minorities. In other words, while these religious intellectuals may be authoritative in the domain of scholarship, this does not necessarily translate to their command of authority in society. While the *ulama* and *ustaz*, including activists in some Muslim organizations and religious functionaries in the official establishment, are often seen as the guardian of the religion, the religious intellectuals are regarded as "outsiders" especially if they are seen to be less strict in their religious persuasion, by way of suggestion or insinuation of their ideological adversaries. Apparently one's intellectuality is less appealing than one's possession of symbolic Islamic image. The mark of piety and even outward dressing, could very much contribute or enhance the authority. Moreover, the tendency amongst the Islamist leaders to use emotive rhetoric and instilling fear and anxiety amongst the congregations will further provide them with the image as the "defender" of Islam.

Even in prominent *pesantren*, the works of religious intellectuals hardly made it to the "official" reading lists, since the curriculum still remained in the traditional format. Even if they belonged to the alma mater of a certain *pesantren*, there is no guarantee that their intellectual credentials would be recognized by their own alma mater. It is interesting to note that even in the institutes of higher learning, the works of these intellectuals are not commonly read and discussed, especially when the curriculum on Islamic thought is still very much biased in its Middle-Eastern sources. The public may identify them via the mass media, but their works are hardly deliberated or discussed openly in the public or given media attention.

Contending religious orientations compete to make their digital presence in the cyberspace (Turner 2007, pp. 117–44). Though much has been said about the role of the new media, it is important to note that monopolizing them does not mean the complete dominance over the discourse, as other discursive receptacles are equally important. Perhaps the significance of the new media is that it enables the religious resurgents and populists type to be at the forefront in the Internet, making their ideas quickly accessible to the Muslim public, especially the young ones. Such active presence in the Internet is starkly absent or ineffective by Muslim religious intellectuals. As such their ideas remained unknown to the larger Muslim audience.

To reiterate, the reason for this relegation is not that the progressive voices are timid or that their intellectual deliberation are weak, but because they encounter a number of obstacles. What is clear is that the progressive circles have weak support base, and their discourse could not go beyond certain circle of readers. Moreover, in a sociocultural milieu of intellectual captivity and the dominance of academic imperialism, local thinkers and scholars are hardly given prominence and recognition. As such Indonesian writers and students seem to be at ease in quoting and referring the authority of exogenous scholarship, rather than local ones.

As such the religious intellectuals' expertise and experience may not necessarily translate into being authoritative as the latter's stamping is dependent on other factors. In the context of the market of ideas, including the religious ones, the mass media and the visibility in the latter, could be enhancing the authority of a personality (be it intellectual or preacher). Often, religious intellectuals, by virtue of their style and content, could only garner a limited audience, or those who are already much affiliated to reformist and progressive audience. Conversely, those without scholarship or substantive ideas articulated in the public sphere could easily be accord the authoritative source of Islam, by virtue of their strict persuasion and affiliation to the mainstream religious establishment.

The Authority Challenged

The religious intellectuals are being challenged, not so much because their works are less rigorous in substance and theory but by the fact that they are deemed as liberal and less committed to the orthodoxy or departing from the mainstream interpretation. Hence it is not uncommon that many of the religious intellectuals are easily labelled as proponents of "Islam Liberal" denoting their aberrant religious thought and possibly working for foreign interest. It will be interesting to survey the kind of criticisms targeted against prominent religious intellectuals, particularly against Harun Nasution, Abdurrahman Wahid (Gus Dur) and Nurcholish Madjid. The latter, in the earlier decades received stinging criticisms from M. Rasjidi (1977) on the issues of *sekularisasi*, who had also launched criticisms against Harun Nasution. The senior Faisal Ismail (2010) and Adian Husaini (2005a) also targeted their criticisms against Nurcholish for the latter's secularistic and pluralistic convictions. Gus Dur in particular is criticized by Hartono

Ahmad Jaiz (1999, 2003, 2006) and Adian Husaini (2000), who are the two leading resurgent writers criticizing a group of writers, scholars and activists whom they had labelled as "Islam Liberal" (Adian and Nuim 2002; Adian et al. 2003; Zarkasyi et al. 2004; Hartono and Agus 2004; Adian 2005a and 2005b).

Generally, the preachers and teachers who are even deemed as *ulama*, have greater avenues and means to penetrate into the Muslim public sphere. The authority they possess is derived mainly from their charisma and privileged position, rather than through their scholarship and intellectual commitment. It becomes uncommon that the two groups (traditionalist and resurgent) claimed that their authority can be traced or affirmed from the Quranic injunction or they are *"pewaris nabi"* (the mantle of the prophet) (Brinton 2011). It is not uncommon to see the religious traditionalists (as represented by *kyai* and *tuan guru*) competing for authority with those revivalists *ustaz* in the urban organizations and communities, as well as with those Muslim scholars/activists as representing the more critical and liberal voices.

Apparently, the role of social media enables certain *da'is* and preachers to get more attention and coverage than the religious intellectuals. By virtue of this mass media exposure, the former is easily deemed to be the "authority" on Islamic matters. In other words, their authority is very much based on their symbolic attachment, the number of followers, and the genealogy of scholars that they harkened or associated with. While it is easy for us to identify reasons for which the Muslim religious intellectuals became relegated, and their authority challenged, the imperative point will be how to bring about the critical Islamic discourse as initiated by this group to the forefront of Muslim public discourse.

The authority they claimed or projected is mostly symbolic in nature than of substance. This group often claim their authority by virtue of "Textual Authority", where their discussions are made on the basis of asserting the scriptural verses. Khaled Abou El Fadl notes this tendency as problematic. To simply quote the scriptural authority as it is suffice and as completely justified, is intellectually unbecoming, if not authoritarian altogether. He explained:

> In the endless stream of dogma that one encounters in Muslim conferences, lectures, and publications, the Qur'an and Sunnah are affirmed as authoritative. This is often presented as if it resolves all issues. However, in reality, this is only the beginning of the inquiry.

> Importantly, one must deal with who is presenting the Qur'an and Sunnah and how they present these sources. Typically, a speaker addressing a particular issue in one of those publications or conferences will quote a couple of Qur'anic verses or hadiths and perhaps an anecdotal story from the religious traditions. Nonetheless, quotations and anecdotes do not make an argument; they simply illustrate it. It is the speaker who makes the argument and it is the speaker who chooses the illustrative quotations and anecdotes. If the speaker is ill informed, simplistic, dogmatic, or ill-intentioned, he or she will seek to exclude the vast spectrum of authoritative texts and opinions in favour of his or her own authoritarianism (El Fadl 2001, p. 41).

What has been described above also has its parallel in the Indonesian case. Instead of deliberating the discourse by the logic of objectivity and reasoning, we see writers and preachers of the traditionalist and resurgent bend invariably used the selected textual authority in which no question or scrutiny is necessary and the quotable quotes are itself the authority that all must accept. This tendency can also be observed in the academia where academic shoddiness is covered by those selected textual authority, as if the quotable references could suffice to explain anything and everything.

The Accomplishment

Despite all the above challenges it becomes imperative to recognize some of the accomplishments of Indonesian Muslim religious intellectuals. The presence and contributions of religious intellectuals is more dynamic and robust in comparison to the intellectuals with no religious affiliations. Yet their discourse in not exclusively about religion but covers other important matters, especially in addressing Indonesian societal, political and cultural issues. However there are areas in which these religious intellectuals, perhaps with the exception of Mansour Fakih and M. Dawam Rahardjo, have yet to demonstrate presence, and these include development issues from the perspectives of human economics and political economy.

Overall their achievement lies in their diagnosis of the current situation as well as providing alternative discourses and narratives to complement or replace existing dominant discourses. Although their discourse, largely academic-like in content and rigour, may not have reached widely to the Muslim public at the grassroots level, it has the potential to reach out further, as long as there is organic engagement and attachment with the Muslim publics, and their presence in the discursive realms of the academia can be sustained.

Without going through the details of their ideas, this discussion highlights some of the key ideas and advocacy made by some leading Indonesian religious intellectuals. Harun Nasution's pioneering scholarship and teaching gave a critical outlook for Islamic Studies in Indonesia, while Mukti Ali points to diversifying the approaches of studying Islam and society. In the New Order era, Islamic intellectual discourse witnessed an exciting development. With the political control tightened by Suharto's regime, Muslim intellectuals and intelligentsia channelled their creative energy to developing an Islamic discourse that is contextually Indonesia, while affirming the primacy of democracy, civil society and the rule of law. While Muslim intellectuals in many Muslim countries were drawn to the discourse of creating an Islamic state, the Indonesian religious intellectuals like Nurcholish Madjid and Gus Dur were at the forefront in deliberating the demands of *realpolitik* of a Pancasila state. This is very much reflected in Nurcholish's "Islam Yes, Political Islam No" (2008, p. 226) remark, including those by Ahmad Syafi'i Maarif (1996) of Islam's compatibility with democracy.

The affirmation of developing Indonesian Islam is well articulated in Abdurrahman Wahid's *Pribumisasi Islam* (2006), including other writers that spoke about the importance of developing *fiqh* Indonesia (Marzuki 2014). The call for the rethinking of Islamic legal thought and practices could be found in the works of Jalaluddin Rakhmat (2007). Azyumardi Azra's (2013) historical studies on the dynamics of Islamization in the archipelago put the interest on the critical study of Islamic nexus of ideas. The blending of critical social sciences in the study of contextual theology were explored in Kuntowijoyo's *Ilmu Sosial Profetik* (2008), Moeslim Abdurrahman's *Islam Transformatif* (1996) and Abdul Munir Mulkhan's *Teologi Kiri* (2002). The interest in Islamic philosophical thought is represented in various writings of M. Amin Abdullah (1995), Mulyadi Kertanegara (2007), Komaruddin Hidayat (2011), while Musa Asy'arie's (1999) cultural philosophy points to the Indonesian cultural and intellectual conditions.

Interestingly, development issues are the least being taken up as they require a specific training. Nevertheless, Islam and developmental issues are well taken up by Dawam Rahardjo (1999), while Mansour Fakih (1989, pp. 165–77) developed a series of writings on people's empowerment and critical consciousness in the hegemonic capitalist development model. Others like Eko Prasetyo (2002) wrote about the need of liberation from this repressive model. Few others took special interest in the sufistic discourse (Alwi 2001; Haidar 2006 and 2016). Three other themes that are popularly taken up are Islamic educational reforms, especially on *pesantren* and the gender issues and politics affecting Indonesian Muslim women. The importance of pluralism in the context of Indonesia's multi-religious and multi-ethnic composition is dealt with by various writers, such as Budhy-Munawar Rachman (2011).

The younger scholars have made their presence in various publications, including translating their academic theses written abroad into Indonesian language (Muhammad Ali 2016). They are generally academics working in Indonesian or foreign universities, many of whom were campus activists during their undergraduate days. The topics and issues that they engaged are far more diverse, although some, due to campus expectations, are circumscribed from engaging in the public sphere. Overall this group can be said to be the "religious intellectuals" in the making, though their promising contribution is yet to be seen. While many of them have attained higher degrees especially in Islamic Studies, and subsequently taken up post in universities, the challenge lies in their drive to function in the public sphere, especially when the syndrome of "academicism" is affecting their versatility and social commitment, apart from the public celebrity pull which eventually affect their rigour. Indeed this next generation of religious intellectuals is interesting to be tracked and assessed in the future.

Another area of accomplishment is their vocal and persistent voices in articulating the rational, universalistic and humanistic dimension of Islam. This is not only addressed to the Indonesian audience, but also to the larger human community, via translations, interviews and forums. Works from Nurcholish, Gus Dur, and recently by Ahmad Syafi'i Maarif, are some of the writings from Indonesian Muslim religious intellectuals that have been translated into English language aimed at a wider audience. This point should be emphasized, more so when prominent figures amongst them have taken up issues and problems of the Muslim world, apart from giving critical insights into the dynamics of Indonesian Muslim society. This is exactly a point made by Soroush, who saw the role of Muslim intellectuals in bringing the universal message to the larger international audience:

> The modern Muslim intellectual stands to serve the needs of other communities as well when he or she begins to question and rethink the premises of both Islamist discourse and modern discourse simultaneously. He can also show to the non-Muslim world how complex Islam truly is, once he brings to the surface the internal dynamics of Islamic discourse that have been silenced or suppressed for so long. As a result our collective understanding of Islam will be broadened and enriched (Soroush 2005, pp. 5–6).

Indeed the Indonesian religious intellectuals have demonstrated that Muslims can enter the public sphere using the common discursive language, with committed concerns over developmental transgression, democratic mutilation, environmental disaster, and other forms of ideological distortions in the realms of culture, religion, education, economy and the like.

Conclusion

The realm of religious discourse is a competing site, where invariably the authority over the discourse is constantly challenged and mediated. The predominance of religious traditionalists and religious resurgents meant that the religious intellectuals need to prove their commitment to the religious tradition inasmuch as they can be critical about it. These religious intellectuals who have produced several substantive works and perspectives, remain at the margin. Their ideas are still in the minority. The intellectual groups are hardly given patronage or aligned with the power establishment. There is no strong base of support; mosques and *madrasahs* are still within the stronghold of religious traditionalists and resurgents. The Muslim public are still largely subscribing to the mode of traditional religious ideas and practices. In a socio-cultural setting where anti-intellectualism pervades, critical intellectual perspectives are deemed as excesses and even malevolent. Apparently the rise of anti-Islam Liberal rhetoric, garnered by the resurgents, has great ramifications on the credibility of the religious intellectuals.

Their struggle and tribulations are examples of the challenge faced by any progressive group in history. Those who support progressive voices first need to consider the milieu in which they operated. Our solidarity to their endeavour and struggle are imperative. Obviously religious intellectuals alone cannot accomplish the task in cultivating and developing progressive ideas for the Muslim public. The presence of intelligentsias as intermediary, disseminator and propagator are therefore crucial. As long as the critical ideas of religious intellectuals do not penetrate deep into Muslim religious education and in the conventional religious discourse, there will be hardly any chance for the widespread reception of reformistic and progressive thought. While this may take time, religious intellectuals need to devise creative strategies to make an effective presence in the Muslim public sphere. Working with the cultural and literary circles may be a possible strategy, apart from maintaining their critical writings to be published and disseminated by committed publishing houses.

Similarly, as long as the mainstream contemporary academic discourse remains largely alienated from the reformistic and critical agenda, such will not augur well for critical discourse to develop. Moreover without institutional and consistent elite's support, the religious intellectuals could never make much inroads into the educational realms, even at the higher levels, including the mass media. Most importantly, their intellectual presence, developed and articulated in consonance with the needs of the people, will in the long run persist in substance and relevance. For those who have the interest to see a progressive Indonesian discourse developing, an alignment with and support to this group is therefore essential. The nurturing of a strong grassroots base, through the formation of various culture circles, that functions as disseminator of ideas, would ensure that critical ideas initiated by religious intellectuals could be appreciated, communicated and extended. To underestimate their roles and potentials will be unwise. Enhancing and buttressing their substantive authority through discursive means is therefore imperative in maintaining a progressive voice against the turn to conservatism, exclusivism and extremism.

REFERENCES

A. Ahmad Hizbullah MAG. 2001. *Koreksi Aqidah KH Said Aqil Sirajd: Jangan Samakan Tauhid Islam dengan Trinitas Kristen.* Yogyakarta: Yayasan Andi. http://kallolougi.blogspot.sg/2011/10/koreksi-aqidah-kh-said-aqil-sirajd.html.

Abdul Munir Mulkhan. 2002. *Teologi Kiri: Landasan Gerakan Membela Kaum Mustadl'afin.* Yogyakarta: Kreasi Wacana.

Abdurrahman Wahid. 2006. *Islamku, Islam Anda, Islam Kita: Agama Masyarakat Negara Demokrasi.* Jakarta: The Wahid Institute.

Adian Husaini. 2000. *Gus Dur Kau Mau Kemana: Telaah Kritis Atas Pemikiran Dan Politik Keagamaan Presiden Abdurrahman Wahid.* Jakarta: Dea Press.

———. 2005a. *Nurcholish Madjid: Kontroversi Kematian Dan Pemikirannya.* Jakarta: Khairul Bayan Press.

———. 2005b. *Islam Liberal, Pluralisme Agama & Diabolisme Intelektual.* Surabaya: Risalah Gusti.

———. 2005c. *Wajah Peradaban Barat: Dari Hagemoni Kristen Ke Dominasi Sekular-Liberal.* Jakarta: Gema Insani.

Adian Husaini and Nuim Hidayat. 2002. *Islam Liberal: Sejarah, Konsepsi, Penyimpangan, dan Jawabannya.* Jakarta: Gema Insani.

Adian Husaini et al. 2003. *Membedah Islam Liberal: Memahami Dan Menyingkapi Manuver Islam Liberal di Indonesia.* Bandung: Syaamil Cipta Media.

———. 2015. *Semesta Cinta.* Bandung: Noura Books.

Ahmad Muntahal Hadi, ed. 2016. *Menolak Pemikiran KH. Said Aqil Siroj.* Pasuruan: Tim Pustaka Sidogiri, 1437 H.

Ahmad Syafi'i Maarif. 1996. *Islam dan Masalah Kenegaraan.* Jakarta: LP3ES.

Alatas, Syed Hussien. 1977. *Intellectuals in Developing Societies.* London: Cass.

Alwi Shihab. 2001. *Islam Sufistik: "Islam Pertama" dan Pengaruhnya Hingga Kini di Indonesia.* Bandung: Mizan.

Azyumardi Azra. 2013. *Jaringan Ulama Timur Tengah dan Kepulauan Nusantara Abad XVII & XVIII.* Jakarta: Kencana.

Bahtiar Effendy. 2003. *Islam and the State in Indonesia.* Singapore: Institute of Southeast Asian Studies.

Brinton, Jacquelene. 2011. "Preaching and the Epistemological Enforcement of 'Ulama' Authority: The Sermons of Muhammad Mitwalli Sha'rawi". *Intellectual Discourse* 19, no. 1: 97–120.

Budhy-Munawar Rachman. 2011. *Islam dan Liberalisme.* Jakarta: Friedrich Naumann Stiftung.

Eko Prasetyo. 2002. *Islam Kiri: Melawan Kapitalisme Modal dari Wacana Menuju Gerakan.* Yogyakarta: INSIST Press.

El Fadl, Khaled Abou. 2001. *And God Knows the Soldiers: The Authoritative and Authoritarian in Islamic Discourses.* Lanham, MD: University Press of America.

Faisal Ismail. 2010. *Membongkar Kerancuan Pemikiran Nurcholish Madjid Seputar Isu Sekularisasi dalam Islam.* Jakarta: Lasswell Visitama.

Fromm, Erich. 2002. *To Have and To Be.* New York: Continuum.

Haidar Bagir. 2006. *Belajar Hidup dari Rumi.* Bandung: Mizan.

———. 2016. *Mereguk Cinta Rumi.* Bandung: Mizan.

Hartono Ahmad Jaiz. 1999. *Bahaya pemikiran Gus Dur.* Jakarta: Pustaka Al-Kautsar.

———. 2003. *Gus Dur Menjual Bapak-Nya: Bantahan Pengantar Buku, Aku Bangga Jadi Anak PKI.* Jakarta: Darul Falah.

———. 2005. *Ada Pemurtadan di IAIN.* Jakarta: Pustaka Al-Kautsar.

———. 2006. *Al-Qur'an dihina Gus Dur*. Jakarta: Hujjah Press.
Hartono Ahmad Jaiz and Agus Hasan Bashori. 2004. *Menangkal Bahaya JIL dan FLA*. Jakarta: Pustaka Al-Kautsar.
Jahanbakhsh, Forough. 2001. *Islam, Democracy and Religious Modernism in Iran, 1953-2000: From Bāzargān to Soroush*. Boston: Brill.
Jalaluddin Rakhmat. 2007. *Dahulukan Akhlak di Atas Fiqh*. Bandung: Mizan.
Jameah. 1999. "Jameah Interview with Dr. Soroush: Published in June 1998 in the Popular Tehran Daily, *Jameah* and Newly Published Book *Siyasat-Namah*". drsoroush.com. https://www.drsoroush.com/English/Interviews/E-INT-19980600 Jameah_Interview_with_Dr_Soroush.htm.
Jurnal Ahmad. 2011. *Koreksi Pandangan Prof. Dr. M. Quraish Shihab dalam bukunya Membumikan Al-Quran*. 24 November 2011. https://ahmadbinhanbal.wordpress.com/2011/11/24/koreksi-pandangan-prof-dr-m-quraish-shihab-dalam-bukunya-membumikan-al-quran/.
Komaruddin Hidayat. 2011. *Memahami Bahasa Agama: Sebuah Kajian Hermeneutika*. Bandung: Mizan.
Kuntowijoyo. 2008. *Paradigma Islam*. Jakarta: Mizan.
M. Amin Abdullah. 1995. *Falsafah Kalam di Era Postmodernisme*. Yogyakarta: Pustaka Pelajar.
Mansour Fakih. 1989. "Mencari Teologi Untuk Kaum Tertindas". In *Refleksi Pembaharuan Pemikiran Islam: 70 Tahun Harun Nasution*, pp. 165–77. Jakarta: Panitia Penerbitan Buku dan Seminar 70 Tahun Harun Nasution bekerjasama dengan Lembaga Studi Agama dan Filsafat.
Marzuki Wahid. 2014. *Fiqh Indonesia: Kompilasi Hukum Islam dan Counter Legal Draft Kompilasi Hukum Islam dalam Bingkai Politik Hukum Indonesia*. Bandung: Marja & Fahmina.
Moeslim Abdurrahman. 1996. *Islam Transformatif*. Jakarta: Pustaka Firdaus.
M. Rasjidi. 1977a. *Koreksi Terhadap Dr Harun Nasution tentang Islam Ditinjau dari Berbagai Aspeknya*. Jakarta: Bulan Bintang.
———. 1977b. *Koreksi Terhadap Drs Nurcholish Madjid Tentang Sekularisasi*. Jakarta: Bulan Bintang.
Muhammad Ali. 2016. *Islam & Penjajahan Barat*. Jakarta: Serambi.
Mulyadi Kertanegara. 2007. *Nalar Religius: Memahami Hakikat Tuhan, Alam, dan Manusia*. Jakarta: Penerbit Erlangga.
Mun'im Sirry. 2013. *Polemik Kitab Suci*. Jakarta: Gramedia.
Musa Asy'arie. 1999. *Filsafat Islam Tentang Kebudayaan*. Yogyakarta: LESFI.
Nor Ismah. 2016. "Destabilising Male Domination: Building Community-Based Authority Among Indonesian Female Ulama". *Asian Studies Review* 40, no. 4: 491–509.
Nurcholish Madjid. 2008. *Islam, Kemodenan dan KeIndonesiaan*. Bandung: Mizan.
Rahardjo, Dawam. 1996. *Intelektual, Inteligensia dan Perilaku Politik Bangsa: Risalah Cendekiawan Muslim*. Bandung Mizan.

———. 1999. *Islam dan Transformasi Sosial-Ekonomi.* Jakarta: LSAF.
Soroush, Abdol Karim. 2005. "Responsibilities of the Muslim Intellectual in the 21st Century". In *Crosscurrents: Alternatives Voices in Our Changing Times,* interview by Farish A. Noor, pp. 15–21. Shah Alam: Marshall Cavendish.
Turner, Bryan S. 2007. "Religious Authority and the New Media". *Theory, Culture & Society* 24, no. 2: 117–34.
Zarkasyi, Hamid Fahmy et al. 2004. *Tantangan Sekularisasi dan Liberalisasi di Dunia Islam.* Jakarta: Khairul Bayan.

4

NEW CONTESTATION IN INTERPRETING RELIGIOUS TEXTS: *FATWA*, *TAFSIR*, AND SHARIAH

Syafiq Hasyim

Introduction

This chapter examines the contestation among Muslim organizations and scholars in Indonesia towards Islamic interpretation. For the longest time, the interpretation of Islam has been dominated by two poles: on the one hand are the traditionalist Muslim scholars as represented by Nahdlatul Ulama (NU), al-Washliyah and Perti (Persatuan Tarbiyah Islamiyah); and on the other hand are the modernist Muslim scholars represented by Muhammadiyah and Persis. Majelis Ulama Indonesia (MUI, Council of Indonesian Ulama)—a quasi-state institution formed in 1975—is a relatively newcomer in the field of Islamic interpretation, and became more visible in the public domain during the post-Suharto era (after 1998). The coming of the reform era stimulates the emergence of a new type of interpretation of Islamic texts, offered by Muslim scholars from organizations considered to be non-mainstream: those with Salafi-Wahhabi leanings, transnational Islamic organizations, and the Jama'ah Tabligh.

This chapter traces the contestation among several Islamic groups and actors in the field of Islamic interpretation. In analysing these differences of opinions, it considers the importance of historical, political and theological variables. The local Indonesian context too is important here to reflect the distinct characteristics of interpretation of Islamic texts compared to other contexts.

The Making of Islamic (Re)interpretation in Indonesia

Interpretation of Islamic texts and traditions is integral to the religion (Waardenburg 1999, p. 2). In truth, Muslim scholars are not just interpreting the foundation texts in Islam, but also interpreting the numerous secondary "interpretations of Islam". Muslim scholars already exposed to the discipline of hermeneutics (*ta'wīl*) such as Mohammed Arkoun (1928–2010), Nasr Hamid Abu Zayd (1943–2010) and Mohammed Abed al-Jabri (1935–2010) would be familiar with this notion of reinterpreting interpretations of Islam. These Muslim scholars produce inclusive Islamic interpretations because they consider different aspects and viewpoints. The act of interpreting the various interpretations of Islam also means that the interpreter will never get through to the true meaning of Islam, which is in the hands of the ultimate owner, God (El Fadl 2010).

The history of contesting the reinterpretation of Islamic texts in Indonesia is very dynamic and encouraging. In the Suharto era (1966–98), modernist and traditionalist Muslims intensely argued and debated on their interpretations of Islam. Muhammadiyah was free to offer their version of Islam as long as it was not related to political Islam. Within Muhammadiyah, prominent scholars at the forefront of promoting the organization's interpretation were Buya Hamka (1908–81), A.R. Fachruddin (1915–95), and Ahmad Azhar Basyir (1928–94). In fact, Buya Hamka changed the strict and puritanical approach of Muhammadiyah towards the promotion of values such as "sincerity, honesty, moderation and resoluteness" (Hamka 1958; Rush 2006, p. 26). A.R. Fachruddin was a Muhammadiyah leader who combined theological, legal and local approaches to Islam. He understood *fiqh al-ikhtilāf* deeply and leaned towards the problem-solving approach. Azhar Basyir used a deep and philosophical approach in interpreting Islam. Both figures introduced a new tradition to the younger generations of Muhammadiyah regarding the meaning of non-theological aspect of *tajdīd* (Fanani 2007). Both figures were very progressive when they came to Islamic interpretation, but were quite careful in their criticism towards the state (Fachruddin 2006).

Adopting a similar tone to Muhammadiyah is Persatuan Islam (Persis) (Federspiel 2009), based in West Java. The leading figure of Persis, A. Hassan (1887–1958), published *Tafsir al-Furqan* (Hassan 1984). Persis develops the reinterpretation of Islam based on a more puritanical approach of Islam than Muhammadiyah. It rejects the model of reinterpreting Islam which blindly follows *madhāhib* (four schools of Islamic law), therefore opening the gate of *ijtihad* (activity of deciding Islamic law from the Quran and Sunnah). Menchik (2016) calls this third largest organization "Islamist". The last Islamic reinterpretation activity within Persis is quite left behind from Muhammadiyah and NU due to the limited number of resource persons who are considered as national Muslim scholars. Persis seems to decline due to contestation with other local Muslim organizations such as PUI (Persatuan Umat Islam) and Mathla'ul Anwar, and newly unaffiliated groups of Islam such as Pemuda Hijrah Bandung, HTI (Hizbut Tahir Indonesia) groups and many others.

NU, Perti and al-Washliyah live within the framework of *madhāhib*. NU and other Islamic groups believe that the interpretive productions of *madhāhib* remain indispensable to Indonesian Muslims and there is therefore no need for opening the gate of *ijtihād* as suggested by Muhammadiyah and Persis. NU only agrees with *ijtihād* within the *madhāhib* in the forms of *qawlī* and *manhajī*. The *qawlī* means the scrutiny of opinions of *madhāhib*, selecting and contextualizing the *aqwāl* (opinions) of previous *ulama* and the *manhajī* (the method) means imitating and using the method of *ijtihād* used by the scholars of *madhāhib*. However, the reinterpretation of Islamic texts gained prominence to become more open, inclusive and progressive within this organization, especially during the era of Abdurrahman Wahid (1994–99). The strict affiliation of NU to *madhāhib* is slowly minimized by Nahdliyyin (followers of NU). The general tendency of reading the texts of Islam among the NU scholars becomes more fluid and adaptive to the new developments in contemporary issues.

In 1975, a state-sponsored Islamic organization, MUI (Majelis Ulama Indonesia, Council of Indonesian Ulama) was established. Suharto was very enthusiastic to consider MUI as an umbrella institution for existing Islamic organizations (Mudzhar 1993; Hasyim 2011). Not only that, MUI was also expected to become the melting pot of various models of Islamic interpretations through its capacity as a *fatwa* body. In fact, MUI had played more as a regimist *fatwa*-maker in the Suharto era. Many of its Islamic legal and religious opinions were intended to support the interest of the state rather than that of the people. In the Suharto era, the regimist inclination of MUI was evident through its institutional tagline as the "guardian of ruling government" (*khādim al-ḥukūmah*).

Independent Muslim scholars like Harun Nasution (d. 1998), Nurcholish Madjid or Cak Nur (d. 2005), Munawir Sjadzali (d. 2004) and Quraish Shihab (b. 1944) also offered reinterpretation of Islamic texts. Nasution, the former rector of UIN Jakarta, was an important figure behind the invention of *pembaharuan Islam* (Islamic renewal). The *Pembaharuan Islam* agenda is a way of interpreting Islam that emphasized the importance of "innovation" based on rationality. Nasution criticized the traditional Sunni-Ashʿarite theology as a hindrance to progress. According to him, Islam should be rationally approached from various and different aspects: political, sociological, historical, theological and others (Nasution 1975). In the same vein, Cak Nur promoted the de-sacralization approach when reinterpreting Islam. He differentiated the sacred aspect of Islam from the secular aspect. Cak Nur's general model of Islamic reinterpretation was to combine traditional and Islamic texts, *al-muḥafazat ʿalā qadīm al-ṣāliḥ wa al-akhdhu bi al-jadīd al-aṣlaḥ* (Madjid 2008; Gaus 2010). While Munawir Sjadzali offered a modern interpretation of the concept of state in Islam (Nafis 1995; Sjadzali 1993), another progressive Quranic exegete, Quraish Shihab, established a scholarship of *tafsīr*, which is progressive and adaptive to contemporary issues and problems (Shihab 2004). Both Muslim scholars and ordinary people continue to refer to their works.

In the last decade, with the rise of identity politics and the prevalent use of social media, the readership of inclusive and progressive Islamic reinterpretation has slowly declined. Generally, Indonesian Muslims continue to enjoy "simplified" thinking and Islamic practices. They prefer to learn Islam from Muslim preachers whose approach are more direct and simple rather than Muslim scholars with depth and profound knowledge on the subject matter. This development might be in line with Harry C. Triandis' view that the general characteristics of a fundamentalist group in any religion are to avoid the complexity of the world, and this happens especially among young people who are searching for the meaning of their religion (Triandis 2009, p. 136). Marty and Appleby (1992) describe them as persons who want to have a simple solution for all problems of their life and Waardernburg (2007, p. 32) depicts this process as fundamentalization of a religion.

Illiberal Politics and Liberal Islamic Interpretation

Do politics shape the way Islamic texts are interpreted? Islamic interpretation in many cases is closely linked to politics. In the context of Indonesia, this connection is obvious and unique. The tendency of being close to power is unavoidable among Muslim organizations and scholars, although politics is deemed to corrupt Islamic interpretation.

Logically, a liberal political system, such as in the United States and Europe, would encourage liberal interpretation of religious texts. In Tunisia and Morocco, the mushrooming of liberal Islamic thought has a similar trajectory to the liberal politics of their system. However, in the context of Indonesian Islam, Suharto's illiberal politics are not identical with the illiberal production of Islamic interpretation among Muslim organizations and scholars. During the Suharto era, progressive Muslims had the edge. Suharto, who embraced *pembangunanisme* (the ideology of developmentalism) had indirectly contributed to the shaping of moderate Islamic interpretation congruent with this ideology.

In addition, the illiberal interpretation of Islam, to some extent, was marginalized because it did not match Suharto's worldview. Muhammadiyah, for instance, developed a reformist approach of interpreting Islamic texts in line with Suharto's ideology of national development. During the New Order, Muhammadiyah did not openly criticize the ruling regime because it received support from it (Fachruddin 2006). In addition, many Muhammadiyah figures were accommodated and recruited into the bureaucracy. For instance, the ministers of religious affairs were Muhammadiyah members. NU members were marginalized and therefore quite critical of Suharto.

NU also developed a solid methodology of interpreting Islamic texts. Rather different from Muhammadiyah, NU under the leadership of Abdurrahman Wahid (d. 2009) was critical of Suharto, but made political calculations before doing so. Gus Dur, for example, criticized the establishment of ICMI (Ikatan Cendekiawan Muslim Indonesia, Association of Indonesian Muslim Intellectuals) as the will of the regime to apply Islamic sectarianism within the government administration.

In terms of interpretation of Islam, however, NU also benefitted from the Suharto era. NU brought an end to political Islam. Gus Dur was firm to develop progressive Islam that does not support an Islamic political state system. This idea, of course, gave a theological foundation to Suharto to implement his policy of separating Islam from politics.

Both NU and Muhammadiyah finally agreed to accept Pancasila as the sole ideology of Indonesia (*asas tunggal*) in 1984 and 1985 respectively. MUI accepted Pancasila earlier than NU and Muhammadiyah. The acceptance of Pancasila as the sole national ideology reflects the agreement of the mainstream Muslims of Indonesia to the state ideology of this country. By accepting Pancasila, it means that all Islamic interpretation should be compatible with the content of Pancasila.

MUI Dominance

Conservative reinterpretations of Islamic texts coincided with the emergence of Islamist organizations after Suharto's resignation in 1998. The polarization of Muslim society into progressive and conservative camps also began to be visible. There were differences regarding the status of sharia law (Suryakusuma 2012, p. 209). The conservative trend did not develop during the Suharto era due to the strong state control against such discourse. Public discussions and debates on sensitive issues of political Islam such as on Islamic state, the superiority of Islam, and many others, began to rise in the post-reform era. Blatant contestation among different groups of Islam began to appear in the public sphere and all these resulted from the opening of democracy in Indonesia. As a consequence, the scholars of NU, Muhammadiyah, MUI, Persis were not the only ones offering Islamic interpretations, but also Wahhabi, Salafi, HTI, ultra nationalist Islam, and many others.

However, MUI emerged as a latecomer for the conservative camp through its role as a semi-official *fatwa*. It established its grip by monopolizing *fatwa*-making on ʿ*aqīdah*-related issues (Islamic belief). For instance, it developed a method of determining *aliran sesat* (MUI n.d.; Hasyim 2015). This can be seen as the first sign of rising conservatism because MUI centralized Islamic interpretation within a non-Islamic state system. In this regard, it has become a single authority in defining right and wrong in the interpretation of Islamic texts related to the issues of belief and faith. The older Islamic organizations, such as NU and Muhammadiyah, can tolerate MUI's full control of ʿ*aqīdah*-related issues because all Muslims need to be in one voice for ʿaqīdah as the main principle of Islam (ʾuṣūl). MUI, NU and Muhammadiyah silently agreed that the place of contestation and debate in Islamic interpretation should only be for issues centring on non-ʿaqīdah. They suggested that various interpretations and dissenting opinions are only tolerable in the field of furūʿiyyah, the issues of branch of Islam.

Since the reform era, MUI dominance in Islamic interpretation was evident in its *fatwa* collection born out of Musyawarah Nasional VIII MUI (National Congress of Ulama, MUI) in 2005. The content of the *fatwa* reflects the position of MUI in Islamic interpretation that tends to be conservative and sectarian. This *fatwa* compilation, for instance, reinstated the banning of Ahmadiyya, as well as prohibiting secularism, pluralism and liberalism (*fatwa* on Sipilis) (MUI 2005; Hasyim 2011).

The MUI *fatwa* compilation in 2005 is an important reference for many Muslim groups in Indonesia. It inspires a number of Muslim vigilante organizations such as FPI (Front Pembela Islam, Islamic Defenders Front), FUI (Forum Umat Islam, Indonesian Muslim Forum) and many others to persecute religious minority groups such as Ahmadiyya and Shia. These organizations follow the conservative and radical path that MUI has paved. Apart from that, MUI *fatwa* inspired other groups of Islam to share its conservative position. This means that there is a market for conservative and extreme interpretations of Islam.

Newly Emerging Contestants for Islamic Interpretation

In the post-reform era, the contestation of various interpretation models to the Islamic texts takes place not only between traditionalist and modernist organizations and scholars. It now involves the so-called non-mainstream groups which in the past were overpowered by mainstream organizations. New actors or contestants emerged since Indonesia has changed politically and sociologically from an authoritarian to a democratic country. The change of political landscape provides more opportunities for all modes of Islamic interpretation to be offered to citizens. However, the emergence of new actors does not eliminate the old actors. On one hand, old actors such as Muhammadiyah, NU, Persis and MUI remain influential and dominant as the reference for Islamic interpretation. On the other hand, new contestants began to have influence in the model of Islamic interpretation in the public sphere of Indonesian Muslims.

The new contestants of Islamic interpretation often contradict the ideas of old contestants in interpreting the Islamic texts. Sometimes, they not only contradict, but also challenge, established types of Islamic interpretation. The following section emphasizes how new actors or contestants become increasingly important.

Sunnah group

I use the term Sunnah to refer to groups that employ the tradition and narrations of the Prophet Muhammad as the fundamental requirement of understanding Islamic texts. The Sunnah groups tend to avoid any forms of "interpretation" because to them, Islam is what the Quran and Sunnah have stated literally and verbally. Interpretations, conversely, are commentaries to the Quran and Sunnah. The Sunnah groups outline how Muslims should obey the text and fully submit to the Quran and Sunnah. Even in instances where new interpretations are required, these must not contradict the literal meanings of the Quran and Sunnah. They avoid *ta'wīl* (hermeneutical approach to the text). I specifically call the group of Sunnah, and not "Quran", because its principle doctrine is that everything not found in the Sunnah should be rejected. The interpretation of the Quran can only be done through the Sunnah. For them, interpretation of *ulama* not categorized as *muḥaddith* (experts on the sciences of *ḥadīth*) and scripturalist are not binding. They follow the Hanbali school of Islamic law because this school claims to be the *madhhab* of Sunnah defender.

The Sunnah groups in Indonesia include those under the supervision of Muslim preachers such as Abdul Qadir Jawas, Khalid Basalamah, Syafiq Riza Basalamah, Firanda Andirja and many others. They began as a small group of followers, through Majlis Taklim and the club of *kajian keagamaan*, but has now grown and expanded. Their way of conducting Islamic teaching is fixed, targeting mainly at urban and born-again Muslims. They connect to the urban Muslim professional groups via companies, offices where they work, and many other ways and they get their *ustadz* to give lectures during Friday prayers and other occasions. A popular preacher, Khalid Basalamah, for instance has regular preaching sessions at the mosque of Blok M Square Mall. He also established Yayasan Khalid Basalamah that organizes activities like Islamic study classes to businesses such as Umrah Tour, restaurants and also centres of *zakat, infaq* and *sadaqah*. Many Salafi and Wahhabi figures have their own businesses, especially in tourism and sharia medicine (*al-ṭibb al-nabawī*).

The Sunnah groups benefit a lot from social media. They record and upload their preachings on YouTube. Interestingly, they are successful in attracting an online audience, as evident from the high viewership on their YouTube accounts. Khalid Basalamah's broadcasts on YouTube are widely viewed by thousands of people and often become viral in social media.

Islamic interpretation concerns the obligation of practising Islam in a pure way based on the literal meaning of Sunnah. All the religious practices not based on the Sunnah are rejected. Therefore, they criticize the Islamic interpretation of NU *ulama* and also other prominent ones such as Quraish Shihab, whose interpretations are not only based on Quran and Sunnah, but also include the opinions of *ulama* from the various disciplines of Islam.

The Sunnah groups that prioritize a puritanical approach in interpreting Islam challenge the theological concept of NU and also other Muslim groups. For instance, they blatantly categorized the Ash'arite theology as heterodox (*sesat*) because it accepts the use of *ta'wīl* in interpreting the attributes of God. The Sunnah groups such as Khalid Basalamah and Firanda Andirja consider those who use the *ta'wīl* as *sesat* (deviant from Islam). Such challenge to the *'aqīdah* system of NU existed in the past, though within limited circles, unlike today where it is rampant in the social media. It stimulates debates and contestation between the Sunnah groups and NU members. The Sunnah groups claimed that they are the real Ahlussunnah Waljamaah (Sunnis) because their beliefs and practices in faith and *'ubūdiyyah* are always based on credible traditions, while NU and other groups claimed to be the real followers because they follow the teachings of Salaf al-Sālih and *ulama*. In a democratic country like Indonesia, such contestations are allowed, as long as they do not promote violence and *takfīrī*.

Hijrah interpretation

Hijrah is a term originally used by Prophet Muhammad to describe the migration of oppressed Muslims from Mecca to Medina in June 622. Medina was a safe and fine city that could allow the Islamic mission to continue. In the Islamic literature, *hijrah* is defined in many ways: (1) as a migration from the abode of *kufur* to the abode of Islam, and (2) as a migration from a situation of injustice to that of justice.

In the current discourse of Indonesian Islam, *hijrah* is interpreted symbolically by a group of people as the migration of person physically and mentally to a better condition. The *hijrah* groups do not have their own method of Islamic interpretation, but depend on the help of other *ulama*. Most *hijrah* groups follow the Salafi/Wahhabi interpretations. Indonesian Salafi figures like Khalid Basalamah, Syafiq Basalamah, and Adi Hidayat have significant followings within their circles. Teuku Wisnu, a prominent *hijrah*-inspired movie actor, studied the texts written by Syafiq Basalamah and other Salafi-Wahhabi inclined preachers. As a result, many Salafi and Wahhabi-oriented *hijrah* groups mimic their teachers when condemning those practising what they consider as *jahiliyya* (ignorance) practices. Teuku Wisnu once said that reciting *al-fatihah* (the first chapter of the Quran for those who passed away—a common practice among Indonesian Muslims) is not found in the practice of Prophet Muhammad's life.

However, the *hijrah* communities are also not monolithic in their ideology and belief. For instance, they adopt a different outward appearance from the general Salafi-Wahhabi groups. One example is the Gerakan Pemuda Hijrah, which is identified by its leader Hanan Ataki. This group is in line with other Muslim groups such as Muhammadiyah and NU in terms of their reference towards the Quran and Sunnah. This community is popular among millennial Muslims in Bandung, West Java, because its approach and subject of preaching touch the hearts of young people. Instead of wearing strict Islamic symbols like Salafi-Wahhabi preachers, Hanan Ataki often puts on a white t-shirt, jeans and *beanie* during his classes. He does not adopt an emotional and agitated tone while preaching, but his audience adores his Quranic recitation and simple explanation of complex issues. His *tartil* pitch plays into the hearts of the audience. Many young people in Bandung idolize and look up to him as their spiritual leader.

The influence of Jama'ah Tabligh towards the *hijrah* communities is obvious among celebrities. One of the first musicians to undergo such Islamic spiritual migration later became a member of Jama'ah Tabligh. Saktia Ari Seno (Salman al-Jugjawy), the former guitarist of the *Sheila on 7* band, Derry Sulaiman, Yuki Pas Band and Reza Noah, declared themselves as converts of Jama'ah Tabligh. They were attracted to the simplicity and clarity of the teachings. Jama'ah Tabligh's messages to its followers are simple: to increase "faḍa'il al-aʿmal" (the pristine deed of Islam), to preach to non-Muslims and to avoid the prohibited practices of Islam. They emphasized on *al-amr bi al-ma'marūf wa al-nahy 'an al-munkar* (commanding rights and forbidding wrongs) (Cook 2004).

Populist orientations of Islamic (re)interpretation

Although the populist orientation is not a new phenomenon in Indonesia, it has gained prominence in the 2017 Jakarta gubernatorial election. This event segregated and polarized the Muslim community not only in Jakarta but also in other provinces. Supporters of this mode of interpretation were not only preaching in Jakarta but in other provinces of Indonesia as well. Ustadz Abdul Somad, for instance, is popular in the outer Islands and Jakarta. The Jakarta gubernatorial election in 2017 was the starting point for the emergence of populist orientation in Islam.

The populist orientation emerged out of the protest by Muslim groups towards the speech made by Basuki Tjahaja Purnama (the governor of Jakarta). The speech was considered to have constituted blasphemy towards the Quran and Prophet Muhammad. Groups calling themselves the 212 or 414 groups or Presidium Alumni 212 were very successful in garnering support from the masses. The court later charged Ahok with a two-year jail sentence. The groups referred to an MUI *fatwa*. Later, this movement set up the GNPF-MUI (Gerakan Nasional Pengawal Fatwa-MUI, the National Movement to Uphold the Fatwa of the Indonesian Council of Ulama), claiming to be the guardians of the MUI *fatwa*. What was meant by the MUI *fatwa* in this context was very limited as it only referred to the *Pendapat dan Sikap Keagamaan MUI*.

The GNPF-MUI also tried to create their own Islamic interpretations on other similar cases. In another instance, they mobilized their supporters to hold the Friday prayer along the Sudirman-Thamrin road. They targeted at the Indonesian government because they believed that through the police, the government disallowed them to perform their prayers there. They were also angry with the MUI elites because they too prevented them from conducting their mass prayers there. Because of this, the GNPF-MUI changed its name to GNPF-Ulama. In traditional Islamic jurisprudence, it is recommended that the Friday prayer be held at a mosque, but GNFP-MUI interpreted this to also mean that the prayer can be held outside the grand mosque. The move elicited responses from both MUI and NU: MUI advised GNPF-MUI not to hold the Friday prayer at the Sudirman-Thamrin road; NU too rejected the plan of holding the Friday prayer at the Sudirman-Thamrin road because this would disrupt public space, which should be protected from being dominated by the interest of any one group. Using an Islamic legal argument, NU states that holding the Friday prayer in a public space is against the principle of *maṣlaḥa*. Consequently, the planned Friday prayer was moved to the Monument Nasional, Jakarta. Although MUI was not happy and NU clearly rejected the plan, the change of the venue from the Sudirman-Thamrin road to the National Monument (Monas) of Jakarta was somewhat a compromise. Finally, the Friday prayer was held without any violence. In addition to that, President Jokowi surprised many by attending the session. It gave the impression that GNPF-MUI's interpretation regarding the venue of the Friday prayer—represented by Rizieq Shihab, Bachtiar Nasir, Ustad Tengku Zulkarnain and some others—attracted significant followings in Jakarta. In addition, the influence of 212 groups became very important and gained significant reference points among a segment of Indonesian Muslims.

Political Islam

There is a group that interprets Islamic texts bearing nuances of political Islam, both in the soft and hard forms. The soft form of political Islam is done through shariatization of life, but stopped short of asking for the establishment of an Islamic state. The PKS (Partai Keadilan Sejahtera, Prosperous Justice Party) belongs to this group. The hard form of political Islam is done through the establishment of an Islamic political system such as HTI via *khilāfat*. In doing so, contesting the interpretation of Islamic texts in the public sphere of Indonesian Muslims occupies a very important place.

As a political party, the role of PKS in Islamic interpretation is rather unique. PKS argues that as a *dakwah*-based party, providing Islamic interpretation is one of its responsibilities, as *dakwah* and politics should be unified and integrated. Through its leaders and *ulama*, PKS produces its own interpretation of Islamic texts which are different from other Islamic political parties such as PKB (National Awakening Party) and PAN (National Mandate Party) that refer to their mother organizations, NU and Muhammadiyah respectively. The PKS *ulama* which is structurally under Dewan Syariah PKS issues *fatwa*, *bayan* (explanation) and *tadzkirah* (warning).

PKS does not follow any *madhāhib* (schools of jurisprudence) but continues to use the works of books written by the *ulama* of four schools of Islamic law, although in the PKS there are those who follow Ḥanafī, Mālik, Shāfiʿī and Ibn Ḥanbal. In many cases, PKS' preference of the Muslim Brotherhood-type of interpreting the politics related-Islamic texts that tends to support the establishment of political Islam is observable. It is understandable if PKS, like other conservative Muslim organizations, agrees with the intervention of the state to regulate religious freedom. PKS, therefore, is very supportive of the state in banning deviant groups (*aliran sesat*) such as Ahmadiyya and Shia. In short, PKS endorses all kinds of Islamic interpretation that support the shariatization of Indonesia.

Adopting a similar model is the HTI (Hizbut Tahir Indonesia, Liberal Party of Indonesia), although in political issues, PKS and HTI do not always share similar perspective. The way HTI interprets Islamic texts is by referring to the thought of its founder, Taqiyuddin al-Nabhani (1914–77) (Osman 2018; Hilmy 2010). The central idea of HTI interpretation of Islamic texts is based on sharia implementation and the proper establishment of an Islamic political system. In this case, they support the concept of *khilāfah*. HTI is dedicated to the strengthening of the *khilāfah* system so that it becomes acceptable among Indonesian Muslims. They consider the *khilāfah* system as the solution to all problems.

HTI also releases Islamic legal opinions on issues concerning belief, lifestyle and economics. All these issues are placed under the framework of the *khilāfah* system. Therefore, the HTI is against secularism and democracy, which they considered as a *tāghût* (satanic) system. Because of this, HTI rejects religious freedom, pluralism, women empowerment, free market and all other systems identified as Western elements. HTI contends that Muslims should follow a sharia-based economic system. The strength of HTI in this regard is its capability in packaging Islamic discourse to win the hearts of intellectuals and young educated people. One example of a personality who fits this mode of thinking is Felix Siauw, who adopts simple interpretations to gain sympathy among the young and educated. Although Siauw's books are not based on strong and sophisticated arguments, or on extensive data and scientific Islamic discipline, they are able to attract the young and educated.

At some levels, HTI also gets support from other groups even from within Muhammadiyah and NU. The support from Muhammadiyah seems to be greater than that from NU. HTI feels that Muhammadiyah provides more space for HTI thought. Despite this fact, NU Garis Lurus does not agree with the establishment of a *khilāfah* system in Indonesia. This group draws many similarities with the HTI mission: for instance, to enforce *al-amr bi al-ma'rūf wa al-nahy 'an al-munkar* and to fight against liberalism, secularism and pluralism. Ustadz Abdul Somad who has NU cultural and theological affiliation often talks about the idea of *khilāfat*. On the one hand, mainstreaming *khilāfat* is a strategic method of HTI to popularize its ideology, but on the other hand, it is HTI's weakness as *khilāfat* is not the solution to all problems.

Conclusion

Recent contestations concerning textual interpretations do not produce new ideas or concepts. Muhammadiyah and NU have, for instance, argued over whether Islamic interpretations should be based on a direct reading of the Quran and Sunnah, or rely on interpretations of savants of the past. Muhammadiyah believes in a direct interpretation of the Quran and Sunnah and rejects fidelity to *madhāhab*; while NU believes in an intermediary (agency) class, through classical jurists. The new actors of Islamic interpretation are also wrestling on similar issues to what Muhammadiyah and NU have contested for decades. The Sunnah groups are offering puritanical interpretations of Islamic texts, while populist Islamic interpretations seek Muslims political support through exploiting their grievances.

Interpreting Islamic texts is closely related to the political, ideological, and pragmatic interests of the interpreter. Such interpretations will be used to support the aspirations of their patrons. A right-leaning interpretation of Islamic texts is always associated with the right of the political spectrum. New participants of the Islamic interpretation domain often capitalized on the social media to disseminate their ideas. They are able to package their ideas to become "instagramable" and "youtubeable". The progressive and moderate type of Islamic interpretation is often left behind by their conservative and Islamist-type counterparts when it comes to social media campaign. In all, the art of Islamic interpretation now is no longer solely about content, but also about how messages are packaged. Mastering these new modern techniques will allow more Indonesians to accept their ideas.

REFERENCES

Cook, Michael. 2004. *Commanding Right and Forbidding Wrong in Islamic Thought*. Cambridge: Cambridge University Press.
El Fadl, Khalid Abou. 2010. *Speaking in God's Name: Islamic Law, Authority and Women*. London: Oneworld Publications.
Fachruddin, Fuad. 2006. *Agama Dan Pendidikan Demokrasi, Pengalaman Muhammadiyah Dan Nahdlatul Ulama*. Jakarta: Alvabet.
Fanani, Ahmad Fuad, ed. 2007. *Muhammadiyah Progressif Manifesto Pemikiran Kaum Muda*. Jakarta: JIMM-LSFI.
Federspiel, Howard M. 2009. *Persatuan Islam: Islamic Reform in Twentieth Century Indonesia*. Singapore: Equinox Publishing.
Gaus, Ahmad. 2010. *Api Islam Nurcholish Madjid: Jalan Hidup Seorang Visioner*. Jakarta: Penerbit Buku Kompas.
Hamka. 1958. *Sejarah Perkembangan Pemurnian Agama Islam Di Indonesia*. Jakarta: Tintamas Djakarta.
Hassan, A. 1984. *Al-Furqan: Tafsir Qur'an*. Pustaka Aman Press.
Hasyim, Syafiq. 2011. "The Council of Indonesian Ulama (Majelis Ulama Indonesia, MUI) and Religious Freedom". *Irasec's Discussion Papers* 12 (December).
———. 2015. "Majelis Ulama Indonesia and Pluralism in Indonesia". *Philosophy and Social Criticism* 41, nos. 4–5: 487–95.
Hilmy, Masdar. 2010. *Islamism and Democracy in Indonesia*. Singapore: Institute of Southeast Asian Studies.
Madjid, Nurcholish. 2008. *Islam, Kemodernan Dan Keindonesiaan*. Bandung: Mizan Pustaka.
Marty, Martin E. and R. Scoot Appleby. 1992. *Fundamentalisms Observed*. Chicago: University of Chicago Press.
Menchik, Jeremy. 2016. *Islam and Democracy in Indonesia: Tolerance without Liberalism*. Cambridge: Cambridge University Press.
Mudzhar, Muhammad Atho. 1993. *Fatwa of the Council of Indonesian Ulama: A Study of Islamic Legal Thought in Indonesia 1975–1988*. Jakarta: INIS.
MUI. 2005. *Fatwa Munas VII Majelis Ulama Indonesia*. Jakarta: Majelis Ulama Indonesia.
———. n.d. *Mengawal Aqidah Umat: Fatwa MUI Tentang Aliran-Aliran Sesat Di Indonesia*. Jakarta: Sekretariat Majelis Ulama Indonesia.
Nafis, Wahyuni, ed. 1995. *Kontekstualisasi Ajaran Islam: 70 Tahun Prof. Dr. H. Munawir Sjadzali, M.A*. Jakarta: Ikatan Persaudaraan Haji Indonesia.
Nasution, Harun. 1975. *Pembaharuan Dalam Islam: Sejarah Pemikiran Dan Gerakan*. Jakarta: Bulan Bintang.
Osman, Mohamed Nawab Mohamed. 2018. *Hizbut Tahrir Indonesia and Political Islam: Identity, Ideology and Religious Political Mobilization*. London: Routledge.

Rahmat, M. Imdadun. 2008. *Ideologi Politik PKS: Dari Masjid Kampus Ke Gedung Parlemen*. Yogyakarta: PT LKiS Pelangi Aksara.
Rush, James R. 2006. *Hamka's Great Story: A Master Writer's Vision of Islam*. Wisconsin: The University Wisconsin Press.
Shihab, Moh. Quraish. 2004. *Jilbab, Pakaian Wanita Muslimah: Pandangan Ulama Masa Lalu & Cendekiawan Kontemporer*. Jakarta: Lentera Hati.
Sjadzali, Munawir. 1993. *Memori Akhir Tugas Menteri Agama Republik Indonesia, Masa Bakti 1988–1993 Kabinet Pembangunan V*. Jakarta.
Suryakusuma, Julia. 2012. "From Both Sides Now: Shari'ah Morality, 'Pornography' and Women in Indonesia". In *Legitimacy, Legal Development and Change Law and Modernization Reconsidered*, pp. 193–213. London and New York: Routledge.
Triandis, Harry C. 2009. *Fooling Ourselves: Self-Deception in Politics, Religion and Terrorism*. London: Praeger.
Waardenburg, Jacques. 1999. *Muslim Perceptions of Other Religions: A Historical Survey*. New York and Oxford: Oxford University Press.
———. 2007. *Muslims as Actors*. Berlin: Walter de Gruyter.

5

ACEH'S SHARIAH OFFICE: BUREAUCRATIC RELIGIOUS AUTHORITY AND SOCIAL DEVELOPMENT IN ACEH

Arskal Salim and Marzi Afriko

Introduction

Islamic law (shariah) has now become part of Aceh's development planning agenda. Based on the special autonomy policy, the province has the full authority to enforce shariah in a comprehensive manner. Numerous discussions arose regarding this notion, especially with the dominance of *jinayah* law enforcement, whether it can bring about any social change (Feener 2013). Many studies have explored the roots and effectiveness of its implementation (Salim 2008, 2015). However, little is known about the bureaucracy that sustained this shariah implementation agenda since its initiation, particularly the development of organizations within the bureaucracy. How organizations have been functioning to convey this vision of shariah implementation in Aceh remains unexplored.

The growth of regional organizational structures indicates a new phase of Indonesia's reform after the fall of Suharto in 1998, where politics have become decentralized. In Aceh, Dinas Syariat Islam (The Department of Islamic Shariah [DSI]) is one of the government offices established aimed at shariah implementation. There are also other offices bestowed with bigger authority, higher status, and independence. Divisions within the DSI cover domains such as Islamic law development, which extends to Aceh's Islamic development vision. In this sense, sharia enforcement should go beyond the scale of law enforcement as what have been studied in several countries (Rehman and Askari 2010). The Aceh government does not revisit shariah implementation goals, though it believes its implementation must be *kaffah* (comprehensive). Shariah enforcement is not limited to the legal renewal; its spectrum is as wide as the definition of Islam itself (Abubakar 2008, p. 19). It is a shared desire that Acehnese people expect, as a "shariah province", where shariah should be reflected not only on the legal reforms, but also on the social and political developments. By investigating the DSI's bureaucratic authority, one notes the powers the Aceh government has assigned to the DSI in assuring and controlling the shariah implementation agenda.

From the beginning, shariah implementation in Aceh relies on a technocratic approach, such as establishing offices, recruiting apparatus, and arranging regulations. The DSI is one of the offices established to strengthen the socio-religious development, as well as to be a distinctive indicator of shariah implementation. The DSI shares some common tasks with the other offices in Aceh, namely the local branches of the Ministry of Religious Affairs. Since the establishment of DSI, the quality and effectiveness of the bureaucracy remains a big challenge in post-autonomous regions, which impedes development (Afadlal 2003).

This chapter argues that the DSI has a share of its weaknesses which affects the low performance of shariah implementation in Aceh. It also attempts to shed some light on the quality of local bureaucracies in post-reformation era, especially relating to shariah implementation, particularly how the DSI office contributes to this failure. This chapter also analyses the challenges facing the DSI office, including the weakness of the DSI legal authority. The quality of legal authority is one of the four components of "acceptance of authority", a concept coined by Conrado R. Santos (1978). Another aspect to investigate is the hierarchy of positions in the DSI office. Although the positions seem to be all filled, they are not effective. It is therefore relevant to also investigate the level of competence or expertise of the DSI personnel, particularly how the relationship between head office personnel and his office staffs affects the offices' overall effectiveness.

The Rationale for the Establishment of the DSI Authority

The Strategic Plan of the Special Province of Aceh 2001–2005 serves as the basis for the implementation of the shariah during the early stages of Aceh's special autonomy. During this five-year development plan, the Aceh government introduced the "development of religion" plan to invoke the special features related to religious life. The development of religion is then translated as the implementation of shariah (Abubakar 2008). This strategic plan also spells out the roles and authority of the DSI office as reflected in its divisions: the division of religious support, the division of justice and the division of Islamic teaching. Each of these divisions has its own sub-divisions. In relation to its mission to strengthen Islamic faith, the DSI established a technical work unit to assign *da'is* to work at the Aceh border as contract labours (non-civil servants). Likewise, the DSI also recruited personnels for *Wilayatul Hisbah* (WH), a unit that was later incorporated into the office of the Municipal Police Service (Satpol PP) to oversee and enforce a number of *qanuns* (law/bill).

The formation of the DSI authority was relatively quick; it was established by the time the Aceh strategic plan 2001–2005 was formulated. Once the central government passed Act No. 18 of 2001 on Special Autonomy of Special Region of Aceh as Nanggroe Aceh Darussalam, the strategic plan was formulated along with the enactment of the Regional Regulation No. 33 of 2001 on Organization of the DSI. There was likely strong political support behind DSI's formation, with the assumption that the strengthening of shariah offices will be an important political capital (Sulaiman 2007). Similarly, some executives in Aceh did not seem to conduct a feasibility study based on legal grounding before the formation of the DSI. Some legal guidance on the establishment of any organization in Indonesia were not followed, such as the Decree of the National Law Development Agency Director No. G-159.PR.09.10 of 1994 on the Technical Guidelines for the Preparation of Academic Paper Legislation. This decree emphasizes the importance of a feasibility study before the establishment of an office, and it was reaffirmed through the

Presidential Regulation No. 68 of 2005 and Law No. 12 of 2011 on the Establishment of Legislation. These decrees and regulations point out how the formation of new shariah offices in Aceh should have followed the legislation related to the structures, duties and functions. In this sense, studies on concepts, goals, objectives, scope and the direction of the DSI should be conducted.

The DSI is a permanent department assigned for the planning and coordinating of shariah enforcement in Aceh. However, the academic script on this planning and coordinating function of the DSI remains unavailable, which would have been important to anticipate its political influence, so that the organization can focus on achieving the goals it has set for itself. Although there is a view that considers an academic script as facultative; there is also a view that sees it as compulsory. An academic script would have ensured a sufficient literature review, and considered various opinions useful in determining the structure of organization before furthering policy goals (Juwana 2006).

In the absence of a long-term vision which should have been laid in the early stage of establishment, the DSI is very prone of making internal structural changes following any change of provincial level leaders. Once the governor is replaced, the DSI director will also change, and the DSI organizational structure will follow. In 2007, the DSI suddenly reduced the work programmes of *Bina Peradilan* (Strengthening the Shariah Court) on the grounds that the *Mahkamah Syar'iyah* (Syariah court) can fulfill that function. The fact that the *Mahkamah Syar'iyah* had just appointed new judges, or that some judges and officials had been transplanted from other areas into Aceh, were not factored in. In another case in 2018, DSI proposed a work programme to form the Technical Service Implementation Unit (UPTD) at the Baiturrahman Grand Mosque, Banda Aceh, which was unrelated to its missions of the implementation of shariah.

The formulation of the DSI authority is part of the government's efforts to draw up the draft policy on the implementation of shariah properly. To date, shariah implementation has been through "trial and error" without incorporating any comprehensive planning. This situation is not unique to Aceh, as similar challenges can also be found in the course of bureaucratic reforms agenda throughout Indonesia (Azizy 2007). It is possible for the DSI that this trial and error will continue should it fails to strengthen its authority and evaluate its works based on strong vision and mission.

Limitations of DSI Authority and its Outreach

The main issue so far is on how the DSI has been performing as the leading sector of religious social development since the enactment of shariah implementation in Aceh. Since its establishment, DSI was perceived by other offices—such as the Bureau of Organization and Governance at the office of the Governor of Aceh and the Office of the Inspectorate of Aceh—as an organization that oversees the implementation of shariah. In 2004, Alyasa 'Abubakar wrote (the first book on shariah ever produced by the DSI) on the formulation of paradigms, policies and activities of shariah, and offered his interpretation of the function of the DSI based on Regional Regulation No. 33 of 2001 on the DSI Organization. He mentioned: "It appears that the main task of DSI is to be a planner and is responsible for the implementation of shariah in the Province of Nanggroe Aceh Darussalam." He referred to Article 3 of the Regional Regulation that "the DSI has some duties to perform the general and special tasks of Regional Government in charge of the implementation of shariah".

Technically, the regional regulation on the DSI did not mention the scope of its authority, especially the part about *"doing the planning of the shariah implementation"*, which should have been spelt out comprehensively. There were no technical guidelines for the DSI to do so, hence the nomenclature given to the DSI was Dinas Daerah (Executive Office). It is therefore inaccurate when Alyasa 'Abubakar said: "Shariah is a big task and cannot be done casually." In the provisions of regional regulations, such as the Government Regulation No. 18 of 2016 on Regional Organization, Article 13 paragraph (4) states that the agency has a specific task to execute special work. Although in this regulation the service is said to be able to accept other "duties" from the governor, the DSI did not acquire this typology of being a service. The DSI was ascribed a "special status" along with the other nine offices based on some regulations on "The Structure of Organization and Management" in Aceh province.

In 2006, all parties in Aceh were looking forward to the enactment of Law No. 11 of 2006 on Aceh Government (UUPA) to accelerate Aceh's development and shariah implementation. There were no new regulations regarding the authority of the DSI, but UUPA clearly imposed the tasks and authority of implementing and coordinating the shariah implementation to regional government heads, such as governors, regents and mayors (Article 42). UUPA then emphasized that the government should formulate regulations on the distribution of government responsibilities related to shariah. The draft of *qanun* (law/bill) was made available in 2013 and was approved by the Governor Zaini Abdullah in 2015 as Qanun 7 of 2015. Unfortunately, this *qanun* did not regulate the authority of the DSI.

The Emergence of the Grand Design for Shariah Islam

In 2014, the DSI, led by Syahrizal Abbas, attempted to implement shariah with a wider dimension. The DSI began compiling the Grand Design for Shariah Islam (GDSI) placing more attention on education, economics, governance, law and custom. DSI had some discussions with the local civil society organizations and the Civil Society Network for Shariah Concerns (JMSPSI), as well as cooperated with many academics to jointly develop GDSI. Some parties involved perceived the GDSI to be DSI's effort to provide a clear road map for the implementation of shariah in the province. At the same time, the DSI also constructed the Humanist Legal Analysis Framework in cooperation with JMSPSI intended for legal use by law enforcement officers.

However, based on some of the proposed drafts, the DSI did not chart any new map concerning shariah enforcement. The DSI tried to escape the narrow interpretation of shariah implementation that focused on the *jinayah* enforcement. DSI mentioned five sectors as a priority, although it remained unclear how these would be connected to other development sectors, and how it would work with multiple stakeholders. To this day, the document has not been used as a reference for the implementation of shariah. Nevertheless, the DSI did put in a lot of effort to make GDSI successful.

Within the GDSI design, the DSI does not propose any new work strategy on the implementation of shariah. The proposed strategies are: (a) redefining the strategic position of DSI within the scope of shariah implementation, (b) remapping the current needs for additional supports to control the implementation of Islamic law, (c) providing a critical review of the new strategic nomenclature for the DSI organization, and (d) thinking more strategically about the coordination and consolidation in implementing shariah. Alyasa 'Abubakar once wrote a normative view that could have been put as the basis for the DSI academic script before the local regulation on the DSI was issued. He divided the responsibility of implementing Islamic shariah into three parties, namely government, society, and individual. However, he did not specify which government office he was referring to. Unfortunately, this manuscript was published after the DSI was established and after the regulation was issued.

Strengthening the Coordination

The DSI also attempted to strengthen the implementation of shariah within the various government offices. Some coordination work was planned so that these offices can synchronize their work. The DSI seeks to achieve joint efforts on a regular basis to achieve common goals (Handayaningrat 2001). The DSI also tried to negotiate its authority by encouraging other offices to engage in the implementation of shariah. Munawar A. Djalil, the DSI Head in 2017, sent a cordial letter to the provincial offices to support the implementation of shariah. However, these offices complained because DSI did not specify the programmes and activities to be implemented. Munawar added that it is therefore crucial that the DSI has the GDSI that provides details of programmes and indicators. The availability of GDSI would help the DSI communicate its programmes more effectively to other parties.

To help consolidate its efforts, the DSI also coordinated with other stakeholders such as the police department, judiciary, *Mahkamah Syar'iyah*, Satpol PP, WH, and other local DSI offices in an annual *Rapat Koordinasi Teknis* (Technical Coordination Meeting/Rakornis). Rakornis is usually conducted for a couple of days to discuss the challenges of shariah implementation from multiple perspectives. The invitees would give their responses and suggestions. The DSI noted this discussion for further consideration or planning. In 2017, Rakornis gathered more attendees, and the DSI invited more stakeholders to report their progress in developing GDSI. Besides inviting the regular stakeholders like in the previous Rakornis, the DSI also invited Aceh Regional Secretary (*Sekretaris Daerah*), Bappeda and the Head of Aceh House of Representative. In addition to hearing comments and suggestions from the attendees and learning from Bappeda Aceh related to Aceh Shariah Development Index, the DSI also sought legal support from the legislative to move the GDSI as part of the Provincial Legislation Programme in 2018.

From the Rakornis, some participants were critical of the DSI. They argue that the DSI is not strong enough to coordinate the programmes beyond their authority. Some invited representatives were not from any of the Aceh regional apparatus; hence their recommendations could not be incorporated into the operational aspects of the DSI. One of the recommendations was "strengthening the cooperation of the enforcement of *jinayah* law" which is surely out of the DSI's authority.

Positions in the DSI

The authority of an organization is also determined by the level of structures that work together. For one, Santos' concept of "acceptance of authority" refers to Max Weber's theory on the existence of hierarchical office while others associated the position with authority of position or sanction, formal position, official authority, and authority of the job. In other words, the level of positions established in any particular organization determines the power of its authority. Structure determines how an organization achieves its goals (Etzioni 2005). Local regulations and *qanuns* have set the general guidance for the DSI regarding its basic structures to work upon. The prevailing question is whether these predetermined positions are able to support the implementation of shariah in Aceh. As a government organization, the DSI's organizational structure is instrumental in regulating and managing the shariah implementation policy in the region.

The reduction in research and development (R&D) working unit

A technocratic system strongly emphasizes on the organization working with available data in order to achieve optimal development outcomes. Government organizations in Indonesia are expected to develop research and development (R&D) units or offices, of which the province of Aceh has yet to have one. R&D is crucial to strengthening the working principle of "evidence based policy making", as regulated by Law No. 25 of 2004 on the National Development Planning System. Unfortunately, the strengthening of R&D agenda was not made a priority for the Bureaucracy Reform agenda in Indonesia, particularly in Aceh. In the Aceh context, and since the implementation of special autonomy and shariah, R&D remains as a major challenge for most organizations.

Twenty years after achieving autonomy status, Aceh shows slow progress in terms of R&D resulting from the low commitment of the local government to work with data.

In relation to shariah implementation, R&D is instrumental for data-driven policy making. In its early phase, DSI had a unit for R&D under the division of programme planning. During the course of time, this sub-division got smaller and now it is completely removed from the structural nomenclature. Although the Regulation of Governor of Aceh No. 131 of 2016 on the Status, Organizational Structure, Duties, Functions and Working Procedures of the DSI office mentions the duty of research, monitoring and evaluation, the nomenclature of R&D sub-division was no longer available in the DSI's strategic planning (Renstra) for programmes and activities. The DSI evaluation mapping did not discuss R&D as an internal strategic issue, or as a challenge in implementing shariah. Instead, it commonly focusses on issues such as the low societal awareness regarding the implementation of Islamic teaching.

The internal structure of the DSI reflects the way in which this organization sees R&D. For R&D to be allotted a sub-division status indicates that these two important programmes are not the DSI's priority. The DSI does not exhibit their commitment for studying, evaluating and measuring the extent to which shariah in Aceh has been implemented. It cannot depend on external institutions such as the Central Bureau of Statistics (BPS) or the Regional Development Planning Agency (Bappeda) to obtain data on shariah implementation. Besides the fact that DSI does not conduct research on its own territory and authority, such cooperation is also complicated because of the DSI's poor coordination record with other institutions.

This "working-without-data" culture puts DSI's authority into question. During the discussion to integrate GDSI draft into the Medium-Term Development Plan (RPJM) for the 2017–22 period in 2017, some data presented by the DSI was doubtful. During the discussions regarding GDSI, the DSI was made aware of the importance of data. The DSI cannot design policies without having a complete picture of the current situation. Some data that it should have been able to provide are unavailable: for instance, there was no data of Acehnese people's Arabic literacy rates provided by either the DSI or Bappeda. Meanwhile, the programme of improving religious understanding and Quranic literacy was set as one of its shariah implementation plans.

Apparently, the proposed programme was executed without being recorded or analysed. In another occasion, during a DSI budgeting consultation exercise in 2018, Bappeda questioned the DSI about the current condition of mosques and *meunasah* which were financially supported by the DSI along with their programmes. The DSI admitted that they never collected such data and did not know where to obtain them.

Thus far, it can be seen that the DSI has not been strategic in designing their programmes, thus their agenda can neither be evaluated nor measured accountably. The DSI seems to carry out numerous programmes throughout the year, but in fact, they are only serving community proposals or requests, unrelated to their strategic plan. This work culture is a major factor that will continue to thwart DSI's authority. Should the DSI continue to work based on the quantity of activities as opposed to the achievement of its strategic plan, it will never accomplish its main mission of enforcing shariah in Aceh comprehensively. Shariah implementation, later on, will only be limited to ceremonial programmes and less impactful activities.

The ups and downs on the power of supervision and propagation

The DSI office has 108 staffs at the headquarters, and 200 contract personnel working as *da'i* at the Aceh borders. Between 2002 and 2007, before the transfer of WH personnel to the Satpol PP department, the DSI controlled this unit. Today, WH is designated for supervising and enforcing shariah law, while the border *da'is* are specially dispatched to teach and preach Islam in six border districts: Aceh Tamiang, Southeast Aceh, Aceh Singkil, Subulussalam, South Aceh, and Simeulue. In these districts, the community live alongside different cultures and religions; therefore the government thinks that the strengthening of the Muslim faith in these areas is crucial.

The separation of the WH from the DSI was widely opposed by the WH personnel, the DSI Head, and the local community who believe that this decision would weaken WH's authority in performing its responsibilities of enforcing shariah in society (Afriko 2010). For the sake of the WH's roles and noble mission, the DSI Head, Munawar once expressed the fundamental differences between WH and Satpol PP as "*Satpol PP nyan yang paroh leumo, WH yang paroh ureung lagee leumo*" [Satpol PP is working to drive the cows that entered the market, while the WH is working to drive people whose mentality are like cows [immoral].

The Satpol PP's tasks are unrelated to shariah implementation, therefore its role is distinct from the WH. In 2007, the Aceh governor, through the DSI Head Ziauddin Ahmad, stated that the WH has more distinctive features compared to its fellow law enforcer watchdog units and it provides better welfare and career trajectories for its personnel (Afriko 2010). Do these special features of the DSI ensure shariah enforcement in Aceh? There is no guarantee for that. Within a decade of shariah implementation, many *jinayah* cases were prosecuted by the WH personnel, in addition to a number of physical clashes with citizens (Human Rights Watch 2010; Ichwan 2013).

Since the initiation of the Border *Da'i* programme by the DSI, there have been two major bureaucratic issues. The first issue relates to the monitoring mechanism for *da'i* performance. By management, the Border *Da'i* programme is directly supervised by the DSI at the provincial level, as this programme is funded through the special autonomy fund at the province level. This affects the nature of the programme which is quite similar to another provincial government programme (e.g. the incentives for local religious leaders). The direct chain of management causes some issues in terms of monitoring, in a way the performance assessment was conducted by the provincial DSI "remotely" through periodic coordination meetings and site visits. The DSI office could have done this assessment more effectively and less costly, but this alternative cannot be carried out due to bureaucratic procedure.

In a report entitled *Da'i Performance Assessment* released by the DSI in 2015, *da'is* working on teaching and preaching Islam at the borders were found to be ineffective. Recruited *da'is* are mostly selected by the provincial government and found themselves unfamiliar with the local socio-cultural contexts at the borders. Nasruddin, the manager of the Border *Da'i* programme, mentioned that there is no guarantee that the best *da'is* selected from the city are the most suitable people to work in remote areas. The *da'is'* mission and approach often clash with local approaches when it concerns religious matters. Additionally, these metropolitan *da'is* often complain about the difficult transportation in their placement borders. Many *da'is* were reported not staying in the borders area during their duty.

All of these dynamics of the Border *Da'i* programme were well captured and recorded by the DSI offices in the district and regency levels. Unfortunately, these offices have no authority to address the issues due to overarching powers attached to the provincial DSI. The absence of reports from the local DSI offices convinces the provincial DSI that the programme is still feasible to run, and does not require significant renewal. By far, the recommendation of the DSI assessment on the Border *Da'i* programme mainly focused on fulfilling the quantity or number of *da'is*. In the past few years, there has been an increasing number of *da'is* for up to 200 personnel (25 in Simeulue district, 19 in South Aceh district, 47 people in Aceh Singkil district, 39 in Aceh Tamiang district, 46 people in Southeast Aceh district, and 24 people in Subulussalam). The report also mentioned a baseless claim from a district DSI saying that the ideal number of *da'is* for one district is 500. The rationale for increasing *da'i* personnels at the borders was not accounted for, because there was no proper assessment conducted for this purpose. It is an intricate challenge to decide how many *da'is* are needed per village, therefore a strategic concept and preliminary assessment are needed prior to sending *da'is* to the borders.

Assessment on the *da'is'* performance tend to focus on their experience and well-being, rather than whether their mission is accomplished, or how impactful was their presence in the village. Due to weaknesses in the monitoring assessment, the effectiveness of this programme cannot be comprehensively measured and analysed. Every year, the Border *Da'i* programme spends more than Rp7 billion, or at least 20 per cent of the total DSI spending. The cost for this type of *dawah* is relatively high, since the DSI only has a budget of over Rp9 billion for coordinating Islamic *dawah* and *syiar* programmes. This high cost, however, does not lead to any measurable indicators in terms of their effectiveness, such as the number of new Muslim converts, the level of religious compliance of the people at the borders, or other indicators. A prevailing question on this matter is: "Is this huge cost worthwhile?"

The second issue of the Border *Da'i* programme is the adaptability of the *da'is* in society. The DSI working plan mentions that this programme employs some strategies to improve the people's religiosity and *aqidah Islamiyah*. To fulfil this goal, the DSI only sets one indicator of "establishing and maintaining quranic learning in *gampong* (village) level", and "distributing incentives for *imeum meunasah* (local Islamic leaders)". With this goal, it is clear that the mission of upholding *aqidah Islamiyah* carried out by the border *da'is* who are rewarded with a monthly salary, is much supported by the work of local Islamic leaders and quran teachers who are only rewarded by incentives. In this sense, these *da'is* are working less while being paid a huge sum of money. Thus, society's support in the implementation of shariah in Aceh is indeed needed, although a better system needs to be made available to distribute the powers between the government and society.

The programme *Da'i at the Borders* was seen as an effort to replace the role of local communities. This programme seems to overlap with the role of local religious leaders on the ground. As a consequence, some complexities arose whether to substitute preaching activities with community empowerment. The differences in the educational background of the community as well as the way of interpreting Islam should have been studied by the DSI before they deployed the *da'is* to the border. The local community needs programmes that empower them, such as leadership training for their village officers, *ulama*, and *adat* leaders. The DSI at the province level could delegate these activities to the local DSI offices to minimize the operational cost. *Da'is* in the area could serve as the trainers for the community while also developing the capacity building and performance assessment tools. The DSI could share responsibilities of strengthening Islamic faith with the local community at the border.

The lack of expertise and insufficient managerial capabilities

Expertise is one of the absolute basic needs that must be fulfilled by every organization. Expertise or "technical knowledge" is an acquired competence in Max Weber's terms of rational organization among the structuralist view (Santos 1978). This technical competence is needed in developing and managing organizational personnel in Indonesia, in addition to managerial competence and socio-cultural competence. Technical competence can be assessed on the basis of academic capacity and professionalism, such as educational backgrounds, degrees, course works, or relevant trainings related to their duties and positions within the organization.

There have been various levels of academic competence among the DSI apparatus. This type of competence can be assessed by two main aspects, namely normative competence (i.e. the ability to translate Islamic development agenda into practice) and technocratic competence (i.e. the ability to perform organizational roles and functions).

The DSI personnel seems to have an average level of technocratic competency. It can be seen from the personnel's relatively little knowledge on the legal authority and position as described above. Although DSI leaders have high academic competence, they do not necessarily possess high-level competence on technocratic matters. Technocratic competence requires specific skills which are mostly non-academic related, such as managerial skills. The DSI is one case where the technocratic competence at the regional level is proven to be low. Since the agenda of bureaucracy reform was started, there have been many studies focusing on measuring the slow development in the region. It has been found that the major cause of this underdevelopment was the political dynamics at the local level (Afadlal 2003). A similar study reported the low bureaucratic competence of Indonesian structural personnel and suggested an intervention to improve it (KSI 2017). Table 5.1 illustrates the comparison of competence among the DSI apparatus in Aceh.

TABLE 5.1
A Comparison of Competence among the DSI Apparatus in Aceh

Competence \ Position	Office Head	Sub-Head	Staff
Technocratic	middle	middle	middle
Normative	high	low	low

The competence of DSI staffs has been an issue since their recruitment in 2003. The DSI office which has the specific task of managing the shariah implementation should have been filled with qualified people whose academic and experience match its mission. The DSI was clearly unprepared for the bureaucratic reform at that time. During the early reform period in post 1998 under the Abdurrahman Wahid regime, there was organizational downsizing and merging from the central to the regional levels. Staffs from the Office of Information and Communication (Infokom), Social Service, Youth and Sports Office, inspectorate staffs, headmasters of madrasas and others were assigned to be the DSI staff. This disoriented beginning of the DSI staff recruitment pinpointed that the special autonomy did not put the implementation of shariah as a major agenda.

During Alyasa 'Abubakar's leadership (2003–7), there were efforts to increase the normative competence of DSI staff by sending them to pursue higher degrees on Islamic law in some universities, including the Islamic University of Ar Raniry, Banda Aceh and some universities in Malaysia. However, this endeavour was not sustained as these staffs were not reassigned to their original posts. Some qualified staffs were assigned to different offices, while the government did not recruit new staffs who can support the DSI tasks. To date, more than fifteen years since its operation, DSI has not been able to deal with this lacking competence.

Due to these limitations, the DSI relied heavily on cooperation with other parties for several activities, such as conducting research, book publishing, and trainings. Nevertheless, this kind of cooperation opportunity was also limited to certain circles. As a result, the DSI did not complete the drafting of GDSI despite four years working on it. This kind of ineffectiveness indicated the weak technical ability of the DSI apparatus, particularly in managing its human resources for strategic planning.

Another contributing factor for the low normative competence of the DSI personnel was their personal interest and understanding on how Islam would be enacted in Aceh's civic life. The DSI apparatus should have an objective perspective and be able to provide a more progressive way of religious social development in the region. There were some examples of cases where personal subjectivity was presented to the public. To start with the latest case, there was a department head from the DSI who spoke at a discussion forum in response to issues of the increasing number of violence against women in Aceh in early 2018. He proposed to increase the punishment for the murder perpetrators to a death sentence, which caused quite a public controversy. This polemic subsided soon after the DSI Head clarified that the mass media had misquoted the original statement.

In another case related to the issue of former Jakarta Governor Basuki Tjahaja Purnama (Ahok) in 2017, where the DSI personnel's view was subjectively portrayed to the public. One of the officials expressed his view that Ahok was considered to have offended Islam. This personal subjectivity put DSI's objectivity into question, because as a government office, it should adopt a neutral stance. The third case was related to the DSI personnel's reaction to the recommendation of Aceh Besar regent—through Regulation No. 451/65/2018—concerning the obligation of air stewardesses entering Aceh to wear hijab (head scarves). One of the DSI personnel commented on this during an exclusive interview between a CNN Indonesia reporter and the Aceh Besar regent, Mawardi Ali on 1 February 2017, which ended in a deadlock. This apparatus expressed his personal view that CNN attempted to embarrass the implementation of shariah in Aceh and referred to the news channel as an "inhibitor" of shariah enforcement in Aceh, calling them "TV Kafirun" (TV Invidel).

Since 2007, media spotlight on the DSI has reduced, with the transfer of WH to the Satpol PP department. The DSI's direct involvement in controlling the enforcement of shariah on civic society was seen by many parties as violating the standards of humanist law. There were some clashes between the WH apparatus and citizens, and also some violations of *jinayah* law carried out by individual WH personnel. Should WH, with these prevailing cases, remain a part of the DSI, it will surely decrease the DSI's authority. When WH can function optimally, it would strengthen the DSI's authority. In this sense, the DSI, as an executive office, overlapped by performing judicial duties.

Office leaders' personal influence

As a government office, the DSI has been led by leaders with various levels of professional training. The DSI apparatus, however, have to follow organizational rules and administrative procedures, just like other personnel in other organizations. Likewise, the chain of communication and command between office leaders and subordinates must work well in its own dynamics. Santos (1978) articulates that leaders, such as directors or managers, are significant figures for measuring organizational authority. This chapter notes that the change of leaders has impacted the internal atmosphere of the DSI. Subordinates who were used to be led by more senior directors felt awkward when their new leaders are younger than them. For instance, the appointment of Munawar A. Djalil as DSI Director in 2017 shocked some DSI officers, although he was formerly a section head at the DSI. Some of the DSI staffs said that "young people can be emotional". The staffs' earlier experience during Syahrizal Abbas' leadership (2013–16) was better. They felt that every single decision was taken only after careful considerations. During Abbas' period, the DSI conducted evaluative policy reviews, especially on the performance of the DSI itself. On the other hand, Munawar's leadership was seen as more assertive; his subordinates perceived that he did not carry out bureaucratic leadership which requires careful and deliberate considerations before making any decision. Bureaucracy as well as authority are needed to reflect on organizational decision making (Bolton and Dewatripont 2013). Premature decisions or weakly-considered determination are seen to be harming public needs.

In the past few years, the DSI leadership situation seems to have improved, with the recruitment of two doctorate graduates as department heads. One of them, Munawar A. Djalil, eventually, became the DSI Head. The appointment of these scholars as head created some problems within DSI; one of the subordinates, Syukri who is older than the director, felt that he is able to plan the DSI activities better. He had expressed his disagreement with the Head's decision on the 2017 Rakornis draft, which should have been discussed with him as the section head and the man in-charge of planning activities. The lower level staffs later decided that they needed to comply with orders and directives from two different figures to keep operations running.

Conclusion

The DSI is a government office with the mandate to develop shariah. It has made some progress in terms of its legal status, structure, position, and efforts to better perform its responsibilities to support the implementation of shariah in the Aceh province. However, some factors impede its authority.

In the current bureaucratic state, the highest executive leader in Aceh is the governor. This person can propose and determine changes in how the shariah is applied, as how Governor Irwandi Yusuf merged the WH unit into the Satpol PP Office in 2007. When he returned to the position for a second time in 2017, he revised the public canning punishment (usually conducted in front of the mosque) to the prison under the Governor Regulation No. 5 of 2018. Many wondered whether he was pressured by the international community to enact the changes, but he argued that he needed to conceal such process from children. He also wanted to ease public fear of potential investors to come to Aceh. He received support from academics and politicians, even though many were against him. For the authority ascribed to DSI, the governor can make improvements to it by revisiting its direction, structure, tasks, and functions. Subordinates generally obey the governor's decision: one personnel commented that "it is up to the governor's direction, if the governor wants, we will follow".

The DSI's current authority is not strategic enough, and certainly will not be able to bring measurable changes. Thus, it is not worth a large organizational budget. Regional budget support from the special autonomy is the major provider for social-religious sector funds in Aceh, and it will no longer be available from 2027 as it will be stopped by the central government. Should the DSI authority not be properly evaluated, the burden of the Aceh government operational spending and its comparison to shariah implementation performance will certainly be onerous.

REFERENCES

Abubakar, A. 2008. *Syariat Islam di Provinsi Nanggroe Aceh Darussalam: Paradigma, kebijakan, dan kegiatan* [Shariah in Nanggore Aceh Darussalam Province: Paradigm, Policy, and Activity]. 5th revision. Banda Aceh: Dinas Syariat Islam Provinsi Nanggroe Aceh Darussalam.

Afadlal, ed. 2003. *Dinamika birokrasi lokal era otonomi daerah* [The Dynamics of Local Bureaucracy in Autonomy Era]. Jakarta: Pusat Penelitian Politik (P2P) LIPI.

Afriko, Marzi. 2010. "Syariat Islam dan radikalisme massa: Melacak jejak awal kehadiran FPI di Aceh". In *Serambi Mekkah yang berubah: Views from Within*, edited by Arskal Salim and Adlin Sila. Jakarta: Alvabet & Aceh Research Training Institute (ARTI).

Azizy, Ahmad Qodri. 2007. *Change management dalam reformasi birokrasi*. Jakarta: Gramedia Pustaka Utama.

Birkland, Thomas A. 2007. "Agenda Setting in Public Policy". In *Handbook of Public Policy Analysis: Theory, Politics and Methods*, by Frank Fischer, Gerald J. Miller, and Mara S. Sydney. Florida, US: CRC Press.

Blau, Peter Michael and Marshall W. Meyer. 2000. *Birokrasi dalam masyarakat modern* [Bureaucracy in Modern Society], translated into Indonesian by Slamet Rijanto. Jakarta: Prestasi Pustakaraya.

Bolton, Patrick and Mathias Dewatripont. 2013. "Authority in Organizations". In *The Handbook of Organizational Economics*, edited by R.obert Gibbons and John Roberts, pp. 342–72. Oxford: Princeton University Press.

Etzioni, Amitai. 2005. "Authority Structure and Organizational Effectiveness". *Administrative Science Quarterly* 4, no. 1: 43–67.

Feener, R. Michael. 2013. *Shariah and Social Engineering: The Implementation of Islamic Law in Contemporary Aceh, Indonesia*. Oxford: Oxford University Press.

Handayaningrat, Suwarno. 2001. *Administrasi pemerintahan dalam pembangunan nasional* [The Governmental Administration in the National Development]. Jakarta: Gunung Agung.

Human Rights Watch. 2010. *Menegakkan moralitas: Pelanggaran dalam penerapan syariah Islam di Aceh, Indonesia* [Upholding Morality: The Violation in Shariah Implementation in Aceh, Indonesia]. New York: Human Rights Watch.

Ichwan, Moch Nur. 2013. "Alternatives to Shariatism: Progressive Muslim Intellectuals, Feminists, Queers and Sufis in Contemporary Aceh". In *Regime Change, Democracy and Islam: The Case of Indonesia*. Leiden: Final Report Islam Research Programme Jakarta.

Jann, Werner and Kai Wegrich. 2007. "Theories of the Policy Cycle". In *Handbook of Public Policy Analysis: Theory, Politics and Methods*, edited by Frank Fischer, Gerald J. Miller, and Mara S. Sidney. US, Florida: CRC Press.

Juwana, Hikmahanto. 2006. *Penyusunan naskah akademik sebagai prasyarat dalam perencanaan pembentukan RUU*. Jakarta: Departemen Hukum dan HAM.

Knowledge Sector Initiative. 2017. *A Policy Brief on Meninjau Ulang Standar Kompetensi Jabatan Pimpinan Tinggi* [Reexamining the Competence Standard of the High Leadership Position]. Jakarta: KSI.

Rehman, Scheherazade S. and Hossein Askari. 2010. "How Islamic are Islamic Countries?" *Global Economic Journal* 10, no. 2: 1–37.

Salim, Arskal. 2008. *Challenging the Secular State: The Islamization of Law in Modern Indonesia*. Honolulu: University of Hawaii Press.

———. 2015. *Contemporary Islamic Law in Indonesia: Shariah and Legal Pluralism*. Edinburg: Edinburg University Press.

Santos, Conrado R. 1978. "A Theory of Bureaucratic Authority". *Canadian Public Administration* 21, no. 2: 243–67.

Sulaiman, M. Isa and Gerry van Klinken. 2007. "Naik daun dan kejatuhan Gubernur Puteh" [The Raise and Down of Governor Puteh]. In *Politik lokal di Indonesia* [Renegotiating Boundaries: Local Politics in post-Suharto Indonesia], by Henk Schulte Nordholt and Gerry van Klinken, translated by Benhard Hidayat. Jakarta: KITLV and Yayasan Obor.

6

MUSLIM FEMALE AUTHORITIES IN INDONESIA: CONSERVATISM AND LEGAL NOTION OF WOMEN PREACHERS ON FAMILIAL ISSUES

Euis Nurlaelawati

Introduction

In Indonesia, Islamic religious authority is split into a number of fields. As Burhanudin (2007) notes, the *ulama* (singular *alim*) is no longer the only authoritative body in the transformation of Islamic knowledge and discourse. Azra and others also noted this and maintained that there is a variety of religious authority in contemporary Indonesia (Azra et al. 2010). Women have taken part quite significantly in leadership and authority of religion. Judging and preaching are two activisms in which women's involvement in both the leadership and religious authority is very evident. The involvement of women is very clearly shown in Islamic judiciary where familial issues are heard. Meanwhile, in terms of preaching, their involvement began to be very significant when a programme which amalgamates Islamic propagation and entertainment known as "dakwahtaintment" on media has flourished. These women preach various Islamic teaching including Islamic law of family.

In Indonesia, family law has received significant attention from the government. Since Muslims are the majority of the population in Indonesia, applied family law has been adopted mostly from Islamic (family) law. Accommodating a number of local practices, state interest, and Islamic legal doctrines, the Indonesian government tackles familial issues by issuing a number of laws (Nurlaelawati 2010). To understand family law in Indonesia, we should refer to what is so-called *Kompilasi Hukum Islam*, henceforth called *kompilasi*, and the Law of Marriage No. 1/1974. The *kompilasi* is a legal reference provided for judges of Islamic courts and Muslims in general, while the Law of Marriage applies to all citizens of Indonesia and is therefore to be referred to by judges of both Islamic court and civil court.[1]

A number of developments on the administration of the judicial institutions have been made. The development in substantial laws on familial issues has also occurred and a number of legal reforms on family law have been made (Nurlaelawati 2010). This is completed by a number of governmental policies on legal procedural issues (Sumner and Lindsey 2010). A number of programmes that provide better justice for litigants, women litigants in particular, such as circuit court, legal aid and *prodeo* are launched (Sumner and Lindsey 2010; Nurlaelawati 2016).

Within the development of judiciary, the legalization of the recruitment of female judges is positive, following the initial appointment in the 1950s.[2] Strengthening their positions as *ulama* and leaders of traditional Islamic schools since the 2000s, female Muslims have also stood as religious preachers, competing with their male counterparts on the public stage. Although the number is not as many compared to their male counterparts in both domains, they have had quite an equal standing in terms of admission and position. With their powers and voices, their involvement in these two domains of state and non-state institutions has been expected to contribute to the realization of advancing women's rights in both domestic and public areas.

The phenomenon of the involvement of Muslim women in the public religious authority historically has been argued by many to be in line with the involvement of women in education. Kloos noted that in the late nineteenth century, there were many institutions of religious learning that offered female students the opportunity for education. He also related this to the colonialism which accelerated this process.

Agreeing with Robinson (2008, p. 269), he said that "in South Asia, religious authorities observed how positions of power were increasingly occupied by non-Muslims. In order to protect the integrity of the Muslim community, they argued, there was no choice but to involve the domestic sphere and (by implication) women" (Kloos 2016). Therefore, reformist religious schools started to educate girls in the 1920s and this, as Hefner (2009a, p. 23) noted, was followed by conservative institutions and the involvement of women in Islamic education, schools and universities, is equal to that of men (Hefner 2009b, p. 63).

There is a number of works devoted to the discussion of women's leadership and authority. Srimulyani (2013) studied about the role of *nyai*, wives of *kyai* whose position parallels that of their husbands in *pesantren* and who also served as foster mothers to young *santri* (Smith and Woodward 2014), in Java, taking the examples of three *pesantern* where three *nyai* were involved in the leadership. She argues that women in the *pesantren* exercise agencies over history. She found that those *nyai* negotiated their public roles, leadership and agency within the compass of some *pesantren* traditions. Kloos (2016) also studied about female leadership. Taking two female leaders of Aceh, he demonstrated that the struggle for gender equality has taken many forms in Indonesia and that to advance women's status, one does not have to be a women rights activist and to refer to secular agenda. As with the previous writers, Widiyanto (2015) observes the significant role and authority of women in promoting peaceful life within religious ties. He discussed how a female activist, Sinta Nuriyah, has contributed to the idea of realizing the protection of religious minorities and that as a Muslim activist, Nuriyah and her ideas wield authority on present day-Indonesian Muslims. Salim and I discussed about the initial appointment of women in Islamic judiciary, its further development, their legal notion and their contribution to the realization of gender equality and justice. We argued that while women have been involved in the legal transaction in Islamic judiciary, gender justice and equality have not been realized (Nurlaelawati and Salim 2017).

This chapter discusses the involvement of Indonesian Muslim women in preaching and observed their legal notion and their contribution to the realization of advancing gender equality and justice and factors leading them to voice conservative and ambiguous legal rules. By focusing on how female preachers deal with familial legal rules, this chapter examines the empowerment of women and their contribution to the realization of justice within Muslim women on the relevant cases. It demonstrates that female preachers are also at the forefront in the public domain, and therefore female authority has been widely admitted within Indonesia's wide community. Nonetheless, the sort of Islamic family law advocated and spoken by these female preachers particularly through the media have not yet significantly directed to benefit women within legal discourses and transactions, that they are not well conversant of Islamic family law introduced by the state and their references to various Islamic legal rules are associated with their educational backgrounds and the public and media demands.

The following sections are based on empirical data and deploy analytical contents and a sociological approach. They are based on data from interviews, observation, and documentation conducted during two periods of research, June to August 2017 and February to May 2018. During these periods, observations on YouTube videos on preaching were collected. The contents of the videos were studied and analysed. Interviews with a few audiences of the show were also conducted. Although few other female preachers are discussed, the focus of the study is on Mamah Dedeh and therefore, even though the focus is not on dakwahtaintment and the media, the materials to be observed are the videos and their contents. As noted above, the involvement of female preachers began to be noticed in line with the use of media in *dakwah* activities and it is the voices of these media-using female preachers that are widely observed by Muslim society.

Family Law on Women Issues and Legal Reforms

Before we delve into the discussion on the female preachers and their legal notions, it is necessary to first have an overview of the Islamic legal rules on familial issues. This is so as to see the extent to which religious preachers understand and refer to these rules.

After independence, a number of seminars on women issues were organized,[3] and a draft on the national law of marriage was launched in 1973 to be discussed within parliament. A draft was then approved and declared to be issued as Law of Marriage No. 1/1974. This law is applicable to all Indonesian citizens regardless of their religion. It should therefore be applied in both civil and Islamic courts when dealing with family issues. Under this law, both civil and Islamic courts across Indonesia have had the same jurisdiction over matrimonial issues and the substantive grounds of their settlements since 1 October 1975. These include, among others, permission for a husband to have more than one wife, marriage dispensation, child custody and alimony, legal status of a child, termination of parental custody, determination of guardianship, appointment of a guardian when a minor is abandoned by the parents, and determination of the origin of a child.

Looking at the rules included in the Law of Marriage, it seems that Islamic family law inspired most of the regulations. There were several articles dropped from the law as they were considered by Muslims to have deviated too far from Islamic doctrines (Cammack 1997). These articles included the ban on polygamy and the permission of inter-religious marriage. These articles raised criticism from Muslim scholars and they urged them to be eliminated (Blackburn and Bessel 1977, pp. 132–36). To accommodate the voices of the Muslim majority, the articles were then abolished.

After being promulgated, the Law of Marriage provides judges of both courts with legal references when dealing with familial issues. However, as others (Harahap 1999) and I (Nurlaelawati 2010) have argued, since the law covers only marriage and divorce issues, judges of Islamic courts have not had sufficient legal references to resolve cases of inheritance and other types of familial issues. Before the issuance of the *Kompilasi Hukum Islam*, this had become a problem for Muslims in particular, as judges had referred to divergent legal doctrines covered in the classical legal books and produced judgments with varied legal references. With the enactment of the *Kompilasi Hukum Islam* in 1991, which generally adopts the classical Islamic doctrine but accommodates a number of reforms with the consideration of state interest and local values, the problem is hoped to be solved. This law has strengthened and added a number of rules not covered in the Law of Marriage, including the limitation of polygamy, minimum age of marriage of sixteen for female and nineteen for male, equal right of husband and wife in property gained within marriage, and others.

Over the course of time, a number of further reforms have been made through many ways, including the amendment of law and judicial reviews over a number of articles deemed to be against the constitutional rights of citizens. These two kinds of reforms were done among others to accommodate women's interest sought by gender activists and intellectuals. One judicial review was sought by Halimah vs Bambang. Halimah felt that she had been unfairly treated in court after her rejection of her husband's petition to divorce her on the ground of continuous dispute. This was after the Supreme Court's decision to accept her husband's proposal to the court that rejected his appeal to review its own decision and after the decision that finally approved her husband's petition to divorce her. Unfortunately, after several hearings and discussions the Constitutional Court rejected her request through its decision identified as 006/PUU-III/2005. What Halimah did sow the seeds of legal development and demonstrate the awakening of Muslim women's legal awareness in general and how human rights and gender notions have spread widely.

To enhance women's rights, White and Mulia (2008) and Burhanudin and Fathurrahman (2004) noted that a number of seminars to disseminate ideas on gender equality and to challenge traditional interpretations of Islamic teaching were held and books and journals[4] which contributed to public debate and influenced the public policy on women and gender issues were published (Nurlaelawati 2016). This was then strengthened by the government which ratified a number of international covenants, including the Convention on the Elimination of All Forms of Discrimination Against Women (CEDAW) and the International Covenant on Civil and Political Rights (ICCPR).[5] CEDAW (Article 2) requires all state signatories to eliminate discrimination on the basis of gender in public and private spheres. ICCPR stresses that men and women should enjoy equal access to all civil and political rights (Article 3) and it requires the guarantee of legal certainty for any legal action (Article 15). The Convention on the Rights of the Child (CRC) is a specific international treaty that affirms the basic rights of children.[6] To ensure the implementation of the protection of the children, the CRC has laid down four principles, including non-discrimination, devotion to the best interests of the child, the right to survival and development, and the respect for the views of the child. The Indonesian Law of Children Protection No. 23/2002 in Article 2 states that awarding of the custody rights to the parents should consider the four principles as specified in the Convention, including the notion or the best interests of the child.

These state-Islamic laws are Islamic laws that should formally be acknowledged and applied in all Muslim societies. Accordingly, it is these laws that would be observed and shared by all religious authorities, including religious preachers. They are then required to be well conversed in these laws to preach during religious congregations. Besides, they may also need to give a good perspective of the various legal opinions about the issue of family law in this context.

The Involvement of Female Preachers in the *Dakwah* Activities

Women in Indonesia have for many centuries been able to gain access to property and to positions in offices.[7] With regards to their involvement in state agencies, several works have indicated that in Indonesia women have been involved in for example, judicial body, including in Islamic judiciary since the first two decades after Indonesia's independence (1945), where female judges began to be recruited to serve in the Islamic courts, although this had attracted protest from many conservative Muslim groups (Nurlaelawati and Salim 2017). Despite the fact that the general court had appointed female judges in the late 1950s, they considered women sitting on the bench of the Islamic courts to be a violation of the Islamic legal tradition, especially in light of the Shafi'i juristic doctrine. In response to this criticism, the Directorate of Religious Justice of the Ministry of Religious Affairs gave a justification of women recruitment and stated that the recruitment was due to legal emergency (*darura*), as Indonesia lacked qualified Islamic judges. At the time many of the male judges employed in the Islamic courts did not meet the full requirements, such as possessing standard knowledge of Arabic and familiarity with classical Islamic legal references.[8]

The involvement of women in religious preaching was actually seen far earlier than in the judiciary. In fact, a number of women were reported to have assumed as leaders in *pesantren* where they would do preaching (Srimulyani 2013). At that time, their preaching was heard and observed by only a small group of Muslims (the inhabitants and students of the *pesantren*). Different from their male counterparts, they did not preach to a wide public audience and thus were not widely heard (Widiyanto 2015). The situation has become quite different since the 2000s when the dakwahtaintment flourished. As with male preachers, female preachers could also perform on stage before a wide public audience. Nonetheless, female preachers that present their preaching are not those who have been known before as *ulama*, but those who are legitimized as preachers through their popularity in the media. As will be shown below, this has resulted in the sharing of their Islamic thoughts and opinions with the wider Muslim community.

The dakwahtaintment started to flourish as several groups of Indonesian Muslims began to Islamize their attitude. This is, as Sofyan (2012, p. 70) argued, in line with the liberalization of media ownership which has led to the liberty and lack of control from the government. Further, the media owners brought about the inclination of ideology, the increasing number of *dakwah* programmes and the mushrooming of religiously-oriented programmes and *sinetrons*—literally, electronic cinema. Many discussed the role of media in the observance of Islamic teachings and rituals and found it to be significant. Eva F. Nisa (2018a, pp. 68–99), for example, looks at how religious messages uploaded on Instagram through posts and captions have significantly affected the way Indonesian Muslim youth observe their religion and accentuate their religious piety (pious) and life goals. She argues that Instagram has recently become the ultimate platform for Indonesian female Muslim youth to educate each other on becoming virtuous Muslims. In her other work, Nisa (2018b, pp. 24–43) also looked at the use of social media in *dakwah* focusing on One Day One Juz (ODOJ) programme, which endeavours to encourage Muslims to revive the spirit of reading the Quran through the mobile application WhatsApp. According to her analysis, ODOJ has brought new colour into the contemporary Islamic public and has contributed to the understanding of the transformation of the religious mediascape in Indonesia.

This phenomenon is in broader perspective relevant to the idea of democratization of *dakwah* itself. As noted by Moazami, Crollius argued that there has been dynamic of *dakwah* which could be traced back to the shift of the *dakwah* concept in the early twentieth century (Jouili and Moazami 2006). Moazami said that "while *dakwah* was traditionally understood as an activity to be conducted under the aegis of the clerics, Reformist thinkers claimed it to be the duty of every Muslim, thereby opening the path for lay persons to be involved in it", and this shift to which he refers as "democratization" of *dakwah*, became beneficial for women and led them to be included in the *dakwah* duty and activities (Jouili and Moazami 2006). In the activism of *dakwah* in Indonesia, a number of names came up, including Abdullah Gymnastiar, Arifin Ilham, Yusuf Mansur, and Jefri Al Buchori (Hasan 2012, pp. 376–78). Although female preachers are not as plentiful as male preachers, they include Mamah Dedeh, Qurratu A'yun, and Lutfiah Sungkar. These names that have appeared since 2000 are then followed by other names that appeared after 2010, including Oki Setiana Dewi and Lulu Susanti.

The phenomenon of the engagement of female in *dakwah* programmes through any way and through the media in particular has been seen by some researchers as the empowerment of women. Mariatul Qibtiyah (2012, pp. 300–10), for example, considered Mamah Dedeh who engaged herself in dakwahtaintment as one of the progressive preachers who brought about progressive Islam. According to her, Mamah Dedeh often answered questions raised by the audience by considering the condition of the questioners and did not stick to Islamic doctrines. However, at the same time many found that the appearance of female preachers like Mamah Dedeh has not benefitted women. In his paper, Sofyan (2012, p. 70) demonstrated that Mamah often subordinated women. For example, he drew attention to some shows mostly in 2012 where the discussions of the relationship between women and men in the family sent the message of women subordination. Yusuf (2016, p. 35) strengthened this view and even considered the show by Mamah Dedeh as one of the TV shows that clearly demonstrated that there has been commodification of religion in the media. He saw Mamah Dedeh as one of the unqualified preachers to be heard widely on media and has been maintained merely due to her unique attitude.

Female Preachers and Legal Notions on Women Issues

There have been many notable *ulama* and religious preachers, such as Sinta Nuriyah, Zakiyah Darajat, and Huzaimah Tahido Yanggo, who are considered to be religiously knowledgeable and holding voice on progressive legal notions. The formation of Ulama Perempuan Indonesia and the Kongres Ulama Perempuan Indonesia, and the holding of KUPI (Indonesian Women's Ulama Congress) have strengthened the existence of the progressive and moderate female *ulama* in Indonesia. These have of course been very popular and internationally heard, but within the Indonesian Muslims circle itself they may not have been evenly heard (Rosidin and Hasani 2017). Common Muslims may not have been aware and in fact although the conference was published widely in the media, this has not been acknowledged by common Muslims as they appeared on formal forums that could only be viewed once. It is therefore not the voices of the common people that have been observed, but rather the voices of female preachers that appeared constantly in the media such as Mamah Dedeh. Hence it suffices to say that Mamah Dedeh and other female preachers that appeared on the television or other media have greatly influenced the understanding of religious doctrines in society, including Islamic law of familial issues. As noted above, although the paper does not focus on the issue of media and dakwahtaintment, it refers to a number of familial issues that are discussed in the media.

a. Gender Asymmetries in the Voice of Women

When delivering their sermons, female preachers that used the media seemed to have voiced quite various and uncertain legal notions. They often referred to the legal opinion of one school of Islamic law for one legal case but to another for another case. Mamah Dedeh, for example, referred to Shafi'i school for the issue of guardianship but then referred to another school in other marital case, while not mentioning the school itself. She also did not refer to Islamic family law that has been provided by the state, although her legal opinions sometimes go with the state's opinion. She often simply states that, in Islamic law, one issue is regulated this or that way, without stating the divergent opinions of the schools of Islamic law. Moreover, female preachers are not controlled by the state in proposing their legal opinions. Accordingly, their legal opinions often do not go with the legal opinions introduced by the state.

Interestingly such legal opinions are also conveyed in dramas, films and other media programmes. One drama entitled "Cinta Bunga", for example, showed how the pronouncement of divorce three times in one go was observed as a triple divorce (*talak ba'in*) by the writer of the story. The drama referred to the view of one legal school that states that a divorce uttered three times in one go is considered a triple divorce which results in the man not being able to revoke the divorce or even marry the wife unless she marries another man and is then divorced (Zuhayli 2001). Meanwhile, if the writer or the drama refers to the state Islamic law, for example Article 120 of KHI, such a divorce is considered as a single divorce with a different effect.

This has also resulted in a shortage of legal opinions that are unreceptive toward gender issues. Let us take an example of a video show of Mamah Dedeh in October 2015 on polygamy.[9] Although she seemed to refer to the state Islamic law, Mamah Dedeh was very permissive towards polygamy and accepted its practice by merely stressing on financial capability. Therefore she supported polygamous marriage as long as it is entered with an economically-capable man and supported by an *ulama* or a *kyai*. She did not give any reason or ground on which polygamy could be done by the *kyai*. She simply felt that the *kyai* are economically capable persons to solemnize polygamous marriages. Another video illustrated another gender-biased legal opinion of hers.[10] The video on 17 August 2016 which discussed the issue of husband's duties and wives' rights, conveyed Mamah's legal opinion that the wives' obedience to their husband is absolute. According to her, wives are not allowed to go out without their husband's permission. Mamah Dedeh did not explain and elaborate on this and gave an impression that the husband's wishes have to be followed at all times. She also stated that wives' denial of their husband's request to have sex is punishable. Here she also did not go into detailed explanations about the issue.[11]

As with female judges, female preachers assume a critical position in the process of Indonesia legal development, particularly on women's rights. They could influence legal thinking and practice of the society. The female preachers on media gained wide viewing and would form both the legal discourse and practice of the society. To some extent female judges, however, have quite different roles in that context. Female judges constitute legal practitioners and their legal opinions have evident impacts on women's legal rights and determine their legal fate. Let us take an example of how female judges did not oppose their male counterparts when hearing cases of polygamous marriage. By meeting the petition of a husband, the female judges have put wives in a subordinate and grieved position. Meanwhile, female preachers are legal advisors whose legal opinions do not directly impact women's legal rights. However, different from female judges whose legal opinions impact certain women, these female preachers with their permissive views about polygamy, may have motivated many husbands to enter polygamous marriages. In other words, with their gender bias, female judges would give limited impacts while female preachers would give wider impacts.

b. Classical Doctrine versus State Law

Different from their colleagues in the Islamic judicial body,[12] the preachers including the female ones are not strictly abided by law. They are not well controlled by the state and the relevant institution. There is a formal institution to monitor and control the media including television.[13] Nevertheless, it seems that the institution does not perform up to the mark. In fact, many shows, dramas and other programmes are often criticized as they convey negative learning for viewers. In the case of religious programmes, the lack of control of that relevant institution is also evident. As have been noted above, some preachers are often not well conversant with religious teachings. Therefore, besides the television broadcaster's motive that would be highlighted, it is the personal views and ideas that dominate the substance of the law conveyed and shared in this religious preaching. Independency is very clear from these female preachers as they do not have to argue against their male counterparts on the stage.

As a result of this tendency of female religious authorities in both judicial stage and public stage, Muslims in Indonesia have remained conservative. The permissive attitude of the judges including the female ones has resulted in conservative observation of Islamic family law in Indonesia. In the case of polygamy, as I have discussed above, many husbands entered into polygamous marriage with the permission of the judges. The judges, including the female ones, often approved proposals of polygamy and stressed mostly on the qualifications to be met by husbands rather than on the reasons why husbands wish to have polygamous marriage. Consequently, they could accept any reasons presented by the husbands although the presented reasons are not permitted in the laws (Nurlaelawati 2015). The conservative attitude of these male and female preachers can also be seen in the cases of underaged marriage. For example, the practice of underaged marriage by a young and famous religious celebrity, Arifin Ilham, was mentioned by some *ulama*, including a famous female religious celebrity, Oki Setiana Dewi. Agreeing with another preacher, Yusuf Mansur, she stated that Arifin is a role model for young men in terms of observation of Islamic doctrine and avoidance of extra-marital sexual intercourse and she also believed that what Arifin did will create goodness and deprive evil in this era of globalization. Although to some extent due to her acquaintance with some progressive religious scholars of Syarif

Hidayatullah State Islamic University, where she did her Masters, Oki Setiana Dewi maintains this sort of conservative legal opinion regarding marriages (Dewi, interview, 2018).

> Such kind of legal comprehension and practice within Muslim society by a number of preachers has actually been notified by activists of children rights protection and Muslim scholars who have quite progressive legal notion, particularly female activists. These groups of Muslims often voice more sound thought of considering a long-term maslaha (public good). Through an international seminar, KUPI/Kongres Ulama Perempuan Indonesia in 2017, they discussed and highlighted the issue of children marriages and proposed more progressive regulations on children issues. Badriyah Fayumi, the leader of KUPI, stated that with the reference to Islamic rationale she hoped to be able to propose to the government an amendment to the minimum age requirement for marriage, which although has been proposed to increase, not been changed (Fayumi, interview, 2018).

Media and the Problem of Expertise: The Challenge against Legal Modernization and Authority within Muslim Society

Not only do such female preachers often convey gendered-biased and conservative opinions, they also are not very knowledgeable about the Islamic law of familial issues in general. During a video show on 28 July 2015 where the issue of the utterance of triple divorce at one go was again discussed, Mamah Dedeh, for example, made a mistake which showed her lack of understanding of the topic.[14] She said that the utterance of triple divorce at one go is considered to be one divorce and she then seemed to refer to the state Islamic law. She did not discuss the details of the various legal opinions within Islamic law leaving this legal issue unclear to the audience. Above all, she seemed to be not conversant about the issue. This is particularly clear when she misspelled the word *muhallil* which means "splitter man". When describing that triple divorce results in prohibition of the husband to marry his wife unless she marries another man, instead of saying *muhallil*, she said *mukholli*, which certainly has a different meaning. Another video demonstrated how she was not well conversant about Islamic family law. The video showed a discussion of guardianship where a distant questioner through phone asked about *wali hakim*. The questioner narrated that he had a female friend who converted to Islam and married a Muslim man. As the woman's father is a non-Muslim, she was formally appointed as the guardian or *wali hakim*. She then asked about other conditions under which a formal *wali hakim* could be appointed to substitute a paternal guardian who refuses to give permission or guardianship to his daughter. Mamah Dedeh slovenly replied that there are a number of conditions on that. Interestingly she mentioned that a father who is worried of being influenced by pronouncing the *ijab* (proposal) formula could be substituted by a *wali hakim*. By saying that, she was referring to *wakil wali*, while the question was concerned about *wali hakim*.

These videos confirmed what a researcher, M. Fachrudin Yusuf, noted about Mamah Dedeh's level of general knowledge of Islamic doctrine. According to Fachrudin, Mamah Dedeh is known as a straightforward person and it is this personality trait that has attracted the audience. Most of her audience are not aware that Mamah Dedeh, in his view, is not well conversed in Arabic articulation and that she is not knowledgeable about Islamic law. With regards to Islamic law, Fachrudin even frankly stated that she answered the legal issues arbitrarily. She puts herself across as a reference to all the religious legal issues addressed in the Muslim society. He said:

> Audiens tahu persis bahwa Mamah Dedeh adalah da'iyah yang dikenal keras tanpa kompromi. Modal itulah yang nampaknya disukai oleh pemirsa Indosiar. Padahal bagi muslim yang ahli baca al-Qur'an, bacaan Mamah Dedeh dapat dikatakan biasa, bahkan cenderung kurang fasih dan belum layak diperdengarkan kepada khalayak umum, apalagi dalam kapasitasnya sebagai ulama. Dalam hal hukum agama, dia tampil dengan begitu hebatnya hingga mampu menjawab semua persoalan yang diajukan si pencurhat. Bagi ahli hukum Islam, jawaban yang disampaikannya seringkali cenderung kurang pas, dia acapkali mengambil dalil secara serampangan, tanpa perangkat metodologis yang memadai (Yusuf 2016).

What Fachrudin noted seemed to strengthen the perception of the eligibility and expertise of new religious intellectuals in general religious teachings. In his work, Hasan (2012, p. 379), for example, states that these preachers may be not as literate as those in the past. They, Hasan continues, however, "are certainly more able to manipulate symbols and its relevance with the rituals and to represent the mass society of today".

Regardless of the fact that such preachers are not well competent in a number of legal issues as demonstrated above, the media, such as television, has a wider influence and acceptance within society and bears new actors of religious authority. As with the printing media, the television contributes to the rise of various religious authorities. The religious authority is no longer limited to the established *ulama* and as noted above, this has resulted in the emergence of *dakwah* democratization. While this may be good, it has, in my view, brought about challenges to legal modernization of the state, particularly in legal unification and the advancement of women's legal status (Nurlaelawati 2010).

The audiences and the viewers of this media come from various backgrounds. Many of them are illiterate in Islamic family law, but are very enthusiastic to learn about it. Unfortunately, they are unaware that not all new actors in religious preaching are conversant in religious knowledge and therefore take for granted what these preachers delivered. This is, of course, not the fault of the observers and listeners. It is the state's and the preachers' duties to ensure the substance of the preaching. When the preachers delivered the messages and teachings in a right tone and direction and the state takes control of the substance of the preaching, the listeners and the viewers would learn the right and proper messages.

The example of how viewers observe uncritically the teachings delivered by Mamah Dedeh could be seen through the videos on polygamy and divorce. As it is clear in a number of judicial cases in the courts, many husbands' understanding of polygamy as their exclusive rights is also clearly evident among the audiences of Mamah Dedeh's preaching programmes. Besides the audiences of the show, the viewers of the video uploaded on YouTube demonstrated their agreement to the conservative legal notion of the preacher. Let us take the example of the comments on the video show of October 2015. Although most female commentators disagreed with Mamah Dedeh, male ones supported Mamah Dedeh through a comment on 12 May 2018 by referring to the Quranic texts and to the notion of *Zina* avoidance, a reason that is always cited by those who tolerate the polygamy practice.

Another video on the spousal relationship illustrates the same observation of the legal opinion of Mamah. As noted above, although her gender sensitivity has improved, she remains gender-biased. The video in response to a question about the legal rule of the husband's fooling around showed that Mamah puts women in a wrong position by saying that when the husband plays around with another girl, the wife should reflect on herself that she did not treat the husband well and that she cannot petition a divorce. To this comment, the viewers responded positively.

This conservative legal opinion of Mamah Dedeh and of the observation of society proved that there are many challenges in the process of legal modernization. The state Islamic law that has been introduced and has offered reforms seems to be challenged by and resisted within Muslim society. While it may be acceptable that religious authority is followed by many groups of persons, it is safe to say that dakwahtaintment on media has failed to play a positive role in modernizing the legal discourse of Muslim society. In fact, this is not only seen in *dakwah* programmes, but also in infotaintment programmes where a number of celebrities' familial issues are gossiped and where celebrity *ulama* are invited to give their legal opinions.

It seems that democratization of *dakwah* which has resulted in the rise of new religious authorities has brought negative impacts to legal modernization in the society. Although the media is considered to have contributed to the literacy of legal knowledge, the involvement of less conversant preachers, including the female ones, has put new challenges to the modernization of legal thinking which would benefit women and other vulnerable groups of the Muslim society in Indonesia.

Conclusion

Women have assumed important positions within religious leadership and authority. They have occupied positions in the courtrooms and preaching stage to disseminate religious teachings, including Islamic law on familial issues. By so doing, they have empowered themselves and equated to men. However, as their male counterparts show in dakwahtaintment, these female preachers have not modernized their way of thinking offered in a number of national laws and international covenants where women are given equal rights as men. This is because even though they are independent and can voice their legal notions freely, female preachers have to adhere to the needs and policies of the media owner where they perform. What is made worst is that female preachers that are widely heard on television are not well conversant in Islamic family law.

Therefore, although in some cases, women have benefitted from the reforms on Islamic family law and the involvement of women in the Islamic judiciary, in other cases on polygamy and spousal relationship, women remain subordinate and weak. The Law on the Elimination of Domestic Violence (UU Penghapusan Kekerasan dalam Rumah Tangga No. 23/2004) provides rules in relation to domestic violence and categorizes violence into four categories: physical, mental, sexual, and negligence (*penelantaran*) of financial support and children care;[15] and a polygamous marriage can be considered as a form of mental violence.[16] Nonetheless, it seems that rather than referring to and considering such conventions and Law No. 23, and viewing polygamy as a form of domestic violence, preachers tend to consult *fiqh* doctrines and Quranic verses and see it as the rights of men who are financially and mentally capable. Hence, while it has been assumed that female preachers would have higher gender sensitivity than their male counterparts, their engagement in *dakwah* programmes in the media where Islamic family law is often spoken and discussed has not yet directed themselves and other Muslim women to modern legal way of thinking where greater gender justice could be achieved.

NOTES

1. There are two court systems in Indonesia—civil court and Islamic court—that have jurisdiction over familial issues. The partition results from the fact that Islamic law is adopted to be applied on Muslims since Islam is common in Indonesia. Since then there have been two separate courts to hear familial cases. However, while civil court also hears criminal cases brought by both Muslim and non-Muslims, Islamic court only hears familial cases. Since 2006, Islamic court has had wider jurisdiction as it also hears Islamic economic cases. See Hisyam (2001).
2. However, it needs to be noted that female authority has long been debated by scholars in Muslim countries. This is due to the popular notions in Muslim society derived from the classical Islamic legal opinion that women are not allowed to assume important positions as they are considered to be weak and sensitive.
3. These seminars were organized by Ikatan Sarjana Wanita Indonesia on 29 January 1972 and Badan Musyawarah Organisasi Islam Wanita Indonesia on 22 February 1972. Earlier, two congresses were also held in Jakarta in 1935 and in Bandung in 1938 to discuss the legal status of women under Islamic law. See Syahuri (2013), pp. 4–6.

4. See also a number of policy reports written by The Asia Foundation on women's empowerment at http://asiafoundation.org/. Among the significant attempts made by these women's rights activists were the proposal for a Counter Legal Draft of the compilation of Islamic laws in Indonesia (KHI) and a proposal for a law on the elimination of domestic violence. Unfortunately, the Counter Legal Draft of KHI was dismissed because its provisions were too controversial. The draft on the elimination of domestic violence was issued in 2004 as Law No. 23/2004. The women's rights activists also supported women in resolving their familial problems and assisted in dealing with legal issues. In fact, they have been involved in assisting women to propose judicial reviews on the rules considered to be gender biases and to have contradicted constitutional values in the Constitutional court.
5. CEDAW was adopted on 18 December 1979, entered into force on 3 September 1981, and ratified by Indonesia in 1984. Meanwhile, ICCPR was adopted on 16 December 1966, entered into force on 23 March 1976, and ratified by Indonesia in 2006.
6. CRC was adopted on 20 November 1989, entered into force on 2 September 1990, and ratified by Indonesia in 1990.
7. This confirmed Fattore, Scotto and Sitasari (2010)'s argument that women's engagement in the public sector is considered to be as important as in the domestic sphere.
8. For an elaborate discussion on this, see Nurlaelawati and Salim (2017). In this chapter, the authors argue that the recruitment of women as judges in the Islamic court was a gradual process which started at the local level with a small number in the first decades after Indonesia's independence, but then gained its momentum and became acceptable. According to Muqaddas (2010), a woman named Arifiah Chairi was first appointed to the district religious court of Tegal in 1954. Another name was mentioned, i.e., Mrs Prayitno, who was formally appointed by the Minister of Religious Affairs to the religious court of Temanggung (Central Java) (through a decree dated 24 July 1957). A decade later, in 1964, there were fifteen female part-time judges and one full-time judge serving the district religious court of Tegal. From the mid-1990s onwards, almost all district religious court offices have employed female judges at one time or another in their history. Since then, although the majority of the judges in district religious courts are male (reaching up to 80 per cent in some cases), the sight of female judges in religious courtrooms is no longer uncommon, making up almost 30 per cent of the total number of judges in every court. This is particularly relevant to the fact that the inclusion of women in Islamic judiciary has received formal base in 1989 when the Islamic Judicature Act was issued. Since then, female graduates from the faculty of Sharia and law could apply for the position of a judge. This was then strengthened by the state policy that states that women should take up 30 per cent of key positions

in several sectors, including in the legislature, local community boards, and the judiciary.
9. See https://www.youtube.com/watch?v=_pFhHMVw2a0.
10. Notes from an observation of a video show on October 2015.
11. Notes from an observation of a video show on 17 August 2017.
12. Another point is that female judges are provided with and are required by their institution to refer to the state Islamic law and to abide by it. By referring to the state Islamic law, cases are resolved and *ijtihad* (legal exertion) is often glorified by the judges. It should be noted that the Islamic law introduced by the state has proposed some reforms which accommodate various demands of women and vulnerable groups of people. However, female judges have to provide strong arguments when arguing against their biased male counterparts. It is often the case that the personal views of the progressive female judges could not be heard, given the reality that there are few progressive female judges in Indonesian Islamic courts. Judges Rosmawardani from Aceh and Nur Lailah from Wates, Yogyakarta are among them. These judges have often fought for justice and equality for women. In fact, these judges hold greater gender sensitivity than their male colleagues in such cases as joint property, guardianship, and divorce. In the case of guardianship in Aceh following the post-tsunami recovery process, Rosmawardani was once prone to appoint female relatives or family members of the children's mother to take over this responsibility. In the case of divorce, she also placed mental violence as having equal strength to physical violence to be taken as a ground for divorce. See Salim (2009), p. 54; Nurlaelawati and Salim (2017).
13. See Law No. 32/2002 on Penyiaran and Peraturan Komisi Penyiaran Indonesia No. 01/P/KPI/03/1012 tentang Pedoman Perilaku Penyiaran.
14. See https://www.youtube.com/watch?v=epWytqXMbT4.
15. See Arts. 5, 6, 7, and 8 of UU PKDRT. See also Munti (2008).
16. In fact, researchers, such as Nurmila (2009) and Brenner (2011), have pointed at such effects of polygamy on existing marriages, most of which ended in divorce. See also Nurlaelawati (2015).

REFERENCES

Amelya, Arai. 2012. "Gugatan Ditolak MK, Halimah tak Akan Rujuk". *Kapanlagi.com*, 27 March 2012. https://www.kapanlagi.com/showbiz/selebriti/gugatan-ditolak-halimah-bambang-tak-akan-rujuk.html (accessed 12 August 2012).

Azra, Azyumardi, Kees van Dijk, and Nico J.G. Kaptein, eds. 2010. *Varieties of Religious Authority: Changes and Challenges in the 20th Century Indonesian Islam*. Singapore: Institute of Southeast Asian Studies.

Blackburn, Susan and Sharon Bessel. 1977. "Marriageable Age: Political Debates on Early Marriage in Twentieth-Century Indonesia". *Archipel* 14: 132–36.

Brenner, Syzanne. 2011. "Holy Matrimony? The Print of Politics of Polygamy in Indonesia". In *Islam and Popular Culture in Indonesia and Malaysia*, edited by Andrew N. Weintraub, pp. 212–34. London and New York: Routledge.

Burhanudin, Jajat. 2007. "Islamic Knowledge, Authority and Political Power: The Ulama in Colonial Indonesia". PhD dissertation, Leiden University.

Burhanudin, Jajat and Fathurrahman. 2004. *Tentang Perempuan Islam: Wacana dan Gerakan*. Jakarta: Gramedia Pustaka/PPIM.

Butt, Simon. 2010. "Islam, the State, and Constitutional Court". *Pacific Rim Law and Policy Journal* 19, no. 2: 279–301.

Cammack, Mark E. 1997. "Indonesia's 1989 Religious Judicature Act: Islamization of Indonesia or Indonesianization of Islam". *Indonesia* 63: 143–68.

———. 2007. "The Indonesian Islamic Judiciary". In *Islamic Law in Contemporary Indonesia: Ideas and Institutions*, edited by Mark E. Cammack and R. Michael Feener, pp. 146–69. Cambridge: Harvard University Press.

Chan, Faye Yik-Wei. 2012. "Religious Freedom vs. Women's Rights in Indonesia: The Case of Muhammad Insa". *Archipel* 83: 113–45.

Dewi, Oki Setiana. Interview. October 2018.

Fattore, Christina, Thomas J. Scotto, and Arnita Sitasari. 2010. "Support for Women Officeholders in a Non-Arab Islamic Democracy: The Case of Indonesia". *Australian Journal of Political Science* 45, no. 2: 261–75.

Fayumi, Nyai Badriyah. Interview. Pondok Gede, Bekasi, October 2018.

Harahap, Yahya. 1999. "Informasi Materi Kompilasi: Mempositifkan Abstraksi Hukum Islam". In *Kompilasi Hukum Islam dan Peradilan Agama dalam Sistem Hukum Nasional*, by Cik Hasan Bisri. Jakarta: Logos.

Hasan, Noorhaidi. 2012. "Piety, Politics and Post-Islamism: *Dhikr Akbar* in Indonesia". *Al Jamiah Journal* 50, no. 2: 376–78.

Hefner, R.W. 2009a. "Introduction: The Politics and Cultures of Islamic Education in Southeast Asia". In *Making Modern Muslims: The Politics of Islamic Education in Southeast Asia*, edited by R.W. Hefner. Honolulu: University of Hawai'i Press, pp. 1–54.

———. 2009b. "Islamic Schools, Social Movements, and Democracy in Indonesia". In *Making Modern Muslims: The Politics of Islamic Education in Southeast Asia*, edited by R.W. Hefner. Honolulu: University of Hawai'i Press, pp. 55–105.

Hisyam, Muhammad. 2001. "Caught Between Three Fires: The Javanese Penghulu under the Dutch Colonial Administration 1882–1942". Ph.D. dissertation, Leiden University, Leiden.

Hukum Online. "Menguak Sisi Gelap Poligami". 23 December 2006. www.hukumonline.com/berita/baca/hol15941/menguak-sisi-gelap-poligami (accessed June 2011).

———. "Syarat Poligami akan Diperkuat". 19 February 2009. www.hukumonline. com/berita/baca/hol21230/syarat-poligami-akan-diperketat (accessed June 2011).

Jouili, Jeanette S. and Schirin Amir-Moazami. 2006. "Knowledge, Empowerment and Religious Authority Among Pious Muslim Women in France and Germany". *The Muslim World* 96 (October): 617–42

Kloos, David. 2016. "The Salience of Gender: Female Islamic Authority in Aceh". *Asian Studies Review* 40, no. 4: 527–44.

Kompas. 2012. "Anak di Luar Nikah Kini Dilindungi Hukum". 19 February 2012. https://nasional.kompas.com/read/2012/02/19/06161689/anak.di.luar. nikah.kini.dilindungi.hukum (accessed 11 July 2012).

———. 2012. "Keputusan MK Kebablasan". 9 April 2012 (accessed 23 July 2012).

Muqoddas, Djazimah. 2011. *Kontroversi Hakim Perempuan pada Peradilan Islam di Negara-Negara Muslim.* Yogyakarta: LKiS.

Munti, Ratna Batara. 2008. *Advokasi Kebijakan Pro Perempuan: Agenda Politik untuk Kesetaraan dan Demokrasi.* Jakarta: Yayasan TIFA dan PSKW Pasca Sarjana UI.

Nisa, Eva F. 2018a. "Creative and Lucrative *Da'wa*: The Visual Culture of Instagram amongst Female Muslim Youth in Indonesia Asiascape". *Digital Asia* 5: 68–99.

———. 2018b. "Social Media and the Birth of an Islamic Social Movement: ODOJ (One Day One Juz) in Contemporary Indonesia". *Indonesia and the Malay World* 46, no. 134: 24–43.

Nurlaelawati, Euis. 2010. *Modernization, Tradition and Identity: The Kompilasi Hukum Islam and Legal Practices of the Indonesian Religious Courts.* The Netherlands: Amsterdam University Press.

———. 2015. "Sharia-based Laws in Indonesia: The Legal Position of Women and Children in Banten and West Java". In *Islam, Politics and Change: The Indonesian Experience after the Fall of Suharto*, edited by Kees van Dijk and Nico J.G. Kaptein. Leiden: Leiden University Press.

———. 2016. "The Legal Fate of the Indonesian Muslim Women at Court: Divorce and Child Custody". In *Law, Religion, and Intolerance in Indonesia*, edited by Tim Lindsey and Helen Pausacker. Routledge: Routledge Press.

———. 2017. "Indonesia". In *Parental Care and the Best Interests of the Child in Muslim Countries*, edited by Nadjma Yassari, Lena-Maria Moller, and Imen Gallala-Arndt. Germany: T.M.C. Asser Press (Springer).

Nurlaelawati, Euis and Arskal Salim. 2017 (republished). "Female Judges at Indonesian Religious Courtrooms: Opportunities and Challenges to Gender Equality". In *Women Judges in the Muslim Countries: A Comparative Study of Discourse and Practice*, edited by Nadia Sonneveld and Monika Lindbekk. Brill. First published by *Al Jami'ah Journal*.

Nurmila, Nina. 2009. *Women, Islam and Everyday Life: Renegotiating Polygamy in Indonesia.* London and New York: Routledge.

Qibtiyah, Mariatul. 2012. "Fenomena Mamah Dedeh: Ekspresi Islam Progresif yang Merakyat di Era Global". Prosiding Seminar Internasional Multkultural dan Globalisasi.

Robinson, Francis. 2008. "Islamic Reform and Modernities in South Asia". *Modern Asian Studies* 42, nos. 2–3 (March): 259–81.

Rosidin and Ismail Hasani. 2017. *Liputan Kongres Ulama Perempuan Indonesia*. Cirebon: KUPI.

Salim, Arskal. 2006. *Praktek Penyelesaian Formal dan Informal Masalah Pertanahan, Kewarisan dan Perwalian Pasca Tsunami di Banda Aceh dan Aceh Besar*. Banda Aceh: IDLO.

———. eds. 2009. *Demi Keadilan dan Kesetaraan: Dokumentasi Program Sensitivitas Gender Hakim Agama*. Jakarta: PUSKUMHAM.

Smith, Bianca J. and Mark Woodward, eds. 2014. *Gender and Power in Indonesian Islam: Leaders, Feminists, Sufis, and Pesantren Selves*. London and New York: Routledge.

Sofyan, Dicky. 2012. "Gender Construction in Dakwahtaintment: A Case Study of Hati ke Hati Bersama Mamah Dedeh". *Al Jamiah Journal of Islamic Studies* 50, no. 1.

Srimulyani, Eka. 2013. *Women from Traditional Islamic Educational Institutions in Indonesia: Negotiating Public Space*. Amsterdam: Amsterdam University Press.

Sumner, Cate and Tim Lindsey. 2010. *Courting Reform: Indonesia's Islamic Courts and Justice for the Poor*. Australia: Lowy Institute for International Policy, pp. 42–44.

Syahuri, Taufirrahman. 2013. *Legislasi Hukum Perkawinan di Indonesia: Pro-Kontra Pembentukannya hingga Putusan Mahkamah Konstitusi*. Jakarta: Kencana.

Weintraub, Andrew N. 2011. *Islam and Popular Culture in Indonesia and Malaysia*, pp. 212–34. London and New York: Routledge.

White, Sally and Musdah Mulia. 2008. "Islam and Gender in Contemporary Indonesia". In *Expressing Islam: Religious Life and Politics in Indonesia*, edited by Greg Fealy and Sally White. Singapore: Institute of Southeast Asian Studies.

Widiyanto, Asfa. 2015. "Female Religious Authority, Religious Minority and the Ahmadiyya: The Activism of Sinta Nuriyah Wahid". *Journal of Indonesian Islam* 9, no. 1 (June).

Yamada, Naoko. 2012. "Interwinning Norms and Laws in the Discourse of Polygamy in Early Twentieth Century West Sumatera". In *The Family in Flux in Southeast Asia: Institution, Ideology, Practice*, edited by Yoko Hayami. Japan: Kyoto University Press.

Yusuf, Muhamad Fahrudin. 2016. "Komodifikas: Cermin Retak Agama di Televisi: Perspektif Ekonomi Politik Media". *Interdisiplinary Journal of Communication* 1, no. 1 (June).

Zuhayli, Wahbah. 2001. *Al Fiqh Al Islamiyy Wa Adillatuhu*. Beirut: Dar al-Fikr.

7

MOBILIZING ON MORALITY: CONSERVATIVE ISLAMIC MOVEMENTS AND POLICY IMPACT IN CONTEMPORARY INDONESIA

Eunsook Jung

Introduction

In 2017, the Jakarta Governor, Basuki Tjahaja Purnama (known as Ahok), was sentenced to two years in prison with a blasphemy charge against Islam. Ahok has become an "easy" target by conservative Muslim groups because he is a Christian of Chinese descent. On the Jakarta gubernatorial campaign trail in 2016, Ahok cited the Quran saying that Muslims should not be duped by religious leaders using the verse to justify the claim that Muslims should not be led by non-Muslims. When this incident was known to the public, conservative Islamic groups held rallies against Ahok several times pushing for a blasphemy charge on him. These anti-Ahok rallies have attracted about 500,000 Muslims although moderate Islamic organizations like Nahdlatul Ulama (The Rise of Islamic Scholars) and Muhammadiyah (The Followers of Muhammad) dissuaded their members from joining the rallies. His blasphemy charge affected an election outcome by favouring his opponent. Some scholars argue that the influence of conservative Islamic movements on the Jakarta gubernatorial election in 2017 signals an illiberal turn in Indonesian politics (Jones 2017; Hadiz 2017). Other scholars argue that Islam and identity politics have been aggressively politicized.[1] The commonality behind these claims is that the influence of conservative Islamic movements on politics encourages politicians to utilize religious cards to win in elections as the voices of conservative Islamic movements are becoming stronger.

This chapter aims to analyse how conservative movements shape policies in contemporary Indonesia. While Indonesia is home to long-existing, mass-based, and moderate Muslim organizations like NU and Muhammadiyah, many new Islamic organizations have emerged since Indonesia's democratization in 1998. Conservative Islamic movements are pushing for the Islamization of Indonesian society by supporting laws and regulations that are in line with their interpretations of Quran and Hadith. The term conservative is defined as "the rejection of a progressive re-interpretation of Islamic teachings and it refers to an adherence to established doctrines and a social order" (van Bruinessen 2015). Conservatives also object to the modern established authority. For example, although democratization provided opportunities for these movements to emerge, they tend to be critical of or are in opposition to democratization and liberalization. Equally importantly, conservative movements are in competition with institutionalized and moderate Islamic movements in terms of Islamic authority as well as political and social influence, resulting in a diverse and fragmented Islamic civil society. Conservative movements include but are not limited to FPI (Front Pembela Islam, Islam Defenders Front), Muslim Student Action Union (Kesatuan Aksi Mahasiswa Muslim Indonesia, KAMMI), and AILA (Aliansi Cinta Keluarga, Family Love Alliance).

In light of this fragmentation, newly emerged movements since Indonesia's democratization face more competition than before in jockeying for influence. In the beginning of Indonesia's democratization, these groups were considered as the periphery of society, where their voices did not matter as long as they did not interrupt the process of democratization. Many expected that these movements would be moderated as Indonesia's democracy became consolidated. However, despite such expectations, these movements have become a critical force in Indonesia's politics.

Given their importance, the chapter focuses on how these Islamic movements shape policy-making. These Islamic movements are gaining more recognition through mobilization compared to institutionalized organizations like NU and Muhammadiyah. When Islamic civil society is occupied by diverse Islamic organizations, how do newly emerged Islamic movements with relatively short history and less institutional resources make their voices heard in policy-making in Indonesia?

I argue that these movements are weaponizing morality. Conservative Islamic movements impose their interpretations of Quran and Hadith as "right interpretations", and claim that whoever disagrees with their interpretations are neither Islamic nor moral. Such framing makes it difficult for Muslims to challenge their claims in fear of being labelled as "unIslamic" or "amoral". At the same time, such framing enables the movements to reach out to a broader audience who are adversely affected by the processes of democratization and economic liberalization. As a result, these organizations enhance the visibility of issues which, in turn, made political parties more susceptible to their demands. This chapter examines and specifies the mechanism by which conservative Islamic movements pressure political parties on Indonesian policy-making by using the moral degradation frame and increasing an issue salience.

This research on the conservative Islamic movements is based on fieldwork conducted in 2014 and 2017. I collected the data from semi-structured interviews with Muslim activists, the official statements of Islamic organizations, the public statements of Muslim activists, the social media of movement organizations, as well as pertinent court cases. In the next section, I discuss how scholars explain the impact of social movements on policies in Indonesia and elsewhere. I then suggest an alternative explanation, based on my research, about morality framing as a strategy of conservative Islamic movements. Following this, I provide a detailed account of the rise of conservative Islamic movements, and then examine the laws and regulations that are initiated by these social movements. In doing so, I analyse the sequences of mechanisms of political influence by conservative Islamic movements.

Contending Theories of Movement Influence

How do conservative Islamic movements influence policy? In order to answer this question, I will draw from social movement theories.

The scholars of social movements have developed theories about how social movements make an impact. Political opportunity structure and framing have been considered useful in understanding the impact of social movements (Benford and Snow 2000; Jenkins 1995; Tarrow 1994). I emphasize framing more than political opportunity structure because framing can create a favourable political opportunity structure. However, I will review the theories that have been proposed by other scholars and will explain how framing helps conservative Islamic movements to be influential.

First, some scholars emphasize the presence or absence of elite allies (McAdam 1996). Social movement organizations build political alliance by supporting political parties in elections. In return for the electoral support, movements insist that political parties attend to their issues during the post-election period (Htun 2003; Warner 2000). Although political parties do not necessarily follow through the promises they made with movements, elite allies add strength to movements by providing resources, information and networks.

Second, institutional access will offer opportunities of influence for social movements (Hertzke 1988; Skocpol 1995; Wilson 1995; Wald et al. 2005). Institutional access can be created with new laws, access to state agencies, resource commitments, or moral authority (Grzymala-Busse 2015). For example, in studying how churches influence public policy, Anna Grzymala-Busse (2015) argues that churches are most influential in policy-making when they have institutional access to secular policy-making. Institutional access can be created with moral authority while moral authority is high when national and religious identities are well fused and are historically grounded. Both Ireland and Italy are catholic countries. The Irish churches are able to block divorce, abortion and access to contraceptives while their Italian counterparts are unable to do so. These differences can be traced to institutional access.

Third, religiously motivated activists are a valuable political resource, making movements more effective. Religious organizations are often filled with like-minded and committed activists whose skills and experience can be transferrable to political arenas. Thus, a spill-over effect from religious organizational experiences to politics can be observed (Wald 2002; Peterson 1992). Participation, civic and organization skills that religious people learned through religious activities can be useful to political action, such as letter-writing, group decision-making, running meetings and making presentations (Leege 1988; Verba et al. 1993).

While these theories are helpful in understanding what makes social movements influential, they tend to focus on allies, access and resources. What they cannot explain is how conservative Islamic movements can be more influential than institutionalized movements when the former have less resources, less allies and less institutional access than the latter. I highlight two important aspects about conservative Islamic movements. First, ideational factors matter. In particular, framing matters. Framing is a meaning-making process, as framing gives meaning to action (Benford and Snow 2000). Constructing and disseminating meaning is important for social movements because it helps organizations to be recognized and supported by the general public. Successful framing can build support (Diana 1996) and influences policy development (Ferree 2003). Many scholars have demonstrated that framing matters. For example, in studying suicide protest in South Asia, Lahiri (2014) argues that movements need to create emotional narratives of events. Similarly, Ferree (2003) argues, comparing Germany and the United States in terms of abortion, that framing that resonates with institutionalized ways of thinking influences policies. In other words, finding a "right" frame that works for culture would be crucial. Second, this research demonstrates that social movement organizations do not necessarily need political alliance to make any influence in policy-making. As long as issues are salient and political parties take social movements seriously because of issue salience, social movement organizations can make an impact. This is in line with Marco Giugni's work as well as Marco Giugni and Sakura Yamasaki's work. Both research projects demonstrate that social movements are impactful when mobilization can be combined with other factors such as a favourable public opinion. However, the presence and absence of political alliances do not necessarily determine policy outcomes (Giugni 2004; Giugni and Yamasaki 2009).

Moral Degradation Framing as a Strategy of Social Protest

Framing is a powerful strategy. It becomes important in order for any movement organizations to influence politics as well as policies. Framing has three core tasks: framing diagnoses a problem in need of redress; framing provides a rationale to motivate understandings about a particular problem; and framing convinces potential participants to actually engage in activism (Wictorowitz 2004). Many scholars have argued that framing is significant in influencing politics.

As conservative Islamic movement organizations lack in resources, institutional access and organizational experiences, achieving an organization's stated goals is even more challenging than well-established large organizations with extended networks. However, conservative Islamic movements can be successful in influencing policies when they increase issue saliency and pressure political parties with their mobilizational capacity.

Conservative Islamic movements framed their activism as "combating national moral degradation". Such framing connects them with the larger Muslim population who are threatened by any changes that are occurring as a result of democratization, economic liberalization and cultural globalization. The moral degradation frame tends to unite anyone who seeks to stop or slow social changes that are occurring. Framing facilitates the recognition of social movement organizations, which allows movements to recruit more sympathizers. Although public recognition does not necessarily lead to any tangible political or policy outcomes, it enhances issue saliency and strengthens organizational power vis-a-vis political parties.

FIGURE 7.1
The Path of Policy Influence by Conservative Islamic Movements

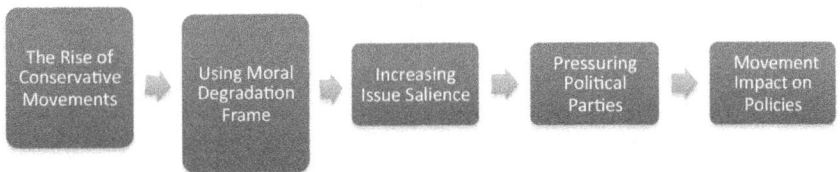

Organizational influence can be categorized into five different areas: agenda setting; access to decision-making arenas; achieving favourable policies; monitoring and shaping implementation; and shifting the long-term priorities and resources for political institutions (Andrews and Edwards 2004). Of all, conservative Islamic movements are successful in agenda-setting, which leads to issue salience. Although their access to decision-making arenas are limited, issue salience will help these movements to pressure political parties to shift their agenda.

In the discussion that follows I build on the framework outlined here in order to explore how conservative Islamic movements have affected policy-making in Indonesia. I have chosen these cases because they illustrate how conservative movements influence politics. All cases highlight the moral degradation frame and issue salience which, in turn, affect political parties' treatment of issues and shape policy-making.

The Landscape of Islamic Movements in Democratizing Indonesia

Although the long tradition of mass-based and moderate Islamic organizations has been embedded in Islamic civil society, Indonesian democratization brought the revival of Islamic organizations ranging ideologically from liberal to conservative. During the reform period (1999–2004), liberal Islamic organizations seemed to gain much influence in Indonesian society because their liberal values aligned well with democratization processes. On the other hand, conservative Islamic organizations were marginalized, and were considered as the unwanted byproduct of political liberalization. However, the trend was, soon, reversed. Conservative organizations grew rapidly following this reform period, and overcrowded Islamic civil society.

Conservative Islamic movements do not share a singular and homogenous identity. They consist of various organizations. Elizabeth Collins (2003) divides conservative movements in Indonesia into four streams based on organizational views on democracy. The first stream is related to the Indonesian Islamic Propagation Council (Dewan Dakwah Islamiyah Indonesia, DDII) and the Indonesian Committee for Solidarity with the Muslim World (Komite Indonesia Untuk Solidaritas dengan Dunia Islam, KISDI), both of which think that Islam itself offers a comprehensive system for politics. In other words, democracy is an unnecessary political system. The second stream is the Muslim Student Action Union (Kesatuan Aksi Mahasiswa Muslim Indonesia, KAMMI) which believes that there is no contradiction between democracy and Islam, as Islamization can be achieved within democracy. They are influenced by the Muslim Brotherhood. It focuses more on Islamic education, and maintains year-round activities for its members, using a cell system. The third stream is the neo-Salafi groups, who believe that *jihad* is necessary to defend Islam, and have created radical Islamic groups. These groups often use violence. Jemaah Islamiyah and the Communication Forum of the Followers of the Sunna and the Community of the Prophet (Forum Komunikasi Ahlu Sunnah wal Jamaah, FKASWJ) belong to this group as well. The fourth stream is Hizbut Tahrir (Party of Liberation), which rejects both the nation-state and democracy, and aims to re-establish the caliphate. Hizbut Tahrir operated clandestinely in Indonesia in the early 1980s but started to act openly only after Suharto fell.

In addition to Collins' streams, I cite two further types of Islamic movement, both of which are heavily influenced by Saudi Arabia. The first type of Islamic movements includes a group such as the Islamic Defenders Front (Front Pembela Islam, FPI) which was established in August 1998, and has been led by Habib Rizieq Shihab, a Saudi-educated scholar of Arab descent. The FPI not only urges stricter adherence to Islamic tenets but also attacks places it sees as emblematic of vice and decadence. The FPI often conducts raids on nightclubs, karaoke bars, and churches. From the beginning, the FPI has been closely associated with individual police and military officers. Some police and military officers are willing to work with the FPI because they found it useful to maintain contacts with Islamic organizations with the capacity to mobilize supporters (Fox 2004; Jahroni 2008). In contrast, a second category of organization shares an ideology with the FPI but does not use their tactics. For example, AILA supports the same ideals as the FPI but uses legal methods to make their voices heard. The AILA, consisting of academics, lawyers, Islamic preachers, and other professions, is at the forefront of Islamic conservative movements. The AILA aims to strengthen Indonesian families.[2] Its main activity so far is to push for criminalizing extra-marital affairs and LGBT acts by submitting a petition to the Constitutional Court. The *Jakarta Post*, a prominent daily English newspaper in Indonesia, once published the commentary titled "AILA is a bigger threat to freedom than the FPI".[3]

These organizations are the main constituencies of conservative Islamic movements in Indonesia. They frame their demands as "defending national morality". Political parties cannot be dismissive about their agenda because they increase issue salience with their mobilizational capacity. Conservative Islamic movements sometimes make alliances either with moderate Islamic organizations or with violent extremist organizations,[4] by framing issues as morality. Therefore, although their voices are not representative of the majority of Indonesians, they can make their voices heard.

This contrasts with mass-based and moderate Islamic organizations which have been cautious with electoral politics. Except for the reform years from 1998–2004, NU and Muhammadiyah have distanced themselves from partisan politics (Jung 2009). Since 2009, NU has been much more actively engaged in elections, especially in the presidential elections, than Muhammadiyah. Nevertheless, both organizations are wary of political parties controlling over Islamic organizations. NU and Muhammadiyah are moderate and mass-based Muslim organizations, whose combined membership is 80 million. Muhammadiyah was established in 1912 while NU was established in 1926. Muhammadiyah, an Islamic modernist organization, owns schools, universities, clinics and hospitals. NU, a traditionalist Islamic organization, consists of many clerics and *pesantren* (traditional Islamic boarding schools). Institutionalized organizations like NU and Muhammadiyah which have supported democratic politics have been successfully incorporated into democratic politics without pushing for an Islamic state. While NU established a political party called PKB (National Awakening Party), Muhammadiyah did not build its own political party. Instead, its former leader formed PAN (National Mandate Party) and tried to attract Muhammadiyah members (Jung 2013). Their efforts to enter into partisan politics were not successful in that these political parties did not gain as many votes as they expected. Around 2004, these organizations kept a distance from partisan politics, and emphasized neutrality toward political parties. They still shape nationalism by opposing the building of an Islamic state, and paying attention to education, health, and religious affairs. However, morality has not been their weapon in influencing politics. The inclusion of mainstream and moderate Islamic organizations made Indonesia's democratization more stable. However, at the same time, radical and conservative Islamic organizations have been marginalized in the mainstream politics (Aspinall 2004).

Combating National Moral Degradation and Policy Convergence

I examine four cases that demonstrate laws and regulations that are initiated by conservative Islamic movements, and explain what roles conservative Islamic movements have played in policy-making. Although political parties are the ones which sign bills, I argue that what pushes political parties to sign particular bills among many is issue salience.

The main contribution of conservative Islamic movements is to increase issue salience. It does not matter which political parties are in power at the national or local level. The ideologies of political parties also do not matter. Political parties in Indonesia can be divided into two categories. One is political parties that have an official allegiance to Pancasila and the other is political parties whose basis is Islamic ideology. Pancasila-based parties are based on religious pluralism,[5] while Islamist parties aim to build an Islamist state.[6] These distinctions are not significant when it comes to policy-making. Both Pancasila-based and Islamist political parties often support issues raised by conservative Islamic movements. As have been discussed earlier, conservative Islamic movements frame their demands as defending national morality. In doing so, they can gain recognition and appeal to a wider audience who are concerned about moral degradation in a fast changing society both politically and economically.

There are three reasons that Pancasila-based parties support the policies of Islamization. First, Pancasila-based parties send a message to voters that they do not need to vote for Islamic parties for Islamic issues. Second, tapping into Islamic issues is a cost-effective strategy for Pancasila-based parties to weed out Islamic parties. Lastly, Pancasila-based parties use Islamic ideology for convincing voters of their morality, as religiosity is highly associated with morality. When Pancasila-based parties accommodate new issues, issue salience increases and issue ownership moves from Islamic parties to Pancasila-based parties. As a result, policy convergence is the likely outcome. The following section will discuss four cases of how conservative Islamic social movements played a role in increasing issue salience.

The Anti-Pornography Law

An anti-pornography bill was introduced in 2006; it proscribed pornographic acts and literature, and restricted social activities involving bodily exposure. It was passed in October 2008 after drastic revisions. As Indonesia already had legislation that regulates the production and distribution of pornography, the necessity of the bill was questionable. The main concern about this bill was because of its broad definition of pornography, which could give authority to the government or certain groups to decide what is right or wrong and what is punishable. It also could restrict freedom of expression, curb cultural diversity and homogenize dress code. Allen (2007) argues that the anti-pornography law was the product of Islamic hegemony against religious diversity. Many believe that this threatens Indonesia's sacred national principles of Pancasila and *Bhinneka Tunggal Ika* (Unity in Diversity). Unity in diversity is the official national motto of Indonesia to impose tolerance from top down.

The pornography debate did not receive much attention until an Indonesian edition of *Playboy* magazine was introduced in 2006. Hardline Islamic groups like the FPI launched violent protests against the headquarters of the *Playboy* magazine. The headquarters had to be moved to Bali. Even the vendors of the *Playboy* magazine were exposed to violence. The FPI's massive violent protests were framed as a "fight against decadent West". In this instance, radical groups were joined by more moderate voices. One of the Muslim leaders called this as "moral terrorism that destroys the way of life of the nation in a systematic and long-term way".[7] In reaction to this, a quasi-government body, the Council of Indonesian Ulama (Majelis Ulama Indonesia, MUI) which initiated "moral reform" (Budiman 2011) based on Islamic moral values, refined the anti-pornography draft and called for its promulgation by the legislature (Salim 2007, p. 122). The bandwagon against moral decadence was thus joined by other moderate Muslim leaders and politicians.

The united forces between radical and moderate Islamic groups behind the banner of guarding morality pressured both Pancasila-based parties and Islamist parties equally. Without a clear initiative of Islamist parties, the bill was able to be passed with some revisions.[8] In fact, of the twenty-nine members of Commission VIII who signed the bill, most of them were from two Pancasila-based parties: Golkar (eight signatories) and PDIP (five signatories). Although Islamist parties participated in the voting, the enthusiastic supporters for this bill were Pancasila-based parties like Golkar and Partai Demokrat (Sherlock 2008). Moreover, the chairmen of both Pancasila-based parties clearly indicated their support for the bill. For members of those Pancasila-based parties, this bill provides opportunities to strengthen their political standing with Muslim voters and modify their profile in Islamic communities. Without the massive protests by FPI and successful framing as defending morality, policy convergence between Pancasila-based and Islamist political parties would not have happened.

Local Sharia Laws

The Indonesian constitution protects religious pluralism, at least for six religions including Christianity, Catholicism, Buddhism, Hinduism, Islam and Confucianism. No national laws are allowed to favour or disadvantage a particular religion. However, more and more district governments in Indonesia have adopted sharia-related regulations since 2001.[9] These laws are made by regional peoples' representative councils (Dewan Perwakilan Rakyat Daerah, DPRD) together with the heads of the regions (Law 10/2004, Art. 1(7)) (Parsons and Mietzner 2009, p. 194). However, local executive heads are the dominant force in drafting and implementing local regulations. The contents of sharia laws vary by region, but often entail punishment for adultery, gambling, prostitution, mandate religious obligations as well as creating a curfew and requiring headscarves for women. Although religious affairs are supposed to be dealt with by the central government, district governments have been issuing these laws by arguing that these laws and regulations are for the purpose of establishing "public order". Public order is highly related with morality. It is viewed that when morality is low, then public order is low.

Currently, seven out of thirty-three provinces (20 per cent) and fifty-one of approximately 497 districts (10 per cent) have adopted sharia laws (Buehler 2011). These are concentrated in Aceh, West Sumatra, West Java, East Java, South Sulawesi and South Kalimantan. Many again assume that Prosperous Justice Party (PKS), an Islamist party, was behind the sharia laws (Dhume 2007). However, sharia laws were not necessarily introduced by local leaders with PKS affiliations. Michael Buehler (2012, p. 220) argues:

> PKS was part of the winning coalition in 7 out of 33 gubernatorial elections held between 2005 and 2008. Not a single sharia regulation was adopted in any of these seven provinces after the elections. Likewise, PKS was part of a winning coalition in 121 out of 427 district head and mayoral elections conducted between 2005 and 2008; 114 of the 121 executive heads supported by the PKS did not issue sharia regulations.

This argument is in line with Robin Bush (2008)'s argument. According to Robin Bush, Pancasila-based parties gained more than 50 per cent of the vote for local legislative elections in 72 out of the 74 districts which implemented sharia laws from 2000 to 2009. In fact, both scholars argue that almost 60 per cent of local executive heads who adopted sharia regulations between 1999 and 2009 are bureaucrats with links to the Golkar Party. Even after 2009, politicians affiliated with secular parties have continued to play a significant role in introducing sharia laws.[10]

There is no ideological consistency in political parties or among politicians that push for the adoption of sharia laws. Instead, the salience of radical Islamic groups matters. The regions with a strong historical presence of Islamic forces are likely to adopt sharia laws. Pancasila-based parties are willingly introducing sharia laws without the strong presence of Islamist parties. It is because politicians are likely to promote sharia laws when they face pressures from interest groups like FPI which functions as a power broker and which can influence voting preferences of individuals (Pisani and Buehler 2016).

Anti-Ahmadiyah Regulations

Ahmadiyah followers have lived in Indonesia since the 1920s and the Indonesian government recognized the Indonesian Ahmadiyah congregation officially in 1952.[11] The Ahmadiyah movement originated in British India in the late nineteenth century (contemporary Pakistan), and shares many of the attributes of Islam. Currently it is believed that Indonesia has 500,000 Ahmadiyah followers (Millie 2012). One of the main differences between them and other Muslims is that Ahmadiyah followers consider Mirza Ghulam Ahmad, the founder of the movement, as one of their prophets.[12]

There has long been disapproval toward Ahmadiyah by both mainstream and radical groups in Indonesia. However, in recent years, anti-Ahmadiyah threats and attacks by hardliners have been growing alarmingly, threatening religious pluralism as well as civil rights in Indonesia (Millie 2012).[13] Despite gruesome violence against Ahmadiyah, both national and local governments failed to halt violence against the Ahmadiyah community. Instead, they issued a ban on Ahmadiyah in dealing with radical groups' violence against Ahmadiyah followers. In 2008, the national government issued a joint ministerial decree regarding Ahmadiyah's propagation. The group was not outlawed but had prohibited its members from promoting its "deviant" teachings. A joint ministerial decree was signed by the Ministry of Religion, the Attorney General and the Ministry of Home Affairs.[14] Bernard Platzdasch (2011) argues that issuing a ministerial degree instead of a presidential decree indicates that the government is trying to please Muslim communities while avoiding the complete alienation of the Ahmadiyah community. Platzdasch terms it an "exquisite maneuver (*permainan cantik*)". When it comes to Islamic issues, all the politicians, including the president, cannot ignore them (Platzdasch 2011, p. 16).

The 2008 anti-Ahmadiyah decree facilitated the introduction of the anti-Ahmadiyah regulations at the local level. Table 7.1 illustrates the names of provinces, municipalities and mayoralties, and local leaders' party affiliations since the 2008 anti-Ahmadiyah decree. All of these localities had direct elections too.

TABLE 7.1
Anti-Ahmadiyah Regulations since 2008

	Date	Locality/Issuer	Name (Party Affiliation)
1.	October 2011	The Mayor of Bekasi	Mochtar Mohammad (PDI-P-Golkar coalition)
2.	March 2011	The Governor of West Java	Ahmad Heryawan (PD-PAN coalition)
3.	March 2011	The Governor of West Sumatra	Irwan Prayitno (PKS-Hanura-PBR coalition)
4.	March 2011	The Mayor of Depok (West Java)	Nur Mahmudi Ismail (PKS)
5.	March 2011	The Mayor of Bogor (West Java)	Diana Budiarto (PKS-Golkar-PDIP coalition)
6.	March 2011	The Regent of Serang	Taufik Nuriman (Golkar-PD-PKS-PDI-P-PPP-Hanura-PKPI coalition)
7.	March 2011	The Regent of Lebak	Mulyadi Jayabaya (Golkar-PDI-P-PKS-PD-PAN-PBR-PPD-PKB-PKPI coalition)
8.	March 2011	The Mayor of Pontianak	Sutarmidji (PPP-PKPI coalition)
9.	March 2011	The Regent of South Konawe	Imran (PD-PAN coalition)

TABLE 7.1 (continued)

10.	March 2011	The Mayor of Banjarmasin	Muhidin (PBR-Gerindra-PKPB coalition)
11.	March 2011	The Governor of Banten	Ratu Atut Chosiyah (Golkar-PDI-P coalition)
12.	February 2011	The Governor of East Java	Soekarwo (PAN-PD coalition)
13.	February 2011	The Mayor of Samarinda (East Kalimantan)	Syaharie Jaang (PD-PKS-PPP-PBR coalition)
14.	February 2011	The Regent of Pandeglang (Banten)	Erwan Kurtubi (Golkar-PD-PKS-PKB-Hanura-PKPB-PPRN-PMB coalition)
15.	February 2011	The Regent of Kampar (Riau)	M. Burhanuddin Husin (Golkar-PKS coalition)
16.	February 2011	The Governor of South Sulawesi	Syahrul Yasin Limpo (PDI-P-PAN coalition)
17.	November 2010	The Mayor of Pekanbaru (Riau)	Herman Abdullah (Golkar-PAN-PBB-PPP-PDS coalition)
18.	September 2008	The Governor of South Sumatra	Alex Noerdin (Golkar-PAN-PD coalition)
19.	May 2008	The Mayor of Cimahi (West Java)	Itoc Tochija (Golkar-PDI-P-PKB-PBB coalition)

Source: This list of provinces, municipalities, and cities are adapted from Crouch (2009, 2012) and Human Rights Working Group et al. (2012). The author added the name of issuer and party affiliation to the list.

Although local governments introduced anti-Ahmadiyah regulations in the name of public order and social harmony (Indonesia Crisis Group 2008), they are religiously inspired. State officials are trying to appeal to conservative local constituencies in the face of radical Islamic groups and powerful religious figures. Anybody who intends to overturn them will be considered anti-Islamic or anti-religious. By 2011, six provinces and twenty-four municipalities and districts introduced anti-Ahmadiyah regulations.[15] Nineteen out of thirty regulations were introduced since the 2008 decree.

TABLE 7.2
Anti-Ahmadiyah Regulations and Party Affiliations

Secular Parties (7)	Secular Parties and Islamic Parties (11)	Islamic Parties (or Islamic Parties Coalition (1)
South Sumatra, South Sulawesi, East Java, Bekasi, West Java, South Konawe, Banten	Cimahi, Pekanbaru, Kampar, Pandeglang, Samarinda, West Sumatra, Bogor, Serang, Lebak, Banjarmasin, Pontianak	Depok

As seen in Table 7.2, except for one locality, Pancasila parties, whether with or without coalition with Islamist parties, won all the localities that implemented anti-Ahmadiyah regulations. In seven out of nineteen localities, local leaders were affiliated with Pancasila-based parties while in eleven localities, leaders were affiliated with coalitions between Pancasila-based parties and Islamist parties. The regulations differ in areas but often include banning of Ahmadiyah activities, outlawing signs for Ahmadiyah mosques and educational institutions, and disallowing the usage of written, oral and electronic media to extend their teaching (Crouch 2011, 2012).

These regulations are not driven by pious politicians in local elections but the product of pressure from radical groups on the Indonesian government. Hardline groups are not shy about claiming credit for what they did. Radical groups are using campaign against Ahmadiyah to capture political and media attention (Fealy 2016). Moderate Islamic organizations also join hardline groups' efforts to eradicate so-called "non-believers of Islam" which they refer to Ahmadiyah. According to a polling on the official NU website, 57 per cent of respondents agreed that FPI was necessary to eliminate immorality and oppose liberal groups while only 25 per cent of respondents said that FPI should be disbanded for ruining the image of Islam (Franklin 2009). For some issue areas, there have been some tactical mergers between moderate and radical groups.

Against Extra-Marital Affairs and LGBT Acts

AILA, a conservative Islamic movement organization, has made itself politically recognized by requesting that the Constitutional Court criminalizes LGBT acts as well as extra-marital affairs. The activists from AILA collaborated with the bigger movement known as Civilized Indonesia Movement (Gerakan Indonesia Beradab, GIB) to spread their beliefs in the name of saving national morality.

Although their attempt to criminalize extra-marital affairs and LGBT acts was thwarted by a December 2017 Constitutional Court decision, AILA continues to work on criminalizing sexual minorities, and to find a way to expand the sphere of the state to scrutinize private lives under the name of protecting national morality. In fact, the Indonesian parliament is reviewing the criminal code that includes the criminalization of LGBT acts. As a result, politically engineered homophobia has become intense drastically in the last several years.[16]

This is a new phenomenon. Indonesia has been tolerant toward sexual minorities. Although the LGBT population has not enjoyed open support, they have never been publicly condemned or punished like what is currently happening. An organization like AILA has changed the atmosphere, accusing homosexuality of child pornography as well as AIDS. The chairperson of AILA, Rita Hendrawaty Soebagio, in her interview mentioned that Indonesia has been experiencing a moral and ethical crisis which was originated from dysfunctional family, and LGBT was the derivative of western feminism movements that caused the crisis in Indonesia.[17] In her view, LGBT is an enemy of Islamic movements, and the bad influence of the West. To her, the pious family (*Keluarga Sakinah*) is the only way to solve this problem. The idea of pious family is strongly rooted in heteronormativity in which homosexuality has no place to stand.

Moderate Muslim organizations as well as all the political parties have also joined the bandwagon of this movement by labelling homosexuality as the biggest national security threat. The Indonesia Defense Minister, Ryamizard Ryacudu, said in his speech that LGBT rights are more dangerous than "nuclear war".[18] Muhammad Nasir,

Minister for Technology, Research and Higher Education, called for a ban on LGBT people on university campuses, claiming that they threaten "Indonesian morals and norms", while the head of the People's Consultative Assembly (MPR), Zulkifli Hasan, agreed with the move, commenting that LGBT sexuality is at odds with "Indonesian culture" (Yulius 2016; Wilson 1995). Many political parties included homosexuality ban as the main agenda of their national congress. Even moderate Islamic organizations Nahdlatul Ulama and Muhammadiyah agreed with such moves. This demonstrates that a small organization with the power of framing can set an agenda and influence the government and politicians. As a result, LGBT communities are currently experiencing unprecedented discrimination in Indonesia.

Conclusion

This chapter examines how conservative Islamic movements have shaped policies in contemporary Indonesia. Despite the consistently low popularity of Islamic political parties and the dominance of the long-existing and mass-based Muslim organizations in Islamic civil society, conservative Islamic movements have become an important driving force in Indonesian policy-making.

Conservative Islamic movements pushed for a closed world view on Indonesian politics that is based on narrow interpretations of Islam. Although they do not represent mainstream views, they are able to mobilize the followers in the name of guarding morality. Their successful framing has silenced the majority of moderate voices, and appealed to people who have been concerned with any changes that have been occurring as a result of political and economic liberalization. As a result, conservative Islamic movements have successfully set an agenda in the name of defending morality. Morality becomes the weapon of the faithful in the conservative Islamic movements. Their mobilizational capacity made their agenda much more salient in public while making both Islamic and Pancasila-based political parties hard to dismiss and disagree with their demands.

In sum, the saliency of conservative Islamic movements is likely to continue. The voices of conservative Islamic movements will become even more intense as there have been mergers between right-wing nationalists and Islamists for Indonesia's parliamentary and presidential elections in 2019. As political parties try to court these conservative movements, the demands of these social movements will prevail even though the popularity of Islamic parties does not necessarily increase. Given this trend, moderate Islamic organizations such as NU and Muhammadiyah have to carefully define what it means to be moderate, and find ways to sustain their values. Otherwise, the influence of NU and Muhammadiyah can be further thwarted.

NOTES

1. *World Politics Review*, 5 March 2018.
2. More hardline Muslim organizations and neo-Salafist teachings have become popular on campuses and also shape what it means to be an ideal family. For more information, see Wieringa (2015), pp. 27–44.
3. *Jakarta Post*, 30 August 2016.
4. For a detailed account about the tactical merger between Islamic civil society and violent extremism, see Jones (2016).
5. It includes Golkar Party, Indonesian Democracy Party of Struggle (PDI-P), National Awakening Party (PKB), Democracy Party (PD), and National Mandate Party (PAN).
6. They include Prosperous Justice Party (PKS) and United Development Party (PPP).
7. *BBC*, 7 April 2006.
8. For more discussions on anti-pornography, see Norshahril (2016).
9. With the second amendment to the Constitution in August 2000, regional governments were granted autonomy, which includes the right to issue regional laws and regulations.
10. For more discussions on sharia laws, see Buehler and Muhtada (2016), pp. 261–82; Buehler (2013), pp. 63–82.
11. About Ahmadiyah communities in Indonesia, see Avonius (2008); Crouch (2009); Munawar (2007); Platzdasch (2011).
12. For discussions about Ahmadiyah and its heresy debates, see Burhani (2013).
13. Mille argues that attacks against Ahmadiyah occurred in West Java more frequently than any other province.
14. Both the Minister of Religion, Maftuh Basyuni, and the Attorney General, Hendarman Supandji, do not have clear party affiliation while the Minister of Internal Affairs, Mardiyanto (2007–9), is affiliated with PDI-P.
15. This figure is compiled from both Crouch (2012) and Human Rights Working Group et al. (2012).
16. About the rise of homophobia, see Boellstorff (2004), pp. 465–86.

17. "Ormas Islam Bersatu Melawan LGBT sebagai Musuh Bersama", Hidayatullah.com, 26 August 2016; "Banyak fakta dan data yang memprihatinkan, yang pada ujungnya menjelaskan ada problem adab dan moral di tengah masyarakat kita. Tak hanya pada anak-anak, tapi hampir di semua lapisan", https://www.hidayatullah.com/berita/wawancara/read/2016/08/26/100035/ormas-islam-bersatu-melawan-lgbt-sebagai-musuh-bersama.html (accessed 1 July 2017).
18. *Tempo*, 23 February 2016.

REFERENCES

Allen, Pam. 2007. "Challenging Diversity? Indonesia's Anti-Pornography Bill". *Asian Studies Review* 31, no. 2: 101–15.
Andrews, Kenneth and Bob Edwards. 2004. "Advocacy Organizations in the U.S. Political Process". *Annual Review of Sociology* 30: 479–506.
Aspinall, Edward. 2004. "The Irony of Success". *Journal of Democracy* 21, no. 2: 20–34.
Avonius, Lenna. 2008. "The Ahmadiyya and Freedom of Religion in Indonesia". *ISIM Review* 22 (Autumn).
Benford, Robert and David Snow. 2000. "Framing Processes and Social Movements: An Overview". *Annual Review of Sociology* 26: 611–39.
Boellstorff, Tom. 2004. "The Emergence of Political Homophobia in Indonesia: Masculinity and National Belonging". *Ethnos* 69, no. 4: 465–86.
Budiman, Nammeke. 2011. "The Middle Class and Morality Politics in the Envisioning of the Nation in Post-Suharto Indonesia". *Inter-Asian Cultural Studies* 12, no. 4: 482–99.
Buehler, Michael. 2011. "Whodunit?: Politicians Affiliated with Secular Parties Implement Most Sharia Regulations". *Tempo*, 6 September 2011, pp. 58–59.
———. 2012. "Revisiting the Inclusion-Moderation Thesis in the Context of Decentralized Institutions: The Behavior of Indonesia's Prosperous Justice Party in National and Local Politics". *Party Politics* 19, no. 2: 210–29.
———. 2013. "Subnational Islamization through Secular Parties: Comparing Shar'ia Politics in Two Indonesian Provinces". *Comparative Politics* 46, no. 1: 63–82.
Buehler, Michael and Dani Muhtada. 2016. "Democratization and the Diffusion of Sharia Law: Comparative Insights From Indonesia". *South East Asia Research* 24, no. 2: 261–82.
Burhani, Najib. 2013. "When Muslims are not Muslims: The Ahmadiyya Community and the Discourse on Heresy in Indonesia". PhD dissertation, The University of California at Santa Barbara.

Bush, Robin. 2008. "Regional Sharia Regulations in Indonesia: Anomaly or Symptom?" In *Expressing Islam: Religious Life and Politics in Indonesia*, edited by Greg Fealy and Sally White. Canberra: Australian National University.

Collins, Elizabeth. 2003. "Dakwah and Democracy: The Significance of Partai Keadilan and Hizbut Tahrir". Paper presented at the Annual Meeting of the American Political Science Association, Philadelphia, PA.

Crouch, Melissa. 2009. "Indonesia, Militant Islam, and Ahmadiyah: Origins and Implications". *ARC Federation Fellowship Islam, Syariah and Governance, Background Paper Series* no. 4 (2009).

———. 2011. "Religious 'Deviancy' and Law". *Inside Indonesia* 105.

———. 2012. "Judicial Review and Religious Freedom: The Case of Indonesian Ahmadis". *Sydney Law Review* 34: 544–72.

Dhume, Sadanand. 2007. "Step up the Fight Against Islamism". *Far Eastern Economic Review* 170: 6–13.

Diana, Mario. 1996. "Linking Mobilization Frames and Political Opportunities: Insights from Regional Populism in Italy". *American Sociological Review* 61: 1053–67.

Fealy, Greg. 2016. "The Politics of Religious Intolerance in Indonesia: Mainstreamism Trumps Extremism?" In *Religion, Law and Intolerance in Indonesia*, edited by Tim Lindsey and Helen Pausacker. Oxen: Routledge.

Ferree, Myra Marx. 2003. "Resonance and Radicalism: Feminist Framing of Abortion in the United States and Germany". *American Journal of Sociology* 109: 304–44.

Fox, James. 2004. "Currents in Contemporary Islam in Indonesia". Paper presented at Harvard Asia Vision 21, Cambridge, MA, 29 April–1 May 2004.

Franklin, Nathan. 2009. "Ahmadiyah Dispute Intensifies". *Inside Indonesia* (March).

Giugni, Marco. 2004. *Social Protest and Policy Change*. Lanham, MD: Rowman and Littlefield.

Giugni, Marco and Sakura Yamasaki. 2009. "The Policy Impact of Social Movements: A Replication Through Qualitative Comparative Analysis". *Mobilization: An International Journal* 14, no. 4: 467–84.

Grzymala-Busse, Anna. 2015. *Nations Under God: How Churches Use Moral Authority to Influence Policy*. Princeton: Princeton University Press.

Hadiz, Vedi. 2017. "Behind the Indonesia's Illiberal Turn". *New Mandela*, 20 October 2017.

Hertzke, Allen. 1988. *Representing God in Washington*. Knoxville: University of Tennessee Press.

Htun Mala. 2003. *Sex and the State*. Cambridge: Cambridge University Press.

Human Rights Working Group, Jakarta Legal Aid Institute, the Institute for Policy Research and Advocacy, Setara Institute, Indonesia Legal Resource Center, Wahid Institute, and the Center for Marginalized Communities

Studies. 2012. "List of Regulation that Prohibit Ahmadiyah Activities Until 2011". In a report submitted to the UN Human Rights Council for the Universal Periodic Review of Indonesia, Geneva, 23 May 2012.

International Crisis Group. 2008. *Indonesia: Implications of the Ahmadiyah Decree.* Asia Briefing No. 78.

Jahroni, Jajang. 2008. *Defending the Majesty of Islam: Indonesia's Front Pembela Islam, 1998–2003.* Chiangmai: Silkworm Books.

Jenkins, Craig. 1995. "Social Movements, Political Representation, and the State: An Agenda and Comparative Framework". In *The Politics of Social Protest: Comparative Perspectives on States and Social Movements,* edited by Craig Jenkins and Bert Klandermans. London: UCL Press.

Jones, Sidney. 2016. "Islamist Civil Society and Violent Extremism in Indonesia: A Tactical Merger? In *Religion, Law and Intolerance in Indonesia,* edited by Tim Lindsey and Helen Pausacker. Oxen: Routledge.

Jones, Sydney. 2017. "Indonesia's Illiberal Turn After the Ahok Case". *Foreign Affairs,* 16 May 2017.

Jung, Eunsook. 2009. "Taking Care of the Faithful: Islamic Organizations and Partisan Engagement in Indonesia". PhD dissertation, Department of Political Science, University of Wisconsin-Madison.

———. 2014. "Islamic Organizations and Electoral Politics in Indonesia: Case of Muhammadiyah". *South East Asia Research* 22, no. 1: 476–94.

Lahiri, Simanti. 2014. *Social Protest in South Asia: Consumed by Commitment.* Oxen: Routledge.

Leege, David. 1988. "Catholics and the Civic Order: Parish Participation, Politics, and Civic Participation". *The Review of Politics* 50, no. 4: 704–35

McAdam, Doug. 1996. "Conceptual Origins, Current Problems, Future Directions". In *Comparative Perspectives on Social Movements,* edited by Doug McAdam, John McCarthy, and Zald Mayer. Cambridge: Cambridge University Press.

Millie, Julian. 2012. "One Year After the Cikeusik Tragedy". *Inside Indonesia* 107 (January–March).

Munawar, Ahmad. 2007. "Faith and Violence". *Inside Indonesia* 89 (January–March).

Norshahril Saat. 2016. *The State, Ulama and Islam in Malaysia and Indonesia.* Amsterdam: Amsterdam University Press.

Parsons, Nicholas and Marcus Mietzner. 2009. "Sharia By-Laws in Indonesia: A Legal and Political Analysis". *Asian Law* 11 no. 2: 190–217.

Peterson, Steven. 1992. "Church Participation and Political Participation: The Spillover Effect". *American Politics Research* 20, no. 1: 123–39.

Pisani, Elizabeth and Michael Buehler. 2016. "Why do Indonesian Politicians Promote Shari'a Laws? An Analytic Framework for Muslim-majority Democracies". *Third World Quarterly* 38, no. 3: 734–52.

Platzdasch, Bernhard. 2011. "Religious Freedom in Indonesia: The Case of the Ahmadiyah". ISEAS Working Paper. Singapore: Institute of Southeast Asian Studies.

Salim, Arskal. 2007. "Muslim Politics in Indonesia's Democratisation". In *Indonesia: Democracy and the Promise of Good Governance*, edited by Ross McLeod and Andrew MacIntyre. Singapore: Institute of Southeast Asian Studies.

Sherlock, Stephen. 2008. "Parties and Decision-making in the Indonesian Parliament: A Case Study of RUU APP, the Anti-Pornography Bill". *Australian Journal of Asian Law* 10, no. 2: 159–83.

Skocpol, Theda. 1995. *Protecting Soldiers and Mothers*. Cambridge: Harvard University Press.

Tarrow, Sidney. 1994. *Power in Movement: Social Movements, Collective Action, and Politics*. Cambridge: Cambridge University Press.

van Bruinessen, Martin. 2015. "Contemporary Developments in Indonesian Islam and the Conservative Turn in the 21st Century". In *Contemporary Development in Indonesian Islam: Explaining the Conservative Turn*, edited by Martin van Bruinessen. Singapore: Institute of Southeast Asian Studies.

Verba, Sidney, Kay Lehman Schlozman, Henry Brady, and Norman H. Nie. 1993. "Race, Ethnicity and Political Resources: Participation in the United States". *British Journal of Political Science* 23: 453–97.

Wald, Kenneth. 2002. *Religion and Politics in the United States*. 4th ed. Boulder: Rowman and Littlefield.

Wald, Kenneth, Adam Silverman, and Kevin Friday. 2005. "Making Sense of Religion in Political Life". *Annual Review of Political Science* 8: 121–43.

Warner, Carolyn. 2000. *Confession of an Interest Group*. Princeton: Princeton University Press.

Wictorowitz, Quintan. 2004. *Islamic Activism: Social Movement Theory Approach*. Bloomington, Indiana: Indiana University Press.

Wieringa, Saskia. 2015. "Gender Harmony and the Happy Family: Islam, Gender, and Sexuality in Post-Reformasi Indonesia". *South East Asian Research* 23, no. 1: 27–44.

Wilson, James. 1995. *Political Organization*. Princeton: Princeton University Press.

Yulius, Hendry. 2016. "LGBT Indonesians on Campus: Too Hot to Handle". *Indonesia at Melbourne*, 26 January 2016. http://indonesiaatmelbourne.unimelb.edu.au/lgbt-indonesians-on-campus-too-hot-to-handle/ (accessed 1 June 2018).

PART II:

Transnational Transmission of Islamic Knowledge

8

SALAFISM, KNOWLEDGE PRODUCTION AND RELIGIOUS EDUCATION IN INDONESIA

Noorhaidi Hasan

Over the last decades, Indonesia has seen the growing impact of Saudi transnational proselytization and religious funding. Owing to the generous support by Saudi Arabia, *dakwah* activities focusing on promoting Salafism proliferated, and this is followed by the establishment of Salafi-oriented foundations and *madrasahs* in Indonesia. During the shifting political stance in the 1990s, the Salafis succeeded in establishing an exclusivist version of Islamic activism in Indonesia within the religious authorities. Due to the intensified Salafi campaign, Indonesian Muslims have been increasingly susceptible to the influences of rigid purification of faith that hardly accepts the diversity of religious expression and culture. This new type of Islamic activism also posed a challenge not only to existing religious authority but also to the legitimacy of established Muslim organizations.

The Saudi campaign impacted schools and university education through the production of Salafi-inspired literature. Translated works by 'Aid al-Qarni, Muhammad Nasir al-Din al-Albani, and Muhammad

Salih al-Uthaimin are among the favourite references taught in Islamic schools and colleges. Salafi-oriented publishers are concerned with the production of such literatures, and they work shoulder-to-shoulder with Salafi preachers who have completed their studies in Salafi centres of learning in the Middle East. The Salafis believe that their main mission is to purify Muslim beliefs and practices and to educate them based on "correct" interpretations of the Quran and Sunnah, in accordance with the example set by the pious forefathers (*Salaf al-Salih*). The first is called *tasfiyya* (purification) and the second *tarbiyya* (education).

This chapter explores the practices of knowledge production, religious authority and education among the Salafi circles in Indonesia, and how they have exerted their influence beyond their own circles. More specifically, I will be looking at how doctrinal competition and ideological conflict are reflected in the discourse and literature produced by Salafi authorities. I will also be examining the role played by Salafi preachers and authorities, both in producing literature and in contextualizing and appropriating Salafi messages into the education system. Before tackling these issues, the historical background of Salafism in Indonesia will be examined.

The Efflorescence of Salafism

The efflorescence of Salafism in Indonesia—evident by the growing number of young Muslim men wearing *jalabiyya* (Arab-style flowing robes) and women wearing *niqab* (a form of enveloping black veil) in public places—might not be isolated from Saudi Arabia's politics of expanding their geopolitical influence throughout the Muslim world. In the 1970s, because of the skyrocketing world oil prices, which gave considerable economic benefits to Saudi Arabia, the kingdom sponsored a variety of *dakwah* activities all over the Muslim world. The purpose of such activities was to ensure the acquiescence of the Muslim world, boost Saudi rulers' legitimacy at home, and fulfill Western political projects (Fraser 1997; Kepel 2002, pp. 69–72; Al-Rasheed 2007). In this way, Salafism was exported and spread, together with the Muslim Brotherhood-inspired *Sahwa* ideology. This campaign was later intensified, particularly in the aftermath of the Iranian Revolution in 1979, and the takeover of the Masjid al-Haram by Juhayman al-Utaybi-led group that same year (Abukhalil 2004; Al-Rasheed 2008; Lacroix

2011). As a result, networks of loyalty and allegiance were established. Clothed in the language of Islamic solidarity and brotherhood, they worked closely together to dominate the religious landscape of the Muslim world.

Within the context of Indonesia, Saudi Arabia moulded close collaborations with the Indonesian Islamic Propagation Council (DDII, Dewan Dakwah Islamiyah Indonesia) and the Institute of Islamic and Arabic Sciences (LIPIA, Lembaga Ilmu Pengetahuan Islam dan Bahasa Arab). Both played a considerable role in recruiting cadres to campaign for Saudi Arabia's ideology, which underwent a change in direction as a result of the political crisis after the Juhayman al-Utaybi's seizure of Masjid al-Haram (Trofimov 2007; Lacroix 2011). Accordingly, the Saudis developed a policy of advertising its commitment to Islam while suppressing radical expressions of political Islam. This policy seemingly became a catalyst for further proliferation of Salafi influence, particularly among youths and university students and staff in that country.

A new variant of Salafism fully supported by the Saudi regime was born out of the concern centred on the need to call for a return to strict religious practices and moral integrity of individuals. Seemingly trivial, superficial issues, such as *jalabiyya, imama, lihya, isbal,* and *niqab* constituted the main themes of day-to-day discussions among followers. The commitment to wear *jalabiyya* for men and *niqab* for women, for instance, is considered to be more important than taking part in political activities. They enthusiastically demonstrated a commitment to religious propagation and a puritanical lifestyle, while refraining from openly discussing politics and excessively applying *takfir* (declaration of an individual as a unbeliever).

Indonesian DDII cadres who studied in Saudi Arabia in the 1980s were inspired by the Salafi movement and organized a systematic propagation method of "quietist Salafism" (Hasan 2007). Upon returning home, they organized workshops (*halqa*) and study circles (*daura*) openly in the areas around university campuses in Yogyakarta. Notable among them were Abu Nida, Ainur Rafiq Ghufron, Ahmad Faiz Asifuddin, Abdul Qadir Jawas, Ja'far Umar Thalib and Yusuf Usman Baisa, to mention but a few names, who soon gained the reputation as the main proponents of Indonesian Salafism. Among the participants in the *halqas* and *dauras* were homegrown-*Darul Islam* (DI)-inspired Negara Islam Indonesia (NII)'s followers who felt exhausted being active in a clandestive movement which was under close surveillance of intelligent agents (Hasan 2006). Although some Salafi proponents had fought the war in Afghanistan, they were also involved in the campaigns against NII and other radical organizations deemed to have been trapped into neo-*khawarij*'s libel which were actively spreading animosity and catastrophy among Muslims.

At the end of the 1980s, and in tandem with the proliferation of quietist Salafism, NII began to lose its foothold in Indonesia. NII leaders, Abdullah Sungkar and Abu Bakar Ba'asyir, escaped to Malaysia in 1985 to avoid being arrested by security authorities because of their harsh criticism against the Indonesian government, which they labelled as *taghut*. This criticism was especially directed at the government's policies to impose Pancasila as the state ideology. In Malaysia, they recruited followers, expanded networks and further developed their militancy and radicalism. From 1985 to 1990, they succeeded in dispatching some 200 members to Afghanistan to participate in a military training (*i'dad ashkari*) camp at Harby Pohantum, which was founded by Shaikh Rasul Sayyaf (Solahudin 2013, pp. 132–34). The purpose of the training was to acquire military knowledge and skills for *jihad* against the government. In Afghanistan, the militants became acquainted with the jihadi Salafi teachings. Their adoption of jihadism stirred up conflicts in the internal *usrah* network (Pavlova 2007; Solahudin 2013, pp. 144–45). Sungkar led an opposition against Ajengan Masduki, then the DI leader who was deemed to be a deviant joining a Sufi Order. Later in 1996, he established al-Qaeda-linked Jamaah Islamiyah (JI), which was active in promoting jihadist Salafism in Indonesia (Abuza 2003).

In the first two decades of the Salafi expansion, both quietists and jihadists successfully attracted a significant following, especially from the the younger generation of Indonesian Muslims. Islamic study circles and workshops, organized by quietists in spaces close to university campuses, were well attended. Likewise, Islamic study circles organized by the jihadist camp also mushroomed in many Indonesia cities. A number of leading Indonesian Salafi authorities, both from the circle of quietists and jihadists, were born out of this context, including Abu Nida, Ja'far Umar Thalib, Yazid bin Abdul Qadir Jawas, Muhammad Umar As-Sewed, Irfan Awwas, Abu Jibril Abdurrahman, and the infamous Abu Bakar Ba'asyir. It is intriguing in this context to understand why so many young people were so eager to participate in the Salafis' Islamic study circles.

Knowledge Production

The key success of the Salafis in attracting a strong following can be explained by their ability to instill habitus through a certain mode of knowledge production. As a "system of durable, transposable disposition, structured structures predisposed to function as structuring structures", habitus guides someone to action or inaction. It becomes social values embedded and established through the *longue-durée* process of socialization. Habitus constitutes a principle which "generates and organizes practices and representations that can be objectively adapted to their outcomes without presupposing a conscious aiming at the ends and or express mastery of operations necessary in order to attain them" (Bourdieu 1995, p. 52). It appears to be the structuring structure that is received through the actor's experiences in internalizing the objective structure of the social world.

The Salafis produce religious knowledge in a broad sense to include not only theology, morality, *fiqh* and in general Islamic reasoning, but also all kinds of non-discursive ritualized, performative and embodied forms of knowledge production, such as prayers, rituals and bodily practices that denote worship and religiousness. Taking religion as a form of mediation (Meyer 2006), in understanding religion as a human practice, it is impossible to separate discursive and non-discursive dimensions and to ignore the mutual interactions between discursive and non-discursive dimensions of knowledge production. Moreover, there is an intricate, mutually constitutive relation between the production of religious knowledge and everyday experiences of the Salafis.

In tandem with its ultimate concern with a purification of Muslim beliefs and practices in accordance with the Quran and Sunnah as well as the understanding and example set by *salaf al-salih*, it is understandable that the Salafis put an emphasis on the teaching of *tauhid,* or more precisely Wahhabi doctrine, in their practices of knowledge production (Hasan 2010). Meaning to accept and believe in the oneness of God and His absolute authority, *tauhid* is considered by the Salafis to be the pillar of Muslim creed. Total submission to God entails a person's sincere determination to implement all of His commands and scrupulously avoid all of His prohibitions. *Tawhid* is taught through the main subject in its curriculum, i.e., Islamic Theology (*'Aqida*). For this subject, Salafis read works such as *Al-Qaul al-Mufid fi Adillat al-Tawhid* [The Useful Opinion on the Evidence of the

Oneness of God], which is the summary of the *Kitab al-Tawhid* [The Book on the Oneness of God] by Muhammad ibn 'Abd al-Wahhab. In some of the Salafi teaching centres, the Salafis are obliged to memorize this text by heart as a precondition before continuing on to study other books.

Having completed this book, the Salafis are usually obliged to study the *Kitab al-Tawhid* or its annotated commentaries such as *Al Qaul al-Shadid 'Ala Kitab al-Tawhid* [The Authoritative Opinion on Book of the Oneness of God] by 'Abd al-Rahman al-Su'udi. Subsequently they should study *al-Usul al-Thalatha* [The Three Principles] by Muhammad ibn 'Abd al-Wahhab before reading *al-Aqida al-Wasitiyya* [The Middle Faith] by Taqiy al-Din Ahmad ibn Taymiyya or its annotated commentary, *Sharh al-'Aqida al-Wasitiyya* [Explanation of the Middle Faith] by Salih ibn Fauzan Ali Fauzan. Having mastered these primary books students are recommended to read other books, including *Nabza fi al-'Aqida* [Fragmentation in the Faith] by Muhammad Salih al-Uthaimin, *Sharh al-'Aqida al-Thahawiyya al-Muyassar* [Concise Explanation of the Faith According to Al-Tahawi] by Muhammad ibn 'Abd al-Rahman al-Khamis, and *Minhaj Firqat al-Najiyat* [Method of the Saved Sect] by Muhammad bin Jamil Zainu.

In relation to the teaching of *tauhid*, the Salafis highlight the importance of the doctrine *al-wala' wa-l-bara'* (allegiance to Islam and renunciation of unbelievers), which implies that any Muslim who claims to have faith in Allah must love, help, and defend Islam and other Muslims while at the same time denouncing infidelity, and segregating himself or herself from the influence of infidels (Hasan 2010). Theoretically, this doctrine entails a clear-cut distinction between the world of believers and that of unbelievers. More importantly, it provides the basis for the Salafis to choose living in small tight-knit communities (*jama'a*), a general practice that is expected to protect them from *bid'a* and reinforce their unity in the face of Muslim enemies.

The understanding of fundamental doctrines provides the foundation for the Salafis to study other subjects including Quranic exegesis, the Prophetic Traditions, Islamic legal theory, jurisprudence, and *dakwah* methodology. For Quranic exegesis, they read, among other things, *Usul al-Tafsir* [Principles of the Quranic Exegesis] by Muhammad Salih al-Uthaimin and *Aysir al-Tafasir li Kalam al-'Ali al-Kabir* [The Simplest Exegesis on the Words of the Eminent Supreme] by Abu Bakar Jabir al-Jazairi. For the Prophetic Traditions, they study *al-Arba'in al-Nawawiyya* [al-Nawawi's Forty Prophetic Tradition Collection] by Imam al-Nawawi or its commentary, *al-Arba'in al-Nawawiyya* by Salih al-Shaykh, as well as *Muzakkirat al-Hadith al-Nabawi* [Treatise on the Prophetic Traditions] by Rabi ibn Hadi al-Madkhali and *Darurat al-Ihtimam bi Sunan al-Nabawiyyah* [Solicitude for the Prophetic Traditions] by Abd al-Salam Abi Barjis Ibn Nasir Abd al-Karim. For Islamic legal theory, the required reading materials include *al-Usul al-Fiqh* [Principles of Islamic Jurisprudence], *al-Usul min 'Ilm al-Usul* [The Principles of the Science of the Principles (of Islamic Jurisprudence)] by Muhammad Salih al-Uthaimin and *al-Waraqat fi Usul al-Fiqh* [Treatise on the Principles of Islamic Jurisprudence] by 'Abd al-Malik ibn Juwaini (Hasan 2010; *cf.* Wahid 2014). This subject is taught to support another related subject, namely, Islamic jurisprudence, in which *Taysir al-Fiqh* [The Simple Version of Islamic Jurisprudence] by Salih bin Ghanim al-Sadlan, *Minhaj al-Muslim* [Method of the Believer] by Abu Bakr Jabir al-Jaza'iri, and *al-Mulakhkhas al-Fiqhiy* [Summary of the Islamic Jurisprudence] by Salih bin Fauzan al-Fauzan are the main required readings. For *dakwah* methodology, the Salafis read *Dakwah al-Du'at* [Islamic Propagation Guidelines for Muslim Preachers] by Ibn Qayyim al-Jawziyya and *Al-Da`watu ila Allah* [Islamic Mission in the Name of God] by Ali Hasan al-Halaby al-Atsari.

The system of instruction in Salafi *madrasahs* is conventional in nature. It is based on an informal teacher-scholar relationship. Every morning, at around 8 o'clock, the *ustadhs* will come to the mosque and occupy different positions and spaces. The most senior *ustadh* will usually occupy the centrepart of the mosque while the other *ustadhs* will sit at the wings. Groups of students sit around them referring to the books held in their own hands while listening to their *ustadhs*. The *ustadhs* read the books and explain the meaning of each sentence while giving illustrations and examples. Sometimes they use small blackboards to make their explanations clearer. Some students make notes in their books while others only listen. In the case of the teaching of Arabic, the students are drilled repeatedly to imitate as fluently as possible the examples of the sentence given by their *ustadhs*. Opportunities to raise questions are given to the students after the *ustadhs* finish their lessons. This activity lasts until the noon prayer. Between the noon prayer and the afternoon prayer, students have lunch and then take a rest. After the afternoon prayer, they will come back to undertake the same activity. This afternoon activity ends around one hour before the sunset prayer at 6 o'clock. Between the sunset prayer and the evening prayer at 7 p.m. the students read and memorize some parts of the Quran, prescribed by their *ustadhs*.

Some Salafi *madrasahs* offer special programmes (*takhassus*) called *Tadrib al-Du'at* (training for preachers) and *Tarbiyat al-Nisa* (education for women). These programmes last for a certain period of time, ranging from three months to one year (Hasan 2010; Wahid 2014). The *Tadrib al-Du'at* is designed to produce ready preachers to conduct *dakwah* activities. The subjects taught consist of Islamic theology, Quranic exegesis, the Prophet's traditions, Islamic history, Islamic law, ethics, and Arabic. The *Tarbiyat al-Nisa* is addressed to women and is aimed at forming their personality according to the Wahhabi doctrine. In this programme, participants study Islamic theology and Islamic jurisprudence besides receiving instructions on behaviour, fashion, gender relations, and the methods of taking care of husbands and children. The materials used are selected from the books required in the aforementioned regular programmes. This sort of sandwich programme played a pivotal role in moulding young cadres of Salafi preachers to spearhead the Salafi *dakwah* expansion among students both at senior high schools and universities.

Conflict within the Salafis

The Salafis are a heterogeneous group. The quietists and the jihadists compete in promoting their respective doctrinal positions and ideological standpoints. This conflict is interestingly productive, meaning that to refute each other's camp, they are active in publishing books, periodicals, pamphlets and other printed materials. Production of religious knowledge is situated and contested. Taking Asad (1986)'s notion of religion as a discursive tradition, it follows that perceptions of Salafis about what proper Islamic knowledge entails and what are the appropriate means through which knowledge is communicated are situated and contextual (van Bruinessen 2003). These perceptions are central to the views and debates about the interaction of Salafis with their social environment. Although there is no single, universal standard about what Islamic knowledge entails, it is a crucial prerequisite in understanding what it means to be Salafi and how Muslim subjects are formed. Hence the means, techniques and practices through which knowledge is being communicated is crucial.

Confident with the positive responses they had acquired from the Indonesian society, the quietists strongly rejected *dakwah hizbiyya* promoted by the jihadists. In numerous articles in *Salafy*, a periodical published by the quietists, *dakwah hizbiyya* is defined as political fanaticism which lacks appreciation towards the truth Salafi system (*manhaj*). It was opposed to the *dakwah salafiyya* for the following reasons: (1) it deviates from the way of faithful Muslims (*sabil al-mu'minin*); (2) its leader comes perilously close to the sins of *bid'a*; (3) its members are committed to the doctrine of *al-wala wa'l-bara* on the basis of their loyalty to a particular leader rather than to the Quran and Sunnah; and (4) it teaches fanaticism (Hasan 2006, p. 141).

The quietists further argued that the main error committed by the *hizbiyya* groups stems from their loyalty to the followers of *bid'a*. This mistake has led to divisions among Muslims because it teaches fanaticism to each separate group, prompting members to renounce any truth that might belong to the others. Adherence to the *dakwah hizbiyya* was even considered to be one of the distinctive characteristics of polytheists (*mushrikin*). This is because those who support it use Islam as a weapon to create fanatical groups for their own political interests, and the result is that Muslims become fragmented and weak.

The criticism was primarily directed at the activism developed by the Tarbiyya movement, which is better categorized into politico-Salafism, to follow Wiktorowicz (2006)'s terms. Yet the implication of the criticism was extended to include the NII and JI that were also perceived to value political engagement over the purification of the individual Muslim's religious beliefs and practices. The quietists not only accused them of being enmeshed in the sinful acts of *bid'a*, but also condemned them as "Agitators of Religion" (Hasan 2006, pp. 141–42). Another big mistake committed by these groups, according to the quietists, is their ambition to revive the caliphate, which proved to have concentrated all Muslim minds and energies on political interests, which can potentially spark bloody conflicts among Muslims. More problematically, the ambition to establish the caliphate is believed to have encouraged the Muslim Brothers to support the Shi'i-inspired Iranian revolution without paying heed to "all the forms of infidelity of this revolution and the hostility of its proponents to the principle of the *ahl al-sunna wa'l-jama'a*" (Hasan 2006, p. 142).

The quietists insisted that one devastating result of the *hizbiyya* has been the spread of a revolutionary spirit among Muslims. They cited a number of events as examples of catastrophes afflicting the Muslim world in the wake of this trend: the rebellion launched by the Jihad group in Egypt that perpetrated the assassination of Anwar Sadat, the Juhayman al-'Utaybi-led group's seizure of the Grand Mosque, Muhammad ibn Surur al-Nayef Zayn al-'Abidin and 'Abd al-Rahman 'Abd al-Khaliq's criticism of the Saudi Arabian royal family and its religious establishment, and the victory of FIS (Front Islamique du Salut) in Algeria. In their eyes, these events provided more than ample evidence about the dangerous spread of the *hizbiyya* for the Muslim world.

Congruent with its non-revolutionary approach, the quietists developed a moderate stance towards existing rulers. In sharp contrast to the jihadists who believed that a ruler cedes his legitimacy through any infraction of the divine law and must be therefore removed, they maintained that Muslims must obey their legitimate rulers, whether just or unjust, on the condition that they are not commanded to commit any sin. In their opinion, the only available way for Muslim citizens to resist legitimate rulers committing errors and acting cruelly is to advise those rulers to return to the right path.

Interestingly, similar to the jihadists, the quietists also advocated a strict application of the sharia. Submission to the sharia is considered compulsory because it is God's law. But they maintained that this is part of the *tawhid al-uluhiyya*, which entails that all kinds of worship are meant for God alone (Hasan 2006, p. 145). According to their interpretation, to believe that those who do not apply the sharia stray necessarily into infidelity (*takfir*), as implied by the jihadists, is a big mistake. Similarly, while denouncing jihadism, they failed to refrain from mobilizing fighters when skirmishes erupted between Muslims and Christians in Maluku. Under the leadership of Ja'far Umar Thalib who established Laskar Jihad in 2000, they ventured to the frontline to fight jihad against Christians in the islands.

In retrospect, the jihadists answered the quietists' criticism by publishing a number of books, including *Potret Salafi Sejati: Meneladani Kehidupan Generasi Pilihan* [*Portrait of True Salafis: Following the Lives of Chosen Generation*] by Tim Ulin Nuha (2007), *Jamaah, Imamah, Bai'ah: Kajian Syar'i Berdasarkan Al-Qur'an, As-Sunnah, Ijma', dan Qiyas* [*Jamaah, Imamah, Bai'ah: Shari'a-based Study on the Basis of the Quran, Prophetic Traditions, Consensus and Analogy*] by Abu Ammar et al. (2010), and *Syubhat Salafi* [*Salafi Ambivalence*] by Tim Jazeera (2011). Published by three Solo-based publishing houses linked to the JI, i.e., al-Qawam, Pustaka Arafah and Jazera respectively (International Crisis Group 2008), the books emphasize that the jihadists' understanding of the doctrines is totally correct as it is based on the fundamental sources of Islam, i.e., the Quran and Prophetic Traditions, plus practices of the Prophet's companions and their sucessors. Abundant quotations from the Quran, the Prophetic Traditions and the epics of the Prophet's companions and their successors are included to convince readers about their interpretation of the doctrines, while delegitimizing that of the quietists. Referring to Muhammad Salih al-Uthaimin, himself an influential Salafi authority among the quietists, they maintain in one book (2010) that those who oppose the righteousness of God's law or prefer to apply man-made law automatically falls into infidelity. The same holds true for those applying democracy as it is diametrically opposed to Islamic system.

Fragmented Authorities

It is of interest to note that while generally depicted as an opposition to *wasatiyya Islam*, the mainstream ideology of Indonesian Muslims, Salafism itself is contested among different authorities and agencies using available modalities and networks. It is in fact the relation between habitus and modalities in the field of contestation that generates practice and appears at the same time as the structuring structure. Within this context we can see the active role played by certain agency to influence or transform the surrounding environment. As a result tensions and conflicts have been always vulnerable, even among the quietists.

Today, there are at least three major active quietist groups led respectively by Lukman Ba'abduh, Dzulqarnain and Abu Turab al-Jawi. Lukman Ba'abduh was deputy commander of Laskar Jihad in Maluku, whereas Dzulqarnain was the head of its *fatwa* section. Abu Turab came to Maluku a little late and was not part of the Laskar Jihad elite group. However, he was able to exert his influence among certain Salafi circles because of his loyalty to Yahya al-Hajuri, the successor of al-Wadi'i in leading Darul Hadith in Yemen. After the death of al-Wadi'i, rivalries and conflicts occurred between al-Hajuri and Abd al-Rahman al-Mar'i al-Adeni. While Ba'abduh sided with al-Adeni, Abu Turab decided to defend al-Hajuri.

Lukman Ba'abduh who built a base in Ma'had As-Salafi in Jember, East Java, managed to draw Muhammad as-Sewed, Ayif Syafruddin, Qamar Suaidi, Abu Hamzah Yusuf and Abdurrahman into his orbit in their competition against Dzulqarnain and his like-minded personalities. Based in Ma'had as-Sunnah in Makassar, the latter built an alliance with Dzul Akmal and Jauhari, the founders of Ma'had Ta'dhim As-Sunnah in Pekanbaru Riau and al-Madinah in Solo, Central Java respectively. They have been active in attacking the manoeuvres of what they called the Lukmaniyun group to rebuild their credential as the true Salafis. Often referred to as RMS (Riau, Makassar and Solo) by their opponents, the Dzulqarnain group even managed to maintain an exclusive access to Fawzan Salih bin al-Fawzan, a leading Salafi authority in Saudi Arabia, who successfully maintained trust and support both from Saudi's religious institutions, such as Haiah Kibar al-Ulama and Lajnah al-Da'imah, and from influential authorities in the Saudi government and universities. Exclusive access to Fawzan Salih bin al-Fawzan is crucial to ensure continued support from Saudi Arabia and, more importantly, their credentials as Salafi authorities in Indonesia.

In contrast to Dzulqarnain, Lukman Ba'abduh and his allies apparently did not succeed in convincing Fawzan Salih bin al-Fawzan to maintain his patronage with them. Their access to Fawzan Salih bin al-Fawzan ended. They were only able to maintain access to Rabi' ibn Hadi al-Madkhali, who has been away from religious and political authority of Saudi Arabia. Al-Madkhali was known as one of the founders of Jamaat al-Salafi al-Muhtasiba (JSM). Both Ba'abduh and Dzulqarnain groups were involved in the competition to claim credentials as legitimate Salafi authorities by crediting their own legitimacy and discrediting the others. The former referred to the latter as the group which was concerned only with MLM, *mutalawwinun, la'ibun*, and *makirun* (being chameleons, just making fun, and rebellious in character).

The dynamics of their competition for the credential as the true Salafis reminds us of similar conflicts in the 1990s around the issue of Sururiyya. They used various media channels, including the Internet, to spread their ideas. While the Ba'abduh group set up Tukpencarianalhaq.com, the Dzulqarnain group prepared to launch pelitaalhaq.com. The latter intensified their campaigns by making alliance with Rodja and Yufid TVs as well as radio stations owned by personalities in Persatuan Pengusaha Muslim Indonesia (PPMI) (Sunarwoto 2016). To justify their support for Rodja and Yufid TVs, they disseminated *fatwas* on the permissibility to display lived photos. They were also not reluctant to wear *peci* (a typical Indonesian black hat). Both lived photos and *peci* remain rejected by the Ba'abduh group.

It is worth noting that despite such a dispute, all proponents of the faction, including Ja'far Umar Thalib, came to actively engage in countering jihadism. Endorsing what Nasir Abbas, former commander of JI, said in his *Membongkar JI; Pengakuan Mantan Anggota JI* [Uncovering JI: Confession of a Former JI Member], Ja'far Umar Thalib strongly criticized the interpretation of Bin Laden on jihad—as a call for killing American and Western civilians—and JI's decision to follow the interpretation. He asserted that Bin Laden did not qualify as a mufti so his *fatwa* should be ignored. According to Thalib, jihad is legitimate only under certain conditions, including the approval from legitimate political authority and only for self-defense mechanism.

Abu Hamza Yusuf came to criticize Imam Samudra, one of the masterminds behind the first Bali bombing who published *Aku Melawan Teroris* [I Fight Terrorists!] (Samudra 2004). In this sort of plea, Samudra asserted that he is the only true jihadist committed to fighting jihad to defend Islam from the attacks of belligerent infidels. Referring to what happened in Palestine, Afghanistan and Iraq, he believed that what he did in Bali was just an attempt to take revenge against "the real international terrorist, America" perpetrating terror against Muslims across the world. In a pamphlet entitled *Membongkar Pemikiran Begawan Teroris* [Revealing the Thought of the Terrorist Mastermind], Yusuf criticized the whole argument proposed by Samudra in the book. According to him, Samudra had misunderstood the Salafi main doctrines and dishonoured the Salafi authorities. He instead idolized problematic figures, such as Safar al-Hawali, Salman al-Awdah, Osama bin Laden, Abdullah Sungkar and Abu Bakar Ba'asyir. As a result, he fell into a false understanding of jihad.

Lukman Ba'abduh took more significant steps toward condemning the jihadists by publishing a book entitled *Mereka Adalah Teroris* [They Are Terrorists] (2005). In this book, he condemns Imam Samudra as a *Khariji*, which is to say (in Salafi parlance) one who destroys Islam by spreading the doctrine of "excommunication" (*takfir*) and perpetrating terror. He further argues that Samudra's main mistake lies in his tendency to follow the thought of so-called *neo-khawarij* activists, whom he identifies as Hassan al-Banna, Sayyid Qutb, Abul

A'la al-Mawdudi, Sa'id Hawwa and like-minded personalities. These thinkers are blamed to have inspired Safar al-Hawali, Salman al'Auda and Osama bin Laden to perpetrate extremism and terrorism among Muslims. Ba'abduh's argument is challenged by Abduh Zulfidar Akaha, a Muslim Brotherhood activist who wrote *Siapa Teroris, Siapa Khawarij* [Who is Terrorist, Who is Khawarij?] (2006). He is of the opinion that Ba'abduh needs not only more evidence to associate radicalism and terrorism with Banna, Qutb, Mawdudi and other Muslim Brotherhood's thinkers, he also needs to be more careful in judging any opinion and analysing any event.

In response to Akaha's criticism, Ba'abduh wrote another book, *Menebar Dusta Membela Teroris Khawarij* [Spreading Lies, Defending Khawarij-Terrorists] (2007), in which he reiterates his criticism of Imam Samudra and other like-minded individuals as a deviant group that is too quick to apply the doctrine of *takfir* to legitimate rulers and Muslims who hold different views. He loses no time in refuting all Akaha's criticism and data, which he blames to be nothing other than lies and libels, especially to prominent Salafi *ulama*, including Bin Baz, Al-Albani, al-Uthaimin, al-Madkhali, and al-Wadi'i, who struggled to promote the Salafi *manhaj*. In Ba'abduh's opinion, these *ulamas* always sought to guide the Muslim *umma* to understand and practise Islam in accordance with the example set by the pious forefathers. In contrast to Muslim Brotherhood's thinkers, they are believed to have never led the *umma* into extremism and terrorism.

Concern with the negative impacts that Imam Samudra's *I Fight Terrorists!* might engender, another quietist proponent, Dzulqarnain M. Sunusi, published *Antara Jihad dan Terorisme* [Between Jihad and Terrorism] (Dzulqarnain 2011, pp. 323–74). He begins his argument by saying that Islam is a religion of mercy and peace that opposes extremism and terrorism. Jihad is emphasized as a mechanism to defend against infidels attacking Muslims, the original ruling of which requires Muslims to participate collectively (*fard kifaya*). It changes into an individual duty (*fard 'ayn*) when it is under the command of a legitimate ruler or when Muslim combatants are in actual confrontation with their enemies in a battlefield. He further explains that this jihad is totally different from terrorism (*al-irhab*). The latter is perpetrated for the cause of human desires and aimed at instigating harm and catastrophe. Referring to the *fatwas* issued by Saudi's Committee of Senior Ulama (Haiat Kibar al-Ulama), he insists that terrorism is absolutely forbidded in Islam and its perpetrators must be brought to trial and punished by death. Dzulqarnain further argues that what Samudra did in Bali is absolutely not jihad. It is just an act of terror perpetrated because of his ignorance of the true meaning and ruling of jihad as well as various conditions to meet before fighting jihad. He concludes that killing innocents is a serious offence against the sharia.

Salafism and Islamic Education

Despite continued competition and conflict among the Salafis, Salafism continues to flourish in Indonesia and extends its influence beyond the Salafi circles, reaching students at senior high schools and colleges. One remarkable impact of the Salafi expansion among students can be seen from the shifting theological discourse in the Islamic literature used in schools and university education from the Ash'arite, which was very popular in Indonesia, to the Salafi theology. According to the Ash'arite doctrine of *tawhid* popularized by Abu Hasan al-Ash'ari (d. 935) and Abu Mansur al-Maturidi (d. 944), God is one, unique, eternal, existent Being; He is not a substance, not a body, not an accident, not limited to any direction, and not in any space. He possesses attributes such as knowledge, power, life, will; He is hearing and seeing and has speech. This theology is especially popular among Indonesian traditionalist Muslims. The shift occurs when the Ash'arite theology was challenged by the concept of the Oneness of God that refers to the doctrine developed by Ahmad ibn Hanbal (d. 855) and Ibn Taymiyya (d. 1328). This concept divides *tawhid* into three branches: *tawhid 'ubudiyya* (unity of worship); *tawhid rububiyya* (unity of lordship); and *tawhid al-asma wa'l-sifat* (unity of Allah's names and attributes).

More and more books used for Islamic education courses at schools and colleges are adopting the concept of the so-called *Tawhid 3*. For example, the textbook for Islamic education courses used in Islamic University of North Sumatra, Andalas University of West Sumatra, and Muhammadiyah University of Mataram. The idea to incorporate *Tawhid 3* into Islamic literature used in schools and university education has grown since 2007. The initiator was, among others, Muhamin, a professor of UIN Malang who argued that the teaching of theology among students should touch their hearts and feelings (Suhadi 2018). For him, insights into the Oneness of God as explained in the concept of *Tawhid 3* are essential to provide a foundation for students to have a correct understanding of their faith that entails in their attitude, behaviour and everyday life.

In our recent research on Islamic literature used in schools and university education in sixteen Indonesian provinces, the topics about purification of faith, the discourse of revitalization of the Prophetic Tradition, and exemplary *salaf al-salih* are imbued in textbooks and Islamic literature spread among students. The popularity of the Salafi books discussing these topics, which lies only behind the so-called popular Islamist and *Tarbawi* literatures, goes hand in hand with the growing acceptance of the ideological books of the Salafi, such as *Kitab al-Tawhid* by Muhammad ibn 'Abd al-Wahhab and *Fath Majid* by Abdurrahman bin Hasan Alu al-Shaykh (Hasan 2018b). These books serve as the main reference used widely by authors of Islamic textbooks for students. As mentioned earlier, *Kitab al-Tawhid* contains the doctrines of monotheism which is strictly defined by Muhammad ibn Abd al-Wahhab as belief in the Only Almighty God and consequently rejecting any forms of polytheism (*shirk*) and sufism. The definition of *shirk* in *Kitab al-Tawhid* includes the practice of prayer in accordance with the exemplary practice of the *Salaf al-Salih*. Within this context, submission to religious leaders, seeking blessings of things and asking for help from other than God are considered an anathema to Islam.

The Prophetic Traditions (hadith) also receive particular attention from the authors of textbooks and Islamic literature used in schools and university education. It is not difficult for the authors to explore more about hadith as Salafi teaching centres, campuses and publishers provide abundant references to hadith. Imam al-Shafi'i College for Islamic Studies in Jember, for instance, is known for its focus on the study of hadith. In fact, canonical hadith books such as *Sahih al-Bukhari*, *Sahih Muslim*, *Al-Adab al-Mufrad*, *Nayl al-Awtar*, *al-Arba'in al-Nawawiyya*, *Riyad al-Salihin* and *Bulugh al-Maram*, to mention but a few, constitute the core references and backbone of the Salafi discourse of Islam. These books have been widely read by the participants in Islamic Study Unit (Rohis) and University-based Islamic Missionary Unit (LDK). Among the Salafi publishers active in publishing such books are Solo-based Al-Ghuroba, Zamzam, and al-Qalam, plus Al-Qamar Media (Yogyakarta), Pustaka Umar (Bogor), Pustaka At-Taqwa (Bogor), Darul Haq (Jakarta), and Imam Adz-Dzahabi (Bekasi).

Most of these books belong to the category of canonical works, standard Islamic references used also by traditionalist Muslims. But the books published by the Salafis include the annotations by Salafi-leading scholars such as Muhammad Salih al-Uthaimin, Nasiruddin al-Albani, and Fawzan Salih bin al-Fawzan. This fact explains the particular element of Salafism embedded in the books. Some Indonesian Salafi proponets have also arisen as the leading annotators, including Yazid bin Abdul Qadir Jawas (Ikhwan 2018). Referring to Salih al-Uthaimin, and Nasir al-Din al-Albani, Jawas in his *Sharh Ahl al-Sunna wa'l Jama'a* (2017) explains about the law of intention in prayer that should not be pronounced. This opinion is intended to refute the followers of the Shafi'ite school of thought. There is no wonder that the Salafi books lie only the third after the popular Islamist and *Tarbawi* books in the map of Islamic literature used in schools and university education in Indonesia.

Conclusion

The spread of the Salafi influence in Indonesia, which was inseparable from Saudi's ambitious campaign for Wahhabization of the Muslim *umma*, went hand in hand with the rise of a new type of Islamic activism and religious authorities. The story began with the dispatch of a dozen Indonesian students to study in the Salafi teaching centres in the Middle East. Upon returning home, they organized *halqas* and *dauras* and established Salafi *madrasahs* across Indonesia. In so doing they recruited loyal followers and sympathizers into their circles. Salafi teaching centres and *madrasahs* had grown up into small Salafi communities and networks in which Salafi way of life constituted an integral element of the Salafis' habitus and everyday life. The production, development, authorization and dissemination of Islamic knowledge in the networks created specific modes of binding and community building.

Salafis are known for their monolithic Islamic worldview, which undermines the diversity of religion and culture. But the Salafi movement that proliferated in Indonesia is far from monolithic. For the last couple of decades, the Salafis have been divided into various groups that were involved in rivalry and conflict around some doctrinal and ideological issues. Some, especially Salafi Jihadists, remain to oppose the state by developing the doctrine of jihadism, while the others (especially the quietists) have become critical of the doctrine and stood at the frontline to refute the legitimacy of the jihadists' ideological position. But this contestation is somehow productive. Many Indonesian Salafi authorities have arisen out of this context, publishing books and pamphlets defending their respective positions.

It is of interest to note that the influence of Salafism has expanded beyond the Salafi circles through the role played by Salafi preachers and authorities both in producing the Salafi literature and in contextualizing and appropriating the Salafi messages in schools and university education. More and more books used for Islamic education courses at schools and colleges are adopting the doctrinal and ideological concepts of the Salafis, including *Tawhid 3*, the revitalization of the Prophetic Tradition in teaching Islam and full commitment to follow the exemplary practices set by the *Salaf al-Salih*.

REFERENCES

Abas, Natsir. 2005. *Membongkar JI; Pengakuan Mantan Anggota JI*. Jakarta: Grafindo Khasanah Ilmu.

Abukhalil, As'ad. 2004. *The Battle for Saudi Arabia: Royalty, Fundamentalism, and Global Power*. New York: Seven Stories Press.

Abuza, Zachary. 2003. *Militant Islam in Southeast Asia: Crucible of Terror*. Boulder: Lynne Rienner Publishers Inc.

Akaha, Abduh Zulfidar. 2006. *Siapa Teroris? Siapa Khawarij?* Jakarta: Pustaka Al-Kautsar.

Al-Rasheed, Madawi. 2007. *Contesting the Saudi State: Islamic Voices from a New Generation*. Cambridge: Cambridge University Press.

———. 2008. "Introduction: An Assessment of Saudi Political, Religious and Media Expansion". In *Kingdom without Borders Saudi Arabia's Political, Religious and Media Frontiers*, edited by Madawi Al Rasheed, pp. 1–38. London: Hurst.

Asad, Talal. 1986. "The Idea of an Anthropology of Islam". Occasional Paper Series. Georgetown: Center for Contemporary Arab Studies.

Ba'abduh, Lukman. 2005. *Mereka Adalah Teroris, Bantahan terhadap Buku "Aku Melawan Teroris"*. Malang: Pustaka Qaulan Sadida.

———. 2007. *Menebar Dusta Membela Teroris Khawarij*. Malang: Pustaka Qaulan Sadida.

Bourdieu, Pierre. 1995. *Outline of a Theory of Practice*. Stanford: Standford University Press.

Dzulqarnain, M. Sanusi. 2011. *Antara Jihad dan Terorisme*. Makassar: Pustaka Assunah.

Fraser, Cary. 1997. "In Defense of Allah's Realm: Religion and Statecraft in Saudi Foreign Policy Strategy". In *Transnational Religion and Fading States*,

edited by Susanne Hoeber Rudolph and James Piscatori, pp. 226–34. Oxford: Westview Press.
Hasan, Noorhaidi. 2006. *Laskar Jihad: Islam, Militancy and the Quest for Identity in Post-New Order Indonesia*. Ithaca, New York: Southeast Asia Program, Cornell University.
———. 2007. "The Salafi Movement in Indonesia: Transnational Dynamics and Local Development". *Comparative Studies of South Asia, Africa, and the Middle East* 27, no. 1: 83–94.
———. 2010. "The Failure of the Wahhabi Campaign: Transnational Islam and the Salafi Madrasa in Post-9/11 Indonesia". *South East Asia Research* 18, no. 4: 705–35.
———. 2018a. "Salafism in Indonesia: Transnational Islam, Violent Activism and Cultural Resistance". In *Routledge Handbook of Contemporary Indonesia*, edited by Robert Hefner. London and New York: Routledge.
———. 2018b. "Penutup: Gagalnya Jihadisme di Kalangan Generasi Milenial". In *Literatur Keislaman Generasi Milenial: Transmisi, Apropriasi, dan Kontestasi*, edited by Noorhaidi Hasan. Yogyakarta: Pascasarjana UIN Sunan Kalijaga Press.
Ikhwan, Munirul. 2018. "Produksi Wacana Islam(is) di Indonesia: Revitalisasi Islam Publik dan Politik Muslim". In *Literatur Keislaman Generasi Milenial: Transmisi, Apropriasi, dan Kontestasi*, edited by Noorhaidi Hasan. Yogyakarta: Pascasarjana UIN Sunan Kalijaga Press.
International Crisis Group. 2008. "Indonesia: Jemaah Islamiyah's Publishing Industry". *ICG Asia Report 147*. Brussels: International Crisis Group.
Jawwas, Abdul Qodir. 2017. *Syarah Ahlusunah wa Al Jamaah*. Jakarta: Pustaka Imam Syafii.
Kepel, Gilles. 2002. *Jihad: The Trail of Political Islam*. London: I.B. Tauris.
Lacroix, Stéphane. 2011. *Awakening Islam: Politics of Religious Dissent in Contemporary Saudi Arabia*, translated by George Holoch. Cambridge, MA.: Harvard University Press.
Meyer, Birgit. 2006. *Religious Sensations: Why Media, Aesthetics and Power Matter in the Study of Contemporary Religion* (inaugural lecture). Amsterdam: VU University.
Pavlova, Elena. 2007. "From a Counter-Society to a Counter-State Movement: Jemaah Islamiyah According to PUPJI". *Studies in Conflict and Terrorism* 30, no. 9: 777–800.
Samudra, Imam. 2004. *Aku Melawan Teroris*. Solo: Jazera.
Solahudin. 2013. *The Roots of Terrorism in Indonesia: From Darul Islam to Jema'ah Islamiyah*, translated by Dave McRae. Ithaca: Cornell University Press.
Suhadi. 2018. "Menu Bacaan Pendidikan Agama Islam di SMA dan Perguruan Tinggi". In *Literatur Keislaman Generasi Milenial: Transmisi, Apropriasi, dan Kontestasi*, edited by Noorhaidi Hasan. Yogyakarta: Pascasarjana UIN Sunan Kalijaga Press.

Sunarwoto. 2016. "Salafi Dakwah Radio: A Contest for Religious Authority". *Archipel* 91: 203–30.
Sunusi, Zulkarnain M. 2011. *Antara Jihad dan Terorisme*. Makassar: Pustaka Assunnah.
Tim Jazera. 2011. *Syubhat Salafi*. Solo: Jazera.
Tim Ulin Nuha. 2007. *Potret Salafi Sejati Meneladani Kehidupan Generasi Pilihan*. Solo: Al-Qowam.
Trofimov, Yaroslav. 2007. *The Siege of Mecca*. New York: Doubleday.
van Bruinessen, Martin. 2003. "Making and Unmaking Muslim Religious Authority in Western Europe". Paper presented to the Fourth Mediterranean Social and Political Research Meeting, Robert Schuman Centre for Advanced Studies, European University Institute, Florence, 19–23 March 2003.
Wahid, Din. 2014. "Nurturing the Salafi Manhaj: A Study of Salafi Pesantrens in Contemporary Indonesia". PhD thesis, Faculty of Arts, Utrecht University, Utrecht, the Netherlands.
Wiktorowicz, Quintan. 2006. "Anatomy of the Salafi Movement". *Studies in Conflict and Terrorism* 29, no. 3: 207–39.
Yusuf, Abu Hamzah. 2005. "Membongkar Pemikiran Sang Begawan Teroris". www.salafy.or.id/print.php?id_artikel=878.

9

OPPOSING WAHHABISM: THE EMERGENCE OF ULTRA-TRADITIONALISM IN CONTEMPORARY INDONESIA

Syamsul Rijal

Introduction

In the name of defending traditionalist Islam, preaching (*dakwah*) has become a widespread activity in contemporary Indonesia. The aim of *dakwah* is to promote the traditionalist Sunni version of Islam and to challenge puritanical and other "deviant" groups. The emergence of *dakwah* is a response to the expansion of global Islamic movements such as Salafi-Wahhabi and Hizbut Tahrir. While many scholars have studied these movements to understand what they perceive as a threat to Indonesian democracy and pluralism, only a few have studied the traditionalist *dakwah* and its various forms in the post-New Order Indonesia (see for instance Alatas 2008; Zamhari and Howell 2012; Woodward et al. 2012). One gap in the existing studies is an analysis of Sunni traditions and doctrines. This chapter finds that some traditionalist preachers and activists have worked together in reasserting traditional

Sunni Islam or what they call *"aswaja"* (the abbreviation of *ahl sunna wa al-jama'a*). This movement seeks to reassert traditionalist Sunni orthodoxy while promoting anti-Wahhabism through various media.

The aim of this chapter is to analyse the religious factor that paved a way for the emergence of this new form of *dakwah*. It argues that its emergence is a response to internal and external threats seen as challenging established religious doctrines and traditional practices. While the Salafi-Wahhabi movement is regarded as the primary "threat", these *dakwah* groups also regarded the Shias, liberal Islam, Hizbut Tahrir, and Ahmadiyah as deviant. The first part of this chapter discusses the general concept of Sunni Islam and its particular meaning for traditionalist Muslims in the Indonesian context. The second part examines the social and political context of the post-Suharto era that gave rise to *aswaja dakwah* and the campaign of anti-Wahhabism among traditionalist Muslims. The third part analyses the variants of *aswaja dakwah* and its characteristics in contemporary Indonesia.

Sunni and Traditional Islam in Indonesia

The term Sunni refers to *ahl sunna wa al-jama'a*, meaning the people of the Prophetic tradition (*sunna*) and community (*jama'a*). In Indonesia, there are numerous Muslim organizations who claimed to represent the Sunni branch regardless of whether they are traditionalist or reformist in their religious orientation. Each group promotes Sunni Islam based on their own interpretation. In the Indonesian context, traditionalist Muslims use the distinctive abbreviation *"aswaja"* to identify their particular brand of Sunni Islam. The term refers to the particular characteristic of Sunni traditionalists that is culturally linked to the largest Islamic mass organization in the country, Nahdlatul Ulama (NU, the Revival of the Islamic Scholars) (Burhani 2012, p. 572). The term was used by NU members to distinguish themselves from the modernist organizations, such as Muhammadiyah, Al-Irsyad and Persis.

Any discussion of traditional Islam in Indonesia would be incomplete without considering the emergence of Nahdlatul Ulama (NU)—the country's largest traditionalist Muslim organization. The NU was established on 31 January 1926 in Surabaya by a number of religious scholars and businessmen from East Java (Fealy and Barton 1996, p. xx; van Bruinessen 1994, p. 17). The aim was to "represent and foster traditional Islam in the Netherlands Indies" (Fealy 1998, p. 17). The

NU views itself as a Sunni Islam group and adheres to the concept of *ahl sunna wal-jama'a* or *aswaja*. For the NU, *aswaja* has three basic doctrines: adopting al-Ash'ari and al-Maturidi in Islamic theology; following one of the four Islamic legal schools (Hanafite, Malikite, Shafi'ite, and Hanbalite), especially, Shafi'ite in *fiqh*; and following sufi schools of al-Ghazali and al-Baghdady (Haidar 1994, p. 74; Burhani 2012, p. 573; Dhofier 1982, p. 158). In general, the traditionalist *ulama* adopted a tolerant view towards non-Islamic local cultures. They understood that such local customs can serve as a means for spreading Islam more widely; therefore, the incorporation of various local customs has appeared in religious ceremonies popular among NU members, such as marriage, circumcision, *maulid* (celebration of the Prophet's birthday), and *ziarah* (visiting the saints' tombs to obtain blessings and intercession) (Saleh 2001, p. 70; Fealy 1998, p. 20). Islamic rituals containing local customs have received criticism from the reformist groups, which regard them as un-Islamic and therefore an unlawful innovation (*bid'ah*).

From the 1920s to the mid-1930s, Muslim traditionalists and modernists engaged in numerous debates. Tensions arose not only in Java but also in Sumatra (Noer 1980, pp. 237–41). However, since the mid-1930s, both groups seemed to have reconciled. The modernists came to realize that they could not eradicate *bid'ah* (innovations) in a short space of time, while the traditionalists accepted that they had to co-exist with the modernists (Noer 1980, p. 260). Furthermore, the discriminatory actions of the Dutch government caused discontent among Muslim groups that led to non-cooperation with the colonial administration. The reconciliation between the two groups was evident through a joint establishment—the MIAI (Majlis Islam A'laa Indonesia or Supreme Council of Indonesian Muslims)—on 21 September 1937 in Surabaya. The purpose of this federation was to promote unity and cooperation between Muslims (Fealy 1998, p. 39; Bush 2009, p. 41).

Since the foundation of the Indonesian nation state, there has been no significant doctrinal dispute between the traditionalists and modernists; however, in the years after independence, NU engaged in politics that led them to a compromise with the state. The NU's political activity was at its height especially after it separated from Masyumi to become a political party in 1952. Between the 1950s and 1970s, NU leaders came to a compromise with Sukarno's restrictive Guided Democracy and Suharto's authoritarian New Order regime (Fealy 2007, p. 154). In

1984, however, NU withdrew itself from party politics and decided to return to *Khittah 1926* (the original platform of the organization). The period from the 1980s to 1990s was the era of intellectual booming for the NU. Many progressive intellectuals and activists emerged and established various institutions such as non-governmental organizations and study centres for promoting pluralism and tolerance (Bush 2009, p. 90). Despite these developments, NU leaders remained active in politics. Their return to formal politics was marked by the foundation of four NU-based parties in 1998, with the largest surviving party being the PKB (Partai Kebangsaan Bangsa, National Awakening Party). Given the rising activity of leading NU intellectuals and leaders in business and politics in the post-Suharto era, NU is no longer "a major force for reform or religious and social liberalization" (Fealy 2007, p. 165).

Aswaja Dakwah and Anti-Wahhabism in the Post-New Order Era

Reforms that followed the fall of Suharto paved the way for freedom of expression in the public sphere. Several Islamic parties emerged and Islamic movements proliferated (Zada 2002; Jamhari and Jahroni 2004; Azra 2004). The ideas of political Islam that had been suppressed by the state were revived and came into public debates (Hasan 2006, p. 14).

Islamic movements that went underground during the New Order era—Salafi, Tarbiyah (Indonesian version of Muslim Brotherhood), Hizbut Tahrir, and Tablighi Jamaat, to name a few—rode on this new found freedom to conduct Islamic activities in public and urged people to support their missionary work. Polemics between Muslim groups articulating different views were expressed through periodicals, books, websites, and public discussions (Meuleman 2011, p. 246). The Salafi groups are the most active of these groups in propagating puritanical Islam in Indonesia. They call on Muslims to return to the original ways of Islam by emulating the Prophet and the early Muslim generations (Meijer 2009, pp. 3–4). Their puritanical views of Islam were reflected in their concerns with "matters of creed and morality, such as strict monotheism, divine attributes, purifying Islam from accretions, and anti-Sufism, as well as typical Arab-style dress, exclusivist tendencies and rigid ritual practices" (Hasan 2010, p. 677). Moreover, the Salafi activists also criticize local Muslim practices that they regard as "unlawful innovation" (*bid'ah*).

The propagation of Salafi doctrine in Indonesia has been a part of the Saudi global campaign for spreading the Wahhabi version of Islam to the Muslim world (Hasan 2010, p. 675). The goal of the Saudi government was to counter both the expansion of Arab socialist nationalism in Egypt in the 1960s and the influence of the Iranian revolution which erupted in 1979 (Hasan 2007, p. 87; Wahid 2014, p. 5). Those influences were regarded as threats to the Saudi Arabia Kingdom. Thanks to the oil boom in the 1970s, the Saudi became active in exporting Salafism to Muslim countries through Muslim organizations that it set up such as Rabitat al-'Alam al-Islami (the Muslim World League) (Gause III 2011, p. 20; Hasan 2005, p. 30). Through Rabitat, the Saudi distributed financial funds for building Islamic schools, mosques, social and *dakwah* facilities, and granting scholarships to Indonesians to study at Saudi universities (Hasan 2005, p. 30; Wahid 2014, p. 5). In Indonesia, the first channel for spreading Saudi Salafism was the Dewan Dakwah Islamiyah Indonesia (Indonesian Islamic Propagation Council, DDII), an organization created for Islamic propagation (*dakwah*) in Indonesia's rural areas (Wahid 2014, p. 5). The first and main educational institution, which was established in Jakarta in 1980 with Saudi funding, was Lembaga Ilmu Pengetahuan Islam dan Bahasa Arab (Institute of Islamic and Arabic Sciences, LIPIA). Hundreds of its graduates went on to study in Saudi Arabia; upon their return to Indonesia, many of these graduates became important Salafi teachers and preachers (Hasan 2005, p. 43). Along with the growing Salafi communities, a number of Salafi leaders established foundations in order to obtain financial support from Saudi Arabia, Kuwait, and other Arab countries (Hasan 2007, p. 91).

With financial support from Saudi Arabia and the Gulf countries, Salafi communities established a number of *pesantren* in various provinces in Indonesia. The International Crisis Group report in 2004 mentioned that there were no less than twenty-nine *pesantren*. While the exact number of *pesantren* is unknown, Din Wahid (2014) assumes that their number has increased probably to fifty *pesantren*. After gaining significant followers, the Salafis established *pesantren* as a means for producing new Salafi preachers and teachers who will spread their knowledge to other Muslims (Wahid 2014, p. 151). The Salafis actively conduct preaching around Muslim communities by delivering sermons in public mosques in the areas where their *pesantren* are based. In some cases, the Salafis even took over the mosque resulting in conflict with the existing committees of the mosque. In his study, Wahid discusses the case of Dewan Da'wah al-Furqan Mosque in Central Jakarta where its officials drove out the Salafis (Wahid 2014, pp. 98–99).

The proliferation of Salafi media technology is another indicator of Salafi expansion. Starting from publishing Salafi periodicals in the 1990s, the Salafi movement has moved to expand their *dakwah* through media technologies after the 2000s. Their motivation was to defend Muslim beliefs and morality from the existing electronic media, which they believed, has been controlled by non-Muslims "wishing to destroy Islamic values, to turn Muslims away from *sharia* and lead Muslims to a false *'aqida* (belief)" (Wahid 2014, pp. 102–3). Among Salafi-inspired radio stations in Indonesia, Rodja is the most popular one. The Salafis started establishing Rodja as an FM radio community in 2005, which was later formally launched as AM radio station in 2007. In 2009, Rodja then expanded its wing to launch a TV channel through Internet streaming and in 2011, through satellites (Rodja n.d.). By using radio and TV, the Salafis have made their ideas accessible to a wider audience in several regions in Indonesia and even worldwide.

The *Aswaja* Response

The increasing *dakwah* expansion of Salafism prompted a critical reaction from traditionalist Muslims, mainly due to the contents of their messages which attacked traditionalist doctrines and practices. Several research reports indicated that the presence of Salafi groups in traditionalist majority areas have triggered conflicts with the local Muslims. Nuhrison (2010)'s research in West Lombok found that the exclusive approach of Salafis and their attacks on local beliefs and practices was the root cause of the conflict. The Salafis, for instance, condemned the celebration of the Prophet's birthday (*maulid*) by the local community in Lombok and judged it as a part of the Hindu heritage. A similar account was shared by many traditionalist preachers and leaders whom I met in Java and Jakarta. Concerned that the increasing expansion of Salafi would diminish their beliefs and traditions, traditionalist Muslim leaders, scholars, and activists have spoken and written against the Salafi movement.

The *aswaja dakwah* can take various forms, ranging from public preaching to utilizing the new media. Traditionalist religious leaders and preachers who engage with local communities include *habaib* and *kiai*, teachers and activists who graduated from *pesantren* and traditional institutions in the Middle East dedicated to guarding their fellow traditionalist community. Many of them have stated that their mission is to protect *aswaja* Islam from the "Wahhabism virus". According to the traditionalist preachers, the Wahhabi *dakwah* has spread widely through the use of modern technologies and has even penetrated NU communities. Some *habaib* and traditionalist preachers mentioned the Rodja Radio and Rodja TV as two of the most important media for propagating the Wahhabi ideology. They claimed that the Wahhabis have used these media to actively propagate Wahhabism and openly criticize the doctrines and religious practices of traditionalist Muslims considered to be *bid'ah*.

The majority of anti-Wahhabi preachers come from Java, especially from East and Central Java. Their concern regarding Wahhabism has led them to strengthen the traditionalist *dakwah* by forming a network among *aswaja* advocates. Their shared mission is apparent in their various *dakwah* groups either through *majelis taklim*, publications, radio or online media. According to the General Chairman of NU (PBNU) KH Said Aqil Siradj, the traditionalists organized *aswaja dakwah* movements on their own initiative without any mobilization and financial assistance from PBNU. He said that *aswaja* had arisen because the traditionalists felt that their long established tradition had been disturbed by the Salafi-Wahhabi preaching (Interview with Said Aqil Siradj, 1 October 2013). This reason was also given by several *aswaja* preachers whom I met in Jakarta and Java.

Aswaja Defenders

Currently, the most vocal *aswaja* advocates are local preachers and religious teachers. To capture their diversity, I classify them into three groups: popular preachers, NU scholars, and online media activists. This classification, however, is not absolute as some preachers are also NU scholars and own media network. In the discussion below, I discuss some of the prominent persons in the campaign to counter Wahhabism.

Popular Preachers: The Case of Habib Noval b. Muhammad Alaydrus

The *dakwah* for strengthening *aswaja* has become a common platform among young preachers, especially *habaib*. Some *habaib* use various media in undertaking their *dakwah* ranging from public preaching, books, magazines, radio to the Internet. In this category, I locate Habib Noval as an example of a young *habib* who actively defends *aswaja* by promoting it through public preaching and publications to the wider public audience. Habib Noval is among the most popular preachers in Solo, along with Habib Syekh b. Abdul Qadir Assegaf, and has thousands of followers. He was born in 1975 into an Arab *sayyid* family in Solo. He received his basic education in secular schools but actively attended religious learning activities such as public sermons and *ratib* chanting in Ar-Riyadh Mosque, Solo. He also studied at the Pondok Pesantren Darul Lughah wad Dakwah (Dalwa), Pasuruan, in East Java for seven months. Returning to Solo, he avidly attended public sermons by the charismatic scholar, Habib Anis b. Alwi Al-Habsyi, from whom he received a deep understanding of religious knowledge. In 2009, he established a sermon group (*majelis taklim*) at his mother's house where he gave sermon regularly. At the beginning, the participants of his *majelis* numbered only about thirty people but later increased to 200; the group grew so large that many people had to sit outside. Two years later, he bought a plot of land for building his *majelis ta'lim*. He said that in his new building, the number of participants increased to around 1,500 people (Interview with Noval Alaydrus, 2 September 2013).

Guarding *aswaja* has become the central theme for Habib Noval's *dakwah* activities. His concern about the growing influence of what he sees as "deviant Islamic movements", such as Wahhabism, motivated him to expand his *dakwah* through peripatetic preaching and utilizing modern media technologies. For Habib Noval, Wahhabism is an extreme ideology that can cause people to become radical and intolerant towards other groups. He argues that the strategic way to counter such groups is through strengthening *aswaja* teachings and traditions so that Muslims themselves can resist the movement (Interview with Noval Alaydrus, 2 September 2013). With this objective in mind, and besides regularly running his study circles and attending sermon invitations, he has promoted *aswaja* through his *majelis'* official website "Majelis Dzikir and Ilmu Ar-Raudhah" at www.ar-raudhah.info/. The website contains his profile and his *majelis*, live streaming, sermon video and mp3 records, and advertisements of his books and religious merchandises produced by his *majelis*. It is also through the website that Habib Noval seeks funding to support his *majelis* by providing a list of four bank accounts to which supporters can donate. Furthermore, the website also has information links to its YouTube and social media (Official Facebook and Twitter).

Habib Noval has also been productive in writing books to defend *aswaja* beliefs. He asserted that his *dakwah* style is more scientific in orientation than merely advising people and religious chanting. His books are usually displayed and sold by his crew in the front yard of the *majelis* where the public sermon is held. His books reflect the content of his regular preaching as the topics of the books are also the topics discussed at his *majelis*. Most of his books contain the *ulama's* arguments and doctrines on traditionalist rituals. One of his current book is entitled *Ahlul Bid'ah Hasanah: Jawaban Untuk Mereka Yang Mempersoalkan Amalan Para Para Wali* [The Doers of Good Innovation: The Answers for Those Who Question the Practices of Saints]. Through this book, Habib Noval seeks to "correct" the Wahhabi's "misconception" that *bid'ah* (innovation) is not identical with a bad or heretical thing. He argues that there are good innovations (*bid'ah hasanah*) in religion such as what traditionalist Muslims have been practising. His books are aimed at traditionalist Muslims so that they can equip themselves with insights on *aswaja* doctrines in order to argue against the Wahhabi group if they are being approached or criticized. Furthermore, he has also produced T-shirts that contain various images and remarks that promote *aswaja* rituals (Interview with Noval Alaydrus, 2 September 2013).

NU Scholars: The Case of Muhammad Idrus Ramli

Idrus is an example of a young and local NU scholar who actively defends *aswaja* through his writings, seminars, and training courses. He was born on 1 July 1975 in Jember, one of the main bases of traditionalist Muslims in East Java. Idrus underwent most of his religious training at the Pondok Pesantren Sidogiri in Pasuruan, East Java, from primary school to senior high school (1986–2004). After graduation, he dedicated himself to teaching in various *pesantren* in Madura, Kalimantan, and later returned to teach in his hometown, Jember. During his studies and teaching, he was active in the local NU division of *Lembaga Bahtsul Masail* (a body for discussing contemporary problems in relation to Islamic law) in Pasuruan and Jember. He is now the chairman of NU's *Lembaga Bahtsul Masail* (LBM) in Jember. Besides, Idrus has also been active in managing magazines and publications serving as editor in chief of media in *pesantren* and the local NU. Since 1998, Idrus has been active as a trainer and speaker in *aswaja* training courses and seminars hosted by local NU branches (Idrus Ramli n.d.). His skills in presentation and debates have made him popular as a vocal defender of traditionalist Islam against other Muslim groups such as Salafi, Hizbut Tahrir, and Shia.

Idrus represents a conservative faction within the NU that strives to revive the Sunni orthodoxy. His preaching activities response to various Islamic groups that challenge the NU doctrine of *aswaja*. Idrus also joined the Forum Kiai Muda Jawa Timur (Forum of Young Kiais in East Java) which criticized the PBNU chairman Said Aqil Siradj and the NU liberal Muslim thinker Ulil Abshar Abdalla for their progressive thoughts deemed to deviate from the *aswaja* principles. In 2009, Forum Kiai Muda invited Said Agil Siradj and Ulil Abshar Abdalla to give clarification (*tabayyun*) on their controversial thoughts. In the forum where Said was a speaker, several young *kiais*, including Idrus, criticized Said for his reference to Shi'ite and Mu'tazilite sources that he claimed was a part of *aswaja* teaching. Likewise, the young *kiais* also criticized Ulil for his controversial ideas, especially with regard to his doubt about the facts of the stories in the Quran, and his attempt to analyse them using human logic and historical assessment.[1]

Idrus opposes various groups such as Shia and Hizbut Tahrir, but sees Wahhabi as the most dangerous since it actively attacks traditionalist Muslims' beliefs and practices. All his books have confronting titles such as "A Smart Guide on How to Argue Against Wahhabi", "The Guide for *Ahl Sunna wa al-Jama'a* in Facing Salafi-Wahabi", and "Open Debates: Sunni versus Wahhabi in al-Haram Mosque". His sharp criticism has offended the Salafis especially in online media. Judging by their titles, Idrus' books are not only aim at fighting back the Salafis, but also provide literatures for traditionalist Muslims to rely on in defending their doctrines and instructing them on how to argue against the Wahhabis. To advance his mission, Idrus also actively organizes *aswaja* training courses for students, religious teachers, activists, especially those who are linked to NU such as PMII cadres and the local NU members in various regions in Indonesia (Idrus Ramli n.d.).

The *Aswaja* Online Media Activists: The Case of Sarkub (*Sarjana Kuburan*—The Grave Scholars)

One of the most innovative and colourful sites is the Sarjana Kuburan (The Grave Scholars, Sarkub). Sarkub is an online network of traditionalist

Muslim activists whose main concern is to spread the teachings of *aswaja* and defend it from the attacks of the Wahhabi and other groups. Founded in Semarang on 30 September 2010, Sarkub also has an official website which was launched on 16 October 2011 at the Ponpes Salafiyah Sladi Kejayaan, Pasuruan, East Java (Sarkub n.d., "Visi Misi Sarkub"). According to Sarkub members, the reason for establishing the Sarkub network was similar to that of several social media users who actively countered the Salafis on the Internet: growing anxiety about the rapid Wahhabi expansion (Interview with Thobary Syadzily, 20 October 2013; Interview with Dian Kusumaningrum, 2 November 2013). Due to criticism from the Wahhabis, who often refer to them as "penyembah kuburan" and "quburiyyun" (grave worshippers), they have decided to call their network "Thariqat Sarkubiyah" (The Spiritual Path of Grave Scholars), popularly known as Sarkub (*Sarjana Kuburan*, Grave Scholars). This name is a direct rejection of Salafi teachings on visiting the saints' graves (*ziarah*). Since Sarkub is an online network, some activists have not met their peers within the network and only meet when they organize a "hanging out meeting" (*kopi darat*) or attend particular religious events (Interview with Mas'ud, 20 October 2013). The network has connected numerous links of *aswaja dakwah* on the Internet either from websites, blogs, social media, or radio.

In its fight against the Wahhabis, Sarkub's approach is more relaxed than other *aswaja* advocates. Its website and community groups in the social media use a distinctive way of *dakwah* by combining a combative style with humour in attacking the Wahhabis. Rather than using serious and deep explanations in their *dakwah*, Sarkub uses an irreverent, mocking, and "fun" approach to counter the Wahhabis. Some Sarkub members in the social media often create humourous posters and images of their traditionalist identity and their rival. In an image spreading through the social media, for instance, the Sarkub team call themselves the "Hunters of Wahhabi". Such image implies that Wahhabi is a deviant and dangerous group that needs to be eliminated from Indonesia.

Thobary Syadzily is a founder and leader of the Sarkub network. He has been called the guardian of *aswaja* in cyberspace by some Islamic magazines (*alKisah* 2013; *Tabloid Media Ummat* 2013). Besides serving as the head of the Pondok Pesantren Al-Husna in Tangerang, Banten, Thobary is also the chairman of the Department of Astronomy (*Lajnah Falakiyah*) of the local NU board in Banten and a member of MUI (Majelis Ulama Indonesia, Council of Indonesian Ulama) in Tangerang. He claims to be a descendant of the great *ulama* of Banten, Syeikh Nawawi Al-Bantani and Syeikh Abdul Karim. He has been conducting a regular Islamic study group (*pengajian*) in his house, countering Wahhabism by analysing the classical religious books (*kitab kuning*) that have been distorted by the Wahhabis. He also relies on classical books in posting religious opinions on the Internet or in delivering his sermons in public. Thobary encourages the traditionalists to preserve classical sources by using them as teaching materials for Islamic education for younger generations so that they are armed with knowledge to counter the *dakwah* of Wahhabi (Interview with Thobary Syadzily, 20 October 2013).

Thobary and his Sarkub are popular among traditionalist Muslim activists and scholars as well as his Salafi opponents due to his active *dakwah* in cyberspace. The Easy Counter site reported that in March 2016, his Sarkub website was visited by about 868 daily visitors, 94 per cent of them were from Indonesia.[2] The number of visitors usually increases when a controversy erupts between the Salafis and traditionalists in Indonesia. With his special team, which he calls the "Densus 99 Anti-Terror Aqidah" (Special Detachment 99 for Anti-Terror of Traditionalist Doctrines), Thobary often debated with Wahhabi-oriented authors whose books have criticized the NU's doctrines and rituals. Moreover, Thobary with Sarkub members also actively attend seminars or discussions in which the speakers are from the Wahhabi. In these events, he often raises questions and debates with the speakers. The results of the visits and debates are posted on their website, and accompanied with photos to show that they have debated with the Wahhabi scholars and discovered flaws in their opponents' arguments. For instance, as posted on the Sarkub website, the Sarkub team attended a book discussion on *The Sacred Graves in Archipelago* (*Kuburan-kuburan Keramat di Nusantara*) by a Salafi-Wahhabi author, Hartono Ahmad Jaiz, at a book fair in Jakarta in 2011. In the book, Hartono states that a visit to the saints' graves to seek their blessings (*ngulap berkah*) is not a tradition of Islam but that of Hinduism and therefore whoever follows this tradition could be judged as infidel (*mushrik*). According to Thobary, he came forward to raise a critical comment during the question and answer session. Quoting from the classical book *Tarikh al-Baghdady*, he rejected Hartono's opinion and argued that some classical *ulama* did allow the practice of seeking blessings at the saints' graves (Sarkub n.d., "Tim Sarkub bertemu Ust Hartono Jaiz").

The event which raised Thobary's profile to prominence was when he accompanied Muhammad Idrus Ramli representing the *aswaja* group in a debate against the representatives of Salafi school, namely Firanda and Zainal Abidin, on 28 December 2013 in Batam.[3] This event was hosted by the local ministry of religious affairs of Batam. The major issue of debate concerned the position of *bid'ah* (unlawful innovation) in Islam. While the Salafi group affirmed their stand on any innovation related to religious practice, the *aswaja* group defended their position as traditionalist by arguing that good innovations (*bid'ah hasanah*) are acceptable in Islam. Both camps presented doctrinal arguments and *ulama's* opinions in justifying their position. The Sarkub team judged the *aswaja* camp as more convincing in the debate and proudly posted the video link on social media (Sarkub n.d., "Tim Sarkub bertemu Ust Hartono Jaiz").

New Conservatism? Buttressing *Aswaja* and Opposing "Deviancy"

Nahdlatul Ulama (NU) has a reputation as one of the largest moderate Muslim organizations in Indonesia. Throughout Indonesia's history, NU has had a number of leaders, scholars and activists who raised progressive ideas in terms of Islamic thought, Islamic law (*fiqh*), and culture as the embodiment of the middle path of NU (Qomar 2002; Ida 2004). One example is the idea of redefinition of *aswaja* by Said Aqil Siradj in 1995 when he had just returned from his studies in Saudi Arabia. Said questioned the established notion of *aswaja* that had been identified as a religious school (*madzhab*). Instead, he defined *aswaja* as:

> a method of religious thinking that covers various aspects of life and stands on the virtues of balance (*tawazun*), the middle path (*tawassuth*), and neutrality in adhering to the faith (*akidah*), being a mediator and glue in the social interaction, and justice and tolerance in politics (Qomar 2002, p. 190).

In this regard, it is apparent that Said views *aswaja* as a method of thinking (*manhaj al-fikr*) rather than a product as his predecessors have emphasized. Through this idea, Said tries to widen the concept of *aswaja* to cover all Muslims so that there is no more dichotomy between Shia and Sunni or between Mu'tazila and Sunni, and so forth (Qomar 2002, p. 190; Feener 2007, p. 156). Said's liberal ideas, especially with regard to his efforts in bridging Sunni and Shia, have sparked criticism not only from Islamist groups but also from the conservative wing within NU. Besides Said, there have been several senior NU progressive thinkers such as the late Abdurrahman Wahid (Gus Dur), the late Muhammad Sahal Mahfudh, Ali Yafie, and Masdar Farid Mas'udi. More liberal ideas have also been promoted by young NU activists such as Ulil Abshar Abdalla, Marzuki Wahid, Jadul Maula, Rumadi, Zuhairi Misrawi, and Ahmad Baso. Those activists continue Gus Dur's ideas, especially on the "indigenization" of Islam (*pribumisasi Islam*) in the Indonesian context; they have also adopted progressive Islamic thoughts from the Middle Eastern thinkers and critical discourses from Western philosophers. Some of these young NU activists call themselves the proponents of "Post-Tradisionalisme Islam" (Islamic Post-Traditionalism) or "Postra" in short. This kind of thought was the result of eclectic ideas taken from Mohammed Arkoun, Abid Al-Jabiri, and Nasr Hamid Abu Zayd (Rumadi 2008; Kersten 2015). Like Gus Dur, they oppose the formalization of Islam and push for the protection of minority rights and Indonesian local traditions.

The new traditionalist group, however, does not engage in NU's progressive debates. In fact, it opposes Islamic post-traditionalism and considers it to be part of the liberal ideas imported from the West. Most of them tend to revive the classical orthodoxy of Sunnism that has been preserved by conservative *kiais* and *habaib*. The orthodoxy includes the adherence to the Ash'arite and Maturidite theology, the acceptance of Sufism, and the adoption of Shafi'i from the four schools of Islamic law. Rather than offering new thinking, the group is more concerned with propagating the established traditional Sunni doctrines, its rituals and practices, and responding to the criticisms that have been posed by the Salafi-Wahhabi group. In general, the group emphasizes that NU practices and rituals (*amaliah* NU) have doctrinal basis (Quranic verses, Prophet's practices, and authoritative *ulama's* opinions) and need to be preserved by Muslims.

The new *aswaja* advocates show a paradox in religious orientation. It is complicated if one uses two fronts: moderate vs. radical Islam in explaining the *dakwah* groups. On the one hand, the *aswaja* resists Islamist movements such as the Wahhabi and Hizbut Tahrir and regards them as extremists, but on the other hand, it also rejects the so-called "deviant sects" such as Shia, liberal Islam, and Ahmadiyah.[4] It seems they have redefined "moderate" into a narrower concept. Habib Noval b. Muhammad Alaydrus is a good example. Considered to be a moderate *habib* in Solo, Habib Noval has been active in reviving *aswaja* teachings as a way of countering Wahhabism. He is also close to *habaib*, *kiais*, and Sufi movements and has been invited by Tarekat Naqshabandi Haqqani to give a sermon in Jakarta. However, when I seeked his opinion on Shia and liberal Islam, he answered without hesitation that these groups were definitely deviant and Muslims should have no tolerance for them. However, as he said, he prefers to use a peaceful *dakwah* in opposing these movements. Furthermore, he has a sympathetic view of the leader of a militant Islamic movement in Jakarta, Habib Rizieq Shihab, and considers him to be a brave figure who has fought to eradicate iniquity (*maksiat*) in Indonesia. He blames the Indonesian media for not being objective in delivering news on Habib Rizieq and his movement (Interview with Noval Alaydrus, 2 September 2013).

While the new *aswaja* advocates generally show opposition to Wahhabism, liberal Islam, and Shi'ism, they have adopted very different responses.[5] Habib Rizieq, for instance, states that he only opposes extreme Shia and Wahhabis and not all their variants. He suggested that Muslims need to be objective about these movements. In the case of the Wahhabis, for instance, he said that some Wahhabis are *mu'tadil* (fair and just), i.e, they appreciate various religious strands within Islam, including the *aswaja* group. For these Wahhabis, he urges Muslim to show respect and engage in dialogues with them. Yet, he opposes *takfiri* Wahhabi who openly criticizes *aswaja* and labels *kafir* (unbeliever) as those who have different views and religious practices. During my fieldwork, I observed Habib Rizieq delivering a sermon on the characteristics of Sunni Islam (*Ciri-ciri Ahlus Sunnah wal-Jama'ah*) in which he described the differences between Sunni and Wahhabi. In his sermon, he criticized "extreme" Wahhabis who apostatized other Muslims as infidels (*kafir*) and accused *aswaja* Muslims as guilty of *bid'ah* (unlawful innovation). Similar case holds also for Shia. Although many *habaib* preachers judge all Shia as deviant, Habib Rizieq only denounces "extreme" subgroup within Shia. The deviant Shia for him is the fanatics (*ghulat*) who regard Ali as God and denounce the companions of the Prophet (Interview with Muhammad Rizieq Shihab, 4 April 2013). Similarly, in one of his sermons, which is available on

DVD, he stated that some Shiis respect the companions of the Prophet and avoid criticizing Sunni believers. He added that some transmitters of Prophetic tradition (hadith) are Shia *ulama* and if people reject Shi'ism it means Sunni Muslims will need to reject the authoritative collection of hadith by Bukhari and Muslim. Because of his objective opinion on this issue, several Wahhabi media have accused Habib Rizieq of being Shia.

The emphatic opposition to Shi'ism has been expressed by a few *aswaja habaib*. The interesting case of this anti-Shia *dakwah* is Habib Ahmad b. Zein Al-Kaff with his organization Albayyinat in Surabaya. While most *aswaja dakwah* oppose Wahhabism, Habib Ahmad has focused his struggle against the spread of Shia groups in Indonesia. Habib Ahmad (2013) states that Albayyinat is a *dakwah* movement based on *aswaja* teaching. He founded the organization in 1988 in Surabaya together with Habib Thohir b. Abdullah Al-Kaff of Tegal, Habib Abdul Qadir al-Haddad of Malang, and Habib Ahmad Assegaf of Bangil (Interview with Ahmad b. Zein Al-Kaff, 13 March 2013). As stated on his website, the reason for opposing Shi'ism is that "the Shia has deviated from the 'true' teachings of the Prophet and they have condemned Muslim leaders who helped the Prophet in spreading Islam. As a consequence, Shia has created anxiety and conflict within society and ruined the stability and security guarded by the government" (Albayyinat n.d). Habib Ahmad claims that the organization has spread to several parts of Indonesia and its activities include providing information to the public on the truth of *aswaja* teaching and the danger of Shia either through publications, book translation, preaching, or training (*kaderisasi*). Albayyinat also has appealed to the government and Muslim organizations to work together in banning the Shia movement. Based on my observations and conversations with several informants, Habib Ahmad has been invited to several *majelis taklim* of *habaib* and *kiais* and usually talks about the danger of Shia. He criticized Muslim leaders and intellectuals such as Said Agil Siradj and Quraish Shihab who have tried to bridge the Sunni and Shia divide in Indonesia. He even suspected that Shia leaders have paid Muslim elites to stop attacking Shia. Furthermore, he also attacked Habib Rizieq for tolerating Shia (Interview with Ahmad b. Zein Al-Kaff, 13 March 2013).

Despite this variation in *aswaja dakwah*, there has been cooperation among *aswaja* defenders to strengthen their Islamic doctrine against external forces. It can be said that the challenge from Islamist movements, most notably the Wahhabi, has created the anxiety that their religious practices will be wiped out. Habib Rizieq (2013) contends that he and other *aswaja* preachers began speaking out against the Wahhabis only recently in the post-Suharto years due to the fact that many of the Wahhabi preachers and their media have been publicly criticizing Muslim traditionalists. Some preachers have built media network among *aswaja*. Habib Noval of Solo, for instance, arranged IT training for *majelis taklim* members to make them media savvy and able to spread their own *dakwah* in cyberspace. Similarly, Idrus Ramli has actively organized *aswaja* training for Muslim youths, including university students, to strengthen *aswaja* doctrine and provide them with the skills to counter Wahhabi and other rival groups. By doing these activities, they are also sending messages to their rivals that the *aswaja* Muslims are powerful and represent a majority in Indonesia.

Contesting the 'True' Sunni Authority

Both *aswaja* and its rival, Wahhabism, claim to follow Sunnism (or the path of *ahl sunna wa al-jama'a*). The attachment to *ahl sunna wa al-jama'a* is significant for Sunni Muslims as it is related to the idea of salvation in the hereafter. This is based on some traditions of the Prophet (hadith) saying that after his own age has passed, Muslims would split into seventy-three groups, all of which would go to hell except one. The single saved group would be those who have constantly observed the Sunna of the Prophet and his Companions (Saleh 2001, p. 63). The Salafi-Wahhabi group claims that their method of understanding and practising Islam is in accord with the method of *ahl sunna wa al-jama'a*. They assert that to be Sunni, "Muslims should consistently follow the instructions prescribed by the Prophet Muhammad and his Companions and join a community that practices his Sunna consistently" (Hasan 2006, p. 135). The Wahhabis, as could be seen from various websites, enjoin Muslims to refer to the basic resources of Islam (the Quran and Hadith), and to follow the path of the pious forefathers (*al-salaf al-salih*). Based on their teachings in religious purification and their opposition to *bid'ah* (unlawful innovation), the Wahhabis claimed that their Sunnism is more authentic than the traditionalist variants. They criticize the traditionalists for adopting practices outside the teachings of *ahl sunna wa al-jama'a* (Hasan 2006, p. 136).

In responding to the Wahhabi challenge, the new *aswaja* groups have advanced various arguments to show that they are the more authentic Sunnis. The first and main argument to maintain their Sunni authority is through textual reasoning. This is carried out through the reference to classical texts of *ulama* who support their position. Some *aswaja* authors, for instance, refer to classical *ulama's* writings, such as of al-Imam al-Murtada al-Zabidi (1732–90 CE) who defined *ahl sunna wa al-jama'a* as based on the Ash'arite and Maturidite thinking. In Islamic theology, both schools represent Sunni orthodoxy (Halverson 2010, p. 30). Al-Zabidi stated that Sunnism consists of *ahl hadith* (followers of hadith), Sufis, and followers of the Ash'arite and Maturidite (Alaydrus 2011, p. 39). Idrus, on his website, states that one of the characteristics of *aswaja* is the adoption of one among four schools of Islamic law (*madzahib*), i.e., Hanafite, Malikite, Shafi'ite, or Hanbalite for everyday religious practice. He argues that, by referring to al-Imam Shah Waliyullah al-Dahlawi (1699–1769), following one particular school (*madzhab*) has been a general practice of the majority of Muslims since the times of the pious predecessors (the first three generations of Islam). This tradition, however, was challenged by the Wahhabi movement emerging in the eighteenth century in Saudi Arabia, which called on Muslims to abandon schools of law and return to the Quran and Sunnah. For Idrus, Wahhabi injunctions are erroneous because they assume the founders of *madzahib* did not base their interpretations and opinions on the Principles of the Quran and Sunnah (Ramli 2013). Hence, according to Idrus, Wahhabism is not a part of Sunnism, but the Kharijite. The Kharijite is the first extreme sect in the early history of Islam that rebelled against the ruling power. Idrus rejects Wahhabism as their teaching justifies *takfir* (accusing one as unbeliever) and the spilling of blood of Muslims whose opinion is different from theirs. Idrus supports his view by displaying several texts of the founder of Wahhabism, Muhammad b. 'Abd al-Wahhab, who endorsed the use of violence (Ramli 2010, p. 42).

Similarly, in defending the religious practices deemed by Wahhabi to be *bid'ah*, *aswaja* preachers and authors resort to authoritative texts of Islam and opinions of the Middle Eastern *ulama*. In the eyes of *aswaja* preachers, the Wahhabis have a narrow and rigid understanding of *bid'ah* that leads them to castigate and lead astray their fellow Muslims. As stated in the Quran, God commands Muslims to consult with knowledgeable persons (*ahl dhikr*) on religious problems. In this case, Habib Noval cites several *ulama's* definition of *bid'ah*. He quotes Imam

Shafi'i's opinion, which divides *bid'ah* into two types: *bid'ah mahmudah* (lawful innovation) and *bid'ah madzmumah* (unlawful innovation). The former is in line with the Quran and Sunnah while the latter is not (Alaydrus 2011, p. 11). Habib Noval refutes the Wahhabi's insistence that all *bid'ah* are deviant. He also quotes various Quranic verses and other *ulama's* opinions in the defence of lawful *bid'ah*. For Muslim traditionalists, lawful *bid'ah* includes *tahlilan, maulidan, salawatan, yasinan, tabarruk, ziarah,* and so forth. Like other *aswaja* books, Habib Noval provides a doctrinal basis for each practice. In the case of visiting the saints' graves, for instance, he contends that it is part of the Prophetic tradition that has been exemplified by his Companion and the pious predecessors (*salaf salihin*). For him, visiting the saints' graves has a very useful impact on both visitors and the dead. He refers to a hadith stating that the Prophet allowed Muslims to visit the saints' graves since such practice can induce visitors to renounce worldly pleasures (*zuhud*) and to remember God (Alaydrus 2011, p. 121). He also refers to some *salaf ulama* such as Ibn Hajar Al-Haitami, Imam Fakhrur Razi and Muhammad Sa'id Ramadan al-Buti to support his argument that visiting the saints' graves is a cherished practice (*amal yang disukai*) and visitors could obtain grace (*rahmat*) from doing so (Alaydrus 2011, pp. 133–136).

The *aswaja* defenders also use historical and factual accounts to uphold their own authority and to reject Wahhabism. Echoing the general reasoning of the NU scholars, the *aswaja* group argues that traditional Islam has long been established in the archipelago thanks to Sufi *ulama*, especially the nine saints (*wali songo*). Most *habaib* commonly told me that most of the nine saints were in fact the descendants of the Prophet (*sayyids*) from Hadhramaut who introduced Islam to Southeast Asia in the earlier phase of Islamization.[6] Rather than attacking the local customs, the saints adopted local cultures as a medium of Islamization provided that they did not go against the principles of Islam. Such argument aims to prove that *aswaja* Islam was rooted in Indonesian history. For the *aswaja* defenders, the Wahhabi and other "deviant" groups came later in the eighteenth century onwards and have destabilized the long established beliefs and practices of *aswaja* as well as the peaceful nature of Indonesian Islam. A late popular preacher in Jakarta, Habib Munzir, contended that Wahhabism is misleading (*mengkufurkan*) Sunni Muslims who practise *tawassul, ziarah kubur, maulid,* and so forth. Habib Munzir stated that in the history of Islam, the followers of Muhammad Abdul Wahhab, who were driven by misguided attempts to purify Islam, destroyed various sacred sites of Islam such as the grave of the grandson of Prophet Husein b. Abi Talib in Iraq, the dome where the Prophet was born, and the domes on the Companions' graves. For the Wahhabis, such sacred sites were a potential source of veneration and idolatry for Muslims due to large number of visitors to the sites (Guntur and Majelis Rasulullah 2013, pp. 73–76). Habib Munzir also stated that the Wahhabis had killed thousands of Muslims in Hijaz (now Saudi Arabia) around 1805 under the pretext of eradicating *bid'ah* (Guntur and Majelis Rasulullah 2013, p. 79).

The *aswaja* preachers have also accused the Wahhabis of attacking their beliefs in Indonesia. While the Wahhabi media are the main concern, there are some cases of mainstream media's religious programme that have caught the attention of *aswaja* preachers and activists. One instance in 2013 was the involvement of national TV channel TRANS7, through its Islamic programme called *Khazanah*, in depicting traditionalist rituals such as visiting the saints' graves as idolatry (*kemusyrikan*). The programme was criticized by the traditionalist Muslims especially from *majelis taklim*, who asserted that the TRANS7 had become a tool of Wahhabi propagation (Sarkub 2013). The Sarkub team and Islamic Defenders Front were among *aswaja* representatives who came to the TRANS7 office demanding clarification and rectification.

Considering the challenges to the *aswaja* community, several sermon groups have raised special topics in countering Wahhabism. In Solo, for instance, Habib Noval has organized a special public preaching (*tablig akbar*) in April 2013 with the theme of "Strengthening Your Faith-Let's Return to the Muslim Saints' Teaching". The opening sentences of Habib Noval (2013) in his public sermon below better illustrated how he responded to Wahhabi challenges:

> Today is the revival era for *ahl sunna wa al-jama'a*, let's revive the true *aswaja*, let's revive the groups of *la ilaha illa-llah* (*tahlilan*), let's revive the groups of *sallal-lahu 'ala Muhammad* (*salawatan*), let's revive the groups of *khatmil qur'an* (Quranic reciting), let's revive *mujelis yasinan*, let's revive visiting the graves, which is recently criticized by TRANS7's Khazanah Program. I urge *aswaja* social organisations to criticise the program so that it could be reviewed or stopped as it offends *aswaja* by stating that those who visit the graves are unbelievers (*mushrik*). They now dare to use TV to attack NU, to attack *habaib*, to

attack *kiais*. Therefore, I ask *kiais* and *habaib* to convey their protest to broadcasting committee since the TV breaks the law of broadcasting … I urge you to "say no to Wahhabi, say no to Salafi" (in English), say no to anti-*tahlilan*, anti-*yasinan*, and anti-*maulidan* … the faith issue (*akidah*) is number one, therefore our priority is to strengthen the faith of *ahl sunna wa al-jama'a*.

Popularizing Traditional Islamic Authority

In the face of attacks from Wahhabi followers, *aswaja* groups have attempted to strengthen their legitimacy by emphasizing traditional authority. One form of reviving such authority is through the revitalization of knowledge connectedness that was historically used in Islamic education before the coming of the modern educational system. William A. Graham (1993) calls this particular transmission of knowledge in the Muslim world as *isnad paradigm*. It links transmitters of knowledge from the current generation back to those in the past through face-to-face learning for authentication (Graham 1993, p. 502; Robinson 2008, pp. 266–67). In this case, the position of descendants of the Prophet is special as they have blood connection to the Prophet and therefore inherit His blessing. This is one of the reasons that make traditionalist Muslims rely more on the religious authority of *habaib* or *kiais*.

The *aswaja* group calls for efforts to revive the importance of *sanad* for the transmission of Islamic knowledge. The lineage of teachers (*sanad*) is usually mentioned in the *ijazah* (certificate) system written by a teacher to his students who have learned a particular subject or text. The *ijaza* is the authorization to teach a certain discipline of Islamic knowledge or textbook either in oral or written form (Graham 1993, p. 511). Although the modern educational institutions provide a formal certificate, the students also receive a special *ijaza* from individual teachers. Some *habaib* narrated that they continued their studies in traditional religious centres such as the *ribath* of Sayyid Muhammad Alawi Al-Maliki in Mecca and Dar al-Mustafa in Hadhramaut, although some of them have already obtained degrees in Indonesia. A popular preacher in Makassar, Habib Mahmud b. Umar Al-Hamid, for instance, spent ten years studying in the Middle East moving from one traditional school to another just to receive a *sanad* and blessings from charismatic scholars without formal certification. For him, the blessings (*baraka*) he gained from his participation in his study as well as his service (*khidmah*) to his teacher is more important than the degree (Interview with Mahmud Al-Hamid, 28 April 2013). The list of well-known teachers (*sanad*) is important for the preachers as they can mention their teachers to their students or public audience as a way of raising their religious authority.

Given the authority of *sanad*, some *habaib* have criticized the Wahhabi for the lack of *sanad*. Habib Munzir, for instance, stated on his website that the traditionalist *ulama*, when they talk about the Prophetic tradition (hadith), have a list of transmitters to the six authoritative collections of hadith (*al-kutub al-sitta*). Hence, he said: "no knowledge without *sanad*, so the *fatwa* without *sanad* is false (*batil*)" (Guntur and Majelis Rasulullah 2013). Habib Munzir criticized the Wahhabi scholars for their lack of *sanad* and therefore their Islamic knowledge should be questioned. He views Syeikh Muhammad Nasiruddin al-Albani (1914–99) as an example of a Wahhabi scholar who has become an authoritative *ulama* in hadith within Wahhabi, but in fact had no strong *sanad* to the Prophet. In response to this, the Wahhabis, represented by Firanda Andirja Abidin, refuted Habib Munzir's statements and said it was a false accusation against the Wahhabi teachers. Firanda accuses Habib Munzir of not being knowledgeable in hadith and trying to fool Muslims in Indonesia (Abidin 2012).

Conclusion

Competition among the groups to represent Sunni has paved the way for the emergence of a new traditionalist movement that aims at defending traditional Sunnism (*aswaja*) from the growing challenges of Wahhabi and other groups. The way *aswaja* groups responded to Wahhabi replicates the way their predecessors responded to challenges from the reformists in the 1920s and 1930s. Although the *aswaja* group has helped to reassert traditional Islam in Indonesia, it also works to revive conservatism and chauvinism within the group. In this case, it has redefined traditional Islam into a more conservative and confronting direction as held by NU's conservative wing. The conservative tendency of *aswaja* includes the assertions of being the "true" Sunnism; opposition to Wahhabism and other perceived "deviant" Muslim groups; and the growing attempts to popularize *aswaja* beliefs and rituals among the wider Muslim population. The group opposes progressive NU leaders and scholars who have redefined Sunnism to be more inclusive.

Within this conservative atmosphere, there emerged a growing need for charismatic and traditional leaders, scholars, and preachers such as *habaib* and *kiais*, who are not only able to provide "authoritative" traditional Islamic knowledge, but also pietistic identity and *baraka* (blessing) for their followers.

I have classified the current *aswaja* defenders into three groups: popular preachers, NU scholars, and online media activists. These *aswaja* defenders mostly come from popular preachers and local NU scholars who share a concern regarding the protection of traditional Islam. The three groups have been active in defending and reasserting traditional Islam through Islamic education, preaching, and new media. Not only have they defended traditional Islam, they have also moved to challenge the Wahhabi and other groups by revealing their rivals' doctrinal weakness and extreme actions, which are considered not in line with "true" Sunni teaching. Furthermore, they have built and consolidated *aswaja* networks to help Muslims resist the internal and external forces that have the potential to challenge traditional Islam. These developments suggest that traditionalist Muslims tend to unite when there is a perceived threat to their community.

NOTES

1. The debates and discussions in this forum could be seen in "Dialog Terbuka FKM Jatim vs KH. Said Aqil Siradj", https://www.youtube.com/watch?v=TvbnCZWG85g (accessed 15 December 2014).
2. For detailed information, see http://www.easycounter.com/report/sarkub.com (accessed 17 March 2016).
3. The video is available at https://www.youtube.com/watch?v=gZCiUGlqgss (accessed 5 November 2014).
4. See for example the vision and mission of Sarkub at http://www.sarkub.com/about/ (accessed 15 October 2014).
5. This is based on my interviews with a number of popular *habaib* preachers in several cities in Indonesia.
6. This narrative can also be found in *al-Kisah*, 24 February 2008.

REFERENCES

Abidin, F.A. 2012. *Ketika Sang Habib Dikritik: Membuka Mata dan Hati, Meniti Jalan Kebenaran.* N.p.: Naashirusunnah.

Alatas, S.F. 2008. "Securing Their Place: The Habaib, Prophetic Piety and Islamic Resurgence". MA thesis, National University of Singapore.

Alaydrus, H.N.M. 2011. *Ahlul Bid'ah Hasanah: Jawaban untuk Mereka yang Mempersoalkan Amalan Para Wali*. Surakarta: Taman Ilmu.

Albayyinat. N.d. "Apa dan Siapa Albayyinat". http://www.albayyinat.net/ind1.html (accessed 20 October 2014).

Ar-Raudhah Majelis Ilmu and Dzikir. N.d. "Tentang Majelis". http://ar-raudhah.info/tentang/ (accessed 2 November 2014).

Azra, Azyumardi. 2004. "Political Islam in Post-Soeharto Indonesia". In *Islamic Perspectives on the New Millennium*, edited by Virginia Hooker and Amin Saikal. Singapore: Institute of Southeast Asian Studies.

Burhani, Ahmad. 2012. "Al-Tawassut wa-l I'tidal: The NU and Moderatism in Indonesian Islam". *Asian Journal of Social Science* 40, nos. 5–6: 564–81.

Bush, Robin. 2009. *Nahdlatul Ulama and the Struggle for Power within Islam and Politics in Indonesia*. Singapore: Institute of Southeast Asian Studies.

Debat Ustadz Wahabi vs Ustadz Aswaja di Batam. 2014. Video File. https://www.youtube.com/watch?v=gZCiUGlqgss (accessed 5 November 2014).

Dhofier, Zamakhsyari. 1982. *Tradisi Pesantren: Studi tentang Pandangan Hidup Kyai*. Jakarta: LP3ES.

Fealy, Greg. 1998. "Ulama and Politics in Indonesia: A History of Nahdlatul Ulama, 1952–1967". PhD thesis, Monash University.

―――. 2007. "The Political Contingency of Reform-Mindedness in Indonesia's Nahdlatul Ulama: Interest Politics and the Khittah". In *Islamic Legitimacy in a Plural Asia*, edited by Anthony Reid and Michael Gilsenan, pp. 154–66. USA and Canada: Routledge.

Fealy, Greg and Greg Barton. 1996. *Nahdlatul Ulama, Traditional Islam and Modernity in Indonesia*. Melbourne: Monash Asia Institute.

Feener, R. Michael. 2007. *Muslim Legal Thought in Modern Indonesia*. New York; Cambridge: Cambridge University Press.

Gause III, F. Gregory. 2011. *Saudi Arabia in the New Middle East*. Council Special Report 63, December 2011. USA: Council on Foreign Relations-Center for Preventive Action.

Graham, William A. 1993. "Traditionalism in Islam: An Essay in Interpretation". *The Journal of Interdisciplinary History* 23, no. 3: 495–522.

Guntur, Mohammad and Tim Majelis Rasulullah. 2013. *Habib Munzir Menanam Cinta untuk Para Kekasih Rasulullah*. Jakarta: Qultum Media.

Habib Noval Alaydrus. 2013. "Tabligh Akbar Masjid Agung Surakarta – Mantapkan Akidahmu". Video File. https://www.youtube.com/watch?v=wl_WL6oxrfM (accessed 20 November 2014).

Haidar, M. Ali. 1994. *Nahdlatul Ulama dan Islam di Indonesia*. Jakarta: Gramedia.

Halverson, Jeffry R. 2010. *Theology and Creed in Sunni Islam: The Muslim Brotherhood, Ash'arism, and Political Sunnism*. New York: Palgrave Macmillan.

Hasan, Noorhaidi. 2005. "Laskar Jihad: Islam, Militancy, and the Quest for Identity in Post-New Order Indonesia". PhD thesis, Utrecht University, Netherlands.

———. 2006. *Laskar Jihad: Islam, Militancy, and the Quest for Identity in Post-New Order Indonesia*. Ithaca: Cornell Southeast Asian Program.

———. 2007. "The Salafi Movement in Indonesia: Transnational Dynamics and Local Development". *Comparative Studies of South Asia, Africa and the Middle East* 27, no. 1: 83–94.

———. 2010. "The Failure of the Wahhabi Campaign: Transnational Islam and the Salafi Madrasa in Post-9/11 Indonesia". *Southeast East Asia Research* 18, no. 4: 657–705.

Ida, Laode. 2004. *NU Muda: Kaum Progresif dan Sekulerisme Baru*. Jakarta: Erlangga.

Idrus Ramli. 2013. "Ikut Sunnah atau Madzhab". http://www.idrusramli.com/2013/ikut-sunnah-atau-madzhab/ (accessed 4 November 2014).

———. N.d. "Profil". http://www.idrusramli.com/profil/ (accessed 20 November 2014).

Jamhari and Jajang Jahroni. 2004. *Gerakan Salafi Radikal di Indonesia*. Jakarta: Raja Grafindo Persada.

Kersten, Carool. 2015. "Islamic Post-Traditionalism: Postcolonial and Postmodern Religious Discourse in Indonesia". *Sophia* 54 (December): 473–89.

Majelis Al-Muwasholah. N.d. "Tentang kami". https://majelisalmuwasholah.com/sekilas-tentang-majelis/ (accessed 5 March 2015).

Meijer, Roel. 2009. *Global Salafism: Islam's New Religious Movement*. New York: Columbia University Press.

Meuleman, Johan. 2011. "Dakwah, Competition for Authority, and Development". *Bijdragen tot de Taal-, Land- en Volkenkunde* 167, no. 2/3: 236–69.

Noer, Deliar. 1980. *Gerakan Modern Islam di Indonesia 1900–1942*. Jakarta: LP3ES.

Nuhrison, M. Nuh. 2010. "Gerakan Paham dan Pemikiran Islam Radikal Pasca Orde Baru (Gerakan Dakwah Salafi di Kec. Lembar, Kab. Lombok Barat, Nusa Tenggara Barat)". In *Direktori Kasus-Kasus Aliran, Pemikiran, Paham, dan Gerakan Keagamaan di Indonesia*, edited by Wakhid Sugiyarto. Jakarta: Kementerian Agama RI Badan Litbang dan Diklat Puslitbang Kehidupan Keagamaan.

Qomar, Mujamil. 2002. *NU "Liberal": Dari Tradisionalisme Ahlussunnah ke Universalisme Islam*. Bandung: Mizan.

Ramli, Muhammad Idrus. 2010. *Buku Pintar Berdebat dengan Wahhabi*. Jawa Timur: Bina Aswaja and LMB NU Jember.

———. 2013. "Ikut Sunnah atau Madzhab". http://www.idrusramli.com/2013/ikut-sunnah-atau-madzhab/ (accessed 4 November 2014).

Robinson, Francis. 2008. "Islamic Reform and Modernities in South Asia". *Modern Asian Studies* 42, no. 2/3: 259–81.

Rodja. N.d. "Profil Radio Rodja dan Rodja TV". http://www.radiorodja.com/ about/ (accessed 25 March 2015).

Rumadi. 2008. *Post-tradisionalisme Islam: Wacana Intelektualisme dalam Komunitas NU.* Cirebon: Fahmina Institute.

Saleh, Fauzan. 2001. *Modern Trends in Islamic Theological Discourse in Twentieth Century Indonesia: A Critical Survey.* Leiden, Boston, and Koln: Brill.

Sarkub. 2013. "KH. Thobay Syadzily: Mengawal Aswaja Sampai Dunia Maya". http://www.sarkub.com/2013/kh-thobary-syadzily-mengawal-aswaja-sampai-dunia-maya/#ixzz2ZI13GGHD (accessed 20 October 2014).

———. N.d. "Tim Sarkub bertemu Ust Hartono Jaiz". http://www.sarkub.com/densus-99-sarkub/densus-hartono/ (accessed 15 October 2014).

———. N.d. "Visi Misi Sarkub". http://www.sarkub.com/about/ (accessed 15 October 2014).

van Bruinessen, Martin. 1994. *NU: Tradisi, Relasi-Relasi Kuasa, Pencarian Wacana Baru.* Yogyakarta: LKIS.

Wahid, Din. 2014. "Nurturing the Salafi Manhaj: A Study of Salafi Pesantrens in Contemporary Indonesia". PhD thesis, Utrecht University.

Woodward, Mark, Inayah Rohmaniyah, Ali Amin, Samsul Ma'arif, Diana Murtaugh Coleman, and Muhammad Sani Umar. 2012. "Ordering What is Right, Forbidding What is Wrong: Two Faces of Hadhrami Dakwah in Contemporary Indonesia". *Review of Indonesian and Malaysian Affairs* 46, no. 2: 105–46.

Zada, Khamami. 2002. *Islam Radikal: Pergulatan Ormas-ormas Islam Garis Keras di Indonesia.* Bandung: Mizan.

Zamhari, Arif and Julia Day Howell. 2012. "Taking Sufism to the Streets: Majelis Zikir and Majelis Salawat as New Venues for Popular Islamic Piety in Indonesia". *Review of Indonesian and Malaysian Affairs* 46, no. 2: 47–75.

Interviews

Interview with Ahmad b. Zein Al-Kaff, 13 March 2013.
Interview with Dian Kusumaningrum, 2 November 2013.
Interview with Mahmud Al-Hamid, 28 April 2013.
Interview with Mas'ud, 20 October 2013.
Interview with Muhammad Rizieq b. Shihab, 4 April 2013.
Interview with Muhsin b. Idrus Al-Hamid, 25 September 2013.
Interview with Noval b. Muhammad Alaydrus, 2 September 2013.
Interview with Said Aqil Siradj, 1 October 2013.
Interview with Thobary Syadzily, 20 October 2013.

10

NURTURING RELIGIOUS AUTHORITY AMONG TABLIGHI JAMAAT IN INDONESIA: GOING OUT FOR *KHURUJ* AND BECOMING PREACHER[1]

By *Muhammad Adlin Sila*

> Empty mesjids cried floods of tears,
> As no worshippers made *sujood* for many years,
> And then crowds came back and thronged their floors,
> You can see angels smile, and the heavens echo with applause[2]

Introduction

Mesjid Kebon Jeruk, an old mosque situated in West Jakarta, Indonesia, is always alive with religious activities. Every Thursday, about 2,000 men will gather at the mosque built by a Chinese woman in 1817, following lectures by an *ustadz* (religious teacher). Dressed in *kurtas*—long-sleeved and hip length shirt traditionally worn by men in India, for which they are easily identifiable—and putting on white hajj caps, they are also dressed in robes, a long and loose shirt commonly worn by the Arabs. Most will have their beards lengthened and moustache shaved. They are followers of Tablighi Jamaat, or Tablighis, literally "a group for preachers", who come from Jakarta, West Java, East Java and the other regions in Indonesia. The Tablighis usually carry large bags of clothing and other supplies with them.

The aforementioned is the most popular poem of the Tablighis that best describes the calling for the Muslims to go back to mosque. In practice, they go out on small group tours to invite Muslims whom they had visited to conduct the canonical prayer in mosque and to bring the message of the Tablighi Jamaat to the Muslims. This activity is called *khuruj* (or *jaula* in Urdu), which according to several scholars (Sikand 2002; Sila 2010 and 2016; and Noor 2012) is both unique and critical to the Tablighi Jamaat. It is unique because *khuruj* (which is called *tashkil* in Indonesia and Malaysia) may take days, weeks or even months (Noor 2012). At the end of the tour, participants will report back orally their experiences to the mosque-based group from which they set out. The act of presenting these reports is called *karguzari*. Sikand (2002) and Noor (2012) have discussed that Tablighi Jamaat became the most widely followed movement and sparked controversy among Muslim scholars. But the two agreed that there is nothing to worry about the Tablighis and their *khuruj* activities. Similarly, Dekmejian (1985) excluded Tablighi Jamaat from the list of Islamic fundamentalist groups since the books they refer to and the religious activities they perform do not contradict with mainstream Islam. They never discuss politics, let alone criticize the ruling government, nor condemn the ceremonies of other Islamic groups as deviant or infidels. The movement is apolitical and non-violent (Noor 2012).

This chapter, however, revisits previous studies and attempts to portray a different understanding of the *khuruj*. It argues that the practice of preaching during *khuruj* challenges the conventional conception of a religious preacher. *Khuruj* is a new technique of preaching or proselytizing, different from traditional preaching methods of more established Islamic organizations such as Nahdlatul Ulama (NU) and Muhammadiyah or even MUI (Council of Indonesian Ulama). My recent ethnographic data when conducting fieldwork in Kebon Jeruk mosque, Jakarta, in 2010 and 2016, shows that Tablighi Jamaat has managed their religious activities, not only *khuruj*, in favour of current needs. I found that *khuruj* has become a breeding ground for the Tablighis to acquire authority. After describing a thoroughly detailed account of the movement, I undertake a discourse analysis of the Islamic movement. I argue that being a preacher (Ind., *muballigh*), in its conventional definition, no longer requires a formal degree in Islamic studies. For the Tablighis, the more *khuruj* they perform, and this includes the number of days and months they go out for *khuruj*, the higher the level of authority they will achieve. To a certain degree, they can provide religious guidance to others. Overall, this chapter re-examines the role of the Tablighis and their contestation toward the conventional conception of religious authority in Islam. As an anthropological inquiry, this chapter touches on issues surrounding what constitutes being authoritative in religious guidance according to the Tablighis, not only the elites but also lay members of Tablighi Jamaat. In short, this chapter explores the topic not entirely from the standard texts. But all the data are derived from lived examples of the Tablighis on the ground.

A Glimpse of Mesjid Kebon Jeruk

What I stated earlier in the introduction describes my impression of Mesjid Kebon Jeruk during my visit in April 2016. There were Tablighis from India, Pakistan, Bangladesh (popularly abbreviated as IPB), Malaysia, Thailand, Australia and the United States. Before choosing Mesjid Kebon Jeruk as my field site, I knew about the Tablighi Jamaat when I visited Mesjid Mamajang Raya, Makassar in the early 1990s. The local authorities granted the movement temporary access to the mosque. I was a young college student of IAIN Alauddin (now UIN, State Islamic University) in Makassar then and wanted to know about the newly established Islamic movement in town. In the late 1990s, when the Tablighi Jamaat was unable to build their own mosque in central Makassar, they officially left Mesjid Mamajang Raya for Mesjid Kerung-Kerung. At the present day, this mosque has become the headquarters of the Tablighi Jamaat in Makassar.

During my visits to the mosque, the Tablighis often mentioned Mesjid Kebon Jeruk as the place they had always wanted to go. Only after several years I was able to visit Mesjid Kebon Jeruk, the first being in 2010, when I began my research on Tablighi Jamaat, until 2016 (Sila 2010 and 2016). Mesjid Kebon Jeruk, to my knowledge, is a mosque that is now the headquarters of the Tablighi Jamaat of Indonesia (Ind., *markaz*). Knowing that the mosque is situated in Glodok business area of Jakarta is interesting as it is predominantly inhabited by residents of Chinese descent who are mostly traders.[3] Being located on Jalan Kebon Jeruk, this mosque is named after its location. This is the largest mosque among about forty-one mosques in Taman Sari subdistrict.[4] Mesjid Kebon Jeruk is known as the headquarter for Tablighi Jamaat in Indonesia. Some political figures have ever visited this mosque.

The Tablighi Jamaat activities are unstructured. Yet, followers of the group try to improve their *khuruj* management. For example, in Mesjid Kebon Jeruk, all Tablighi activities fell under the supervision of the mosque steering committee. The present chairman, Haji Tjetjep Firdaus Abd, is one of thirteen leaders of Tablighi Jamaat or so-called Syuro council within the Tablighi Jamaat in Indonesia nationwide. The nature of this council is collegial. Although Haji Tjetjep chairs the council, his religious expertise is equal to that of other council members. It is someone by the name of Sheikh Saad Al-Kandahlawi, based in India, who is seen as the supreme leader of the Tablighi Jamaat.[5]

Judging from the year of its establishment, Mesjid Kebon Jeruk is one of the oldest mosques in Jakarta. The authenticity of the mosque architecture is still maintained until now, especially when viewed from the mosque's central room. While the back and upper floors of the mosque are additional spaces that were built later. The extension of the mosque is done to accommodate the increased number of the Tablighis coming from outside Jakarta and abroad. The question to be asked further is when the Tablighis came to this mosque and chose it as their headquarters (Ind., *Markaz*). I met Haji Tjetjep Marzuki who then explained the history of the entry of the Tablighis to the mosque as follows:

> There was a Pakistani named Maulana Rahman preaching at the Krukut Mosque, still in the Glodok area now, in 1975. This Pakistani preacher then chose preaching in Mesjid Mosque Kebon Jeruk. After the preaching finished, the mosque committee gave him an honorarium, but he refused. The attendance who saw the incident were amazed at him. Then this Pakistani knew one of the congregations had a broken hand. He then offered treatment to this person. After rubbing this sick person's hand for several times, he was healed. Seeing this amazing thing, another congregation asked if his son could be healed as well. Rahman, the Pakistani, dipped his finger into a glass and read a prayer.

The water that had been prayed was then handed over to the person earlier. After the person's son drunk the blessed water, the child was then recovered. Seeing the audience's sympathetic and respectful attitude over him, Maulana Rahman decided to choose Mesjid Kebon Jeruk as the centre of his preaching during his stay in Indonesia.

Before the Pakistani Tablighi came, Mesjid Kebon Jeruk provided limited services for religious gatherings (Ind. *Pengajian*) for male and female audiences, such as by inviting preachers (Ind. *Muballigh*). In return, the mosque committee gave honorarium to the preachers. This is a very common religious gathering that we can find anywhere in Jakarta mosques. At the time, the mosque had already welcomed the arrival of many guests from abroad including from South Asian countries, Arab, and Africa since the 1970s. But they came for short visit and then left the mosque. Only in 1975, Maulana Rahman came and decided to choose this mosque as the transit for the Tablighis coming especially from India, Pakistan and Bangladesh—popularly abbreviated as IPB—before they scattered throughout Indonesia to do *khuruj*.

When I did this research at this mosque, I met not only the Tablighis coming from these three countries, but also found a few Tablighis from Australia and America. In the last five to ten years, Indonesia has become the world's most well-known Muslim country attractive to the Tablighis. By 2015, there had been about 216 Tablighis coming from abroad. In June 2016, there were already 130 Tablighis from abroad. In reverse, the number of Tablighis from Indonesia going out for *khuruj* overseas increases every year. According to the statistics from Ahmad Subagyo, the Tablighis who began their travel from Mesjid Kebon Jeruk to overseas numbered to 75 groups each comprising five to eight people. Interestingly, they went abroad at their own expense and accepted no honorarium. They travelled to countries like South Asian countries (IPB), Latin America, Africa and Europe.

The Tablighis from overseas have resulted in twofold benefits for the Tablighis in Indonesia. First, they could share their overseas experiences and attracted many interests from others to go abroad for *khuruj*. And second, they could build mutual understanding over the differences of religious orientation between the two and learn how to show respect to each other. For example, I interviewed one Tablighi named Farid who has an NU background. He acknowledged that prior to his interaction with the Tablighis from Pakistan, he only knew one *madzhab* or school of religious thought that is the Shafie School. "From my meeting with foreign Tablighis, then I knew that there are many *madzhab* embraced by Muslims", he asserted.

Mesjid Kebon Jeruk: The Breeding Ground for *Khuruj*

The Tablighis coming from various provinces in Indonesia take turns providing services like giving a call to prayer (a*zan*) and leading the prayer as an imam in Mesjid Kebon Jeruk. This practice has been in place since the last ten years. There is a steering committee in Mesjid Kebon Jeruk which is responsible for ensuring that every province could get their turn to provide some assistance to the mosque. When this research began in early March 2016, the Tablighis from Medan and Aceh, numbering 150 people, took turns providing services to the mosque. Their duties range from keeping the mosque clean, cooking and providing meals for other Tablighis in the mosque, being responsible for reception of the guests (*istiqbal*), leading the prayer for five times a day (*Imam*), and delivering speech (*bayan*) especially after sunset prayer (Ind. *Maghrib*) for about an hour. According to one of the receptionists, every day he received registration (*tasykil*) from the Tablighis wanting to go out for *khuruj* for several days (either three or forty days) or for several months (usually four months) to various regions in Indonesia and abroad (distant places, to borrow the term from the Tablighi Jamaat).

The decision about which country to preach and for how many days and months they are permitted to be away, was read out after *bayan* deliberation after the sunset prayer was over. After dawn prayer (Ind. *Subuh*), Haji Tjetjep Marzuki asked all the Tablighis to gather in the big compound located at the terrace of the mosque to listen to his farewell speech. In this occasion, all the top Syuro council leaders were seated next to Haji Tjetjep Marzuki. On 25 April 2016, during the speech led by Haji Tjetjep Marzuki, there were about eight people who arrived from Pakistan, seven people from Singapore, one from Jordan, and five from Bangladesh. Interestingly, members of Tablighi Jamaat from Bangladesh came with their wives. This phenomenon contradicts criticisms levelled towards Tablighi Jamaat that male Tablighis generally leave their wives and families when they perform *khuruj*.

In his speech, Haji Tjetjep Marzuki reminded all Tablighis to put into practice six main principles of the organization while going for *khuruj*. The Tablighis called these *Ushulus Sittah* (six principles) (Sikand

2002; Sila 2010 and 2016; and Noor 2012). The six principles are as follows: (1) Glorifying the phrase *thasyibah* saying, "There is no God but Allah and the Prophet Muhammad is His Last messenger" (Laa Ilaha Illallah Muhammadar Rasulullah (Ind. *syahadat*), (2) Upholding five daily prayers that are essential for spiritual altitude, piety, and a life free from the ills of the material world. It must be performed with full submission (Ar. *khusyu* and *khudhu'*), (3) Practising science and remembrance to God or *dhikr*, by performing prayers, reciting the Quran and reading Hadith, (4) Respecting every Muslim when meeting and visiting them in their house through door-to-door approach to persuade them to go to mosque, (5) Improving intentions and sincerity (Ind. *An-Niat* and *ikhlas*), (6) Striving in the name of Allah (*fisabilillah*) when going out for *khuruj*.

I wrote down the order of these six principles from a book circulated among the Tablighi congregation.[6] But as I found, in applying these six principles, the Tablighis are encouraged to start from the fifth principle: namely improving intentions and sincerity before starting the *khuruj*. This fifth principle, I think, is the most important one. A senior Tablighi, sitting next to me in the mosque while listening to the speech delivered by another Tablighi, reminded me that:

> It will be useless to go out for *khuruj* unless you renew your intention in advance. *Khuruj* is not an easy task because you will leave your comfortable life behind: your job, your wife and kids. That is why it requires sincerity to what you have decided. Although it is for a while only. So, prepare yourself. Talk to your family. If they want to come with you, take them with you. If they do not want, you must grant them financial allowance before you leave. That's much better and obligatory.

The above expression over financing the family left behind by the Tablighis is extremely important as the committee of Mesjid Kebon Jeruk had become the target of complaints and dislikes from other Muslims in the past (Noor 2012). Family members of the Tablighis left behind for *khuruj* were the ones who made these complaints, mostly concerning financial issues. That is the reason why the mosque committee advised the Tablighis to make sure that they are financially stable before deciding to go out for *khuruj*. However, to use the family as an excuse not to go out for *khuruj* is also unacceptable. As one of the doctrines of Tablighi Jamaat that I often hear from the expositions of Haji Tjetjep, saying: "Do not make the family an excuse not to go out for *khuruj*, for it is assured that it is Allah who will provide sustenance for your children and your wife. It is recommended to make the *khuruj* 3 days in 1 month, 40 days in 1 year and 4 months once in a lifetime."

I found that during the registration process, those planning to go out for *khuruj* must fill out a form conforming their past experiences on *khuruj* and should undergo a set of interviews led by senior Tablighis. I did not manage to get the statistics, but from the registration process only a few chose forty days, and mostly to the outer islands in Indonesia. The majority chose three days for *khuruj* in nearby mosques.

As mentioned earlier, the case of Tablighis from Bangladesh who brought their wives along is not a new phenomenon. Their wives also participated in *dakwah* but to female attendees. The Tablighis from Bangladesh are a good example that can be imitated by the Tablighis from Indonesia who generally go for *khuruj* without bringing their wives. But I found that the reluctance of the Tablighis from Indonesia to bring their wives while *khuruj* is generally due to financial consideration. A Tablighi from Palembang left only a provision for his wife and family of a sum of money equivalent to the four-month period that he spent while abroad doing *khuruj*. When I asked specifically the exact amount, he mentioned that an amount of around Rp12 million (or US$838) is enough to last him four months while in Bangladesh, the country he chose, and he left a sum of Rp4 million (or US$279) for his family during his absence. He admitted that the amount is relatively enough for the cost of travel in Bangladesh for four months. Yet for forty days in Indonesia, the money to be spent is between Rp1.5 million (or US$104) and Rp2 million (or US$139), and the money for their family is around Rp1 million (or US$69.83). But this depends on which areas are chosen and the life necessities of each Tablighi member (Interview with Ihsan, a Tablighi from Palembang, 5 April 2016).

As *khuruj* requires a wholehearted and strong commitment, the committee provides counselling to strengthen the motivation of the Tablighis before going out for *khuruj*. This counselling service is carried out at every congregational prayer from dawn to sunset. But there are certain days namely Thursday, Friday and Saturday where I spent several times observing how the Tablighis attended the so-called *i'tikaf* (staying up late inside the mosque for performing certain cycles of prayer or *raka'at* and reciting the Quran until dawn). I chose these three days on purpose as all the Tablighis from Jakarta, Bogor,

Depok, Tangerang and Bekasi (Jabodetabek) generally gathered in the mosque. As I described earlier, I witnessed around 2,000 people who came to the mosque and reported their arrival at the reception of the mosque (*Istiqbal*). Yet the greatest gathering of the Tablighis all over Indonesia is conducted every four months. I did not manage to attend the gathering, known locally as *ijtima'*, but I heard from Ahmad Subagyo who was at the gathering in 2015 said that the total number of attendance at the *ijtima'* then was around 5,000 people.

Mesjid Kebon Jeruk: The Point of Assembly for the Tablighis

Since the 1970s, Tablighis from overseas considered Mesjid Kebon Jeruk as their top destination. But only in 1975, the chairperson of the mosque, Zulfakar, established this mosque as the transit place for the Tablighis coming from abroad, especially from India, Pakistan and Bangladesh. At the present day, Mesjid Kebon Jeruk has become the host institution for foreign Tablighis planning to perform *khuruj* across Indonesia; it can help process temporary residence permit for foreign Tablighis (Interview with Haji Ahmad Sungkar, Mosque Board of Kebon Jeruk, 25 April 2016). Mesjid Kebon Jeruk also provides temporary accommodation from foreign Tablighis. They are permitted to stay there as long as they wish before joining other Tablighis from Indonesia to do *khuruj* to various regions in the country. Although they have to determine which regions in Indonesia they will visit, they have to be adaptable to suit local needs. "The Tablighis coming from overseas are really helpful for us, especially in terms of financial supports", said Ahmad Subagyo, who is responsible for processing temporary residence permit for foreign Tablighis (Interview with Ahmad Subagyo, Division of Foreign Tablighi, Mesjid Kebon Jeruk, on 26 April 2016). As they are regarded as foreign workers, the Tablighis who come from overseas are asked to lodge their permit proposal to the Indonesian government before their arrival.[7] Once they receive the legal basis, they are permitted to do *khuruj* anywhere in Indonesia.

In short, Mesjid Kebon Jeruk serves many functions. The mosque is regarded as the headquarters of Tablighi Jamaat and as the host institution for the Tablighis coming from various countries. For the first function, Mesjid Kebon Jeruk becomes a point of assembly for all Tablighis in Indonesia. Through this function, the mosque invites all Tablighis to join religious gatherings provided in the mosque ranging from *i'tikaf* (individual performance of prayer for the whole night) every week to *ijtima'* (great gathering) every four months. For the second function, the mosque provides immigration services not only for overseas Tablighis but also for the Tablighis from Indonesia wanting to go overseas. Looking at the many functions of Mesjid Kebon Jeruk, the number of Tablighis who come to this mosque has doubled with the Tablighis from overseas, leading to overcapacity at the mosque.

Nonetheless, all the services in the mosque run well. There were around 150 Tablighis who took turns to provide services voluntarily in this mosque every month. As at March 2016, the Tablighis from Medan and Aceh volunteered to provide services in the mosque. In the following month, the Tablighis from other provinces got their turns, and so on. Their duties ranged from maintaining the mosque clean, serving as kitchen hand, becoming receptionist (*istiqbal*), preaching (*bayan*) after sunset prayer or *Maghrib*, afternoon prayer or *Isha* and dawn prayer or *Subuh*.

Not only that, these volunteers also contributed as much as Rp50 million (US$3,492) to cover operational costs for the month they stayed in the mosque. It is obligatory for each foreign Tablighi to contribute as much as Rp6 million to the committee for every week stayed. According to Ahmad Subagyo, that is the only fee that foreign Tablighis have to pay in return for the services he provides. "When they go for *khuruj* we keep their passports. The reason is because, we are responsible for what they are doing here in Indonesia. They are carrying the name of Mesjid Kebon Jeruk whenever they go for *khuruj*. So, they must be [in] our watch. If anything happens with them, we are responsible", added Ahmad Subagyo. Although foreign Tablighis join the route of *khuruj* of the Tablighis from Indonesia, they are given an opportunity to choose other routes as long as they are granted permission from the steering committee of Mesjid Kebon Jeruk.

It is widely known that wherever they perform *khuruj* activities, the Tablighis will stay for a few days, weeks or months (three days, forty days, or four months) in a mosque. No matter how many days they spend, the Tablighis normally go out for *khuruj* in a group of five people, and they undertook several roles: (1) *Amir* (group leader), (2) *Mutakallim* (spokesperson), (3) *Dalil* (guide or host), and (4) *Makmur* (giver or lecturer). For beginners, the Tablighis will normally perform three days of *khuruj*, usually for those who are still employed in the government or private company. They will visit a mosque on a Friday afternoon and leave the mosque on Monday morning. For foreign Tablighis, and senior Tablighis from Indonesia, they generally choose forty days. Yet whenever they start *khuruj*, it is obligatory for the Tablighis to report their arrival to the committee of the mosque they visit. If permission is given, they will start their *khuruj*, and if not, they will have to find another mosque. Once they are given permission, they will join the congregational prayer straight away and greet everyone they meet in the mosque. At the interval between prayer times, they visit other Muslims who are still at home during the weekends to perform prayer in congregation in the mosque. Their target is the men around the mosque. During *khuruj*, these Tablighis sleep, eat and bathe in the mosque. Sometimes they bring stoves with them (Ind. *Kompor*). That is why they are connotatively called *Jamaah Komporiun*, from the Indonesian word *kompor*, or stove.

At meal times, the Tablighis invite other congregants to have meals together. They were only permitted to eat using their hands; no spoon and fork were allowed because that was how the Prophet ate. This common dining has become an identity marker of Tablighi Jamaat. It was evident when I had meals with them and had something to drink with my left hand. Soon afterwards, one Tablighi advised me to use my right hand. He asked me, "Are you new?" I replied "Yes". In sum, having meals together among the Tablighis is not only about being sociable, but also about identity making.

From this *khuruj* activity, Tablighi Jamaat has been accused of taking over the mosque, as they spend most of the time there. The chairman of one local mosque I met in Jakarta once said:

> We are pleased with the method of preaching among the Tablighis in inviting Muslims to pray in congregations in the mosque so that the mosque becomes full. The only thing we do not agree towards them is that our mosques are taken over and our members are then invited to join their movement.

This comment is true as I found that the Tablighis succeeded in persuading a number of local people to join *i'tikaf* in Mesjid Kebon Jeruk. The invitation to join *khuruj*, even after my research was over, came to me many times. They usually advise me to come more often and it will be much better if I could invite other colleagues to also join *i'tikaf* in Mesjid Kebon Jeruk.

Nurturing Religious Authority among the Tablighis: Why It Matters?

> The only solution to this problem, as the Maulana saw it, lay in separating them from their milieu, and it was decided that they should be withdrawn from it in groups for a period of time, and gathered together in mosques or religious institutions away from bad spheres of influence ... They changed their way of dressing and grew beards, shaking off one by one almost all their pre-Islamic customs that they had retained after their conversion (Khan 1994).

This assertion underlines the basic rationale for *khuruj*. To be in a mosque is the best way to be in a good milieu. The wearing of *kurtas* for men and growing beards are simply done in favour of identity making, let alone it has religious legitimization from the Hadith. All the Tablighis agree that performing *dakwah* or proselytizing is not solely the duty of *ulama*, *kyai*, *habib*, *syaikh* and *ustadz*. As the trademark of Tablighi Jamaat, Haji Tjetjep illustrated to me that *khuruj* is a form of "training" for the Tablighis to master *dakwah*. Haji Tjetjep said that: "To make them perfect in religious proficiency is by and large through *khuruj*. Metaphorically, to be a good tree and fruit is when you feel safe under it" (Interview with Haji Tjetjep Marzuki, Syuro council of Tablighi Jamaat and Chairman of Mesjid Kebon Jeruk steering committee, 7, 8, and 9 April 2016).

I found that the overseas Tablighis do not necessarily replace the roles played by their Indonesian counterparts. On the contrary, their existence enriched the Indonesian Tablighis' *dakwah* experience. Generally, they want to explore and share their *khuruj* experiences in Indonesia with those in their home country, and also in various countries they have ever visited. Not all the Tablighis from abroad have expertise in religion. But the mosque's committee usually invites those who wish to share stories of their *dakwah* experience in various countries outside Indonesia.

I observed that one Jordanian Tablighi shared his difficulties while performing *khuruj* in one of the Muslim countries, and how he overcame the challenges. Such stories inspired other Tablighis to do *khuruj*. Because not all of the Tablighis from overseas are able to speak Indonesian, the mosque's committee appoints some local Tablighis who are able to speak Urdu or Hindi to become the interpreter for them, especially those who had studied in India, Pakistan and Bangladesh. There are about 500 to 600 of the Tablighis who have studied in these countries for eight to twelve years (Interview with Ahmad Subagyo, 27 April 2016).

Does their religious authority matter within the Tablighi circle? Yes, and as my study shows, although the Tablighis are not considered to be fundamentalist (groups calling all the Muslims for the need to return to the Quran and Hadith), they believe that in order to fully implement the teachings of the Prophet Muhammad, one must study from learned persons who have experienced the meaning of the text in real life for reliable authority. For the Tablighis, learned persons are those who have performed *khuruj*, and they may not be the masters of the Islamic doctrine. They are not always scholars of religion or experts on holy texts.

For some Tablighis, joining the movement requires much sacrifice. The decision to join this religious movement was not easy for Haji Tjetjep Marzuki, and he confessed that when he decided to go to India and Pakistan, he was an employee of the national bank and had five children. He said that, "Allah is Omniscient and Maintenance. Alhamdulillah, thanks God, I remained an employee and I even invited my friends to participate with me to preach [Islam]." After his retirement, Haji Tjetjep Marzuki dedicated his whole life to *khuruj*. After the passing of his wife in 2012, he lived alone in a room in Mesjid Kebon Jeruk. He shared:

> I remember the first day I followed *khuruj* overseas while being employed at a national bank as a director. I received 1 month leave from my office. My attire was still casual at the time with t-shirt and jeans. But as time went on I started to wear *kurtas* and white cap onwards. After that, in every gathering in a mosque I visited during *khuruj*, the crowd always asked me to share my religious experiences and ask for religious guidance. To be honest, I have no formal educational background on Islamic studies. I am not a *pesantren* graduate. I have never been affiliated with any formal *tarikahs* nor profess *biat* to any *mursyid*. But when delivering a sermon, I could talk hours and hours about spiritual knowledge. That is simply coming from my experiences going out for *khuruj* in every foreign country. Since I retired, I have been on the board of *syuro* council in the Tablighi Jamaat in Indonesia.

It is evident from the above that *khuruj* is a mechanism that Haji Tjetjep Marzuki and other Tablighis must undergo in pursuit of religious authority within the Tablighi Jamaat circles. I observed during the interval between sunset prayer (*Maghrib*) and night prayer (*Isha*), which is one hour apart, that those who had returned from distant places or foreign countries performing specifically four-month-*khuruj* were asked to share about *khuruj* in general and also the spiritual, sometimes mystical, experiences they encountered.

As Noor (2012, p. 170) notes, due to their cultural roots from India and an apolitical standpoint, many Muslims in Indonesia shun away from the Tablighi Jamaat. Their *dakwah* method makes the movement unpopular. Muslim clerics I met usually overlook the religious capacity of the Tablighis. "They are in fact lay persons but become preachers in their *khuruj*. This is against the standard criteria of being conventional preacher", said one member of MUI. As a countermeasure to these challenges, Muslims have witnessed attempts to centralize religious authority. In the Indonesian case, these developments are evident with the publication of the list of 200 preachers (Ind. *muballigh*) by the Ministry of Religious Affairs before the month of Ramadan in June 2018. Some Indonesian Muslims considered this an attempt by the government to determine who has the authority to become preacher. But the list sparked a heated debate, so it was then submitted to MUI for review, and it grew. One trusted source said that within MUI, the list of *muballigh* has now reached more than 1,000. There were some requests for the government to intervene in the recruitment process of *muballigh*, because there were those who possess no adequate religious knowledge but claimed to be a *muballigh* providing religious guidance. They argue that MUI should be the sole religious authority in Indonesia which could provide religious counselling and issue a *fatwa* (religious pronouncement). In Malaysia or Singapore, for example, the *fatwa* issued by their respective *ulama* councils is very powerful and reliable in providing legal certainty.

Conclusion

On the one hand, the Tablighis have redefined religious authority, but on the other hand, it has also paved a second wave of contesting traditional authority. In the past throughout the Muslim world, Muslim scholars have attempted to reform the traditional structure of Islamic authority to be more democratic and pluralistic (Inam 2013). Today, the formation of religious authority within Muslim communities could be constructed based on non-traditional means. Among the Tablighis, a general acceptance of the increasingly important role of individual conscience in the religious experience can become a new way of nurturing religious authority. This new religious authority, as mentioned by Burhani (2018, pp. 148–52), has challenged the structure of religious authority championed by MUI.

The growing crisis of authority within Muslim communities in Indonesia is not new (Mandaville 2007). It has already been in place not only in Indonesia but across the Muslim world. As Robinson (2009) postulates, the crisis of authority in Islam started as late as the beginning of European colonialization of the Middle East between 1800 and 1920. Yet varying degrees of religious authority in many parts of the Muslim world are resulted from the current social, political or philosophical advances. This in turn has contributed to the crisis of religious authority and permeated countless facets of Muslim life.

Theoretically, the best way to describe religious authority is Weber's *charismatic authority*. I think the embodiment of *charismatic authority* can be seen among religious leaders like Haji Tjetjep Marzuki over the Tablighis in Mesjid Kebon Jeruk, who often claims invisible spiritual powers above tedious processes of teaching. The so-called "pure charisma" is the kind of the ideal type of *charismatic authority* which is intrinsically religious (Hofmann and Dawson 2014, pp. 350–51). This *charismatic authority* usually arises from the issue on what constitutes reliable religious authority over the right interpretation of the scriptures. Conservative authority may wish to lead society in a certain path, but sometimes devotees may be reluctant to follow.

The question on who is more innovative and who is more conservative in this issue is also diverse. Occasionally, religious leaders want to encourage their followers to embrace new components into the tradition, though others are against new innovations. Currently, the Indonesia government has been striving to encourage two of the largest and most established Muslim organizations, NU and Muhammadiyah, to do more in introducing Indonesian Islam, which is adaptive with local traditions. NU with its jargon of "Islam Nusantara" (Islam in the archipelago) and Muhammadiyah with its "Islam Berkemajuan" (Developing Islam) have become the national theme discussed widely in any academic discourse both offline and online.

NOTES

1. The original source of this chapter is derived from an ethnographic study conducted in 2010 and 2016. I did fieldwork in Makassar, South Sulawesi in March and April 2010 and in Temboro, Magetan, East Java in May 2010. In Makassar, I observed and participated in Mesjid Kerung-Kerung located in central Makassar, while in Temboro, I stayed in Pesantren Al-Fatah owned by the late Kyai Uzairon. In 2016, I focused on doing fieldwork in Mesjid Kebon Jeruk, West Jakarta, well-known as the breeding ground of the Tablighis in Indonesia nationwide. My findings in Makassar and Temboro have been published as a chapter in the book entitled *Gerakan Keagamaan Transnasional* published by Puslitbang Kehidupan Keagamaan in 2010, while the findings in Mesjid Kebon Jeruk have been published as a journal article in the peer review journal *Harmoni* published by Puslitbang Kehidupan Keagamaan in 2017. The publication of this chapter would not have been possible without the help of Dr Najib Burhani and Dr Norshahril Saat, from the ISEAS – Yusof Ishak Institute, in editing and giving comments on the first draft of this chapter.
2. http://www.muftisays.com/forums/32-poems--quotes/1337-a-beautiful-poem-on-tablighi-jamaat-section-2.html (accessed 21 July 2018).
3. When I visited this mosque for the first time, I took the local bus. I think this is the best mode of transportation to reach the mosque as there is no parking area around the mosque. Mesjid Kebon Jeruk is located between Jalan Hayam Wuruk and Jalan Kebon Jeruk, two main streets in Taman Sari Subdistrict, Jakarta Barat.
4. Source: The branch of Religious Ministry at subdistrict of Taman Sari, 2016.
5. I participated in the daily activities of the Tablighis in the mosque from Thursday afternoon to Sunday morning, and got involved in their *khuruj* activities generally for three days in nearby mosques. I set up a series of in-depth interviews with members of Syuro council including Haji Tjetjep. I prioritized social interaction with the Tablighis capturing the understanding of the subject (emic view) in a very natural way (naturalistic approach) (Spradley 1979). In the beginning, I introduced myself and my original institution to the steering committee of Mesjid Kebon Jeruk and stated the purpose of my visit. This disclosure or open identity process and expression of the purpose of this research aims at building trust and good relationship with research subjects (Neuman 2003, p. 374). On the first day of the research, I met Ahmad Subagyo, a senior member of Tablighi Jamaat and that of the steering committee of the mosque. I considered him as a gatekeeper who served to be a guide (field assistant) for me during the study. He introduced me to everyone considered being able to provide the information that I needed. However, I did not depend solely on Ahmad Subagyo in obtaining access to other informants. Sometimes I

walked alone and got acquainted with other Tablighis whom I met during my stay at the mosque.

Thanks to Ahmad Subagyo's assistance, I could get acquainted with many senior Tablighis and other members of the mosque steering committee including Haji Tjetjep Marzuki. Not only that, I stayed next door to the private room of Haji Tjetjep Marzuki. This made it easier for me to conduct participant observation in the mosque and to set up in-depth interviews with the Tablighis coming from various backgrounds and social status. If you see a wooden board in front of the mosque, the status of the mosque as part of the state-protected cultural heritage (Ind., *Cagar Budaya*) is vaguely written on it. The Indonesia's Ministry of Culture and Museum in Jakarta has endorsed this mosque as a cultural heritage which must be preserved. That is why Mesjid Kebon Jeruk is now registered as the asset of the local government. In short, what I want to say is that this mosque existed long before the arrival of the Tablighi Jamaat to Jakarta, Indonesia. From the inscription I found in the middle of this mosque, it is written that it was a Chinese Muslim who built this mosque dated in 1817. The woman's name is Hajjah Fatimah Hwu. According to the story I gathered in the field, at that time a Chinese Muslim named Chan Tsin Wa or Tschoa and his wife, Fatima Hwu, initiated the construction of the mosque for Chinese Muslims living around Glodok at the time. A local resident I talked to said that Hajjah Aisah, the descendant of Hajjah Fatimah Hwu, then granted the mosque on 30 December 1991 to be used for other Muslims.

6. The book is entitled *Al Qaulul Baligh fit Tahdzir min Jama'atit Tabligh*, written by Shaykh Hamud At Tuwaijiri.
7. The following are the documents that must be provided when applying for a temporary residence permit: (1) letter of recommendation from home institution; (2) curriculum vitae; (3) copy of degree; (4) photocopy of passport; and (5) letter of invitation from educational institution if they are teaching. Interview with Taufik, Head of KUB, Regional Office of the Ministry of Religious Affairs of DKI Jakarta Province, 27 April 2016.

REFERENCES

Ali-Nadwi, Sayyid Abul Hasan. 1999. *Riwayat Hidup Dan Usaha Dakwah Maulana Muhammad Ilyas*. Yogyakarta: Ash-Shaff. Republished by Penerbit Al-Hasyimiy Bandung, December 2009.

Burhani, Ahmad Najib. 2018. "Plural Islam and Contestation of Religious Authority in Indonesia". In *Islam in Southeast Asia: Negotiating Modernity*, edited by Norshahril Saat. Singapore: ISEAS – Yusof Ishak Institute.

Bustamam-Ahmad, Kamaruzzaman. 2008. "The History of Tablighi Jamaat in Southeast Asia: The Role of Islamic Sufism in Islamic Revival". *Al-Mesjidah* 46, no. 2, M/1429 H.

Dekmejian, R. Hrair. 1985. *Islam in Revolution: Fundamentalism in the Arab World*. Syracuse: Syracuse University Press.

Denzin, Norman K. and Yvonna S. Lincoln, eds. 1994. "Introduction: Entering the Field of Qualitative Research". In *Handbook of Qualitative Research*, pp. 1–18. Thousands Oaks, CA: Sage Publications, Inc.

Hofmann, David C. and Lorne L. Dawson. 2014. "The Neglected Role of Charismatic Authority in the Study of Terrorist Groups and Radicalization". *Studies in Conflict & Terrorism* 37, no. 4: 348–68.

Inam, Hüseyin. 2013. "Power and Authority in Religious Traditions in Islam: Reflections about Issues of Power and Authority in the Traditions and the Present Situation of Muslims in Europe". *European Judaism: A Journal for the New Europe* 46, no. 1: 66–74.

Khan, Maulana Wahiduddin. 1994. *Tabligh Movement*, pp. 5–12. The Islamic Centre, Nizamuddin, New Delhi: Al Risala Books. First published 1986.

Mandaville, Peter. 2007. "Globalization and the Politics of Religious Knowledge: Pluralizing Authority in the Muslim World". *Theory, Culture & Society* 24, no. 2: 101–15.

Neuman, W. Lawrence. 2003. *Social Research Methods: Qualitative and Quantitative Approaches*. 5th ed. United Kingdom: Pearson Education Inc.

Nisa, Eva F. 2014. "Insights into the Lives of Indonesian Female Tablighi Jama'at". *Modern Asian Studies* 48: 468–91.

Noor, Farish A. 2012. *Islam on the Move: The Tablighi Jama'at in South-East Asia*. Amsterdam: Amsterdam University Press.

Reid, Anthony and Michael Gilsenan, eds. 2007. *Islamic Legitimacy in a Plural Asia*. United Kingdom: Routledge.

Robinson, Francis. 2009. "Crisis of Authority: Crisis of Islam?" *Journal of the Royal Asiatic Society* 19, no. 3 (3rd series): 339–54.

Sikand, Yoginder. 2002. *The Origin and Development of the Tabligh-Jama'at (1920–2002): A Cross-country Comparative Study*. New Delhi: Orient Longman.

Sila, Muhammad Adlin. 2010. *Perkembangan Gerakan Keagamaan Transnasional: Kasus Tablighi Jamaat di Pesantren Al-Fatah, Temboro Magetan, Jawa Timur*. Jakarta: Puslitbang Kehidupan Keagamaan, Badan Litbang dan Diklat Kementerian Agama RI.

———. 2016. "Masjid Kebon Jeruk: Menjadi Markaz dan Penjamin Jama'ah Tabligh dari Seluruh Dunia". *Jurnal Harmoni*. Puslitbang Kehidupan Keagamaan, Badan Litbang dan Diklat Kementerian Agama RI.

Spradley, James P. 1979. *The Ethnographic Interview*. New York: Holt, Rinehart and Winston.

Interviews

<u>Mesjid Kerung-Kerung, Makassar</u>
H. Syuaib Gani, 1, 2 March 2010.
Zulkifli Maidin, 2, 3 March 2010.
Zulkarnain Maidin, 7, 8 March 2010.
Sabir Maidin, 10, 11 April 2010.
Yakub, 13, 14 April 2010.

<u>Pesantren Al-Fatah, Temboro Magetan</u>
KH. Uzairon atau Gus Ron, 10, 15 May 2010.
KH. Ubaidillah atau Gus Bed, 12, 13 May 2010.
KH. Imdadun atau Gus Imdad, 15, 16 May 2010.

<u>Mesjid Kebon Jeruk, Jakarta</u>
Ahmad Subagyo, 26, 27 April 2016.
Ihsan, 5 April 2016.
Haji Tjetjep Marzuki, 7, 8, and 9 April 2016.
Haji Ahmad Sungkar, 25 April 2016.

11

RELIGIOUS EDUCATION, SUFI BROTHERHOOD, AND RELIGIOUS AUTHORITY: A CASE STUDY OF THE SULAIMANIYAH

Firdaus Wajdi

Introduction

Studies on Indonesian Islamic organizations and scholars in their connection with their authority is well recorded (Azra, Dijk, and Kaptein 2010; Din 2012; Hefner 2016; Hoesterey 2011; Jabali 2006; Kaptein 2004; Kingsley 2014; Zulkifli 2013). This chapter offers a distinct perspective based on the experience of Islamic transnational organizations. It considers how transnational organizations from Turkey build religious education institutions, change their names to get support from the local government, and utilize Sufi teachings to maintain their authority. This chapter adopts the concept of "opportunity spaces" by M. Hakan Yavuz (2003 and 2004), who applies it when analysing the Muslim social movements in Turkey. The concept is useful to understand the reasons for the popularity of Turkish Muslim movements in Indonesia. An explanation of the concept will begin the chapter.

A discussion on the establishment and transformation of the Islamic education institution of the Sulaimaniyah, formerly known as *asrama*, and then later changed to *pesantren*, follows. The name change not only illustrates its focus on *tahfidz* (the person who memorizes the Quran) with the unique Ottoman Turkish methodology—that promises a faster way to memorize the whole Quran compared to other methods—as a flagship programme, but also its way of gaining authorization from the Ministry of Religious Affairs (Kemenag). Later in the article, the Sufi elements of the Sulaimaniyah will be described. The Sufi brotherhood of the Naqshbandi Sulaimaniyah is where the religious authority in the form of charismatic authority, established since the very beginning by Sheikh Süleyman Hilmi Tunahan as the 33rd Sufi master in the Naqshbandi line. This is a Sufi ritual which connects all followers across the globe. This chapter demonstrates that religious authority in Indonesia is not only contested among local Muslim organizations, but also by the transnational religious movement and among them, the lesser known Turkish Sufi movement, the Sulaimaniyah.

Opportunity Spaces and the Establishment of the Sulaimaniyah in Indonesia

Indonesia is the most populous Muslim country in the world. With a population of over 250 million, approximately 80 per cent of whom are Muslim, Indonesia just like any other Muslim majority country, has experienced an Islamic revival with influence from overseas. While foreign Islamic revival influences in the 1970s and 1980s came almost entirely from Saudi Arabia, Egypt and Iran, in the 1990s a new kind of influence, from Turkey, joined in promoting a revival of piety in Indonesia, coming mainly as private citizens without the government's backing. The Turkish organizations mainly focused on what they called *hizmet*, a religiously inspired service to the Islamic community (Marty 2015). This *hizmet* was commonly in the form of education but in some cases also included health and other social and religious services. Turkish piety movements that came to Indonesia were also sympathetic to Sufi teachings and practices and some even promoted them.

One of the Turkish revivalist movements of the twentieth century that arrived in Indonesia is the Sulaimaniyah movement, named after its founding figure, Süleyman Hilmi Tunahan (1888–1959). The Sulaimaniyah movement focuses solely on religious education for the Muslims. It started off as an informal community whose members studied religion under their Sufi master, Süleyman Hilmi Tunahan, whose intention was to preserve religion in modern Turkey. This group later established the *Kuran kursu*, a boarding school for Quran and Islamic studies. By focusing mainly on the establishment of such Quran seminaries, the Sulaimaniyah movement has now become the most successful dormitory-providing movement in Turkey.

Reviewing the growth of the Sulaimaniyah movement in Turkey, Yavuz (2003) concentrates on their use of "political" and "economic" opportunity spaces which shaped the evolution of the movement. By "opportunity spaces", Yavuz (2003, p. 24) refers to "a forum of social interaction that creates new possibilities for augmenting networks of shared meaning and associational life". Opportunity spaces, as he understands them, can take many forms, including civic and political forums, electronic and print media, cyberspace, cultural foundations, a private education system, and the economic market. Opportunity spaces allow the movement to grow and establish its branches in the society. In terms of political opportunity spaces, the Sulaimaniyah applied a policy to engage the Turkish government, particularly after 1949, which was known as the multi-party system era. In this period, the Turkish government began to accommodate requests to raise the country's religious identity, and to allow the establishment of Quran seminaries. By equipping its preachers with the skills to work for the Directorate of Religious Affairs (Diyanet İşleri Başkanlığı (DİB)), the Sulaimaniyah was able to better engage the government. Consequently, Sulaimaniyah preachers began to dominate this office (Yavuz 2003 and 2004).

In Germany, the Sulaimaniyah made productive use of economic opportunity spaces among the Turkish workers, who were relatively free from the influences of the Turkish government and had the means to provide charity funds to support the movement and its activities. Benefitting from this, the Sulaimaniyah were able to pursue their aims at protecting the new (second) generation against leftist-atheism and radical political Islam. The transnational movement also provided opportunities for expansion. Since the beginning of the 2000s, the Sulaimaniyah have run the most successful dormitory network in Turkey and have built the second largest mosque network in Germany.

In 2005, the Sulaimaniyah established the United Islamic Cultural Centre of Indonesia (UICCI) in Jakarta. Its focus is to provide students, who live in any of its boarding schools, with Quran studies. The Sulaimaniyah are also known for teaching the Ottoman method of Quran memorization which has attracted wide support, both from the local Muslims and the Indonesian government (the Ministry of Religious Affairs to the Ministry of Social Affairs). Since the Sulaimaniyah started their *hizmet* (religious service) in Indonesia in 2005, they have established thirty branches across Indonesia. They are very active in establishing branches compared to the other Turkish Muslim movements (such as the Nuchu and the Fethullah Gulen).

The Sulaimaniyah are able to spread their network as far as Australia. In 1971, they began their *hizmet* in Melbourne and Victoria. They were able to meet the demands for religious education for Turks living abroad—in this case Turks who had immigrated to Australia or who were born in Australia but had Turkish ancestors. When it first started, Melbourne was where the largest concentration of Turkish immigrants were found. The Sulaimaniyah then set up another branch in Auburn, NSW, where Turkish Muslims established the Gallipoli Mosque, one of the largest mosques in Sydney. Based on my observation and interviews, however, in Australia, unlike in Indonesia, there is no huge demand from young Indonesian students for Sulaimaniyah boarding schools with luxurious facilities and for opportunities to study in Turkey later.

In Indonesia, the UICCI (Indonesian Sulaimaniyah organization) utilized education opportunity spaces and expanded its reach because of the popularity of its private Islamic education, especially Quran memorization. While there are many groups that provide private Islamic education in Indonesia, the Sulaimaniyah movement has been able to compete by offering free Islamic studies tuition and high-quality dormitories. They also offer a distinctive Turkish Ottoman Quran memorization method, which, they claimed, yields much faster results than the other methods currently used in Indonesia. The Sulaimaniyah's unique method for memorizing the Quran, its study system, and its institutional setting met the educational needs and piety aspirations of a significant number of young Indonesian Muslims, especially those from less affluent backgrounds. The Sulaimaniyah *hizmet* in its several forms has enabled the movement to attract significant approval and patronage in Indonesia. Local supporters (*ikhwan*) of the Sulaimaniyah movement are also contributing to the establishment of schools in cities across Indonesia (for example in Kalimantan, Aceh and Medan) and supporting their local schools. While access to the growing Islamic education opportunity space in Indonesia has been shown to have facilitated the Sulaimaniyah's establishment there, it is worthwhile to point out the historical and social factors that have made possible the expansion of that "opportunity space" in Indonesia.

High-Quality Free Islamic Boarding Schools

One of the obvious *hizmet* of the Sulaimaniyah is the high-quality boarding schools. This idea started from their founding father, Sheikh Süleyman Hilmi Tunahan who converted his house into a place of study for his students. That was during the time when the Turkish government issued a regulation to limit and prohibit faith education, including Islamic education. This practice to study Islamic education in a dormitory was then continued by the followers and students of the Sheikh. As will be discussed shortly, I would also argue that the focus to provide high-quality boarding schools for Islamic education is adopted by the Indonesian Sulaimaniyah movement, so that they can be accepted in Indonesia.

During my ethnographic research in Turkey and Indonesia. I met several people who said that there are many ways to establish a dormitory for the students. Sometimes one rich businessman can donate an existing building to be used as a dormitory. In this case, the dormitory sometimes was named after the person or a family member of the donor. Alternatively, a group of Muslims worked together to build a dormitory for the students. In this case, commonly, the dormitory was named after the city where it is located. Also, the Sulaimaniyah can take over an unused building to be utilized as a dormitory. So, in this case, the Sulaimaniyah might just keep the old name of the building but then redesign the management and education system using the Sulaimaniyah method.

The Sulaimaniyah boarding schools have been characterized as modern. In addition, the boarding schools are provided to Muslims for free, and this is due to the Sulaimaniyah's ability to raise funds for their *hizmet* programmes. In Indonesia, the Sulaimaniyah boarding schools are called *pondok pesantren*, following the popular name of the Islamic boarding schools in the country. The high standard of the curriculum and the highly qualified teachers in the Sulaimaniyah's *pondok pesantren* refute the negative image of Islamic schools in Indonesia as being "second class" and "dumping grounds" for children who do not go to general schools (Parker 2008, p. 2).

The Islamic education in Indonesia was influenced from overseas by countries such as Egypt, Saudi Arabia, and Iran (Machmudi 2018, p. 91). While these countries have representatives in Indonesia in the form of Islamic education institutions and have been familiar to Indonesian society for a long time, the influence of the Turkish organizations is not widely known, primarily because it is so recent.

The Sulaimaniyah prides itself as a provider of alternative Islamic education that combines some of the best features of existing forms of Islamic education: modern facilities and general curriculum studies plus the moral education of residential *pesantren* life, all without any fee. A follower of Sheikh Süleyman Hilmi Tunahan said that the spiritual leader himself was the initiator of the dormitory education system. Tunahan converted his house into a shelter for people who were studying the Quran and pursuing further Islamic knowledge under his supervision. The dormitory was considered a safe haven away from the difficult situation in Turkey under the Kemalist secular government. The dormitory system also allowed ongoing interactions between the teacher and students, and the students were able to put their knowledge into practice; it would become one of Süleyman's educational philosophies that knowledge should not be merely acquired, but also practised.

As the Sulaimaniyah had developed in Turkey, they were able to build luxurious dormitories for religious students. The dormitory provided first rate facilities, not only for studying but also for general living. On one occasion, during my fieldtrip to Istanbul, I managed to visit a dormitory spanning four levels, catering for 250 students. The facilities included study rooms, a library, and bedrooms, and foods were also supplied. All the students needed to focus on was their studies. This modern type of dormitory system first spread from Turkey to Germany and is now expanding across the globe, beginning in Indonesia only in 2005. Even though Indonesia is a developing country, where traditional religious education institutions provide only moderate living conditions, the Sulaimaniyah continues to build relatively luxurious boarding schools. When I asked one of the *abis* about this, he replied: "We want to make the religious students proud of being religious students."

As observed, Indonesian Muslims represent a large market for Islamic education of all sorts. In fact, the market is already crowded with numerous products and providers, old and new. These include traditional *pesantren*, modern *pesantren*, special *tahfidz* institutes, and full-day Islamic schools, as well as some Islamic education institutions that are affiliated with overseas organizations, such as LIPIA (Saudi Arabia), Alumni of Al Azhar (Egypt), Muthahhari schools (Iran), and Fethullah Gülen-affiliated schools (Turkey). It is important for newcomers to carefully position themselves to compete in such a saturated market. The Sulaimaniyah has been able to move into a market niche constituted by middle- to lower-middle-class Muslim families in search of quality general education for their children combined with classical Islamic studies. The Sulaimaniyah's mission (*hizmet*) is to offer high quality and institutionally modern Islamic education system free of charge, regardless of the prospective student's background. And the Sulaimaniyah offers high standard facilities, not only to support learning but also to make their students proud of their Islamic education from the Sulaimaniyah, which makes them strong competitors in the market. Moreover, the opportunities they offer for their students to travel overseas are attractive to many. Their unique way of operating distinguishes them from the other existing Islamic education providers in Indonesia. Their formula seems to have worked well, considering the number of branches and dormitories established in Indonesia and the rapidly growing number of students attending their institutions.

By the time the Sulaimaniyah movement arrived in Indonesia, it was already a well-established transnational religious movement with standardized institutional practices. In Indonesia, the movement adapted to local needs. One example of this was the way in which the movement presented its Islamic boarding schools to Indonesians. Initially, the Sulaimaniyah dormitories were called *asrama Turki*, which literally translates from the Turkish word *"yurt"* (Ind., *asrama*). After several years, the Indonesian Sulaimaniyah organization recognized that this term did not properly represent their idea of a boarding school, neither was it attracting Indonesian Muslims. This was primarily because the word *"asrama"* means "shelter" rather than "Islamic boarding school". The Sulaimaniyah movement adopted the local term *"pondok pesantren"*, meaning "Islamic boarding school", for its schools in Indonesia. This enabled the movement to connect its dormitory, character-focused, religious education with similar, well-respected, and widespread indigenous religious educational institutions in Indonesia. This facilitated popular local understandings of the Sulaimaniyah educational approach. It also meant that Sulaimaniyah boarding schools were entitled to receive support from the Ministry of Religious Affairs. In Indonesia, the Ministry of Religious Affairs is tasked with providing support to educational institutions or *pondok pesantren*. Notably, however, the Sulaimaniyah movement made a distinction between its *pesantren* and other *pesantren* in Indonesia. To highlight its unique educational programme, specifically speed-learning to recite the whole Quran from memory, the Sulaimaniyah movement officially renamed its centres "Pondok Pesantren Tahfidz Sulaimaniyah" (Sulaimaniyah Quran Memorization Islamic Boarding Schools). This name was first used for the UICCI Rawamangun school in East Jakarta.

The concept of "glocalization" can be employed here to help us understand the development of transnational religious movements in general, and the Sulaimaniyah movement in particular. The term "glocalization" has its roots in the Japanese term "*dochakuka*" (Giulianotti and Robertson 2006). It first appeared in the late 1980s and originally referred to the adaptation of new farming techniques in different parts of the world. It was popularized and developed by Roland Robertson, according to whom glocalization points to the ways local cultures may critically adapt to, or resist, global phenomena. In addition, glocalization "reveals the way in which the very creation of localities is a standard component of globalization" (Giulianotti and Robertson 2006, p. 172; 2007, p. 134). The term was later used to refer to globally dispersed social and cultural changes (Sharma 2008).

The concept of glocalization can be used to understand how transnational religious movements adapt to local situations. Mandaville (2009a and 2009b) argues that transnational Islam is inevitably altered through its encounter with local cultural sensibilities and pre-existing religious conceptions and practices. Therefore, one can observe something more akin to the "glocalization" of Islam, with complex interplay between transnational organizations and influences and the societies and settings into which they enter (Mandaville 2009b, pp. 14–15).

In my account of the Sulaimaniyah in Indonesia, I show that the concept of glocalization can be used to understand the establishment of a global standard, and the subsequent interactions with the Indonesian context. The Indonesian cultural and social context is different in many aspects from that in Sulaimaniyah's country of origin, Turkey, and indeed from those in other places where the Sulaimaniyah have established their branches. The Sulaimaniyah in Indonesia have shown their ability to adapt in order to be more welcomed by the locals. The following section will discuss transnational religious movements and Islamic revival in the Indonesian context, focusing specifically on the Sulaimaniyah movement.

During my ethnographic data collection, the Sulaimaniyah boarding schools acknowledged that they changed their name from the *"asrama"* to *"pesantren"* to get positive responses from Indonesians who could not understand the concept of *asrama* and tend to question the authority of the Sulaimaniyah in teaching the religious subject within an *asrama* instead of a *pesantren*. Therefore, the Sulaimaniyah changed their schools' name to *pesantren* and they received more applicants. This shows that the glocalization of a Turkish *asrama* has resulted in the development of the religious authority that the newcomer received from both the government and community. First, the Sulaimaniyah received endorsement from the Ministry of Religious Affairs, and then when the community knew that the Ministry supports the Sulaimaniyah boarding schools, Indonesian families started to put their faith in the Sulaimaniyah's religious services.

Curriculum and Level of Education

The Sulaimaniyah offers four levels of religious education: *ibtidai* (beginner), *ihzari* (intermediate), *tekamul alti* (pre-advanced), and *tekamul* (advanced). The aim of *tekamul*, the highest level of schools, is to train *abis* (teachers). In addition, there are boarding schools created with the special purpose of training *huffaadz* (people who have memorized the whole Quran). All the boarding schools are coordinated by members at the Sulaimaniyah headquarters in Umraniye, Turkey. In terms of curriculum content, the general curriculum is provided by the general education system run by the government of Indonesia or by modern Islamic schools. The UICCI only aids in general studies subjects in the form of enrichment programmes. However, the religious education curriculum is fully provided by the UICCI, following the Sulaimaniyah's established system of Islamic education.

The religious curriculum of the Sulaimaniyah is divided into four different programmes, according to the levels of education mentioned.

Each level normally takes one academic year to complete. The first level is called *ibtidai* (beginner level), where the students mainly study the grammar of Quran recitation (*tajwid*) and basic Islamic ritual (*fiqh*). In the second level, called *ihzari*, the students begin to study the exegesis of the Quran, Islamic law and Islamic mysticism (*tasawwuf*). In addition, at this level the students also learn the basics of both the Arabic and Turkish languages. *Tahta tekamul* (or *tekamul alti*) is the third level, which literally means "before the completed level". At this level, the students undertake advanced Quranic studies, and learn about Islamic jurisprudence and Islamic law, and Arabic literature as well as the Turkish language. The final level, *tekamul*, is where the students deepen their understanding of the Quran and Hadith, as well as focus on Islamic mysticism. It should be mentioned here that the Indonesian Sulaimaniyah organization (UICCI) provides only the first and second of these educational levels, while the two more advanced levels (*tahta tekamul/tekamul alti* and *tekamul*) are taught in Turkey. The UICCI regularly sends its students to the Sulaimaniyah boarding schools in Turkey to complete their degrees.

The final key component of the UICCI curriculum is the learning experience of the students. The most important feature of this for the UICCI students is living and studying at the dormitories in Indonesia, and then completing their studies in Turkey. Candidates for places at UICCI must meet entry requirements and pass an interview in order to be selected. The selection criteria are strict and challenging as many candidates are competing for limited places. The dormitory does not only serve as the main classroom for students, it is also the place where students experience and practise what they have learned from their Islamic education. For example, learning rituals, such as praying, fasting, and preaching (*dakwah*), are organized by the teachers to make it part of the daily routine activities. The application of the *tasawwuf* ritual of *rabita* also has been routinized within the dormitory lifestyle. This dormitory life is where the Sulaimaniyah members also put into practice their religious knowledge and transform the religious authority.

Sufi Brotherhood among the Sulaimaniyah Movement

The Sulaimaniyah readily acknowledge that they are linked to the Nakşibendi Sufi order. This has been confirmed by many scholars, including Yavuz (2003, p. 11) and Chernov-Hwang (2009, p. 194). The first evidence comes from the fact that the charismatic leader of the Sulaimaniyah was the 33rd *mursyid kamil* (an initiating master of the highest level) of the Nakşibendi Sufi order. *Tasawwuf* and Sufi practices like *rabita* (oath taking), *zikir* (litany recitation), and *khatim* (*zikir* in a group run three times a week), have been important elements of the Sulaimaniyah's education. These are taught in the Sulaimaniyah boarding schools, and importantly, *zikir* and *khatim* are practised by all members of Sulaimaniyah.

The Sulaimaniyah takes the initiation pledge (T. *rabita*, A. *bai'at*) to Sheikh Süleyman. This creates a spiritual connection between the disciples (*telebe*) and the Sheikh and with other disciples of the Sheikh (in other words with the rest of the global Sulaimaniyah community). Through this bond, spiritual connection is opened. In the Sulaimaniyah's tradition, the pledge is called "*rabita*". Originally derived from Arabic, this word was used in Turkish with the same meaning as *bai'at*, namely "to bond" or "a bonding". Among the Sulaimaniyah, it means a connection (bond) between Sheikh Süleyman Hilmi Tunahan and his students. This is because in taking *rabita*, a person officially becomes a part of the Sulaimaniyah brotherhood, thus by connecting oneself to the Sufi master, one connects to the rest of the Sulaimaniyah membership all over the world.

The members of Sulaimaniyah also regularly practise Sufi rituals, principally *zikir* rituals (consisting of multiple repetitions of short phrases from the Quran or reciting the ninety-nine "beautiful" names of God), both in individual and in group devotions. Thus, Sufi brotherhood undergirding the Sulaimaniyah movement helps to create a strong and solid commitment among the Sulaimaniyah to live according to the way of *hizmet* (religious service).

While *rabita* and *zikir* rituals are individual practices, *khatim* is normally practised in a group and includes people who are not initiates. The basic form of the *khatim* is a long recitation of *zikir* litanies, which can be divided equally among the members if it is practised in a group. The group practice is meant not only for personal spiritual benefit but also to foster the connection among Sulaimaniyah members or between the Sulaimaniyah members and outsiders. When outsiders attend, they can learn about Sufi spirituality as it is understood and practised by the Sulaimaniyah.

According to van Bruinessen (1994, p. 19), Sufi orders fulfil a number of functions, not only religious but also non-religious. Each *tarikat* is a social network, and membership in a *tarikat* can bring one social contacts which are potentially useful for finding work, a place to stay, help during difficulties, and so on. For some members, the *tarikat* is also a substitute for, or supplement to, family bonds, offering the emotional warmth and protection the initiate does not find elsewhere. Dominguez Diaz (2011, p. 230) has argued that ritual practice can showcase the identity of religious groups, as well as serve as a mechanism for personal religious transformation. The Sulaimaniyah have been able to preserve this classic form of Sufi spiritual community and esoteric practice in modern Turkey and extend it around the world today. They have been able to combine their variant of esoteric Sufism with other exoteric teaching in a way that is both familiar and attractive to Indonesians, despite the movement's foreign origins.

This examination of Sufi linkages underpinning the Sulaimaniyah global movement and the ways these linkages have supported the growth of the Sulaimaniyah in Indonesia, lends further weight to the estimation that *tarikat* Sufism has a future as part of Indonesian Islam and can be successfully wed to modern institutional forms (Howell 2012). It also shows that the Sufi brotherhood is the arena where this new actor of Islamic revivalist deals with the religious authority. The Sufi master has the charisma, which is continuously maintain through the *rabita*, connection of the Sufi brotherhood.

Conclusion

The Sulaimaniyah has successfully utilized its opportunity spaces in the form of Islamic education with its own characteristics. It has the Ottoman-style Islamic curriculum, and luxurious dormitories and facilities for the Indonesian religious students. The boarding schools allow students to learn Islam, Arabic, and the Turkish culture, as a way to prepare them for the highest education level (*tekamul*) in Turkey. The completion of the *tekamul* level of education gives the Sulaimaniyah members authority to teach religion. This distinguishes from those students at the Sulaimaniyah who never completed the *tekamul*, as they cannot be a teacher (*hoca*). So, here one can understand that the Sulaimaniyah has developed its own system of religious authority through Islamic education system started in Turkey and then developed elsewhere overseas, including in Indonesia with its generic transnational system. This commitment has been preserved in all branches of the Sulaimaniyah making this commitment a huge global trend in general.

Another means of making and developing Islamic authority is through the connection and bond of Sufi brotherhood. Sulaimaniyah members consisting of the students, teachers, and sympathizers are bonded by *rabitha* or Sufi brotherhood. This bond started with the common understanding that their sheikhs are charismatic Sufi masters within the Naqshabandi group. The connection gives a global identity for the Sulaimaniyah members worldwide. This has made the Sulaimaniyah focused more on global connection rather than local connection when it comes to religious authority as they believe that such authority comes only from their sheikhs, connected among the members through Sufi brotherhood. Furthermore, it is also important to note here that the Sulaimaniyah still acknowledge the Ministry of Religious Affairs as one of the religious authorities in Indonesian Islam. The Sulaimaniyah glocalize themselves with changing their *asrama* into *pesantern* has shown the importance of the local source of religious authority.

REFERENCES

Azra, Azyumardi, Kees van Dijk, and Nico J.G. Kaptein, eds. 2010. *Varieties of Religious Authority: Changes and Challenges in 20th Century Indonesian Islam*. Singapore: Institute of Southeast Asian Studies and Leiden: International Institute for Asian Studies.

Chernov-Hwang, Julie. 2009. *Peaceful Islamist Mobilization in the Muslim World: What Went Right*. New York: Palgrave-Macmillan.

Cornell, Vincent J. 1998. *Realm of the Saint: Power and Authority in Moroccan Sufism*. Austin: University of Texas Press.

Din, Wahid. 2012. "Challenging Religious Authority: The Emergence of Salafi Ustadhs in Indonesia". *Journal of Indonesian Islam* 6, no. 2: 245–64.

Dominguez Diaz, Marta. 2011. "Performance, Belonging and Identity: Ritual Variations in the British Qadiriyya". *Religion, State and Society* 39, nos. 2–3: 229–45.

Giulianotti, Richard and Roland Robertson. 2006. "Glocalization, Globalization and Migration: The Case of Scottish Football Supporters in North America". *International Sociology* 21, no. 2: 171–98.

———. 2007. "Forms of Glocalization: Globalization and the Migration Strategies of Scottish Football Fans in North America". *Sociology* 41, no. 1: 133–52.

Hefner, Claire-Marie. 2016. "Models of Achievement: Muslim Girls and Religious Authority in a Modernist Islamic Boarding School in Indonesia". *Asian Studies Review* 40, no. 4: 564–82.

Hoesterey, James Bourk. 2011. *Sufis and Self-Help Gurus: Islamic Psychology, Religious Authority, and Muslim Subjectivity in Contemporary Indonesia*. Proquest: UMI.

Howell, Julia Day. 2012. "Sufism and Neo-sufism in Indonesia Today". *Rima* 46, no. 2: 1–24.

Jabali, Fuad. 2006. "Dissemination of Religious Authority in 20th Century Indonesia". *Studia Islamika: Indonesian Journal for Islamic Studies* 13, no. 1: 165–69.

Kaptein, Nico J.G. 2004. "The Voice of the `Ulamâ': Fatwas and Religious Authority in Indonesia". *Archives de sciences sociales des religions* 49, no. 125: 115–30.

Kingsley, Jeremy. 2014. "Redrawing Lines of Religious Authority in Lombok, Indonesia". *Asian Journal of Social Science* 42, no. 5: 657–77.

Machmudi, Yon. 2018. "The Middle East Influence on the Contemporary Indonesian 'Campus Islam'". In *Islam in Southeast Asia: Negotiating Modernity*, edited by Norshahril Saat. Singapore: Institute of Southeast Asian Studies.

Mandaville, Peter G. 2009a. "Transnational Islam in Asia: Background, Typology and Conceptual Overview". In *Transnational Islam in South and Southeast Asia: Movements, Networks, and Conflict Dynamics*, edited by Peter G. Mandaville. Seattle, Washington: The National Bureau of Asian Research.

———. ed. 2009b. *Transnational Islam in South and Southeast Asia: Movements, Networks, and Conflict Dynamics*. Seattle, Washington: The National Bureau of Asian Research.

Marty, Martin E. 2015. *Hizmet Means Service: Perspectives on an Alternative Path within Islam*. 1st ed. Berkeley: University of California Press.

Parker, Lyn. 2008. "Introduction: Islamic Education in Indonesia". *Review of Indonesian and Malaysian Affairs* 42, no. 1: 1–8.

Sharma, Chanchal Kumar. 2008. "Emerging Dimensions of Decentralization Debate in the Age of Glocalization". MPRA Paper no. 6734. Haryana, India: Kurukshetra University. Online at http://mpra.ub.uni-muenchen.de/6734/.

van Bruinessen, Martin. 1994. "Traces of Kubrawiyya Influence in Early Indonesian Islam". *Bijdragen Tot De Taal- Land- En Volkenkunde* 150, no. 2: 305–29.

Yavuz, M. Hakan. 2003. *Islamic Political Identity in Turkey*. New York: Oxford University Press.

———. 2004. "Opportunity Spaces, Identity, and Islamic Meaning in Turkey". In *Islamic Activism: A Social Movement Theory Approach*, edited by Quintan Wiktorowicz. Bloomington, Ind.: Indiana University Press.

Zulkifli. 2013. "The Ulama in Indonesia: Between Religious Authority and Symbolic Power". *Miqot: jurnal ilmu-ilmu keislaman* 37, no. 1.

PART III:

The New *Santri*

12

POP AND "TRUE" ISLAM IN URBAN *PENGAJIAN*: THE MAKING OF RELIGIOUS AUTHORITY

Yanwar Pribadi

Introduction[1]

After the fall of the New Order administration in 1998, a complex entanglement between communal piety, religious commodification, Islamic populism, and Islamism has occurred in many Indonesia's Islamic institutions. This happens mostly due to the shift among urban middle-class Muslims, from conformed religious expressions to transnational ideas of Islam resulting from the global market economy. These rapidly growing yet fluid groups have continuously attempted to pursue "true" Islamic identity. They have claimed for recognition of their identity to be the most appropriate one and promoted it to be the ideal socio-cultural identity for the whole nation.

The 1998 political transformation has fuelled Muslims' public expression of identities—that includes ethnic, religious, and social class, as indicated in a rapid consumption and commodification of religious practices and observances—and the creation of religious identities, piety,

Muslim pride, and brotherhood through the commerce of Western and local brands. Although these kinds of religious practices were excluded during the New Order era, it is increasingly politicized in the newly democratized and decentralized regional political sphere (Millie et al. 2014, p. 195; Fealy 2008, pp. 15–39; Lukens-Bull 2008, pp. 220–34).

Due to the desire of modern Muslims who find scripturalist Islam as a "dry" subject (Howell 2010, p. 1042), many religious activities nowadays are expressed and practised openly in the public sphere, including at the state-owned mosques and on television, in order to be more inclusive (Millie et al. 2014). However, several contemporary trending religious activities, such as urban *pengajian* (religious congregations in urban spaces), are frequently exclusive—attended by tens of participants and mostly located in houses of the participants alternately—and appear to challenge the traditional, moderate face of Indonesian Islam. Despite its exclusiveness, the materials and issues discussed in such *pengajian* touch upon global and local religious affairs.

Global Islamic revival in the last several decades has fragmented the traditional forms of religious authority, generated new figures of public piety, and created new public spaces in which Islamic teachings are constituted and contested (Hoesterey 2012, p. 38). This has become an underlying reason why Muslims across the globe are attracted to worldwide religious issues. An advanced level of education and the rise of new communication media have also contributed to the emergence of a public sphere, whereby a large number of people has an opinion on political and religious issues. It results in a challenge to authoritarianism, a fragmented religious and political authority, and an increasingly open discussion of issues related to the "common good" in Islam (Salvatore and Eickelman 2004, p. xi).

Besides, we are also witnessing various forms of Islamization and re-Islamization in Muslim stronghold, which are not necessarily a setback. They appear to have been in a long and on-going Islamization process for centuries, and they have gained public support due in part to the euphoria of democracy (Pribadi 2018, p. 9). In Indonesia, alongside the rising consciousness of Muslims to demonstrate their religious self in the public sphere, Islam has increasingly been transformed into public attention and become parts of political expression, legal transaction, economic activity, and social and cultural practices (Hasan 2009, p. 230).

This chapter explores the complex entanglement between communal piety, religious commodification, Islamic populism, and Islamism in urban religious congregations, known as *pengajian*. It then examines the making of religious authority in the increasingly democratized and Islamized Indonesia. Based on an ethnographic fieldwork in the City of Serang (Kota Serang), Banten Province in 2017–18, I investigate the religious expressions among urban middle-class Muslims who participated in a number of exclusive *pengajian*, i.e. *pengajian* voluntarily held in urban areas by loose groups of Muslim, in which there exists an entanglement between communal piety, religious commodification, Islamic populism, and Islamism among members of the groups, and where their ideas of religiosity are scrutinzed. It neither focuses on the contents/materials discussed in the *pengajian* nor the *ustadz* (teachers of Islamic knowledge and Quran reciting in the *pengajian*), but rather investigate religious understanding, perceptions, practices, and ideas of religiosity among urban middle-class Muslims who participated in four exclusive *pengajian* groups.

These urban *pengajian* groups are located in four housing complexes; three of which have only female members, and only one has both male and female members. Each *pengajian* group consists of tens of participants,[2] ranging from ten to fifty persons. Although it is exclusive to the residents of each housing complex, the membership is loose and not official, thus it does not require membership cards. Nevertheless, the current members frequently attempt to recruit new members around the housing complex. Most members are neither officially affiliated with Islamic mass organizations nor with (Islamic) political parties. However, most of the *ustadz* (both male and female) claim that they are inspired by or following the Salafist doctrines which reject *bid'ah* (religious innovation) and support the implementation of *sharia* (Islamic law). While many members are regarded as "the purists" (meaning the Salafists who avoid politics, particularly electoral politics), most *ustadz* can be considered as "the activists" who get involved in politics. One *pengajian* is held every week, another one is held every two weeks, while the two other *pengajian* are held once a month. They are located in houses of the participants alternately. While one *pengajian* is exclusive for women (including the *ustadzah*),[3] two *pengajian* with female members have both male and female *ustadz* and another one with mixed members only invites male *ustadz*. I observed the *pengajian* by appointment, often sat separately from the participants, except in the mixed participants one. However, I was mostly still able to see the attendees and hear the whole *pengajian*, as well as conduct the interviews with the members in separate places, mostly in their own residence.

I argue that since the fall of the New Order in 1998, the making of religious authority in Indonesia's urban areas has been frequently marked by the complexities of interactions between local expressions of Islam and foreign influences, mostly Salafism originated from Saudi Arabia and Egypt, in complex and fluctuated relationships. The entanglement involves the contestation between variants of Indonesian Islam and fragmentation of the *ummah*. In the context of Islamic populism and Islamism, members of *pengajian* groups appear to follow populist ideas in socio-political issues such as, among other things, identifying and condemning a collective enemy. The enemy is usually the rich non-Muslim of foreign descent—mostly the Chinese, or the Westerners—who are accused of destroying Islam. In terms of ideology, many middle-class Muslim groups tend to follow populist ideas on social and political issues. They are concerned with social issues related to socio-religious affairs and conflicts in other Muslim-majority countries, such as the Palestine issue and the civil war in Syria. The local political issues related to, among other things, elections and political parties are also part of their interests. In this context, members of these *pengajian* groups claim to practise "true" Islam. In the matter of communal piety and religious commodification, these groups seem to openly participate in religious observances and indulge in a consumptive behaviour of (sacred) commodities, such as being enthusiasic over religious attire and religious journey, including the increasingly popular *umrah* (a pilgrimage that can be undertaken at any time of the year). In this context, they practise the so-called "pop Islam".

In the next section, I explore the contemporary scene of urban Muslims in post-authoritarian Indonesia. The third section elucidates various aspects in "pop Islam" that highlights communal piety and religious commodification. Next, I discuss how urban Muslims practise "true" Islam that stresses on the rise of Islamic populism and Islamism. Then I narrow the focus on the making of religious authority by these urban Muslims. The last section is the conclusion.

Urban Middle-Class Muslims in Contemporary Indonesia

During the New Order era, the political domination of the state over the society was extensive. The military-dominated Suharto regime and its supporters moved to limit political participation to concentrate power and generally remain vigilant to neutralize Islamic forces (Macintyre 1991, pp. 2, 3; Hamayotsu 2002, p. 356). For most parts of the country, the government at all levels neglected Muslims' socio-political interests and attempted to apply development policies in one, rigid way. Therefore, it seems obvious that all post-New Order democratic administrations will face challenges from newly-reborn generations of Muslim who were marginalized back then. In responding to state power and policies, the new generations tend to employ populist ideas in many aspects of life. There have even been people wishing to take over the state to apply sharia law, or to capture specific institutions as a means to impose their views on society and to suppress the contending views of other Muslims (Ricklefs 2013, p. 19).

In contemporary Indonesia, the relationship between Islam and politics involves, among other things, an on-going process of democratization, identity politics, and the creation of civil society, which have been more complex than before. Indeed, Islam has penetrated into the dominant nationalist and secular political parties. Almost all parties have accommodated religious aspirations and shied away from criticizing controversial religious issues to show the strength of religious influence on Indonesian politics today (Tanuwidjaja 2010). As a result, Islamic parties are no longer the lone channel for Islamic aspirations, thus they seem to have failed to gain popular support or to capitalize these sentiments (Sakai and Fauzia 2014, p. 41; Hicks 2012, p. 40).

Islamism, or political Islam, in Indonesia has been an emerging issue since the early years of post-New Order. Scholars argue that the ample enlargement of Islamists in Indonesia is a result of ordinary Muslims turning into Islam as a reference to regulate their life (Sakai and Fauzia 2014, p. 43). Though the Islamist movement in the country has infiltrated transnational features, the advancement of the local-based movement is due to an effective use of local repertoires of reasoning (local history, *adat*, rituals and memory), rather than through scriptural arguments (Alimi 2014). Moreover, the rampant expansion of television and other media's preaching programmes and local *pengajian* gives opportunities for Muslims to gain Islamic knowledge independently for ethical self-improvement (Sakai and Fauzia 2014, p. 43; Muzakki 2008; Howell 2008). Therefore, instead of directly getting involved in political Islamic movements, many Muslims in Indonesia are seeking to implement an Islamic way of life amidst the challenging and secularizing world (Sakai and Fauzia 2014, p. 43). This is especially true for urban middle-class Muslims.

As Hasan (2009, p. 237) has put it, the rising consciousness of urban middle-class Muslims to engage in debating and objectifying their religion entails the availability of religious spaces in big cities. In view of the growing demands for such spaces, elite housing complexes and shopping centres provide meeting places for people to listen to Islamic public lectures (*majelis taklim*). Luxury Islamic centres were built in big cities, such as Jakarta, Surabaya, Bandung, Yogyakarta, and Makassar, where urban middle-class Muslims participate in reciting Quran while discussing various aspects of Islam.

Contemporary urban Muslims are in constant search of the world, that is religiously defined and provides moral order and spiritual sanctuary to human beings, as Peter Berger called it "the sacred canopy" (Berger 1967). To urban Muslims, Islam represents various sacred canopies that fertilize communal bond and piety, as well as impose morally sacred orders at the cosmological and everyday mundane activities. We have become accustomed to see how religiously Muslim societies attempt to cope with an ever secularizing world. The world, except for Western and Northern Europe, is "as furiously religious as ever" (Berger 1992, p. 32). This state of affairs runs against the assertion of secularization theorists who predicted the significant decline of religion as an influential determinant of social action when people experience modernization and rationalization. Modernization has also triggered a myriad of countertrends as evidenced by the movements of religious revival worldwide (Kitiarsa 2008, p. 3; Pohl 2006, p. 393). However, religiosity is often built on discontent. Rapid social transformation marked by industrialization, urbanization, and modernization can generate notions of uprootedness and disenchantment among certain segments of society, such as the youth, the *petite bourgeoisie*, and other members of the middle class who experience frustration for social mobility and set to protest against the modern way of life (Ismail 2006, pp. 11-13). In terms of education, many young Islamic activists coming from newly urbanized middle-class families have not necessarily experienced formal religious training (Tan 2011). Instead, many of them have been educated in secular institutions where the command over knowledge and skill is revered as the key to meritocratic social advancement.

In Serang, the rise of urban Muslims is due to the fact that the city has developed rapidly since it became the capital of the new Province of Banten in 2000. After the downfall of the New Order regime in 1998, Indonesia has witnessed the emergence of new provinces and the changing patterns of regional politics. As of 1998, there were only twenty-seven provinces, while there were thirty-four provinces in the archipelago by 2019. The new administrative regions are expected to provide public goods such as transportation, jobs and opportunities, and access to education, and thus the regions will become an increasingly complex and specialized provider of goods and services. Consequently, new middle-class groups are emerging, while the old ones are getting stronger.

As a medium-sized regency (*kabupaten*) turned into a new provincial capital, Serang has witnessed the growth of middle-class Muslims in which they have contributed to the rise of Islamic commercialism and consumerism. Various goods and services under the label of Islam have been established to create an image of Serang as a new Islamic city. At the same time, the proliferation of new loose Islamic groupings indicates the strengthening of Islamic communal piety. Both communal piety and religious commodification are obvious characteristics of Islamic pop culture, or so-called "pop Islam", which is a blend of Muslim faith with pop culture. Hoesterey (2012, p. 45) points out that the consumption and public display of Islamic products have become increasingly important avenues through which passionate urban middle-class Muslims around the world search for meaning and express piety. He mentions several phenomenon of pop Islam in Indonesia, including Islamic-themed novels and films, Islamic fashion and aspiration of class mobility, self-proclaimed "sexologists", celebrity preachers and their personal brands, New-Age Sufi networks among urban elites, and Muslim "spiritual trainers". Heryanto (2011, p. 61) proposes that the current and massive development of Islamic pop cultures in Indonesia is largely an extension of the success of Islamic politics in post-New Order.

Furthermore, the impact of media industrialization on religious expression in Indonesia has been substantial. The expansion of new communication technology, such as radio, television, print media, and the Internet, has facilitated the flourishing of pop Islam—the process of which has involved the appropriation of religious goods (Hasan 2009, p. 245). Moreover, there has been an intersection between commerce and Islamic expression to address societal issues experienced by middle-class Muslims. This, in turn, projects an image of Indonesian Islam that blurs existing political divisions in Indonesian society (Rakhmani 2014). I will elucidate the convolution between communal piety and religious commodification in the next section.

"Pop Islam": The Strengthening of Communal Piety and Religious Commodification

In the newly developing Serang, the Muslim community has contributed to the rising consumption of religious goods, ranging from services for religious trips, cosmetics, beauty care, clothing, to food. The religious market in post-New Order Indonesia has reached a broader scope, created massive impacts on the society and attracted high demand from the people. In short, the emergence of new administrative regions in the country has contributed to the growth of middle-class Muslims, the prevalence of communal piety, and the commodification of Islam.

> When my husband got a new job in Serang in 2001, I was very sad because I had to leave my *pengajian* group in Bogor. I had difficult times finding friends whom I could learn Islam and share my religious thoughts and experiences with. I have encountered a number of *pengajian* groups, but none made me feel comfortable due to the differences in teachings, subjects, and group affiliations. Things changed and went well when I moved to a [then] newly-built complex housing in 2007. I had new neighbours who introduced me to a *pengajian* group in which I am an active member up to now. We learn *tahsin* (rules governing pronunciation in Quranic recitation), *hadith* (sayings and acts of the Prophet Muhammad as recorded and transmitted by his contemporaries), and other Islamic teachings. Of course, we also share our thoughts in other casual issues, such as where to find a good *hijab* (veil) store, a recommended *umrah* travel agency, and other things (Sri, a forty-eight-year-old housewife and a member of a *pengajian* group).

Islam has become a pop, chic, youthful, and cool trend among urban middle-class Muslims. Since the 1980s, religiosity has gradually grown into a significant factor amidst the overt political tension against the Suharto administration. It was also a symbol of religious identity politics after the demise of the authoritarian regime. As Hoesterey and Clark (2012, p. 207) have said, popular culture has become a significant arena in Indonesia through which Muslims constitute and contest ideas about Islam and piety. Elsewhere, the rise of pop Islam has provided Muslims with an important platform for breaking with traditional gender roles, building social capital, and acquiring the participatory skills necessary to bring "civil society" into their communities (Mushaben 2008, p. 507).

Many female members of the *pengajian* groups are aspiring housewives who seek both worldly comforts and an enlightment of everlasting afterlife. Most of them believe that *pengajian* serves as a media to bring them closer to God. Not all participants who come to these occasions can read Arabic or understand the meaning of the verses in the Quran. Nevertheless, they are attracted by the tantalizing *pahala* (religous reward/merit for moral conduct) they might obtain by attending the forum. Therefore, in addition to the regular *pengajian* in their neighbourhood, they also attend other *pengajian* occasionally held in other places, such as in neighbouring mosques or at events organized by local government offices and mass organizations. By attending many *pengajian*, these women also feel the need to look charming in appearance as it serves as a display of wealth, power, status, and social class. In this case, it is not surprising that Islamic brands and products of cosmetics, beauty care, and fashion have enjoyed a success of their sellings through rampant and attractive marketing. Clearly, urban *pengajian* is a perfect display of communal piety and religious commodification.

> My husband wants me to look pretty. I do not mind with that. So, I always try to look attractive in front of him. Being beautiful in front of other members in the *pengajian* is also important because I do not want to abase my husband. But, being beautiful is not cheap. Muslim women need cosmetics and beauty care. I was happy that I could find cosmetic stores and beauty care centres easily. But, things went complicated when I started wearing *hijab* in 2014. I could not just go to any beauty care centre. I had to find the ones for Muslimah. At first, I had to go to Jakarta or Tangerang to find what I was looking for. Nowadays, Serang also has several good Muslim beauty care centres. I am happy with that (Maya, a thirty-five-year-old small-and-medium entrepreneur and a member of a *pengajian* group).

As we have noticed, religiosity has been a significant issue among Muslim communities in Indonesia for the last several decades. Being a Muslim means that one not only has to perform religious duties and to avoid immoral and misconduct activities, but also to proudly and persistently demonstrate his or her Islamic identity. In these *pengajian* groups, being religious can literally mean as showing an "Islamic" appearance. For women, distinctive religious garbs, such as expensive *hijab* and long and loose-fitting *hijab* are the principal symbols.[4] For the men, growing beard and wearing *celana cingkrang* (shorter trousers below the knee but above the ankle are considered the most appropriate trousers for Muslim men) are the primary identities. They like to claim that wearing and showing Islamic clothing in appearance are the first steps to become "true" Muslims. They also prefer to talk—or actually to mention—in broken Arabic for certain terms, instead of using Indonesian terms. Moreover, consuming commodities recommended by the religion is also very important for their religiosity. Examples of such commodities are dates fruits, *habbatus sauda'* (black caraway/black cumin), and camel milk; all of which are non-native Indonesian products. For these people, these habits, along with the participation in religious activities, are now considered to be the most appropriate religious expression of Islamic identity.

These phenomena, however, are not exclusive to Indonesia. Vatikiotis (1991, p. 36) argues that it is not striking that in the Muslim world, religion acts as a determinant of political identity, a focus of loyalty, and a source of authority. Islam continues to act as a key mobilizing ideology and social movement frame in Muslim-majority states. Islam, however, is not only a subject of political contention, but also its object (Bayat 2010, p. 8). In short, contemporary urban middle-class Muslims in Indonesia are more dynamic, prone to adopt transnational ideas of Islam, but at the same time are more exclusive and tend to oppose the traditional expression of local Islam.

In Indonesia, Islam has become parts of extensive consumer culture and served much as an important identity marker or sign of social status and political affiliation. Its strength lies in the fact that it has developed into some sort of a network that enables numerous people from different social backgrounds to share and make connections, both in real and virtual life. Through this network, the messages of global Islamic revival have significantly amplified, influencing multiple socio-political fields and encouraging a collective "true Islam" identity. Wearing proper Islamic dress, watching Islamic television programmes, gathering in Muslim cafes and beauty salons, wearing a veil, attending study circles with popular preachers, doing "Islamic" sports, such as archery and horse riding, or going for a pilgrimage to Mecca, have indirectly linked an individual to a larger social group and *ummah* in a general sense. The network, in turn, provides credible paths for upward mobility and also becomes a market for commercial products (Hasan 2009, p. 231). Kitiarsa (2008, pp. 6–7) indicates that commodification helps to redefine religion as a commodity market which is further expanded by the transnational connections of religious organizational and market networks. The market for religious and spiritual renewal products is rather diverse. On one hand, many Muslims avidly select brands and products that symbolically linked to Islam instead of the ones without a religious tag. On the other hand, some of the most successful commercially delivered piety-promotion programmes combine religious teachings with an element of secular culture to enhance their appeal and demonstrate their relevance to modern life (Howell 2013, pp. 402–3).

Most members of the *pengajian* groups do not have formal Islamic education backgrounds. Very few of them studied in *pesantren* (Islamic boarding schools) and other Islamic learning institutions. Many of them are also highly educated (at least bachelor degree graduates) and come from outside Serang—though they have lived in the city for quite a while. In spite of their characteristics being closely associated with communal piety and religious commodification, these people are also avid supporters of Islamic populism and Islamism. They tend to long for an ideal world by creating their own Islamic way of life and are likely to reject the existing Islamic tradition that is deemed to be inappropriate for "true" Muslims. In politics, they believe in populist ideas in choosing people-oriented parties or candidates for official posts and those who demonstrate the best religious populist ideas, such as approaching religious leaders, attending religious ceremonials, or participating in religious festivities, and combining them with good networking among local elites and local leaders. As supporters of Islamic populism and Islamism, they also promote "true" Islam. The next section will further elaborate on this.

"True" Islam: The Rise of Islamic Populism and Islamism

"True" Islam for some Muslims in Indonesia means a "return to Quran and Sunnah" (the practice of the Prophet, which is derived from the hadith); the practices of which in everyday affairs, in terms of Islamic populism and Islamism, are often highly political as we will see in this section. According to Ismail (2006, p. 2), the term "Islamism" is used to encompass both Islamist politics as well as re-Islamization, the process whereby various domains of social life are invested with signs and symbols associated with Islamic traditions. In short, Islamism is not only an expression of a political project, but it also covers the invocation of frames with an Islamic referent in social and cultural spheres. In Indonesia, this is particularly true.

Gellner (1981) proposes two models of Muslim societies: the High Islam of urban Muslims and the Low Islam of rural Muslims. The former is scripturalist and ascetic, suitable for the character of city people, while the latter is ecstatic, meeting the needs of village dwellers. With greater urbanization, Low Islam declines and High Islam becomes ascendant. This occurs because High Islam captures the urban strata's desire for learning and upward mobility. This desire is ruined by the weakness of the state to modernize the country, and thus Islamism is viewed as an affirmation of the scriptural-based spirit expressing frustration with the blocked road to modernization.

In the Indonesian context, much of the debate about the compatibility of Islam and modernity rejects the idea of secular modernist that to achieve modernity entails the privatization of religion and the removal of religious discourse from the public sphere. According to Amir (2009), the Muslim modernists call for the combination of *iptek* (*ilmu pengetahuan dan teknologi*—science and technology) and *imtaq* (*iman dan taqwa*—faith and devotion) to build the nation underpinned by strong Islamic faith. Furthermore, Rudnyckyj (2009) looks at how rapid transformations in the social and economic realms after 1998, have provoked intense ethical reflections in Indonesian society. He shows that Islam spreads through means that reflect its compatibility with modernity. In a Muslim-dominant country like Indonesia, Islam is an integral part of the founding ideologies, and ideological elements of Islam are drawn by both political parties and organizations in civil society (Hui 2013, p. 5).

The supporters of "true" Islam in Indonesia are generally peaceful, in the sense that they are not attempting to transform Indonesia into an open battlefield of wars between Muslims and non-Muslims. Nevertheless, they frequently make use of intolerant ways in arguing, promoting, and disseminating their own expression of Islam against certain groups, whether Muslims or non-Muslims, who are not of the same opinion about Islam. These intolerant acts often cause religious strains. Therefore, besides showing a peaceful and moderate look, as Hadiz (2016, p. 14) puts it, Indonesia can easily exemplify the danger of rising religious violence and intolerance within a democracy, especially due to the activities of vigilante groups that employ religion to justify their presence.

Islamic populism in Indonesia is an urban phenomenon. The rise of urban middle-class Muslims in Indonesia cannot be detached from the marginalized position of Muslims in the country. Hadiz (2016, p. 4) argues that the main project of the new Islamic populism lies on the favourable repositioning of the marginalized *ummah* within the confined nation-state through possible strategy of contestation, in which it does not necessarily involve the call to establish a sharia-based state. Eventually, these urban groups help to establish and sustain the emergence of new Islamic populism.

In Serang, the promotion and dissemination of "true" Islam is due to the emergence of new religious movements that attempt to transform and even replace "local Islam" with "foreign Islam". Serang, and also Banten in general, is well-known for its long history of mysticism and the traditionally-influenced Islamic orientation of its society (Pribadi 2013). However, Salafi-inspired Muslim groups have been changing the religious landscape in the city.

> I used to attend *tahlilan, yasinan,* and other *bid'ah* activities. I was not aware that such practices could lead to *shirk* (the sin of polytheism). A friend of mine started to ask me to join his *pengajian* group in 2013. Now I feel that I have learned a lot from the group. We learn about *fiqh* (Islamic jurisprudence), the Prophet's *Sunnah,* and other Islamic teachings that differ significantly from those of my previous *pengajian.* Sometimes I regret that I did not join this group earlier. This is the real Islam because we return to Quran and *Sunnah* only, not to invented traditions. But Banten is still highly influenced by deviated (*menyimpang*) Islam. It is not right (Hartono, a fifty-three-year-old civil servant and a member of a *pengajian* group).

Hartono is not the only example of a new urban middle-class Muslim in Serang, or in the country, who shares a similar view on Islam. Nowadays, many Muslims like him seem to have counteracted other Muslim groups openly. They are being out of control in voicing their concerns, and of these concerns, some have turned into politicizing the issues and causing troubles. Moreover, a number of sharia-inspired regulations advocated by populist regional leaders have the potential to jeopardize civil liberties of women and other minority groups. Yet, in many cases, Muslims who believe that moral decadence is caused by the absence of sharia in everyday life, have truly supported these regulations.

Rinaldo (2008, p. 26) has suggested that the new ideas on Islam revolved around piety. While Indonesian Muslims, like other Muslims in many countries, have often been more casual in their practice of Islam, these new ideas emphasized on the true practice of the religion through an adherence to certain religious norms. She argues that since the late 1980s, many Indonesians have come to observe Islam more carefully as an essential to being a Muslim. Many of the new ideas about Muslim piety have concerned women, including an increasing call for women to wear proper Muslim clothing and to behave in modest ways. Moreover, some middle- and upper-class women are also attached to the *Tablighi Jamā'at* movement in Indonesia. Their passion to return to the true path of Islam has made them aware of their capacity to exercise agency within the movement's structural plight. The most notable contribution of these women is their effort on undertaking recruitment and sustaining this shared-meaning religious network with their colleagues. They are not only a tool of the men's movement, but also the social agent (Amrullah 2011). The women's movement has also become the focus of new religious movements, the re-Islamization supporters, and even the proponents of Islamic populism and Islamism.

> Indonesia must support the establishment of a free and independent state of Palestine because Muslims in that country are our brothers. Our current leaders in Indonesia do not care about Islam, and in fact, they downgrade it. If they pay no attention to Muslims in our own country, how would they care about Muslims in other countries? We need people's leaders who will take Islam back to glory. Revolution must begin now, so that a good Muslim can lead the country, side-by-side with the people, and is not being submissive to *asing* and *aseng* (foreign powers, refer to the West and China respectively), and so we can become the householder (*tuan rumah*) in our own country (Rukmini, a forty-four-year-old housewife and a member of a *pengajian* group).

Since the 2014 presidential elections, popular political polarization in Indonesia that divides the citizens into secularist-nationalist faction and Islamist-nationalist cohort has escalated. Political tension has fluctuated, heating up every now and then, and cooling down again (Rachmatika 2014; Kwok 2014; Pepinsky 2014). The level of tension is influenced by mixed political factors such as differences in political preferences (political parties, political candidates) and views on nationalism, multiculturalism, and religion.

The situation in Jakarta rapidly spills over to other regions, including Serang. Most members of the *pengajian* groups in Serang claim that they are not interested in politics, in the sense that they are not members of any political party. Nevertheless, many, if not most, of them share opinions about the notion that the head of state, regional head, and leading public officer must be a Muslim; sharia must be implemented in daily life; the limitation of foreign influence; and the abolition of communism, liberalism, and religious pluralism. A recent study demonstrates that Islamist political attitudes have increased after a massive Islamist mobilization in late 2016 and early 2017 (*Aksi Bela Islam*—Action for Defending Islam)—combining both street demonstrations and an electoral challenge—directed against the incumbent Chinese-Christian governor of the Special Capital Region of Jakarta, Basuki Tjahaja Purnama (Ahok). Scholars argue that Muslim attitudes surrounding the main message of the mobilization (that is, the exclusion of non-Muslims from political office, in this case Ahok) significantly intensified during and after the mobilization. This suggests that many Muslims have absorbed the message propagated by the mobilization leaders (Mietzner, Muhtadi, and Halida 2018, p. 161).

It is not striking that non-Jakarta citizens have also been influenced by the manipulative approach promulgated by politicians and Islamist leaders. In Serang, many Muslims participated in the demonstrations, including some members of the *pengajian* groups which I observed.[5] An *ustadz* in one *pengajian* group told me that he participated in the demonstrations.

> The Action for Defending Islam must be followed by Muslims because Ahok has scorned Islam. He must be imprisoned for hurting the feelings of all Muslims in Indonesia. As an *ustadz*, I must invite my *ummah* to participate in the actions, including my students and my *jemaah* (participants in religious congregation). This is a *jihad* (holy wars) against the *kafir* (Umar, a fifty-two-year-old *ustadz*).

It is clear now that the spirit of "true" Islam is a determinant factor that reinforces the rise of Islamic populism and Islamism in Indonesia.

There is also a distinct sign that Islamization is still continuously taking place in the country. It has to be noted, however, that Islamization does not necessarily denote the rise of Islamism. As Ufen (2009, p. 309) has suggested, in many instances, Islamization in Southeast Asia signifies the strengthening of a conservative Islam, instead of the Islamists. Moreover, he argues that most Muslims in some areas in the archipelago have undergone Islamization for decades after the fall of the New Order. This development has been partially facilitated by the state and the political elites since independence. The state certainly has circumscribed the activities of particular religious actors. Nevertheless, most part of this process genuinely appears to be a result of the dynamics in civil society. In the country's current party system, Islamization of politics is moderate, whereas in the society-wide, there is a mushrooming of conservative Islam.

The entanglement between communal piety and religious commodification on the one hand, and Islamic populism and religious commodification on the other hand, has been dynamic and complex as they are frequently overlapping. The making and appropriation of religious authority is apparent. That is what the next section is all about.

The Making of Religious Authority

Banten is well-known for its long history of mysticism and its societal Islamic orientation. The province also has an established tradition of being the centre of various esoteric sciences (Pribadi 2008, p. 1). In colonial Banten, at least four social groups existed and cut across the village's hierarchy. The first group was the *kolot-kolot* (the elders), who enjoyed authority over the villagers because they performed a ceremonial function in the village administration. The *panghulu* (head of mosque functionaries), or *amil* (village official in charge of collecting *zakat*), should be regarded as the second one. They were appointed and co-opted by the colonial government. Additionally, there were two other groups: the religious men (*kyai* and *haji*) and the *jawara* (local strongmen). In the past, the group of religious men was regarded as socially prestigious. They had charismatic power and were admired by the local people. Their position in the society was more independent, compared to the *panghulu* or *amil* (Kartodirdjo 1966, pp. 54–58).

In contemporary Banten, particularly in urban Serang, the primary holder of religious authority is the *kyai* who had performed pilgrimage to

Mecca (*haji*) and has led a *pesantren*. In relation to mosque management, the *kyai* also usually act as mosque functionaries and *amil* who collect *zakat* (alms). Many of them are also members of the Council of Indonesian Ulama (MUI) in various chapters in Banten as well as members of different Islamic mass organizations. They represent local expressions of Islam. Therefore, compared to colonial Banten, the position of the *kyai* in contemporary Banten is even greater. This is comparable to the situation in East Yogyakarta where the religious political authority are in the hands of the *kyai*, though the Sultan is still the ultimate religious and political authority (Woodward 2011, p. 40).

Nonetheless, by utilizing their capabilities and resources, the *ustadz* and participants in the urban *pengajian* in Serang seem to have, openly or not, challenged the *kyai* as the primary religious authority in order to secure their own interests. Meanwhile, through the networks of *pesantren* and Islamic mass organizations, the *kyai* have cautiously responded to the challenge by distancing themselves from such religious activities, such as those held in urban *pengajian*. The *ustadz* and their followers represent an overt Middle Eastern influence of Islam but they are also known to be very adaptive and responsive to socio-political transformations. They might form mutually beneficial relations with the state and the *kyai* not only when the power and influence of both parties are too strong to oppose, but also when making such alliance is seen to be a favourable option. While many residents in elite housing complexes are in favour of the *ustadz*'s way of preaching and many inhabitants in the outskirt of the city are fond of the *kyai*'s *dakwah* style, most city dwellers in non-elite urban housing complex (*perkampungan di tengah kota*) have neither specific preference in religious observances and streams (*aliran*) nor in the preachers. These fuzzy areas have become an open field for the viable and aggressive *ustadz* and their followers to proselytize people through their evangelical mission. This creates an odd situation, as most people without adequate religious education backgrounds are now in limbo, trying to decide who and what to follow because they are in constant search of religious conformity.

The state of affairs is, however, not unique to Indonesia. I have argued that Muslim politics encourage people to be involved in alliances and competitions over the interpretation of Islamic and cultural symbols, as well as the control of the state and public institutions (Pribadi 2018, p. 7). The alliances and competitions with definite goals to ensure the upholding of Islam that have been constantly articulated, are common in Muslim-majority states, although they are varied in its conception and form. The relationship between Islam and politics is highly intricate, especially when it transforms into public symbols, discourses, and practices. Nevertheless, in Indonesia, substantive challenges to the state authority under the banner of Islam have yet to be realized (Pribadi 2018, pp. 9, 11).

In the 1990s, the country had a concern over the notion of *ghazwul fikri* (invasion of ideas), which is a term to refer to various forms of Western cultural invasion, i.e. American movies, music, fashion, food, and most importantly certain styles of religious thought and attitude, such as secularism, liberalism, and religious pluralism. Against this Arab-style political Islam, prominent intellectuals pleaded a "cultural Islam", an expression of Islamic values in Indonesian cultural form. Both sides appeared to share the perception that Indonesian Islam was under threat of being subverted by foreign influences and the assumption that local cultures are largely passive recipients of global flows (van Bruinessen 2015, pp. 61–62). Nowadays, it is exactly the proponent of Arabization who is concerned and has actively attempted to avert the notion of Islam Nusantara propagated by traditional factions of Indonesian Islam (mostly the Nahdlatul Ulama). The traditional factions are also supported by wide segment of the public who oppose Arabization, including leading intellectuals associated with secularism, liberalism, and religious pluralism, such as those who gather at the Liberal Islam Network (JIL).[6]

The Indonesian Muslim society today is marked by deep disagreements over qualified religious authorities and how the ordinary Muslims should take the pronouncements of individual scholars seriously (Hefner 2005, p. 6). The images of Indonesian Islam remain a contested discourse. It is certainly a product of foreign influences. As van Bruinessen (2015, pp. 62–63) has put it, Indonesian Islam is not a product of relative isolation from foreign influences, but a result of an active interaction over centuries with highly diverse powerful cultural flows, including the Middle East and the West, in which they have become the dominant and competing sources of the flow of ideas, with minor visible roles of China and South Asia. This is in line with Woodward's (2011, p. 270) notion that religion, culture, and nationality are as contested today as they were more than seventy years ago, when Indonesia was founded.

In the *pengajian*, the participants are told about local Bantenese Islamic tradition deemed as heretical belief, such as *panjang mulud* and *tahlilan*. *Panjang mulud* is local Bantenese-style (especially some parts of Serang, Cilegon, and Pandeglang) commemoration of the Prophet Muhammad's birthday (on 12 *Rabi' al-awwal*, the third month in the Islamic calendar). Most *ustadz* under the influence of Salafism disapprove this commemoration, considering it as heretical. *Panjang mulud* in Serang usually attracts many onlookers. There is a parade of decorative cart adorned with boiled eggs as the main ornament, as well as food, clothes, and money. Children are generally attracted to participate in such occasions, and thus even though Salafi-inspired Muslims in Serang reject such celebrations, their children can be seen taking part in the amusing events.

During Ramadan, most mosques in Serang hold *tarawih* prayers in twenty *raka'at* (a single unit of Islamic prayer). Meanwhile, most Salafi followers hold eight *raka'at* only. Therefore, though the parents in *pengajian* groups are teaching their children to perform eight *raka'at* of *tarawih* prayers, the kids usually do twenty *raka'at* during *tarawih* prayers in neighbouring mosques. Some parents are aware of this conflicting circumstance, while some others are not.

> I know that the teachers in the mosque near my house come from Pandeglang. They are from *pesantren* and like to attend *tahlilan*. But, they are good people. Therefore, I send my children to learn to recite Quran there. I once also studied at a *pesantren*, and I know that *pesantren* people are usually able to recite Quran well. At school, my children are still not fluent in reciting Quran because there are too many students. However, they can do it better at the mosque (Hendra, a forty-six-year-old civil servant and a member of a *pengajian* group).

Apparently, promoting "true" Islam is a certain means to claim and reinforce their own Islamic identity. All the above mentioned examples seem to indicate that the attitude of the member of *pengajian* groups would last very long with their strong sense of identity. In fact, they have been pushing for a counter-culture against the local traditional Islamic culture, which is very influential in Bantenese society. Nevertheless, the local people do not openly attack these groups since the *kyai*—as their main supporters—are still highly respected by many segments in the society. For many people, opposing a *kiai* is regarded as a serious breach of etiquette with both social and spiritual consequences (Tihami

1992, pp. 99–100; Wilson 2003, p. 246). This situation still holds true in Banten.

It is clear that Banten has a kind of mixed Islamic worldview. On the one hand, traditional Islam—that has roots since the Sultanate era—still prevails in contemporary age. Thus, the traditions and customs of *tahlilan, panjang mulud, ziarah* (pilgrimages to sacred graveyards), and others are still practised by many Muslims in Banten. On the other hand, the religious revivalism by rebellion against the Dutch colonial government in the nineteenth century seems to have re-emerged and generated an increasing number of religious activities. It is not only because people are pious adherents of Islam, but also due to the socio-political disruption in the post-New Order period. This disruption has concomitantly generated re-Islamization or the return to the "true" Islam. As a growing city, Serang is one of the most conspicuous places whereby "local Islam" represented by lower-class Muslim dwellers meets and interacts with "foreign Islam" represented mostly by the middle-class Muslims, in which the latter are the supporters of Islamic populism and Islamism on the one hand, as well as communal piety and religious commodification on the other hand.

While there are Muslims who engage in violent acts to achieve their goal of establishing an Islamic state and supporting Islamic populism and Islamism, there are others who share the same goal but prefer peaceful means, such as through education and political elections (Tan 2011, p. 9). Since 1998, there have been continuous efforts to idealize Muslim-majority states or Muslim-majority areas by various Muslim organizations and political parties, such as the Indonesian chapter of Hizb ut-Tahrir (HTI),[7] Prosperous Justice Party (PKS), as well as other Salafi-inspired groups in Indonesia and Banten, to bring the myth of the Islamic state into existence as a religiously-based governance by God through political means.[8] Meanwhile, the traditional Islamic groups and proponents of secularism, liberalism, and religious pluralism have attempted to fight against this "idealization". For instance, the key champion of these groups, the Indonesia's fourth President Abdurrahman Wahid (1940–2009), claimed that Indonesia should be an example of a compatibility of Islam and democracy by resisting both religious majoritarianism and anti-religious secularism (Seo 2012, p. 1047). However, it is not an easy task, as the MUI issued a *fatwa* (non-binding religious opinion) No. 7 on Pluralism, Secularism, and Liberalism (2005) that rejects those three thoughts (Nasir 2014). The making and contest for religious authority is clearly taking place, not only at the central level, but also in regional public spheres.

Conclusion

As a region influenced by the Sultanate of Banten in the past, Serang is generally known as a traditionally religious region. Thus, the communal concerns on the religious issues in Serang are influenced by the surrounding cultural and religious environments and experiences. However, the arrival of new urban middle-class Muslims, mostly those who have migrated from the bigger and more developed cities, as well as the emergence of new generations of Muslims in Serang and other surrounding towns living in the city, have significantly changed the landscape of cultural and religious expression of Islamic tradition in Serang.

Urban *pengajian* groups in housing complex have been a vital place to discuss, practise, and propagate the combination of pop and "true" Islam by aspiring middle-class Muslims who mostly do not have Islamic education backgrounds and are relatively new to the ideas of Islamic teachings. This trend has gained popularity in the urban areas in the country since the fall of the New Order administration. The making of religious authority has continuously involved complex interactions between two sides: the local expressions of Islam and the foreign understanding and practices of Islam. As a result, there has been a fragmentation of the *ummah*, a condition that is deteriorated by the rampant popular political polarization since the 2014 presidential elections. The city of Serang is only one example, while the same circumstance is also happening in other urban areas in the country.

NOTES

1 Some materials in this chapter are taken from Pribadi (2019a), pp. 103–20 and Pribadi (2019b), pp. 82–112.
2 The names of the people are fictitious and camouflaged due to their preferences to remain anonymous.
3 I was not allowed to enter the house where this particular *pengajian* occurred. Though the content was not necessarily secretive, both *ustadzah* and the participants believed that separation between male and female members in an assembly was a necessity. However, the hosts usually half-opened the

door and still gave me permission to listen and follow the talk from the outside.
4   Rachel Rinaldo (2008, pp. 23–39) finds that PKS women's pious practices are part of the creation of a particular kind of middle-class subjectivity. Based on an examination of two constitutive elements of this habitus, clothing and marriage, she reveals how these pious Islamic practices enact class and gender differences, and simultaneously produce "modern" selves.
5   See Aas Arbi (2016) for the protest on 4 November 2016 and *Suara Pembaruan* (2013) for the protest on 2 December 2016.
6   For an account of the JIL, see Nurdin (2005), pp. 20–39.
7   Ken Ward argues that HTI retains some elements of the clandestine life since its founding, but the Indonesian political mainstream or security authorities have shown surprisingly little hostility towards them. See Ward (2009), pp. 149–64.
8   Both Woodward et al. (2013, pp. 173–89) and Hwang (2010, pp. 635–74) demonstrate that the PKS appears to have, in pursuit of electoral purposes, moderated its hardline positions in their strategy and ideology on the acceptability of local culture. The moderation process is complicated due to the division in the party between the pragmatist who targets non-devout voters and the purist who prioritizes ideological authenticity.

REFERENCES

Aas Arbi. 2016. "Ribuan Muslim Banten Ikut Aksi Bela Islam ke Jakarta". *Radar Banten Online*, 4 November 2016. https://www.radarbanten.co.id/ribuan-muslim-banten-ikut-aksi-bela-islam-ke-jakarta/ (accessed 3 August 2018).

Alimi, Moh Yasir. 2014. "Local Repertoires of Reasoning and the Islamist Movement in Post-Authoritarian Indonesia". *Indonesia and the Malay World* 42, no. 122: 24–42.

Amir, Sulfikar. 2009. "A Message from Ashabirin: High Technology and Political Islam in Indonesia". In *Mediating Piety: Technology and Religion in Contemporary Asia*, edited by Francis Khek Gee Lim, pp. 71–89. Leiden and Boston: Brill.

Amrullah, Eva F. 2011. "Seeking Sanctuary in 'the Age of Disorder': Women in Contemporary Tablighi Jamā'at". *Contemporary Islam* 5: 135–60.

Bayat, Asef. 2010. *Life as Politics: How Ordinary People Change the Middle East*. Amsterdam: ISIM/Amsterdam University Press.

Berger, Peter. 1967. *The Sacred Canopy: Elements of a Social Theory of Religion*. Garden City, NY: Doubleday.

———. 1992. *A Far Glory: The Quest of Faith in an Age of Credulity*. New York: Doubleday.

Fealy, Greg. 2008. "Consuming Islam: Commodified Religion and Aspirational Pietism in Contemporary Indonesia". In *Expressing Islam: Religious Life and Politics in Indonesia*, edited by Greg Fealy and Sally White, pp. 15–39. Singapore: Institute of Southeast Asian Studies.

Gellner, Ernest. 1981. *Muslim Society*. Cambridge: Cambridge University Press.

Hadiz, Vedi R. 2016. *Islamic Populism in Indonesia and the Middle East*. Cambridge: Cambridge University Press.

Hamayotsu, Kikue. 2002. "Islam and Nation Building in Southeast Asia: Malaysia and Indonesia in Comparative Perspective". *Pacific Affairs* 75, no. 3: 353–75.

Hasan, Noorhaidi. 2009. "The Making of Public Islam: Piety, Agency, and Commodification on the Landscape of the Indonesian Public Sphere". *Contemporary Islam* 3: 229–50.

Hefner, Robert W. 2005. "Introduction: Modernity and the Remaking of Muslim Politics". In *Remaking Muslim Politics: Pluralism, Contestation, Democratization*, edited by Robert W. Hefner, pp. 1–36. Princeton: Princeton University Press.

Heryanto, Ariel. 2011. "Upgraded Piety and Pleasure: The New Middle Class and Islam in Indonesian Popular Culture". In *Islam and Popular Culture in Indonesia and Malaysia*, edited by Andrew N. Weintraub, pp. 60–82. London and New York: Routledge.

Hicks, Jacqueline. 2012. "The Missing Link: Explaining the Political Mobilisation of Islam in Indonesia". *Journal of Contemporary Asia* 42, no. 1: 39–66.

Hoesterey, James B. 2012. "Prophetic Cosmopolitanism: Islam, Pop Psychology, and Civic Virtue in Indonesia". *City & Society* 24, no. 1: 38–61.

Hoesterey, James B. and Marshall Clark. 2012. "Film Islami: Gender, Piety and Pop Culture in Post-Authoritarian Indonesia". *Asian Studies Review* 36, no. 2: 207–26.

Howell, Julia Day. 2008. "Modulations of Active Piety: Professors and Televangelists as Promoters of Indonesian Sufism". In *Expressing Islam: Religious Life and Politics in Indonesia*, edited by Greg Fealy and Sally White, pp. 40–62. Singapore: Institute of Southeast Asian Studies.

———. 2010. "Indonesia's Salafist Sufis". *Modern Asian Studies* 44, no. 5: 1029–51.

———. 2013. "'Calling' and 'Training': Role Innovation and Religious De-differentiation in Commercialised Indonesian Islam". *Journal of Contemporary Religion* 28, no. 3: 401–19.

Hui Yew-Foong. 2013. "Introduction: Encountering Islam". In *Encountering Islam: The Politics of Religious Identities in Southeast Asia*, edited by Hui Yew-Foong, pp. 3–16. Singapore: Institute of Southeast Asian Studies.

Hwang, Julie Chernov. 2010. "When Parties Swing: Islamist Parties and Institutional Moderation in Malaysia and Indonesia". *South East Asia Research* 18, no. 4: 635–74.

Ismail, Salwa. 2006. *Rethinking Islamist Politics: Culture, the State and Islamism*. London and New York: I.B. Tauris.

Kartodirdjo, Sartono. 1966. *The Peasants' Revolt of Banten in 1888, Its Conditions, Course, and Sequel: A Case Study of Social Movements in Indonesia*. 's-Gravenhage: Martinus Nijhoff.

Kitiarsa, Pattana. 2008. "Introduction: Asia's Commodified Sacred Canopies". In *Religious Commodification in Asia: Marketing Gods*, edited by Pattana Kitiarsa, pp. 1–12. London and New York: Routledge.

Kwok, Yenni. 2014. "The World's Most Populous Muslim Nation is About to Decide Its Political Future". *Time*, 8 July 2014. http://time.com/2964702/indonesia-election-2014-joko-widodo-jokowi-prabowo-subianto/ (accessed 6 August 2018).

Lukens-Bull, Ronald. 2008. "Commodification of Religion and the 'Religification' of Commodities". In *Religious Commodifications in Asia: Marketing Gods*, edited by Pattana Kitiarsa, pp. 220–34. London and New York: Routledge.

Macintyre, Andrew. 1991. *Business and Politics in Indonesia*. North Sydney: Allen and Unwin.

Mietzner, Marcus, Burhanuddin Muhtadi, and Rizka Halida. 2018. "Entrepreneurs of Grievance: Drivers and Effects of Indonesia's Islamist Mobilization". *Bijdragen tot de Taal-, Land- en Volkenkunde* 174, nos. 2–3: 159–87.

Millie, Julian, Greg Barton, Linda Hindasah, and Mikihiro Moriyama. 2014. "Post-Authoritarian Diversity in Indonesia's State-Owned Mosques: A Manakiban Case Study". *Journal of Southeast Asian Studies* 45, no. 2: 194–213.

Mushaben, Joyce Marie. 2008. "Gender, HipHop and Pop-Islam: The Urban Identities of Muslim Youth in Germany". *Citizenship Studies* 12, no. 5: 507–26.

Muzakki, Akh. 2008. "Islam as a Symbolic Commodity: Transmitting and Consuming Islam through Public Sermons in Indonesia". In *Religious Commodifications in Asia: Marketing Gods*, edited by Pattana Kitiarsa, pp. 205–19. London: Routledge.

Nasir, Mohamad Abdun. 2014. "The 'Ulamā', Fatāwā and Challenges to Democracy in Contemporary Indonesia". *Islam and Christian-Muslim Relations* 25, no. 4: 489–505.

Nurdin, Ahmad Ali. 2005. "Islam and State: A Study of the Liberal Islamic Network in Indonesia, 1999–2004". *New Zealand Journal of Asian Studies* 7, no. 2: 20–39.

Pepinsky, Tom. 2014. "The Key to Understanding Indonesia's Upcoming Elections? The Jokowi Effect". *The Washington Post*, 17 March 2014. https://www.washingtonpost.com/news/monkey-cage/wp/2014/03/17/the-key-to-understanding-indonesias-upcoming-elections-the-jokowi-effect/?noredirect=on&utm_term=.18c2697df044 (accessed 6 August 2018).

Pohl, Florian. 2006. "Islamic Education and Civil Society: Reflections on the Pesantren Tradition in Contemporary Indonesia". *Comparative Education Review* 50, no. 3: 389–409.

Pribadi, Yanwar. 2008. "Jawara in Banten: Their Socio-Political Roles in the New Order Era 1966–1998". MA thesis, Department of Islamic Studies, Leiden University.

———. 2013. "Another Side of Islam in Banten: The Socio-Political Roles of Jawara during the New Order Era 1966–1998". *Journal of Indonesian Islam* 7, no. 2: 314–36.

———. 2018. *Islam, State and Society in Indonesia: Local Politics in Madura*. London and New York: Brill.

———. 2019a. "Fragmentasi Umat dan Penciptaan Otoritas Keagamaan: Tanggapan terhadap 'Islam Lokal' dan 'Islam Asing' di Indonesia". *Jurnal Masyarakat dan Budaya* 21, no. 1: 103–20.

———. 2019b. "Komodifikasi Islam dalam Ekonomi Pasar: Studi tentang Muslim Perkotaan di Banten". *Afkaruna: Indonesian Interdisciplinary Journal of Islamic Studies* 15, no. 1: 82–112.

Rachmatika, Pandu. 2014. "Why Avoid Political Polarization?". *Jakarta Post*, 21 June 2014. http://www.thejakartapost.com/news/2014/06/21/why-avoid-political-polarization.html (accessed 6 August 2018).

Rakhmani, Inaya. 2014. "The Commercialization of Da'wah: Understanding Indonesian Sinetron and Their Portrayal of Islam". *The International Communication Gazette* 76, nos. 4–5: 340–59.

Ricklefs, M.C. 2013. "Religious Elites and the State in Indonesia and Elsewhere: Why Takeovers are so Difficult and Usually Don't Work". In *Encountering Islam: The Politics of Religious Identities in Southeast Asia*, edited by Hui Yew-Foong, pp. 17–46. Singapore: Institute of Southeast Asian Studies.

Rinaldo, Rachel. 2008. "Muslim Women, Middle Class Habitus, and Modernity in Indonesia". *Contemporary Islam* 2: 23–39.

Rudnyckyj, Daromir. 2009. "Power Pointing Islam: Form and Spiritual Reform in Reformasi Indonesia". In *Mediating Piety: Technology and Religion in Contemporary Asia*, edited by Francis Khek Gee Lim, pp. 91–112. Leiden and Boston: Brill.

Sakai, Minako and Amelia Fauzia. 2014. "Islamic Orientations in Contemporary Indonesia: Islamism on the Rise?". *Asian Ethnicity* 15, no. 1: 41–61.

Salvatore, Armando and Dale Eickelman. 2004. "Preface: Pubic Islam and the Common Good". In *Public Islam and the Common Good*, edited by Armando Salvatore and Dale Eickelman, pp. xi–xxv. Leiden and Boston: Brill.

Seo, Myengkyo. 2012. "Defining 'Religious' in Indonesia: Toward Neither an Islamic nor a Secular State". *Citizenship Studies* 16, no. 8: 1045–58.

Suara Pembaruan. 2013. "Starbucks Bikin Larangan Merokok 7,26 Meter dari Gerai". *Suara Pembaruan*, 4 June 2013. http://sp.beritasatu.com/metropolitan/ratusan-masyarakat-banten-melakukan-long-march-dari-serang-menuju-jakarta/117629 (accessed 3 August 2018).

Tan, Charlene. 2011. *Islamic Education and Indoctrination: The Case in Indonesia*. London and New York: Routledge.

Tanuwidjaja, Sunny. 2010. "Political Islam and Islamic Parties in Indonesia: Critically Assessing the Evidence of Islam's Political Decline". *Contemporary Southeast Asia: A Journal of International and Strategic Affairs* 32, no. 1: 29–49.

Tihami, M.A. 1992. "Kiyai dan Jawara di Banten: Studi Tentang Agama, Magi, dan Kepemimpinan di Desa Pasanggrahan Serang, Banten". MA thesis, Department of Anthropology, Universitas Indonesia.

Ufen, Andreas. 2009. "Mobilising Political Islam: Indonesia and Malaysia Compared". *Commonwealth & Comparative Politics* 47, no. 3: 308–33.

van Bruinessen, Martin. 2015. "Ghazwul Fikri or Arabization? Indonesian Muslim Responses to Globalization". In *Southeast Asian Muslims in the Era of Globalization*, edited by Ken Miichi and Omar Farouk, pp. 61–85. Basingstoke: Palgrave Macmillan.

Vatikiotis, Panayiotis J. 1991. *Islam and the State*. London and New York: Routledge.

Ward, Ken. 2009. "Non-Violent Extremists? Hizbut Tahrir Indonesia". *Australian Journal of International Affairs* 63, no. 2: 149–64.

Wilson, Ian Douglas. 2003. "The Politics of Inner Power: The Practice of Pencak Silat in West Java". PhD thesis, Murdoch University.

Woodward, Mark. 2011. *Java, Indonesia and Islam*. London and New York: Springer.

Woodward, Mark, Ali Amin, Inayah Rohmaniyah, and Chris Lundry. 2013. "Getting Culture: A New Path for Indonesia's Islamist Justice and Prosperity Party". *Contemporary Islam* 7: 173–89.

13

THE RISE OF COOL *USTADZ*: PREACHING, SUBCULTURES AND THE *PEMUDA HIJRAH* MOVEMENT

Wahyudi Akmaliah

Introduction

Like many other women her age, Juliah Indah, an urban girl studying at Al-Azhar University in Jakarta, is active on Instagram (a social media platform). Yet, unlike many others, she is a "micro-celebrity" with 95,100 followers online. I first met her when she took an internship at the Research Center for Regional Resources at the Indonesian Institute of Sciences (PSDR-LIPI) as part of the mandatory requirements for her study in International Relations in October 2017. She introduced me to a young Islamic preacher, Ustadz Hanan Attaki, whom she and many of her friends were fans, and who is also known by his acronym UHA. For her, most Islamic preachers tend to deliver Islamic sermons and doctrine in a patronizing manner by expecting their followers to agree with them. She also regards their messages as missing many essential points. Juliah, however, regards UHA differently. In only a matter of one minute, he can make her understand the essence of his lectures uploaded to his Instagram. UHA's sermons leave a strong imprint in her memory. She can clearly recall his words, which at times bring her to tears. She often listens to the sermons while driving in Jakarta. For Juliah, he is the coolest *ustadz* (Interview, 4 October 2017).

The Islamic preaching scene in Indonesia has evolved significantly. Decades ago, there was a preacher by the name of Zainuddin MZ, who held the title of a preacher for *One Million Ummah* (Dai Sejuta Umat) through the circulation of his cassettes, and that he signed a contract with Virgo Record during Suharto regime. He transformed Islamic preaching from the traditional way into a pop culture and reached out to a mass audience (Zainuddin 1997). Following this, the change of the television landscape from having only one state channel to a few private television stations at the beginning of the 1990s opened up opportunities for Islamic televangelists (Muzakki 2012; Rakhmani 2016). Furthermore, unlike the one-directional media of television and radio, social media has changed the pattern and form of communication. Social media is highly fluid and multi-directional. Social media, which has a democratic and egalitarian character, is able to access information on specific events in real-time and is faster in transmission than both radio and television broadcasts. This pattern allows new Islamic preachers to enrich the lives of their audiences. Their presence inevitably has challenged the established religious authorities—primarily Muhammadiyah and Nahdlatul Ulama (NU) (Eickelman and Anderson 2003).

Many scholars have discussed the role of the Internet with regards to Islamic preaching (Lim 2005; Barker 2005; Hosen 2008; Barendregt 2009). These scholars show the continuity of how Islamic preaching has developed with the growth of digital technologies. Slama (2017, pp. 98–99), through his study of social media, focuses on the WhatsApp mobile application, which he considers to be the most popular social media chatting platform in Indonesia for Islamic preachers to converse with their members. WhatsApp is used not only for members to discuss issues related to Islam in their everyday life, especially after their meetings in person during gatherings (*pengajian*), it also serves as an avenue for preachers to solve their followers' problems. Separately, the application became the backbone of a social movement in the country that aims "to revive the spirit of Quran reading" which has succeeded in recruiting more than 140,000 followers, nationally and internationally, through the One Day One Just (ODOJ) movement (Nisa 2018b; Muslim 2017).

Social media platforms—such as Facebook, Twitter, Instagram, and YouTube—can host unlimited number of followers and users. Because of this structure, both institutions and individuals from diverse Islamic groups compete for followers, in order to shape and channel their interests. Weng (2018) shows the intersection between online and offline activities by highlighting the figure of Felix Siauw, who employs three digital platforms (Facebook, Twitter, and YouTube). He asserts that Felix Siauw uses social media platforms to influence young Indonesian Muslims with HTI ideology. On Facebook usage, Halim (2018) investigates the community of *pesantren*, mainly in South Sulawesi. On the one hand, the community uses it as a medium for teaching and their appropriation with technology modernity. On the other hand, it is a networking tool to maintain a reputation among other *pesantren*. Meanwhile, Nisa (2018a) focuses on young Indonesian Muslim women and their usage of Instagram for various kinds of Islamic preaching lucratively.

Various scholars examine the contribution of social media to Islam and how digital media platforms are related to political Islam and revolutions in the Middle East (Bunt 2003; Bräuchler 2003; Lim 2013). Enriched by these studies, this chapter examines UHA and his movement. I look at the *Pemuda Hijrah*, which uses both Instagram and YouTube as a form of Islamic preaching to reach out to young Indonesian Muslims. In contrast to established Islamic learning styles, they changed their methods of preaching following the subculture's lifestyle and the symbols associated with it: they adjust their clothes, appearance, and rhetorical styles to attract young audiences. Because of this, UHA's followers have increased dramatically. Indeed, his followers are often on a lookout for his latest sermons. Due to the massive number of UHA's followers, he rarely delivers sermons at the Al-Latief Mosque—his home base as well as the space of the *Pemuda Hijrah* movement. All of UHA's sermons were organized at the most significant and substantial mosque. The mosque of Transtudio in Bandung became one of such places to accommodate his classes.

This chapter explores data from UHA and the *Pemuda Hijrah's* digital platforms, both Instagram and YouTube. It also features accounts from interviewees who worked behind the scenes for him (Campbell and Vitullo 2016). I strengthen this by attending some of the gatherings organized by the *Pemuda Hijrah*. This chapter raises three questions: what is the context that makes UHA and the people behind him establish the *Pemuda Hijrah*? What is their *dakwah* when approaching young Muslims in Indonesia? How does his preaching method demonstrate contemporary Islamic practices in Indonesia? This chapter argues that the city of Bandung is the primary site of the subculture movement in Indonesia. It provides the necessary context that encourages UHA and his campaign to wield significant influence, both during offline Islamic gatherings and through the online means of posting texts, videos, and images through social media posting. By employing the subculture lifestyle, which is increasingly prosperous, they are not only successful in differentiating themselves from other Islamic preaching methods, but also in reaching out to new audiences. Nevertheless, they continue to face challenges from other subculture groups in Bandung, and also from their own members.

Paradoxes of Bandung: Between Cosmopolitanism and Conservatism

The Dutch colonial government established Bandung by incorporating "historical orientation to global modernity and cosmopolitan culture" (Martin-Iverson 2011, p. 7) for tourism, trade, and education. Recommended by Ir R. Van Hoevell, it was a transit city for the Europeans before going to other cities. Until today, the city retains various aspects of European heritage. Prominent buildings that are a part of the colonial legacy include Gedung Merdeka (Independence Building) and the buildings around Braga and Asia-Africa Street. The city has long been a popular place for students and foreign tourists since Indonesia gained independence from the Dutch in 1945 (Iskandar 2003). Also, due to its relatively close proximity to Jakarta (i.e. it is approximately 180 km southeast of Jakarta), the city has been regarded as an essential city by every Indonesian president, such that numerous state events were organized there. Up to now, one of the most prestigious meetings that took place in this city was the Bandung Conference on 18–24 April 1955. It was hosted by President Sukarno to invite new countries, independent from their former colonial masters, to form a new block to discuss Afro-Asian cooperation.

Bandung, which is home to many state and private universities, has become the centre for a range of cultural practices, including counterculture from various urban communities. Some scholars (Iskandar 2003; Takeshita 2011; Kim 2017) divide the cultural practices into three periods dealing with the emergence of subculture. Firstly, the pop culture period of the 1970s. A group of young people in Bandung, consisting of Sonny Suriaatmadja, Denny Sabri Gandanegara, and Remy Sylado, created a local magazine, *Aktuil*. It contained counter-narratives towards information produced by the mass media and provided an alternative to western pop cultures such as westernized rock music and lifestyle. During the 1960s and the 1970s, this magazine was trendy among young people, especially in several big cities. For two years (1973–74), the magazine broke sales records by selling 126,000 copies and became a trendsetter (Iskandar 2003; Takeshita 2011; Kim 2017).

The 1980s were referred to as the street culture period. The skateboard community, for instance, formed the embryo of the BMX bicycle society after the establishment of a small skate park in Lalu Lintas (Taman Ade Irma Suryani). Members wore t-shirts, jeans, and sneakers supplied by those who had established independent clothing shops' distro. This community later became associated with the underground music communities (punk, hardcore, and metal groups) in the third period of the 1990s, as the independent music and fashion scene well-known in cultural studies and sociology developed the subculture with the spirit of "Do It Yourself" (DIY) (Iskandar 2003; Takeshita 2011; Kim 2017). The term is a part of their independent culture and lifestyle as a counter-narrative in Indonesia, imported from underground ideologies (Wallach 2008). Bandung became the site of creative industries developed by the city's youth with their divergent interests.

The cosmopolitan outlook of Bandung has led to some scholars exploring the religious practices of the city. These scholars are interested in whether the practice of Islam is "moderate" and reflective of their lifestyle, or whether it tends to be more conservative. Mudzakkir (2016) uses Ahmad Hasan and his Islamic organization, Persis (Persatuan Islam/Islamic Union) as a case study. According to him, in the early twentieth century, Persis was an Islamic organization that fought against traditional practices that did not adequately follow the strictures of the Quran and Hadith. Ahmad Hasan and his organization became involved in numerous tensions with many Islamic Muslims groups, including challenging a number of Islamic religious, traditional groups (*kiai*), especially from Nahdlatul Ulama. Rosyad (1995) confirms the strong influence of Persis in their dealings with the Islamic Tarbiyah during the post-Suharto regime, and the group later changed its name to Prosperous Justice Party (Partai Keadilan Sejahtera/PKS). For Rosyad (1995), the presence of Tarbiyah is a continuation of a long-standing *tajdid* (renewal) tradition in Islam following the Koran and Sunnah. Inspired by Ikhwanul Muslimin (Muslim Brotherhood) in the global context, it would like the Tajdid movement to solve various problems of the Muslim community.

In the province of West Java, which Bandung is a part of, sharia law is implemented. However, it is not enforced in Bandung, thus earning it the title of a moderate city. However, Millie and Safei (2010) have criticized the "Religious Bandung" programme proposed by Mayor Dada Rosada. The public in the city considered him as being too secular because he does not have a *santri* background (i.e. coming from an Islamic boarding school). He approached some Islamic leaders who perceived that Islam had been marginalized in Bandung's public life. The programme somehow targeted the city's night entertainment and cultural life, which had existed for years. K.H. Athian Ali Da'i warned the night clubs that they do not represent the face of Islam. In order to prove himself as a religious person, Dada closed the red-light district of Saritem, which is located close to the Bandung train station. For Millie and Safei (2010), this is an example of how conservative Muslim groups have used Islamic identity to enforce their interest on public morality. In another case, Dada banned Dewi Persik's *dangdut* musical performance. Millie and Safie (2010) asked "whether this very same plurality will be threatened by its practical implementation".

The above outline shows the socio-cultural paradox of Bandung. On the one hand, it showcases urban lifestyles, with the subcultural practices influenced by the West. On the other hand, on religious matters, there are Islamic hardline groups, reinforcing conservative values in the name of Islam during Mayor Dada's administration. This paradox explains the emergence of UHA and other Islamic pop preachers such as Evie Effendi and Handy Bonny in Bandung. By marrying symbols of subculture and lifestyles, as well as the conservative values in Islam, they differentiate themselves from other Islamic preachers in Indonesia.

Ustadz Hanan Attaki (UHA) and the *Pemuda Hijrah*

UHA was born in Aceh on 31 December 1981. After finishing his junior and senior high school education in Ruhul Islam Islamic boarding school (Pondok Pesantren) in Banda Aceh, he studied Quran exegesis (*tafsir*) for his BA in Al-Azhar University, Egypt. He then moved to Bandung to join his wife, Haneen Akira. She found a job with Ma'had Al-Imarat in 2007, an Islamic institution established through cooperation between the Muhammadiyah central leadership and Asian Muslim Charity Foundation, which focuses on teaching Arabic (Interview with Bejo, 14 April 2018). As a newcomer to Bandung, he found it challenging to find a job. He applied for many jobs at Islamic institutions and boarding schools in Bandung, but he could not get a job as an Islamic teacher. With the Arabic mastery, he translated a book with the hope of getting it published, but this too was turned down by many publishers.

Moreover, the book he translated was already proposed by another translator (Hanan Attaki 2017a).

He started to write a book entitled *Tadabur Al-Quran* [Reflecting and Understanding the Meaning of the Quran]. After working hard for one month on the book, he could not find a publisher. Hence, he decided to self-publish for a total of 300 copies. The profits made from the book were later used as the capital to fund his cell phone business, which he established sixty stores in Bandung. Nevertheless, he lost his money from this business (Hanan Attaki 2017a) and went back to teaching religion at Jendela Hati and STQ Habiburrahman, focusing on memorizing the Quran. He then moved to the Salman House of Quran at the Institute of Bandung Technology (ITB), and became its director (Wink 2018). His background as an Al-Azhar graduate, his mastery of the Arabic language, and his ability to recite the Quran well led to his prominence as a religious teacher in Bandung. He also became an Islamic teacher as well as a preacher in many mosques in Bandung.

While delivering sermons at the Al-Latief Mosque, he saw some young people among his followers. One of those was Fani Krismandar, also known as Inong. Due to this first meeting with UHA, members of Al-Latief Mosque and Inong suggested the formation of a new movement. Before meeting Inong, UHA was like other Islamic preachers coming back from the Middle East: in fashion sense and teaching styles, often wearing Arabic garments, cloak, and turban. His Islamic teachings mainly deal with the Quran and Hadith, without contextualizing the social background of the audiences. UHA gave numerous sermons in mosques throughout Bandung, but his outreach remained relatively small. Inong helped him by establishing *Pemuda Hijrah*, which contributed significantly to his rise at the national level.

Inong is a famous skateboarder in Jakarta, Surabaya, Yogyakarta, and other islands apart from Java. Born in 1982, he started skateboarding in 1992 and graduated from the college of visual design communication of Widyatama University. He has participated in many national and international skateboarding competitions. Through these competitions, he received sponsorships from the clothing label UNKL 247, a reputable company known for upholding street culture nationally and globally (Luvaas 2013). The company chose him to be both an ambassador rider and a creative designer. His most significant contribution was to raise the profile of youth street culture, attracting the youth towards skateboarding and surfing (Interview with Inong, 14 April 2018). One of Inong's most influential contributions to the skateboarding culture in Bandung was a movement known as "We Build This City", which was financially supported by UNKL 247.[1]

Two factors led him to seriously reconsider his career as a skateboarder. Firstly, many injuries impacted his ability to perform jumps and other tricks. The physical toll on his body led him to take up surfing as a substitute. Secondly, the death of his father made him spend more time taking care of his mother at home. This fostered a sense of inner tranquility. He then initiated a new company, 247 plies, under the brand of UNKL 247. He also became a more reflective person bringing him to the mosque, where he frequently listened to sermons. He finally decided to choose UHA as his favourite preacher (Interview with Inong, 14 April 2018). Therefore, when UHA wanted to create a *dakwah* community, Inong was a willing member. Given his knowledge in design and experiences dealing with street culture, he was able to assist in raising UHA's profile and establishing the *Pemuda Hijrah*.

The *Pemuda Hijrah* Tagline and Their Audiences

In March 2015, with Inong and a few others, Hanan Attaki established *Pemuda Hijrah*. In order to give the movement an image of not being too Islamic, Inong proposed the name *Shift* as an alternative to *Hijrah* from the Arabic word. The word "shift" refers to the computer keyboard key symbolizing to "move" and to "transform", and represents Hijrah in Islam. However, when *the Shift* was used to create an Instagram account, it was already taken up by other people. The *Shift* then became the symbol of *Pemuda Hijrah* (Interview with Inong, 14 April 2018). Meanwhile, the term "Hijrah" initially comes from Prophet Muhammad's migration from Mecca to Medina in 622 CE to escape violence and persecution by the Arab elites of Mecca. The event has then been extended to mean "the withdrawal from the un-Islamic path to a new 'correct pathway'" by many Islamists (Nisa 2018b, p. 74). However, fundamentalist thinkers and their followers, mainly Sayyid Abū al-A'lā Mawdūdī (1903–79) and the Jamā'at-i Islāmī in Pakistan and Sayyid Quṭb (1906–66) of the Muslim Brotherhood in Egypt, considered Hijrah as an ideology (Yusuf 2009).

In the Indonesian context, Hijrah represents the identity of Islamist movements such as Salafi groups, Hizbut Tahrir Indonesia, and the Tarbiyah movement. Hijrah has also become the tagline of UHA's sermons. Specifically, the meaning of Hijrah for him, as cited by Saefullah (2017, p. 276), is not only the physically movement from the land of infidels (*kuffar*) to the land of the believers (such as the migration of

Prophet Muhammad), but also as a metaphoric meaning by ridding one of sins and all things God forbids, or in other words, total repentance (*taubatan an-nasuuha*). UHA and the *Pemuda Hijrah* concentrated on reaching out to youth audiences. Inong divided his proselytizing targets into four types: mainly activists, sympathizers, neutral or uncommitted people, and those who are against the movement, or "the contra people". They only focused on the third and fourth categories due to the presence of many Islamic organizations concentrating on the first two. Consequently, many Islamic preaching groups do not involve young people. UHA also asserted this during his delivery of a sermon in Pondok Pesantren (Islamic Boarding School) of Daarul Amanta, Kediri, East Java, on 17 December 2016. He reaffirmed the young as his target audience. His speech was then recorded and uploaded by *Lampu Islam.Net* on YouTube on 1 October 2017.[2]

FIGURE 13.1
Map of the *Pemuda Hijrah's* Islamic Preaching Target Audience

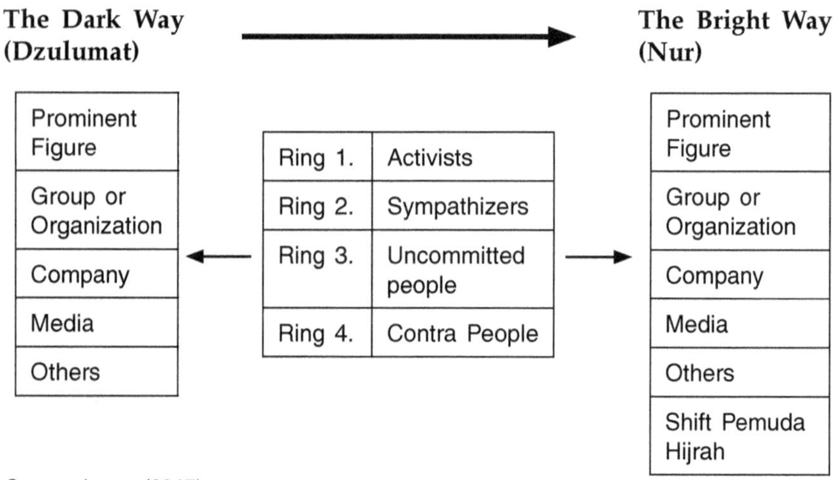

| The Dark Way (Dzulumat) | → | The Bright Way (Nur) |

| Prominent Figure |
| Group or Organization |
| Company |
| Media |
| Others |

Ring 1.	Activists
Ring 2.	Sympathizers
Ring 3.	Uncommitted people
Ring 4.	Contra People

| Prominent Figure |
| Group or Organization |
| Company |
| Media |
| Others |
| Shift Pemuda Hijrah |

Source: Inong (2017).

Therefore, understanding youth culture is significant for this movement. Inong's presence and his experience with street culture provided the most significant contribution in developing *Pemuda Hijrah's* impact. He did so not only by capitalizing on his knowledge and experience, but he also explored the current youth national and global cultural trends deeply. Firstly, he conducted offline activities, such as interviewing students in Bandung. With his team, Inong often interviewed students regarding their perception of Islam and social issues, such as wearing the veil, Islamic law, Islamic organization, as well as the informants' hobbies. This qualitative research then contributed to the team's design of Islamic preaching contents and how these can represent the youths, especially on social issues related to love, entertainment, and family. Moreover, UHA also changed his appearance to be identified as a young hipster by wearing beanies and t-shirts.

Secondly, he also utilizes online activities to deliver his messages. Here, they focus on Instagram and YouTube because these are popular among the youths, visually attractive, and easily accessible. Although Facebook is the most popular social media platform in Indonesia, Instagram is the most popular platform among the youths. According to Hansa Salva, Director of Taylor Nelson Sofres (TNS) Indonesia, about 90 per cent of Indonesian youths use Instagram. Instagram users also consist of people of other age groups: 59 per cent of the users are between 18 and 24 years old; 30 per cent are between 25 and 34 years old; and the rest belong to the 35–44 age group. In terms of gender proportion, Instagram users are mostly women (tempo.co 2016). Meanwhile, for YouTube, it is an open channel for the public to upload and share videos.

These two considerations encourage them to create accounts on Instagram and YouTube: mainly @pemudahijrah for their social movement and @hanan_attaki for UHA's Instagram; and Hanan Attaki as well as *Pemuda Hijrah* for YouTube. The name "@pemudahijrah" on Instagram came about unintentionally. One of his team members wanted to use the name "Shift", however, it was already being used. He then chose "@pemudahijrah". This username was previously rejected by Inong because he felt that it was too early to use the name as the *dakwah* strategy, which may give a negative perception of Islamic preaching to the Indonesian public. Nevertheless, in this case, Inong was proven wrong. The *Pemuda Hijrah* becomes the new trend in the Hijrah movement in Indonesia.

Micro-*Ustadz* Celebrity

Both the online and offline activities have raised UHA's profile as well as that of *Pemuda Hijrah* in Indonesia. According to a survey conducted by the Center for the Study of Islam and Society (Pusat Pengkajian Islam dan Masyarakat/PPIM), UHA has been categorized as a moderate religious teacher on social media, on par with prominent figures such as Mamah Dedeh, Abdullah Gymnastiar, Yusuf Mansur, Quraish Shihab,

Din Syamsuddin, Said Aqil Siradj, Ma'ruf Amin, Mustofa Bisri, Maulana, Syafi'i Maarif, Teh Ninih, Haedar Nashir, Oki Setiana Dewi, and Ulil Abshar Abdalla (Convey Indonesia 2018). In comparison to these other prominent religious figures who have established their careers for years, how does UHA obtain popularity even though he was never featured on national television? In part, the death of Jefri Al Buchori on 26 April 2013 created a vacuum for Islamic preachers representing Indonesian Muslim youths. Nevertheless, this argument alone is not enough to explain the rise of UHA, without factoring his use of pop culture and capitalizing on Bandung's subculture environment.

UHA's offline activities were able to attract a young audience for two reasons. Firstly, excellent infrastructure and a friendly environment were provided for, such as spaces for prayers, and improvements to the design of the Al-Latief Mosque for youths to hang out with their friends. In every corner of the mosque, there are many electrical points where people can charge their smartphones freely. This mosque with such a friendly environment entices the youths to visit, and they do not have to demonstrate Islamic attributes such as *peci*, *sarung*, and *koko* shirt (traditional Malay-Indonesian men Muslim shirt which is worn during religious occasions). Many of them enjoy coming to the mosque for their daily prayers without any judgments imposed on what they are wearing. During my three-day observation at the mosque, there were roughly 200 people at the *Maghrib* (dusk prayer) and *Isya* prayers (evening prayer). As a small mosque located in an urban area, those numbers are quite significant.

Secondly, the youth community is also welcomed to join activities at the mosque. One of the reasons why many youths are interested to join the classes is because they are invited by their friends to do so. Hendra, a young man who works at a motorcycle servicing shop, shared that he became a member of the Shift movement due to a friend's invitation. He felt that UHA's sermons and some of the Islamic teachers from the Al-Latief Mosque suited him. This also happened with Yoga, a young man who works at Ace Hardware and came to the classes due to his friend's invitation. Both Hendra and Yoga were then invited to involve their friends to join the classes. Meanwhile, Pevi Permana, the first Indonesian professional skateboarder recognized internationally, was invited by his friend, Inong. Inong had been inviting him for two years, coming to his office and home every week before he finally accepted the invitation and attended an Islamic study group session (*kajian*). He later got deeply involved in *Pemuda Hijrah* (Pevi Permana 2017).

One significant event that reaches out to a broad audience is "Brigez Berzikir untuk Indonesia" [Brigez utter Allah's name repeatedly in remembrance for Indonesia]. Ustadz Arifin Ilham—a veteran religious preacher—led the *zikir* attended by around 1,500 people from the Brigez motorcycle gang who were committed to repent (*bertaubat*) in the Agung Mosque located in Bandung. In front of Arifin Ilham, they promised to do useful activities and rid any negative perceptions in the society towards them (detik.com, 23 February 2015). UHA and the Shift movement initially created this event as a pilot project. This event then encouraged other motorcycle gangsters to organize similar events (Hanan Attaki 2017b).

Regarding their online activities, UHA and the *Pemuda Hijrah* upload both videos and photos which match popular taste within the subculture community life. They produce two products: a short video well-known as *a one-minute booster;* and a lengthy sermon. For the one-minute booster, the video contains UHA's speeches (accompanied with background music) focusing on social problems faced by young people and how to resolve them by bringing themselves back to Allah and Islamic teachings. The longer videos provide recordings of UHA's sermons and that of other Islamic preachers within the Shift movement in various mosques. The photos are used to make announcements of the weekly Islamic teachings at the Al-Latief Mosque. The photos, which are uploaded to Instagram, draw on the symbols and references often practised in contemporary pop culture found in youth magazines such as the *Rolling Stone* and the *Hai*. The *Pemuda Hijrah* is seeking to transform the image of Islamic gatherings, which are often regarded as being too normative and old fashioned.

UHA and the *Pemuda Hijrah* have many followers on both Instagram and YouTube. Currently, the @hanan_attaki account has over 7.9 million followers, and the @pemudahijrah account has over 1.9 million followers. The reason why UHA's followers are more prominent compared to @pemudahijrah is due to Inong's desire to centralize UHA's figure image amid Indonesian society, which idolizes personalities more than organizations. Consequently, the Shift movement, as a mechanism to build *Pemuda Hijrah*, must take a step back from his popularity. The online activities have established UHA as one of the most popular Indonesian Islamic preachers or micro-*ustadz* celebrity. Senft (2008) applies the theory micro-celebrity to discuss how people utilize "new style of online performance" that can "amp up" their popularity through digital platforms such as videos, blogs, and social networks like social media. Indeed, Marwick and Boyd (2010, p. 121) explain the term clearly as the people who have "an audience they can strategically maintain through ongoing communication and interaction".

Challenging Religious Authority and Its Impact

The UHA example demonstrates how a preacher can obtain his popularity through digital media platforms in the Indonesian public. With creativity and innovation and coupled with offline efforts, anyone can be micro-celebrities. Their fate will be decided by how netizens perceive their content videos. Because of this, social media has replaced the role of television that previously supported popular preachers or televangelists such as Abdullah Gymnastiar, Arifin Ilham, Yusuf Mansur, and Mamah Dedeh. The phenomenon of micro-*ustadz* celebrity can provide alternative religious teachings suitable for a society dominated by Muhammadiyah and Nahdlatul Ulama (NU). Unlike television channels that have some requirements and procedural administration before running programmes, the limited intervention in social media can bring challenges. There are three possibilities of how the emergence of UHA and the *Pemudah Hijrah* can be disruptive.

Firstly, what is the fate of moderate Muslims in Indonesia? Many scholars argue that Indonesia is in the midst of a "conservative turn". The series of Aksi Bela Islam demonstrations against Basuki Tjahaja Purnama as the Governor of DKI Jakarta that led him to be jailed for two years is an example of how Muhammadiyah and NU could not stop conservatism. It shows that new religious authorities have a voice within Indonesian Muslim society. In regards to this, by observing UHA's videos, I find that most of them do not carry any statement inclined towards conservatism or Islamic politics, and most of his sermons discuss problems of youth's daily life with Islamic resources as the solution. Nevertheless, his short statement in a sermon that supported the 212 movements indirectly demonstrated his political interest or an Islamist supporting trans-Islamic ideology.[3] However, the use of pop culture and subculture symbols create what Muller (2015) regards as a "pop-Islamist".

Secondly, he is threatening the subculture community. The *Pemuda Hijrah* movement, on the one hand, is a form of transformation of the proselytization of Islamic preaching in Indonesia. On the other hand, this method can challenge the subculture lives which have different aims. To manage these conflicting interests, Inong often oversees the symbols employing subculture's taste. However, he once posted pictures containing symbols of a Punk music underground community, as a form of resistance. Ucok Homicide, one of the voices of the Bandung underground music scene, recorded his objection due to unrelated use of its symbol. Moreover, some of their previous friends who have already become Hijrah members have a different orientation. Instead of keeping the underground's principles that treat the military and fascism as their most prominent, they partly support the Front Pembela Islam's (FPI) violence and illegal activities in Bandung (Interview with Ucok Homicide, 17 April 2018). The emergence of the *Pemuda Hijrah* then has caused tension. Although they are not changing what their members are wearing, however, they are trying to replace those subculture communities' ideologies with those that are in line with UHA and the *Pemuda Hijrah's* perspective.

Thirdly, it has an impact on personal relations. When people become members of the *Pemuda Hijrah*, they must leave behind their negative past. Conversely, they must follow the Quran and Hadith strictly following their preacher's views. Apart from personal transformation, they also have the mandate to invite the people around them to the movement. This may result in changes to the relationships they have with their closest friends and family. It happens with how Linda (Interview with Linda, 17 April 2018), one of my informants who works in one of the non-governmental organizations in Bandung, deal with her boyfriend, who got involved with *Pemuda Hijrah* since 2014. After following the *kajian*, his life changed dramatically, and he stopped her from listening to music and required her to wear the veil. The rise of the Ahok case in 2016 becomes a heated discussion between them, and tensions arose. Later, they discussed the role of women at home. Because of this, they broke their engagement in 2016, even though they had been best friends since they were in junior high school. Linda felt she could not live together with her former fiancé.

Conclusion

This chapter discusses the emergence of UHA and his organization, the *Pemuda Hijrah*, in the Indonesian public sphere. The integration of both social networks online and offline has seen them emerge as a new alternative religious authority that differentiates them from other well-known Islamic preachers. UHA was able to adjust to the psychology of the youth audience. Instead of talking about what is and is not permitted in Islam, they discuss youth's social problems and seek solutions to bring them back to both Allah and the Quran and Hadith. To attract an audience from a diverse background, they also employ pop culture and subculture products, such as movies, music, and fashion. Offline activities support online practices and complement one another. The two offline activities are establishing a youth-friendly environment in the mosque and inviting both ordinary people and social media influencers who wield a strong following in their communities.

This creative *dakwah* approach is currently not found in other Indonesian cities where the youth populations are predominant, such as Jakarta, Yogyakarta, Surabaya, Semarang, and Makassar. Bandung's history being a Dutch colonial city contributed to its cosmopolitanism landscape. Consequently, this legacy was inherited by the emergence of a pop culture to counterbalance the Sukarno presidency. The power of cosmopolitanism as a social capital created many subcultures and their associated industries with the spirit of DIY. Although the Bandung society accommodates cosmopolitan values, their religious expression tends to be conservative. The presence of Persis is part of this conservative narrative.

Nationally, UHA has become a micro-*ustadz* celebrity rivalling other Islamic preachers in Indonesia. He has become the idol of many young Indonesian Muslims and sets an example of how to be a good Muslim. Nevertheless, his Islamist leanings have remained a question compared with the most prominent Muslim organizations that represent moderate Islam.

NOTES

1. Due to Bandung streets being unconducive for skateboarding, with his friends, Inong built some of the infrastructure of Bandung streets to make them suitable both for the pedestrians and skateboarders. Pretending to be official workers in Bandung city, they built the guard rail in the Bandung pedestrian street. This guard rail serves to protect the pedestrian walk while allowing the pedestrians to hold the rail and walk along the road. Nonetheless, to a skateboarder, it is helpful for gliding. It is the same with the dustbin box, which is created from an iron material. Besides storing garbage, the dustbin box serves as a base for skateboarders to jump. This idea has not only been adopted in many other cities in Indonesia, but it is also an inspiration to develop the indigenization of street culture in Indonesia with many differences and difficulties compared to that overseas (Inong 2014).

2. From the beginning, I see *dakwah* in Indonesia as tending to progress slowly and reaching a dead end, especially for the youth. Islamic preaching focused mainly on events, while most of the members previously are possibly Hijrah (move on to be a religious person). Because of this, few people obtain God's guidance, although there are many events related to it. Some mosques have identified with the youth in Bandung. Some of these mosques are the mosque of Salman ITB, Istiqomah, and Al-Furqon, located in the Indonesia University of Education (Universitas Pendidikan Indonesia/UPI). When the mosque of Istiqomah holds an event, the attendees come from both the mosques of Salman and Al-Furqon. Conversely, when Al-Furqon has an event, the members come from the other two mosques. So these events are rotating among them. Because of this *dakwah* concept, it creates a gap between those youths who need God's guidance but do not know how to achieve it, and those who have received God's guidance and know how to access it (Hanan Attaki 2017b).

3. Therefore, I would like to support our friends, especially *dakwah hijrah* (*proselytization hijrah*). The segment audience for *dakwah hijrah* is not for those who have already moved on (*hijrah*). Those are well-known as *dakwah tarbiyah;* coaching, and educating. Meanwhile, the *dakwah hijrah* is for those who do not understand Islam. Indeed, those who fear Islam. Also, those who did not participate in the 212 movement and expressed hatred to the event. They are not our enemy. They are the goal target of our *dakwah*. Therefore, if there is proposed the question of why we must have do protest and created the crowded mass by practicing the Jum'at praying on the street, instead of praying in the mosques, they are not our enemy. They are our *dakwah* market. If they are not joining yet, we have still homework. Instead of shouting in oration for those who are not joining as *munnafik* (hypocrite) and the rests are involving are *mukmin haqqa* (a true believer), it can break among Muslim solidarity. Therefore, we do proselytize them with different treatment comparing to *tarbiyah* proselytization. We must be patient with many changes (Hanan Attaki 2017b).

REFERENCES

Barendregt, Bart. 2009. "Mobile Religiosity in Indonesia: Mobilized Islam, Islamized Mobility and the Potential of Islamic Techno Nationalism". In *Living the Information Society in Asia*, edited by Erwin Alampay, pp. 73–92. Singapore: Institute of Southeast Asian Studies.

Barker, Joshua. 2005. "Engineers and Political Dreams: Indonesia in the Satellite Age". *Current Anthropology* 46, no. 5 (December): 703–27.

Bräuchler, Birgit. 2003. "Cyber Identities at War: Religion, Identity, and the Internet in the Moluccan Conflict". *Indonesia* 75: 123–51.

Bunt, Gary R. 2003. *Islam in the Digital Age: e-Jihad, Online Fatwas and Cyber Islamic Environments*. London: Pluto Books, 2003.
Campbell, Heidi A. and Alessandra Vitullo. 2016. "Assessing Changes in the Study of Religious Communities in Digital Religion Studies". *Church, Communication and Culture* 1, no. 1: 73–89.
Convey Indonesia. 2018. "Sikap Intoleran Gen Z: Kemudahan Akses Pembelajaran Agama Secara Instan". *Convey Indonesia*, 10 November 2018. https://conveyindonesia.com/api-dalam-sekam-intoleransi/2017/11/10/sikap-intoleran-gen-z-kemudahan-akses-pembelajaran-agama-secara-instan/ (accessed 8 May 2018).
detik.com. 2015. "Alasan 1.500 Anggota Geng Motor Brigez Tobat Bareng Arifin Ilham". detik.com, 23 February 2015. https://news.detik.com/berita/2839747/alasan-1500-anggota-geng-motor-brigez-tobat-bareng-arifin-ilham?nd771104bcj (accessed 13 May 2018).
———. 2015. "Tentang Para Pemuda Hijrah di Masjid Al-Lathiif, Skater sampai Eks Vokalis". detik.com, 11 August 2015. https://news.detik.com/berita/d-2988601/tentang-para-pemuda-hijrah-di-masjid-al-lathiif-skater-sampai-eks-vokalis/komentar (accessed 13 May 2018).
Eickelman, Dale F. and Jon W. Anderson. 2003. "Redefining Muslim Publics". In *New Media in the Muslim World: The Emerging Public Sphere*, edited by Dale F. Eickelman and Jon W. Anderson, pp. 1–18. Bloomington and Indianapolis: Indiana University Press.
Featherstone, Mike. 1991. *Consumer Culture and Postmodernism*. London: Sage.
Halim, Wahyuddin. 2018. "Young Islamic Preachers on Facebook: Pesantren As'adiyah and its Engagement with Social Media". *Indonesia and the Malay World* 46, no. 134: 44–60.
Hanan Attaki. 2017a. "Kisah Ustadz Hanan Attaki: Rumah 700 Juta Terbeli dengan Shalat Ashar". *Tentara Siber Islam*, 1 August 2017a. https://www.youtube.com/watch?v=nd7jZUTEFvE (accessed 28 April 2018).
———. 2017b. "Sejarah Berdirinya Pemuda Hijrah | SHIFT – Ust. Hanan Attaki Lc". *Lampu Islam Net*, 1 October 2017b. https://www.youtube.com/watch?v=DF5SgxCz0iY&t=1664s (accessed 28 April 2018).
Hosen, Nardisyah. 2008. "Online Fatwa in Indonesia: From Fatwa Shopping to Googling a Kiai". In *Expressing Islam: Religious Life and Politics in Indonesia*, edited by Greg Fealy and Sally White, pp. 159–73. Singapore: Institute of Southeast Asian Studies.
Inong, Fani. 2014. "Historic Route". *Holiday Route*, 7 December 2014. https://www.youtube.com/watch?v=_AX9KY9iFuE (accessed 5 May 2018).
Iskandar, Gustaff. 2003. "Fuck You! We're from Bandung!". *Commonroom.info*. http://bcfnma.commonroom.info/2003/fuck-you-were-from-bandung-mkii/ (accessed 6 May 2018).

Kim, Yujin. 2017. "Making Creative Movement: Transformation of Urban Culture and Politics in Bandung, Indonesia". *Geographical Review of Japan Series B* 90, no. 1: 17–25.

Lim, Merlyna. 2005. "Archipelago Online: The Internet and Political Activism in Indonesia". PhD dissertation, University of Twente.

———. 2013. "Many Clicks but Little Sticks: Social Media Activism in Indonesia". *Journal of Contemporary Asia* 43, no. 4: 636–57.

Luvaas, Brent. 2013. "Material Interventions: Indonesian DIY Fashion and the Regime of the Global Brand". *Cultural Anthropology* 28, no. 1: 127–43.

Martin-Iverson, Sean. 2011. "The Politics of Cultural Production in the DIY Hardcore Scene in Bandung, Indonesia". PhD dissertation, University of Western Australia.

Marwick, Alice E. and danah boyd. 2010. "I Tweet Honestly, I Tweet Passionately: Twitter Users, Context Collapse, and the Imagined Audience". *New Media & Society* 13, no. 1: 114–33.

Millie, Julian and Agus Ahmad Safei. 2010. "Religious Bandung". *Inside Indonesia*, 23 May 2010. http://www.insideindonesia.org/religious-bandung (accessed 7 May 2018).

Mudzakkir, Amin. 2016. "The Politics of Islamic Identity in West Java". *Wahid Foundation*, November 2016. http://wahidfoundation.org/index.php/news/detail/The-Politics-of-Islamic-Identity-in-West-Java (accessed 5 May 2018).

Muller, Dominik M. 2015. "Islamic Politics and Popular Culture in Malaysia: Negotiating Normative Change between Shariah Law and Electric Guitars". *Indonesia and the Malay World* 43, no. 127: 318–44.

Muslim, Acep. 2017. "Digital Religion and Religious Life in Southeast Asia: The One Day One Juz (ODOJ) Community in Indonesia". *Asianscape: Digital Asia* 4: 33–51.

Muzakki, Akh. 2012. "Islamic Televangelism in Changing Indonesia: Transmission, Authority, and the Politics of Ideas". In *Global and Local Televangelism*, edited by Pradip Ninan Thomas and Philip Lee. London: Palgrave Macmillan.

Nisa, Eva F. 2018a. "Creative and Lucrative Da'wa: The Visual Culture of Instagram amongst Female Muslim Youth in Indonesia". *Asiascape: Digital Asia* 5: 68–99.

———. 2018b. "Social Media and the Birth of an Islamic Social Movement: ODOJ (One Day One Juz) in Contemporary Indonesia". *Indonesia and the Malay World* 46, no. 134: 24–43.

Pevi Permana. 2017. "Hijrah – Story of Pevi Permana". *Ammar TV*, 23 April 2017. https://www.youtube.com/watch?v=2TTQLeZWlSk (accessed 12 May 2018).

Rakhmani, Inaya. 2016. *Mainstreaming Islam in Indonesia: Television, Identity, the Middle Class*. London: Palgrave Macmillan.

Rosyad, Rifki. 1995. *A Quest for True Islam: A Study of the Islamic Resurgence Movement among the Youth in Bandung, Indonesia*. Canberra: ANU Press.

Saefullah, Hikmawan. 2017. "Nevermind the *Jahiliyyah*, Here's the *Hijrahs*': Punk and the Religious Turn in the Contemporary Indonesian Underground Scene". *Punk & Post-Punk* 6, no. 2: 263–89.
Senft, Theresa M. 2008. *Camgirls: Celebrity and Community in the Age of Social Networks*. New York: Peter Lang.
Slama, Martin. 2017. "A Subtle Economy of Time: Social Media and the Transformation of Indonesia's Islamic Preacher Economy". *Economic Anthropology* 4: 94–106.
Takeshita, A. 2011. "Popular Culture in Indonesia During the New Order: Reading Process of Constructing the 'Newness' as Reflected in Entertainment Magazines for Young People". PhD dissertation, Osaka University.
Tempo.co. 2016. "Pengguna Instagram di Indonesia Anak Muda Mapan, Terpelajar". Tempo.co, 14 January 2016. https://nasional.tempo.co/read/736014/pengguna-instagram-di-indonesia-anak-muda-mapan-terpelajar (accessed 5 May 2018).
Wallach, Jeremy. 2008. "Living the Punk Lifestyle in Jakarta". *Ethnomusicology Journal* 52, no. 1 (Winter): 98–116.
Weng, Hew Wai. 2018. "The Art of *Dakwah*: Social Media, Visual Persuasion and the Islamist Propagation of Felix Siauw". *Indonesia and the Malay World* 46, no. 134: 61–79.
Wink. 2018. "Biografi dan Profil Lengkap Ustadz Hanan Attaki – Pendiri Pemuda Hijrah". *Biografiku*, 18 January 2018. https://www.biografiku.com/2018/01/biografi-dan-profil-lengkap-ustadz-hanan-attaki-pendiri-pemuda-hijra.html (accessed 3 May 2018).
Yusuf, Imtiyaz. 2009. "Hijrah". In *The Oxford Encyclopedia of the Islamic World*, edited by John L. Esposito. http://www.oxfordislamicstudies.com/article/opr/t236/e0307/ (accessed 27 April 2018).
Zainuddin, MZ. 1997. *Dakwah dan Politik 'Da'i Berjuta Umat'*. Bandung: Mizan.

14

NEW RELIGIOUS PREACHER IN THE CHANGING RELIGIOUS AUTHORITY: THE OFFLINE AND ONLINE PREACHER OF USTADZ ABDUL SOMAD

Hamdani

Introduction

The proliferation of new Islamic preachers in Indonesia has seriously undermined conventional religious authorities. The media savvy of Abdullah Gymnastiar (popularly known as Aa Gym) serves as an example. Marketing himself to be an Islamic self-help psychology and celebrity guru through his TV channel and publishing company, he has significantly shifted traditional and hierarchical forms of religious authority towards a more familiar and relational kind of authority (Hoesterey 2008, p. 98). He masterfully commanded the media and learnt from secular sources of self-help manuals for Sufi wisdom (Watson 2005, p. 773). Another example is Felix Siauw. Despite coming from a Catholic background with limited understanding of Islamic tradition, he has successfully drawn a large audience of Muslim youth in many occasions both online and offline. Hew (2018, pp. 64–65) found that Felix has more than four million followers on Facebook, two million followers on Twitter, one million followers on Instagram, and 20,000 subscribers on YouTube in 2017. He is one of the leading social media preachers in Indonesia today (Hew 2018, pp. 64–65).

The new media allows the Muslim public to choose which religious authority fits their intellectual capacity and preference. Like various TV channels which are offered by a service provider, customers can choose which programme suits their taste and individual leanings. As a result, they have the freedom to determine which religious agents are qualified and fulfill their social and spiritual needs. Turner (2007, p. 118) argues that in terms of access, the new media is basically democratic. In a democratic atmosphere, Muslims can find suitable religious opinions in accordance with their own preference in which Hosen (2008, p. 164) called "Fatwa Shopping". When people feel that a religious edict (*fatwa*) does not fit their wish, they attempt to seek a second opinion. This fact reveals an opening trend of religious authority whose reception shows a surprising diversity in religious life. The democratizing potency of mass media technologies, according to Eickelman and Anderson (1999, p. 2), will have a good effect on strengthening civic pluralism, civil society and a challenge to authoritarian domination in Muslim-majority countries.

The emergence of new preachers is certainly as natural as the emergence of new celebrities in the entertainment world. People continuously expect newcomers to give an alternative or replace the old players. In the last few decades, Indonesian Muslims have known popular preachers such as Hamka, Qosim Nurseha and Zainuddin MZ. From a variety of Muslim preachers, the appearance of Abdul Somad shows a distinct episode in the various spectrum of traditional, moderate, conservative and radical leanings of preachers. His sermons often indicate a traditional understanding of a Muslim agent who interprets religious teachings as traditionalist *nahdliyyin* (members of Nahdlatul Ulama, NU) treat religious texts and realities. At some other times, he has shown his formalism approach and radical thoughts regarding social and political issues. While he has many fans both online and offline, Somad also triggers controversies occasionally which has created many opponents. Therefore, he gets many compliments and at the same time criticisms from the Muslim public. However, his way of preaching has opened the eyes of Muslims concerning a new method and proclivity of transmission of religious knowledge in the midst of an old fashion way of Islamic preaching.

The investigation of this topic does not only reveal the complexity of religious authority in the Muslim world, but also the dynamic constellation of Indonesian Muslim actors due to the shifting social and political structure. In this case, the transformation is from an authoritarian regime of New Order to a more democratic atmosphere in which people can freely express their ideas and use various media. With the emergence of new media, established pillar of traditional authority is shaken by new actors whose influence emulates the old regime of religious guardians. Traditional authority which mostly relies on oral and print media has been challenged by a new community of internet-based network under the command of new intellectual elites. The new trend of changing religious authority has been identified by many scholars (such as Eickelmen and Anderson 1999; Watson 2005; Turner 2007; Mandaville 2007; Hew 2018; Slama 2018; Nisa 2018). As Nielsen (2016, p. 2) found that traditional Muslim authorities have lost ground after the appearance of new actors whose popularity has been supported by the use of new media and gained many followers. In the *dakwah* world, Ustadz Abdul Somad represents a new actor capable of reviving religious teachings in accordance with majority of public demand with an interesting mass communication. Although he comes from a traditional Islamic background, his speech does not fully represent his original training.

The influence of Abdul Somad in reshaping religious knowledge reveals the changing orientation of traditional agents into multi-faceted expressions of a new actor who speaks to a new audience. The emergence of Somad in various social media platforms has attracted many Muslim audiences who presumably found a suitable preacher in fulfilling their spiritual needs and moral guidance. Somad's followers on Facebook has reached one million, and two million on Instagram. In the YouTube channel, his videos have been viewed by more than fifty million viewers as of February 2018. For this achievement, the media termed him as "Da'i Sejuta View" (the preacher with a million viewers) on par with KH Zainuddin MZ's call, "Da'i Sejuta Ummat" (the preacher with a million audience) (Karni 2018, pp. 28–31). This raising star probably signifies an intertwining pattern of social and political life under the rivalry of authority among actors who continuously attempt to gain the people's support and a greater influence.

Profile of Ustadz Abdul Somad

Born on 18 May 1977 to parents of Malay and Batak descent, Somad was groomed into a religious person. In the small district of Silo Lama, Asahan, North Sumatra, the little Somad grew up with his parents, Bahtiar and Rohana. His father was a palm oil farmer, while his mother was a housewife (Interview with Ustadz Abdul Somad via WhatsApp Messenger, 26 July 2018). Through his mother, Somad has blood links with the great figure Sufi of Sumatra, Syaikh Abdurrahman or Syaikh Silau Laut. His mother raised her children using Sufi values; for example, she recited *Surah Al-Fatihah* (the first chapter of the Quran) a hundred times every night as a regular pray for the success of Somad's life (*Gatra* 2018, p. 36).

From a young age, Abdul Somad studied in Islamic schools. His grandfather seemingly designated his path towards *dakwah*. It was said that two hectares of coconut field were prepared by his grandfather to support this aim. "It is intended to spread God's messages. He [Somad] should attend Islamic schools", said his grandfather (*Gatra* 2018, p. 36). That was why he was sent by his parents to his elementary school (SD) in Al-Washliyah Medan and he graduated in 1990. In the same foundation, he continued his studies at MTs Mu'allimin Al-Washliyah and graduated in 1993. His parents later sent him to Pesantren Darul Arafah, Deli Serdang, North Sumatra. He spent only a year there before moving to Madrasah Aliyah Nurul Falah in Indragiri Hulu and graduated in 1996 (Mamnun 2016).

He pursued his undergraduate studies at the State Islamic University (UIN) Sultan Syarif Kasim Riau. However, he did not continue his study at this institution because he decided to take up a scholarship from the Egyptian government to study at Al-Azhar University, Cairo. He was one of the 100 recipients of the scholarship out of 900 Indonesian applicants. After he graduated from Al-Azhar University, he pursued his master degree at the Institute of Dar Al-Hadith Al-Hassania, Morocco. This time, he was also granted a scholarship from the Morocco government after competing with many applicants. At this university, he deepened his understanding of the science of Hadith and wrote a thesis on the "Rijal al-Muwatta wa al-sahihaini alladzina dhu'afa'ahum al-Nasa'i fi kitab al-Dhu'afa wa al-Matrukin: jam'an wa dirosatan" (Comprehensive Analysis of Narrator of al-Muwatta and Shahihain (Compilation of Hadith) which are regarded weak by Imam Nasa'i in his work: Dhuafa and Matrukin) (*Somadmorocco* 2010).

Somad's intellectual capacity and sense of humour has been perceived by his friends since his student days in Egypt and Morocco. This combination later became his "selling point" in preaching. During his studies at Al-Azhar University, he performed remarkably well as proven by his *"jayyid"* (good) grades since the first semester until the end of the course (*Gatra* 2018, p. 36). His ability to deliver a religious speech was known during his student days at Morocco. The audience enjoyed his speeches when he was invited by the Indonesian Embassy to give a short sermon (*kultum/kuliah tujuh menit*, a seven-minute speech) during the month of Ramadan. He was able to fluently recite many quotes from the Quran and Hadith, names and history of *ulama*. He also peppered his talk with jokes (Interview with Nasrullah Jasam, a friend of Somad, Jakarta, 10 May 2018). However, Somad admitted his intellectual capacity with a humble confession by revealing his experience at Al-Azhar University, Egypt, where he did his undergraduate studies. He said: "Saya ini otaknya pas-pasan" (I'm not a smart person) and that was why he could not take part in many activities (student organizations) like other smart students. He also said that he was able to obtain *"jayyid"* (good) grades only after working hard and concentrating on his studies (Talk Show tvOne 2018).

Back to his hometown, Somad applied for a teaching position at the State Islamic University (UIN) Sultan Syarif Kasim (Suska) in 2008. He was accepted by the Faculty of Ushuluddin (Theology) and taught the science of Hadith. His name, in full family name and academic title, was written in the university's list of lecturers as Abdul Somad Batubara, Lc., D.E.S.A (UIN Suska Riau undated). At his workplace, he also delivered religious speeches on many occasions, such as during the reunion of the alumni of UIN Suska, Jum'ah sermons, public lectures, and during the welcoming of Ramadan. Since Somad was very well-known to the public, the university benefitted not only from his fame when advertising their campus, but the student enrolment had also increased, particularly in the Faculty of Ushuluddin (*Gatra* 2018, p. 31). In the Islamic university, Somad was an important asset such that other lecturers defended him when the public found out about his involvement with the radical political movement, Hizbut Tahrir Indonesia (HTI). In a statement published by the media and broadcasted on YouTube, several lecturers from the "Asosiasi Dosen Indonesia" (ADI, Association of Indonesian Lecturers) testified that Somad was a good lecturer and had never been involved in the radical political movement (MPC-ADI Suska Riau 2017).

His popularity has intensified in the last few years since his sermons were uploaded to YouTube. A creative team supporting him, Tafaqquh, has played an important role in publishing Somad's videos in various social media channels (Interview with Ustadz Abdul Somad via WhatsApp Messenger, 26 July 2018). His viewership on social media has increased significantly since then, and his popularity extends beyond Indonesian cities to other Asian countries such as Malaysia and Brunei Darussalam. The way he preaches is favoured by many Muslims, not only because of the topics of choice, but also due to his eloquent speech combined with a humorous style. He admits that his idols are Syaikh Muhammad Mutawalli Sya'rawi (a prominent Egyptian preacher) and Hamka (a respected Sumatran preacher) (Interview with Ustadz Abdul Somad via WhatsApp Messenger, 1 August 2018). To the Indonesian public, the art of preaching combined with humour attracts a strong audience. KH Zainuddin MZ, an Indonesian preacher whose popularity was sustained by his eloquent speech and humour, is a good example. In addition, the benefit of using social media is that the audience can watch the sermons at their own convenience and share it among their networks. Therefore, Somad's popularity has been increasing such that he has become too busy and cannot accept any invitations, even from President Jokowi (*Berita Indonesia* 2017). He admits that his schedule has been fully booked until May 2020 (Interview with Ustadz Abdul Somad via WhatsApp Messenger, 1 August 2018).

Somad's popularity and his social impact has been recognized by the public. It is not a wonder that people have great expectations of him to become an even greater figure. Due to his great influence, *Republika Daily* nominated him as one of the "Tokoh Perubahan 2017" (Agent of Change 2017). On 10 April 2018, he accepted the award which was delivered by Zulkifli Hasan, the chairperson of People's Consultative Assembly (MPR) (Republika.co.id 2018). At the regional level, Somad was awarded a title of honour "Datuk Seri Ulama Setia Negara" which pledges him as a committed agent in delivering Islamic teachings and being loyal to the state. This title was awarded by the Institute of Malay Culture (LAM, Lembaga Adat Melayu) in Pekanbaru, Riau on 20 February 2018 (Tribun Pekanbaru.com 2018). Additionally, Somad has also been nominated as a potential candidate for Vice President, presumably representing Muslim voters. Recommended by the elites of the 212 pro-movement, Prabowo Subianto and Ustadz Abdul Somad were paired as president and vice president candidates to win the 2019 presidential election, which of course did not materialize as Prabowo later named Sandiaga Uno as his running mate (Tempo.co 2018). A few months before the recommendation, Abdul Somad's name also unexpectedly emerged in the list of presidential candidates in a survey by the National Survey Media (Median, Media Survey Nasional) on 1–9 February 2018 (Suluh Riau.com 2018). This indicates that the public has big expectations of Ustadz Abdul Somad to take opportunities beyond his current position.

The Ideology of Ustadz Abdul Somad

Born in a traditional Muslim family, Somad grew up following the Sunni theology which is affiliated to the *"Ahlussunnah wal jama'ah an-nahdliyah"* faction. It is a religious ideology adopted by NU which includes several aspects of Asy'ariyah and Maturidiyah theology. It recognizes four schools of thought (Maliki, Hanafi, Syafi'i and Hambali) in Islamic jurisprudence (*fiqh*) and the mysticism framework based on Imam Al-Ghazali and Imam Junaid Al-Baghdadi's doctrine (Tim PWNU Jawa Timur 2007, p. 3). This ideology idealizes some important principles of religious framework such as *tawasuth* (moderatism), *tasamuh* (tolerance), *tawazun* (balance), *i'tidal* (justice), and *amar ma'ruf nahi munkar* (enjoining good and forbidding evil) (Tim PWNU Jawa Timur 2007, pp. 57–60). In terms of cultural perspective, the *aswaja an-nahdliyah* adopts a receptive approach to local culture based on the principle of *"al-muhafadzah 'ala qadim al-shalih wal akhdzu bi al-jadid al-ashlah"* (preserving good old traditions and accepting new and better traditions) (Tim PWNU Jawa Timur 2007, p. 31). Hence this religious credo accommodates many local cultural practices such as *tahlil* (death ritual), *slametan* (traditional feast), reading of the book of Barzanji, performing *wayang* (puppet) and other traditions (Haidar 1994, p. 333). This worldview also recognizes four spirits of social and religious life: *ruhut tadayun* (religious spirit), *ruhul wathaniyah* (spirit of nationalism), *ruhut ta'addudiyah* (spirit of pluralism) and *ruhul insaniyah* (spirit of humanity) (Tim PWNU Jawa Timur, pp. 47–50). In layman's terms, it is often conceptually simplified into the concept of three *ukhuwah* (unity/fraternity), which are: *ukhuwah Islamiyah* (Islamic unity), *ukhuwah wathaniyah* (national unity) and *ukhuwah Insaniyah/Basyariyah* (unity in humanity) (Affandi and Rohani 2017, pp. 175–76).

In his sermon, Somad conveys that *Ahlussunnah wal Jama'ah* is the middle path between two extremes: *jabariyah* (fatalism) and *qadariyah* (free will). This theology essentially refers to the people who follow the tradition of Prophet Muhammad and who are also known as *ahlussunnah* (the people of the Prophet's Sunnah), the antithesis of *ahlul bid'ah* (the people of religious innovations) which refers to the people who hold onto theological perspectives that contravene the credo (Ajl 2017 and Somad 2017a). Somad also consistently emphasizes that tolerant practices of traditional Muslims such as performing *tahlil* (prayers for the deceased), celebrating *maulid* (the Prophet's birthday) and visiting graves (*ziarah kubur*) as religious and cultural practices that do not contravene Islamic teachings (Tafaqquh 2016). These practices have been criticized by puritan Muslims as religious innovations which are forbidden. In this regard, Somad convincingly explains the lawfulness of these practices by utilizing religious texts and reasoning to back his arguments.

However, Somad's traditional views are not automatically parallel with mainstream *nahdliyyin* (NU agents). His opinions indicate his inclination to conservative ideas and phobia to liberalism, secularism, pluralism, and shi'ism which are misunderstood or exaggerated as a serious threat to Indonesian Muslims. This proclivity has been showed by the current marginal faction of NU which called themselves as the "NU Garis Lurus" (lit. Straight Line of NU), which claims to be the righteous faction of NU. Somad's inclination towards the "NU Garis Lurus" can be observed from his response towards a question on which NU cleric should be followed, whose reputation was not contaminated by the "virus of secularism and liberalism": KH Luthfi Bashori, KH Idrus Romli and Buya Yahya (Somad 2017b). This statement has certainly triggered criticism from many people, particularly *nahdliyyin*. While the "NU Garis Lurus" does not represent the majority of NU, Somad's statement has been perceived by some as worsening and dividing the NU organization (Rohman 2018). This perception is much more dangerous than Wahabi agents attacking the NU's religious practices (Zain 2017). Somad should withdraw his statement because it will confuse many people and erode the authority of NU organization, said a commentator (Rohman 2018).

Another one of Somad's surprising statements is his mockery of an NU agent, Ahmad Ishomuddin, in his response to the question on the MUI agent from Sumatra. Somad had unexpectedly humiliated the young and bright NU leader by saying that he was fired from the MUI office after testifying for Ahok's case. Further, he attempted to shame

Ishomuddin by questioning three things: his doctoral degree, circumcision and pilgrimage (Ishomuddin 2018). These allegations were denied by Ishomuddin in a calm response by stating that all of the accusations were baseless. He had already performed *hajj* (pilgrimage) and was circumcised in his childhood. In addition, he had never claimed to own a doctoral degree, including when he testified for the case of HTI, in which he addressed himself as Ahmad Ngishomuddin, M. Ag., or KH Ahmad Ishomuddin (Redaksi 2018a). One of NU's elites, Yahya Cholil Staquf, commended Ishomuddin's mature response.

> On the one hand, there is someone like Pak Kyai Ahmad Ishomuddin who is capable of responding to a mockery in a calm and relaxed manner. Because Pak Ishom knows, those who humiliate him merely "talk without evidence", expressing their hatred with black campaigning and slander. Pak Ishom may have learned from Gus Dur and Kyai Said Aqil Siroj who have been treated badly by people, but they did not take it personally and can enjoy life. Slander, mockery and hate speech have been treated as a refresher and sweetener of life (Redaksi 2018b).

Somad's support of HTI often links him to their radical ideas to replace the current political system. Although he has displayed efforts to present a sense of nationalism and acceptance of Pancasila recently, the digital traces which are documented in YouTube continue to give an impression of his support for Islamism and formalization of sharia. In the congress of Khilafah (global Islamic leadership) in Riau on 26 May 2013, Somad clearly showed his support of the idea of establishing a *khilafah* and appealed to the audience to get their children to take an oath (*bai'at*) to the *khilafah* who will lead the world. He believes that the *khilafah* is the solution to all problems. By quoting a Prophetic saying, he strengthened his argument: *"Ya Ibna Khawalah, idza ro'aita al-khilafah nazalat al-ardha al-muqoddasah"* [O Ibn Khawalah, if you find a *khilafah*, it must be descended from the holy land]. He also mentioned another Prophetic saying: *"Man mata wa laisa fi 'unuqihi bai'at, mata mitatan jahiliyyah"* [Those who died without taking an oath (to *khilafah*), he/she will die in *jahiliyah* (un-Islamized]] (Somad 2013). Somad's statement about *khilafah* can be found in a question and answer session when an audience asked him about *khilafah*. By quoting a Prophetic saying, he divided the five periods of *khilafah* chronologically and predicted the end period of *khilafah* to be as successful as the Prophet Muhammad's period. It is the period of the Prophet Muhammad, *khulafaur rasyidin* (four credible leaders), monarchy, dictator and *khilafah* as the Prophet's practice. On this occasion, he encouraged the audience to struggle for it (Cahaya Islam 2017).

Somad's proximity to hardliner groups whose reputation tends to wreak havoc, gives an impression of his support for intolerant groups. Since the 212 movement, these groups have a more solid network and political leverage to gain support from the Muslim public. Somad's worldview which is inclined to Islamism and formalism has the same frequency as these groups. His religious and political insights are seemingly close to that of Rizieq Shihab based on his statement when asked about Rizieq Shihab. He has shown his admiration to the leader of the Islamic Defenders Front (FPI, Front Pembela Islam), describing him as a brave religious leader who has lived up to the principle of *"amar ma'ruf nahi mungkar"* (enjoining good, forbidding evil) (Ceramah Terbaru 2017). He also defended Rizieq Shihab and his organization which notoriously present Indonesian Islam with angry faces and violent approaches as part of their implementation of the Prophet's attitude in dealing with non-believers. According to Meong Channel (2017), "Muslims should be angry, according to Somad, if God's laws and his religion is undermined or attacked by the infidels, and the act of being angry is in fact considered to be an *ibadah* (good deed)". At the end of 2017, Somad visited Rizieq Shihab in Mecca during his minor pilgrimage (*umrah*) and met him for about two hours (*Kumparan News* 2018). Rizieq, who had been staying in Mecca since the middle of 2017, is a government fugitive for pornography allegations and nine other cases (Tempo.co 2017).

Although his sermons reflect a good mastery of comparative school of thought in Islamic jurisprudence, Somad's statements frequently fell under the conservative categories of Islamic interpretation. Certain Muslim audiences were surprised with his statement on the impermissibility of celebrating Mother's Day, use of "Merry Christmas" greeting by Muslims, drinking coffee at Starbucks, having a non-Muslim leader in Muslim society, framing Syrian civil war as merely a Sunni-Shia conflict, and resentment to Shia and liberal Muslims. These views might represent the "conservative turn" of Indonesian Islam (van Bruinessen 2014). When the MUI issued the unlawfulness of secularism, pluralism and liberalism in 2005, according to van Bruinessen, it signified the conservative proclivity of Indonesian Muslims. This *fatwa* was a result of radical Muslims joining the MUI with the support from conservative factions of the Muslim population (van Bruinessen

2014, p. 28). On several occasions, Somad also criticized the idea of secularism, pluralism and liberalism. Without a deep understanding of these concepts, he elaborated on them based on his own understanding and believed that they were Western concepts that contravene Islamic teachings (Amil Islam 2017).

Although he was not involved in the 212 movement, Somad's political orientation is easy to identify. One of his agitated oration on YouTube has clearly demonstrated his position through the Ahok controversy. In front of a crowd, Somad zealously provoked the masses to voice their zero tolerance towards non-Muslim leaders. "No infidel agent dares to be a leader in a majority Muslim community. There is no compromise in this issue", he screamed (Al-Faqih 2016). Through his sermon, he showed his rejection to having non-Muslim leaders by referring to Surah Al-Maidah verse 51 (prohibition to appoint Jews and Christians as *aulia* [interpreted as leader]), although he has shown tolerance towards different religion in other occasions. He said the idea which supports non-Muslim leaders is secular and liberal, and should be challenged (*Hot News* 2017). The Ahok controversy, according to Somad, has a positive impact in differentiating between human and Satan, friend and enemy (*Bisyarah Channel* 2017). This simplistic perspective on the *muamalah* (non-definite or worldly) aspect has been constantly repeated with a similar exclusionary tone concerning the Ahok's case using a black and white approach. That is why Somad assumes that Muslims who defend Ahok are deviant Muslims. "They are wrong, sinful and aberrant", while those who are against Ahok are right, fine and authentic Muslims (Gaata TV 2017).

Religious Authority and Preachers

Fragmentation of authority is a common global trend in the Muslim world: from the authoritative *ulama* as the primary locus of authority to the new religious intellectuals (Kramer and Schmidtke 2006, p. 175). As Kaptein (2004, p. 128) argues, religious authority is no longer the sole domain of the *ulama* as religious specialists par excellence. Moreover, the concept of religious authority is very much subject to changes in the political, social, educational, and religious spheres in Indonesia. Turner (2007, p. 132) found that mass education has created a systematization of Islamic teachings through various media resulting in a distinct religiosity. It is self consciousness and reflexive religiosity which question traditional forms of knowledge that have been preserved by traditional elites. The advance of literacy and extensive global market for religious texts have enhanced the demand for print texts and website access. This new development has encouraged competition between the traditional *ulama*, new intellectuals and the state to control official religion (Turner 2007, p. 132). In other words, the traditional voice of *ulama* has acquired a new competitor, not only from the circumference of the *ulama* themselves, but also from outside the circle (Kaptein 2004, p. 128). Felix Siauw, for example, has been a popular preacher and has many followers particularly among Muslim youth, even though he has recently converted to Islam and graduated from an agricultural university. It is similiar with Irena Handono, who has a Catholic background and was a church-activist-turned-popular-Muslim-preacher after converting to Islam when she was twenty-six.

The democratic nature of the Indonesian public has led to the exponential proliferation of emerging religious preachers. Besides the credible *ulama* which have competence in Islamic studies and have been recognized by the Muslim public such as Ahmad Mustofa Bisri, Maimun Zubair, Quraish Shihab, and Ahmad Syafi'i Maarif, there are newcomers which are younger and lack deep knowledge of Islamic sciences such as Abdullah Gymnastiar, Arifin Ilham, Yusuf Mansur, Mamah Dedeh, Felix Siauw and Abdul Somad whose followers continuously grow in the midst of contested authority. Other trends include the emergence of preachers from several categories such as child preachers, Chinese-convert preachers, ex-rock preachers, and ex-church activist preachers. However, the competence of the newcomers has often been questioned by Muslim scholars due to their lack of mastery of Islamic sciences and contribution of radical ideas to the Muslim audience. In response to this trend, the government issued a list of approved Islamic preachers to anticipate and overcome such problems. One of the MUI (Indonesia's Ulama Council) agents admitted that the "policy could suppress the emergence of preachers who do not really understand Islam, thereby giving people a wrong understanding about it". The growing trend of incompetent preachers was also worrying as this could lead to a degradation of the quality of religious understanding of Indonesian Muslims. Hosen (2017) labelled such unqualified preachers with "Ustadz Jadi-jadian" (lit. not real) or "Ustadz Karbitan" (lit. immature or forced preacher) due to their inclination to answer questions beyond their knowledge and claiming themselves as well-versed preachers.

However, unlike new preachers whose competence in Islamic studies are still limited, Ustadz Abdul Somad has sufficient mastery of Islamic sciences. His educational background in *pesantren*, Al-Azhar University and the Institute of Dar Al-Hadith Al-Hassania has convinced many people of his authority to speak for Islam. His memorization and eloquence in citing the Quran, Hadith and the opinions of the *ulama* has impressed the Muslim public as the ideal *ulama* who has the capacity to "impose rules which are deemed to be in consonance with the will of God" (Gaboriau 2010). During a religious event which invited Somad as preacher, he was given the label of *ulama* which was inscribed on a big banner as "Ulama Besar dari Riau" (Great Ulama from Riau). When Somad was invited to Jakarta, Vice President Jusuf Kalla praised Somad, commenting that his sermon was based on evidence and that the way he conveyed was easy to understand (Riana 2018). Ustadz Shamsi Ali, an Indonesian imam in a New York mosque, also argued that Somad has extensive knowledge and reference in Islamic teachings. His way of communication has a strong character (assertive) and is exciting (humorous) (Shamsi Ali 2017).

However, Somad's inclination to Islamism and formalism makes him fail to communicate his teachings to the moderate factions among Indonesian Muslims. The moderate paradigm of NU and Muhammadiyah which emphasizes the use of non-violence and accepts the current Indonesian political system does not accommodate Somad's worldview. The religious authority of NU and Muhammadiyah as the biggest Muslim organizations in Indonesia has been challenged by this new agent who slowly undermines the established institutions of religious movement with his growing followers and sympathizers. Somad's relations with conservative and radical groups have created a network and community which has endeavoured to distance from old traditions and set up their own internal conception of authority, authenticity and continuity (Turner 2007, p. 127). His connection with FPI, HTI and the 212 movement's pro-elites has proven his different platform from NU and Muhammadiyah's agenda of moderating Indonesian Islam.

Amid obscuring the conception of the *ulama* in the public discourse, Somad has taken advantage in manipulating the Muslim public by imposing Islamic interpretations based on his own understanding. While for a long time the authority of the *ulama* was presumed, the current developments of the Muslim world have contested that concept (Hatina 2009, pp. 2–3). Hassan Al-Turabi, for example, defines the word *ulama* as "those versed in the legacy of religious (revealed) knowledge ('ilm), which means anyone who knows anything well enough to relate it to God" (Ibid., p. 2). According to Azra (2002), the most fundamental requirement to be an *ulama* is to have an excellent knowledge of *fiqh* (Islamic law) and classical Islamic knowledge based on Al-Quran, Hadith and *kitab kuning* (lit. Yellow Books, classical works written by Muslim scholars centuries ago). The mastery of these disciplines is necessary to make decisions regarding Islamic jurisprudence. Also, the *ulama* must have a good understanding of the sources and methodology to issue *fatwa* (religious edict) (Nor Ismah 2016, p. 493). Although people assume Somad to be an *ulama*, however, in a humble confession he admitted that he is not. "I am not an *ulama*. I am just a preacher. On a scale of 1 to 100, I must be on the lowest level."

Somad's habit of answering all questions in his sermons from the pulpit has given two impressions. Laymen and supporters deemed him as a well-versed cleric on Islamic knowledge who has never disappointed them. Among his fans, Somad has successfully combined scholarship and comedy through mass communication. "The young Hamka was born", commented his follower (Indonesiana.id 2017). However, some of his statements triggered controversies in the public such as his comments on Rina Nose, his condemn of Syria's leader, Bashar al-Assad, and his statement on the history of Red Cross. In a question and answer session, Somad insulted Rina Nose (a young celebrity) for taking off her veil in a pejorative manner. To him, covering the female *aurat* (nakedness) is obligatory and it is a form of personal spiritual change known as *hijrah* (religious transformation). In this regard, he suggested that Muslims do *hijrah* in a total mentality (Islam Channel 2017). Somad also simplified the conflict in Syria as a religious, faction-based conflict. He said that Bashar al-Assad represents the Syi'ah, while the rebellion fights for Sunni Islam. The Association of Syam Alumni of Indonesia (Alsyami) attempted to clarify this issue, but was ignored by Somad. Without referencing to credible sources, Somad argued that the symbol of the Red Cross symbolizes Christian theology missionary. These statements certainly do not reflect a good scholarship and was presumed by the Muslim public as arbitrary views which will lead the audience to misleading assumption of realities.

Conclusion

Since religious preachers have played an important role in the transmission of religious knowledge to the Muslim public, their role in the formation of religious understanding and moral configuration of Indonesian Muslims cannot be ignored. The deepening religiosity of Indonesian Muslims in the last few decades has involved a variety of preachers who conveyed religious messages and have shaped Muslim spirituality. The emergence of Ustadz Abdul Somad in the era of new media does not only signify the changing patterns of religious authority, from traditional to a more intertwined trend of religiosity, but it has also demonstrated a successful experiment of new media as the tool of *dakwah* (propagation) that at the same time magnifies a personality's influence. While authority, according to Kaptein, can be referred to notions, in text, in groups of persons and in institutions, the authority of individual in the case of Ustadz Abdul Somad is inevitably contested among the Muslim public. The more he answers questions from his audience, the more the public recognizes his competence or disputes against him.

It is a new pattern whereby a preacher's reputation is sustained over the recognition he receives and at the same time, the rejection of his authority is due to his statements or opinions on certain issues. Controversial statements by Ustadz Abdul Somad on *khilafah* (a global Islamic political system), Starbucks, Mother's Day, "Merry Christmas" greeting, Ahok's case and other issues can be identified as examples of how he has been appraised and treated differently among pro and contra Muslim public. Some observers say that he has an excessive ambition to answer all questions regardless of whether he has sufficient knowledge or not concerning the issue. In the transparent and democratic trend of social media, Somad's strengths and weaknesses can be easily analysed by experts and trigger a controversy leading to negative sentiments against him. It is therefore not a wonder that Somad is often barred or tried to be banned by his haters to deliver sermons in certain places such as Bali, Hong Kong and Semarang.

Despite his Sufi and traditional background, Somad's views reflect a complex religious and political standpoint which is possibly influenced by the new wave of Islamism, radicalism and populism religious movements. His ideas on the formalization of Islamic Shari'a and his campaign for the concept of a *khilafah* system do not represent the mainstream thought of traditional or *nahdliyyin* Muslim community who accept the secular Indonesian political system (Pancasila). He also frequently constructs the simplification of political realities which have been presumably produced by the elite's conspiracy against Muslim aspirations. Whether it is a personal preference or impulse to fulfill certain audience's favourite topics of preaching, Somad's statements have led to a variety of paradox ideas which frequently confuse some audience. While he has encouraged diversity (*kebhinekaan*) and unity (*ukhuwah*), at the same time he has discouraged pluralism and triggered social fragmentation by strengthening the politics of identity. It is interesting that such paradox ideas were conveyed from the pulpit and favoured by current Muslim audience both online and offline.

REFERENCES

Affandi, Haryanto and Edi Rohani, ed. 2017. *Pengantar Studi Aswaja An-Nahdliyah*. Yogyakarta: LKiS.

Ajl, Almunai. 2017. "Tiga Dasar Akidah Aswaja Bersama Ust Abdul Somad Di Masjid Al-Falah, Selangor", 9 October 2017. https://www.youtube.com/watch?v=GrVVUKoPKVo (accessed 6 June 2018).

Al-Faqih, Erwin Yulianto Nurhuda. 2016. "Tangkap Ahok..!!", 26 November 2016. https://www.youtube.com/watch?v=cp0T5ve-nn0 (accessed 2 June 2018).

Amil Islam. 2017. "Tabligh Akbar: Pluralisme dan Liberalisme, Ustadz Abd Somad", 6 November 2017. https://www.youtube.com/watch?v=ypOwcozIEuQ&t=610s (accessed 2 June 2018).

Azra, Azyumardi. 2002. "Biografi sosial-intelektual ulama perempuan: Pemberdayaan historiografi". In *Ulama perempuan Indonesia*, edited by Jajat Burhanuddin. Jakarta: PPIM.

Berita Indonesia. 2017. "Ustaz Abdul Somad Menolak Undangan dari Presiden Jokowi dan Menteri, Begini Alasannya", 29 October 2017. https://www.youtube.com/channel/UC8gn4CjSqK5MxfIUwNGIScw (accessed 4 June 2018).

Bisyarah Channel. 2017. "Terimakasih Ahok, Ustadz Abdul Somad", 30 June 2017. https://www.youtube.com/watch?v=zuORErR6vGs (accessed 2 June 2018).

Cahaya Islam. 2017. "Perlukah Kita Perjuangkan Tegaknya Khilafah Atau Menunggunya", 19 November 2017. https://www.youtube.com/watch?v=ZZT0TRVT8p4 (accessed 9 June 2018).

Ceramah Terbaru. 2017. "Pandangan ustadz abdul somad tentang Habib Rizieq Syihab", 23 September 2017. https://www.youtube.com/watch?v=74wdE3q2_js (accessed 9 June 2018).

Eickelman, Dale F. and Jon W. Anderson. 1999. "Redefining Muslim Publics". In *New Media in the Muslim World: The Emerging Public Sphere*, edited by Dale F. Eickelman and Jon W. Anderson. Bloomington: Indiana UP.

Gaata TV. 2017. "Hikmah dibalik peristiwa Ahok dan Rina Nose", 22 November 2017. https://www.youtube.com/watch?v=4lJlAaaAICY (accessed 2 June 2018).

Gaboriau, Marc. 2010. "Redefinition of Religious Authority among South Asian Muslims from 1919 to 1956". In *Varieties of Religious Authority: Changes and Challenges in 20th Century Indonesian Islam*, edited by Azyumardi Azra, Kees van Dijk and Nico J.G. Kaptein. Singapore: Institute of Southeast Asian Studies.

Gatra. 2018. "Habis Energi Bahas Caci Maki", 14 February 2018, p. 36.

Haidar, M. Ali. 1994. *Nahdlatul Ulama dan Islam Indonesia: Pendekatan Fikih Dalam Politik*. Jakarta: Gramedia.

Hatina, Meir, ed. 2009. *Guardians of Faith in Modern Times: ʿUlamaʾ in the Middle East*. Leiden: Brill.

Hew Wai Weng. 2018. "The Art of *Dakwah*: Social Media, Visual Persuasion and the Islamist Propagation of Felix Siauw". *Indonesia and the Malay World* 46, no. 134: 61–79.

Hoesterey, James B. 2008. "Marketing Morality: The Rise, Fall and Rebranding of Aa Gym". In *Expressing Islam: Religious Life and Politics in Indonesia*, edited by Greg Fealy and Sally White. Singapore: Institute of Southeast Asian Studies.

Hosen, Nadirsyah. 2008. "Online Fatwa in Indonesia: From Fatwa Shopping to Googling a Kiai". In *Expressing Islam: Religious Life and Politics in Indonesia*, edited by Greg Fealy and Sally White. Singapore: Institute of Southeast Asian Studies.

———. 2017. Facebook Status, 7 August 2017. https://www.facebook.com/NadirsyahHosen/ (accessed 2 August 2018).

Hot News. 2017. "Nasehat Ustad Abdul Somad Untuk Ahok", 27 November 2017. https://www.youtube.com/watch?v=LvVsUutrgCU (accessed 2 June 2018).

Indonesiana.id. 2017. "Buya Hamka Dulu, Ustadz Abdul Somad Sekarang", 10 November 2017. https://indonesiana.tempo.co/read/119101/2017/12/08/satriwansalim/buya-hamka-dulu-ustadz-abdul-somad-sekarang (accessed 2 June 2018).

Ishomuddin, KH Ahmad. 2018. "Parah!!! Ust Abdul Somad Lecehkan Rais Syuriah NU", 17 March 2018. https://www.youtube.com/watch?v=ooPipQ_pdWc (accessed 2 June 2018).

Islam Channel. 2017. "Ustadz Abdul Somad Menghina Rina Nose", 19 November 2017. https://www.youtube.com/watch?v=yAUVrRxau0w (accessed 2 June 2018).

Ismah, Nor. 2004. "Destabilising Male Domination: Building Community-based Authority among Indonesian Female Ulama". *Asian Studies Review* 40, no. 4 (2016): 491–509.

Kaptein, Nico J.G. 2004. "The Voice of the `Ulamâ': Fatwas and Religious Authority in Indonesia". *Archipel* 125 (January–March 2004): 115–30.

Karni, Asrori S. 2018. "Ambil Untung Panggung Somad". *Gatra*, 14 February 2018, pp. 28–31.

Kramer, Gudrun and Sabine Schmidtke, eds. 2006. *Speaking for Islam: Religious Authorities in Muslim Societies*. Leiden: Brill.

Kumparan News. 2018. "Cerita Pertemuan Ustaz Abdul Somad dan Rizieq Shihab di Mekah", 2 January 2018. https://kumparan.com/@kumparannews/cerita-pertemuan-ustaz-abdul-somad-dan-rizieq-shihab-di-mekah (accessed 9 June 2018).

Mamnun, Tasbihul. 2016. "Profil Dan Biodata Ustadz Abdul Somad, Lc. MA Lengkap", 15 February 2016. https://profilbiodataustadz.blogspot.co.id/2016/09/profil-dan-biodata-ustadz-abdul-somad.html (accessed 4 June 2018).

Mandaville, Peter P. 2007. "Globalization and the Politics of Religious Knowledge: Pluralizing Authority in the Muslim World". *Theory, Culture and Society* 24, no. 2: 101–15.

Meong Channel. 2017. "Kenapa Fpi dan HTI Brutal?", 25 July 2017. https://www.youtube.com/watch?v=tdUpyyxiJJs (accessed 6 June 2018).

MPC-ADI Suska Riau. 2017. "Penegasan Ketua MPC-ADI UIN Suska Riau Tentang Ust. Abdul Somad, Lc., MA", 30 December 2017. https://www.youtube.com/watch?v=F2FdUmUOFnw (accessed 4 June 2018).

Nielsen, Richard A. 2016. "The Changing Face of Islamic Authority in the Middle East". *Middle East Brief*, no. 99 (May): 1–8.

Nisa, Eva F. 2018. "Creative and Lucrative Daʿwa: The Visual Culture of Instagram amongst Female Muslim Youth in Indonesia". *Asiascape: Digital Asia* 5, nos. 1–2: 68–99.

Redaksi. 2018a. "Na'udzubillah, Abdul Somad Fitnah KH Ishomuddin Belum Sunnat, Tujuannya Apa Ya?", 18 March 2018. http://www.suaraislam.co/naudzubillah-abdul-somad-fitnah-kh-ishomuddin-belum-sunnat-tujuannya-apa-ya/ (accessed 9 June 2018).

———. 2018b. "Tetap Santun Hadapi Fitnah, Berikut Pujian Gus Yahya Cholil Staquf untuk Kiai Ishomuddin", 18 March 2018. http://www.suaraislam.co/tetap-santun-hadapi-fitnah-berikut-pujian-gus-yahya-cholil-staquf-kiai-ishomuddin/ (accessed 1 June 2018).

Republika.co.id. 2018. "Pesan Ustaz Somad pada Acara Tokoh Perubahan Republika 2017", 10 April 2018. https://www.republika.co.id/berita/nasional/umum/18/04/10/p6z3mf348-pesan-ustaz-somad-pada-acara-tokoh-perubahan-republika-2017 (accessed 6 June 2018).

Riana, Friski. 2018. "Yang Bikin Jusuf Kalla Terkesan Dengar Ceramah Ustad Abdul Somad". Tempo.co, 4 February 2018. https://nasional.tempo.co/read/1057178/yang-bikin-jusuf-kalla-terkesan-dengar-ceramah-ustad-abdul-somad (accessed 2 June 2018).

Rohman, Amamur. 2018. "Ustaz Somad dan Salah Kaprah NU Garis Lurus", 16 January 2018. https://geotimes.co.id/opini/ustaz-somad-dan-salah-kaprah-nu-garis-lurus/ (accessed 3 June 2018).

Shamsi Ali, Imam. 2017. "Ustaz Abdul Somad yang Saya Kenal". Detik.com, 28 December 2017. https://news.detik.com/kolom/3788813/ustaz-abdul-somad-yang-saya-kenal (accessed 2 June 2018).

Slama, Martin. 2018. "Practising Islam through Social Media in Indonesia". *Indonesia and the Malay World* 46, no. 134: 1–4.

Somad, Abdul. 2013. "Pentingnya Penegakan Syariah & Khilafah (Muktamar Khilafah Riau 1434)", 26 May 2013. https://www.youtube.com/watch?v=wZADo9cnpDk (accessed 9 June 2018).

———. 2017a. "Aqidah Ahlussunnah Waljama'ah (Masjid Jami' Kuala Lumpur, 16.12.2017)", 18 December 2017. https://www.youtube.com/watch?v=m9gHpN2R6ok (accessed 6 June 2018).

———. 2017b. "Ikuti Ulama NU Garis Lurus - Ustadz Abdul Somad, Lc., MA", 5 July 2017. https://www.youtube.com/watch?v=aD-iAtO952A (accessed 1 June 2018).

Somadmorocco (blog). 2010. "Biografi", 28 July 2010. https://somadmorocco.blogspot.com/search?q=biografi (accessed 4 June 2018).

Suluh Raiu.com. 2018. "Daftar Capres Alternatif, Ustadz Abdul Somad Muncul di Dalamnya", 23 February 2018. http://m.suluhriau.com/read-210411-2018-02-23-daftar-capres-alternatif-ustadz-abdul-somad-muncul-di-dalamnya.html#sthash.3pyK9a3B.dpbs (accessed 1 June 2018).

Tafaqquh. 2016. "Bid'ah & Maulid Nabi (1) - Ustadz Abdul Somad, Lc. MA", 23 December 2016. https://www.youtube.com/watch?v=iRHX1iL1uBQ (accessed 1 June 2018).

Talk Show tvOne. 2018. "Fakta TvOne – Ustadz Somad Blak-blakan Soal Persekusi", 11 September 2018. https://www.youtube.com/watch?v=-7w5o0D-qmA (accessed 20 June 2019).

Tempo.co. 2017. "9 Kasus Rizieq 1 Berstatus Tersangka, Ini Daftar Lengkapnya", 31 January 2017. https://nasional.tempo.co/read/841367/9-kasus-rizieq-1-berstatus-tersangka-ini-daftar-lengkapnya (accessed 9 June 2018).

———. 2018. "Ijtima Ulama GNPF Rekomendasikan Abdul Somad Cawapres Prabowo", 29 July 2018. https://nasional.tempo.co/read/1111556/ijtima-ulama-gnpf-rekomendasikan-abdul-somad-cawapres-prabowo?BeritaUtama&campaign=BeritaUtama_Click_3 (accessed 31 July 2018).

Tim PWNU Jawa Timur. 2007. *Aswaja an-Nahdliyah: Ajaran Ahlussunnah wal Jama'ah yang Berlaku di Lingkungan Nahdlatul Ulama*. Surabaya: Khalista.

Tribun Pekanbaru.com. "Ustadz Abdul Somad Resmi Sandang Gelar Datuk Seri Ulama Setia Negara", 20 February 2018. http://pekanbaru.tribunnews.com/2018/02/20/ustadz-abdul-somad-resmi-sandang-gelar-datuk-seri-ulama-setia-negara?page=all (accessed 4 June 2018).

Turner, Bryan S. 2007. "Religious Authority and the New Media". *Theory, Culture & Society* 24, no. 2: 117–34.

UIN Suska Riau. Undated. Daftar Dosen Tetap PNS Fakultas Ushuluddin. https://uin-suska.ac.id/dosen/ushuluddin/ (accessed 4 June 2018).

van Bruinessen, Martin. 2014. "Perkembangan Kontemporer Islam Indonesia dan Conservative Turn". In *Conservative Turn: Islam Indonesia Dalam Ancaman Fundamentalisme*, edited by Martin van Bruinessen. Bandung: Mizan.

Watson, C.W. 2005. "A Popular Indonesian Preacher: The Significance of Aa Gymnastiar". *The Journal of the Royal Anthropological Institute* 11, no. 4 (December): 773–92.

Zain, Moch. 2017. "Hati-Hati, Abdul Shomad Ajak Warga Nahdliyyin Membenci NU", 1 October 2017. https://www.erhaje88.com/2017/10/hati-hat-abdul-shomad-ajak-warga-nahdliyyin-membenci-nu.html (accessed 1 June 2018).

15

SANTRI, CINEMA AND THE EXPLORATORY FORM OF AUTHORITY IN TRADITIONALIST MUSLIM INDONESIA

Ahmad Nuril Huda

Introduction

The common stereotype that depicts Islam as "an authoritarian religion" is a mistake, for it resulted from a partial understanding about the nature of religious authority in Islamic societies (Berkey 2010, p. 105). While the construction of religious authority in Islam consists of varying degrees of textuality, discursive methods and personified knowledge (Mandaville 2007), the stronghold of Islamic religious authority since the formative period of Islam has never been singular (Crone and Hinds 1986). It is in fact always contingent, plural and relational (Kramer and Schmidtke 2006, p. 2). This is because the normative texts of Islam are mute until they are interpreted (textuality), and thus dealing with them requires expert knowledge that is premised on a certain level of literacy and requisite training (discursive methods). This requirement has in turn pluralized Islamic authority into diverse categories of classified producers and transmitters of that knowledge, such as the religious scholars, the Sufi leaders, and the political figures (personified knowledge). Moreover, since Islam has no church-like institution and ordained clergy, what counts as authoritative knowledge of Islam has always been contested among diverse epistemological, social, cultural, and political orders.

In the modern times, the traditional construction of Islamic religious authority has seen a vigorous process of fragmentation, triggered by the advent of new media technologies and the rise of mass education in the Muslim societies, among other causes. This fragmentation in Islamic authority is marked by the emergence of new types of Muslim actors who do not necessarily have "formal" religious qualifications, but have vigorously created alternative sites of learning to speak of and for Islam (Eickelman and Anderson 1999), that subvert, break with, and even attack the traditional structures of scholarship, ideologies and authorities in the Muslim world (Devji 2005). For example, in the case of Indonesia today we might see the rise of popular Islam, which I define here as the daily understanding, articulation, and practice of what counts as Islam by a large number of ordinary Muslims in everyday lived circumstances, largely mediated through practices of popular culture, the global market economy, and modern lifestyles. Recent works on this area have shown the rising popularity of online *fatwas* (Hosen 2008), celebrity Muslim preachers (Hoesterey 2008) and the wide circulation of popular music (Barendregt 2006), magazines (Jones 2010), novels (Arnez 2009), television dramas (Rakhmani 2016) and films (Heryanto 2014) which offer ordinary narratives of Islamic piety. This form of democratization of Islamic knowledge beyond the hands of trained Muslim scholars to critical audiences of Muslims in public domains has in turn helped the production of a Muslim public sphere; that is, the everyday public realm in which various identity groups of Muslims compete with each other for political influence (Eickelman and Anderson 1999).

Yet, there is a tendency among Muslims and scholars alike to exclusively associate the nature of Islamic authority to the prescription of correctness (Asad 1986),[1] that is, to confine the conceptualization of Islam to the realm of orthodoxy. In Indonesia, this is evidenced, among others, by the rise of older attempts of formal implementation of religious law (sharia) by the early 2000s (Salim 2008). This may imply that the popular narratives of Islamic piety as articulated by the ordinary Muslims through popular culture practices are less authoritative, thus less Islamic, than, for example, the juridical practices of Islam theorized and produced by the "legitimate" Muslim jurists and religious scholars. In my view, however, such attitude is misleading simply because Islam, as a lived religion, is never a mere congeries of rituals and practices prescribed by the normative texts and legitimate jurists, but is also about transformation, adaptation and coherence of those rituals and practices within particularly individual, social and historical contexts.

In this regards, the late Harvard historian Shahab Ahmed (2015) has provided illuminating insights into how we could better comprehend the nature of authority in Islam. He writes that authority that is operative in Islam (and in other religions) is not only prescriptive, but also explorative. In other words, while the prescriptive authority gives to its proponent a license to prescribe, the exploratory authority grants its bearer a license to explore (by) himself a range of possible meanings of being Muslim (Ahmed 2015, p. 282). Ahmed, however, reminds us that since exploration is the business of setting out into the unknown and the uncertain, not everyone is able to carry out such a business. Conversely, in order to explore, one has to bear in mind that they have the "authority" to do so, and fulfil the "meaning-making" purposes from that exploration (Ahmed 2015, p. 283). Examples of the projects of exploratory practices and discourse include the philosophers and Sufi saints, who arrogate to themselves the highest epistemological authority to interpret God's words, yet at the same time do not seek a singular correct truth of Islam on the basis of their authority. In short, conceptualization of the authoritative in Islam does not only consist of the regulation and requirement of correct practices, but also accommodates exploratory discourses and practices by (a collection of) Muslim individuals in search of truth and meanings.

Taking a cue from Ahmed, this chapter aims at examining the extent to which the current rise of cinematic practices among the *santri* communities in present day Indonesia resonates with the projects of exploratory discourse and practices that inform the construction and fragmentation of religious authority in modern Islam. In particular, I will focus on the cinematic practices of Sahal, my *santri* interlocutor who has vigorously organized various forms of cinematic practices, such as film-making, film-screening and film-discussion in the Nahdlatul Ulama (NU) headquarters and across the provision of *santri* communities.

However, before embarking on my examination, I first need to briefly discuss some characteristics of the *santri* communities.

An Overview of the *Santri* Communities

In the most popular sense, the term *santri* refers to "young students of Islam". Yet it may be used to designate devout Muslims who practise and obey the core teachings and rituals of Islam (Geertz 1976 [1960], p. 127). Here, my use of it loosely refers to both connotations. The *santri*, however, is never a monolithic term, but represents various practising Muslim groups who often compete with each other for public attention and political influence. Their varieties range from traditionalist,[2] modernist,[3] Islamist[4] to many other groups. To limit the focus of this chapter, my use of the term *santri* strictly refers to traditionalist Muslim groups affiliated, both structurally and culturally, with NU (the biggest traditionalist Muslim organization in Indonesia), unless clearly stated, for example, "the non-NU *santri*".

The central backbone of *santri* communities is the *pesantren*. It is easily recognized as a compound of buildings where the young *santri* live to learn and practise Islamic doctrines, ethics, and rituals. In the past, *pesantren* were mostly established in rural villages, mainly offering traditional system of Islamic education, and largely catering to students of low-class economic backgrounds. Today's *pesantren*, however, are existent in both urban and rural areas, open to male and female students, combine the teaching of classical Islamic texts with varying degrees of general education, and attended by students of various economic and social backgrounds. The young *santri* may live in their *pesantren* until they reach the age of marriage, but most commonly, they would leave when they complete their high school degree, either to pursue their college studies, or to return home. While the *santri* who have finished their studies may work in various sectors, whether formal or informal, many of them are commonly assigned to religious offices, and often tasked with giving religious services and education in their communities. Subsequently, collections of these *pesantren* graduates would have formed a larger community of *santri* that is linked through cultural, spiritual and intellectual bonds.

Each *pesantren* is led by a *kyai*, a religious male scholar required to serve as a living model of the pious Islamic life in his own *pesantren*. According to the *pesantren* culture, the *kyai* holds an absolute authority, and accords a total obedience from their *santri*, an obedience that may extend beyond the *santri's* time at the *pesantren*. In many cases, the *kyai* is often seen as "a little king", in the sense that his leadership can be bequeathed to his male descendants or relatives, signifying to a certain extent domination of patriarchy in the *pesantren* and in the *santri* communities at large. Other examples of the *pesantrens* patriarchal culture include the implementation of a gender-segregation system. The patriarchal structure in *pesantren*, however, should not necessarily be seen as originating from Islamic teachings, but a marriage between Islamic values and Javanese and other local cultures in Indonesia (Srimulyani 2012). At present though, a few *pesantren* in Indonesia are led by a *nyai*, the female equivalent of *kyai*, breaking down the dominant power and authority of the *pesantren's* male leadership (ibid).

As a learning institution, the main activity in the *pesantren* is the transmission of Islamic knowledge. Its main curriculum is the teaching of *kitab kuning* (lit. yellow book), loosely defined as the classical Arabic-scripted texts of Islam (van Bruinessen 1990). The "classical" here does not refer to "original texts of Islam of the Meccan and Medinan communities", but to authoritative texts of the forefather of Muslim scholars from "the medieval period of Islamic history, specifically from the twelfth to seventeenth centuries C.E. in which being Muslim and being Sufi were nearly synonymous" (Lukens-Bull 2005, p. 15).[5] Learning methods of *kitab kuning* by the *pesantren* people are structured upon a combination of time discipline, patience and a strong reliance on the *kyai's* reading of the texts, signifying the salience of *kitab kuning* as the fundamental source of their religious knowledge, and the genealogical link of their religious tradition to the authoritative form of Islam established by the forebears of local Muslim scholarship. Thus, despite the addition of state-sanctioned secular curriculum in many of today's *pesantren* for the sake of modernization (Hefner 2009), the *kitab-kuning* curriculum remains profound among the *pesantren* communities.

Nearly all traditionalist *pesantren* are closely tied, either culturally or politically, to NU. It is a mass-Muslim organization, established in 1926 by a number of *kyai* from *pesantren* in East Java, largely in response to earlier establishment of similar modernist organizations, such as Muhammadiyah and Al-Irsyad in 1912. Yet despite the strong roots of the *pesantren* in NU, nearly all *pesantren* are independent from

NU arguably due to the undisputed authority of each *kyai* among his *pesantren* members and local communities. At the same time, as an assemblage of Muslim communities, NU is by no means a pastorhood-like institution whose members are (allowed to be) able to dominate the claim over production of truth in society, a situation that is a seemingly characteristic of Islam writ large. In fact, not only is it usual among the NU people to have different opinions over religious, social and even political issues, but they also consist of various factions ranging from conservative and moderate, to "hybrid" forms of neo-modernist, post-traditionalist and liberal Islam.

With regards to political behaviour, relations between NU and the state has fluctuated throughout history. However, it is safe to say that the *pesantren* people are generally loyal supporters of democratic values and nationalistic ideas (Feillard 1997), and that their political behaviour in the public domain is parallel to the renowned dichotomy between NU and Muhammadiyah (Bush 2009). Nevertheless, the arrival of Islamic transnational movements in the last few decades in Indonesia has challenged the traditional domination of NU and Mumammadiyah in the country's Muslim public sphere. The most notable examples of these movements include the Islamist political party, Partai Keadilan Sejahtera (Prosperous Justice Party, PKS) and its affiliations, which are the Indonesian versions of Ikhwanul Muslimin, Hizbut Tahrir Indonesia, and the Salafi movement. Many scholars of Indonesian Islam assign their arrival to mark the conservative turn of Indonesian Islam (van Bruinessen 2013). The current changes to the Muslim public sphere in Indonesia has influenced the rise of cinematic practices among the *santri* across their communities, an exploration that I shall venture below.

The Rise of Cinematic *Santri* in the Indonesian Muslim Public Sphere

In 2008, *3 Doa 3 Cinta* [3 Prayers 3 Loves] became the first Indonesian commercial film to be directed by a *santri* filmmaker,[6] and was also the first film to vividly portray a character of a *santri* with a heart-beating desire for a film camera and film-making practice.[7] The film marked a rise of what I call the cinematic *santri* among the *pesantren* people. It refers to a substantial segment of a younger generation of *santri* who recently began to organize various forms of cinematic practices, such as film making, film screening, film workshops, and film discussions across the *santri* communities. By using all means possible, many of these young *santri* have made films about, but not limited to, the everyday life of Muslims in *pesantren*. Some of these films have only been circulated within the *pesantren* circle, but most of them have also experienced alternative public screenings, such as through social media, local film festivals, and "independent" mobile cinema practices. They also concerted the development of film-making infrastructure and the expansion of cultural sites of cinematic activism in the local regions where the NU community forms the majority group. By and large, their cinematic discourses revolve around the significance of voicing in public spaces traditions and interpretations of the NU-*santri* communities' characteristics of Islam, not seldom *vis-à-vis* those of other Muslim groups in the country.

Historically, in spite of the widespread taboo of film technology among the conservative majority of the *santri*, film is not entirely foreign to the former. Since the 1960s, the more moderate groups of NU-affiliated cultural producers have played an active role in the country's film arena, following the establishment of *Lesbumi* in 1962, largely in response to the increasing domination of Lekra, a cultural organization associated with the now-deceased Indonesian communist party, over the country's artistic and cultural fields (Sen 1994). After the political suspension of *Lesbumi* in 1966,[8] NU never totally turned away from cinema. In conjunction with the popularity of Islamic "nine-saints" films in the 1980s, for example, a few of NU religious figures took active participation in public discourse on how films can be used for *dakwah*. At the same time, a call for Islamic film productions was often heard from the *pesantren* grounds, usually as a reaction to the influx of "indecent films" (of domestic and overseas production) assumedly featuring sex, violence and incorrect representation of Islam (van Heeren 2012, pp. 116–18).

Today's cinematic practices of the *santri*, however, are a phenomenon very much belonging to the post-Suharto Indonesian Muslim publics. While educational reforms of *pesantren* and rapid transformation and proliferation of digital technologies in the *santri* communities are crucial to the ability of the *santri* to engage with film technologies, it is the rising visibility of Islam in Indonesian public space that has largely triggered the *santri* to use cinema for political purposes. To understand this situation, we need to look back at the increase of new Muslim middle classes across Indonesian urban societies in the 1980s (Hefner 2000). Economically, they owed their growth to the New Order's strong economic progress during the 1980s and 1990s, in parallel with the rise of Asian new riches (Robinson and Goodman 1996). Yet politically, their public voices were defined by the New Order's strict policies on expressions of political Islam, forcing them to cultivate their piety through education, popular media and other cultural practices. As the ban on political expression by Islamic groups was lifted following the transitional years of the *reformasi* era, which was also coincidentally marked by the explosive growth of the audio-visual media industry and popular culture practices (Sen and Hill 2007), the *santri* became new Muslim actors who have brought forward a novel form of Islamization (Heryanto 2008, p. 14), involving an attempt to blend symbols of Islamic piety with materials and spaces of modernity.

Unlike the middle class, according to liberal assumptions (Robinson and Goodman 1996, p. 3), this new Muslim affluence is inclined to religious dispositions (Barendregt 2006, p. 174), linking their Islamic piety with global practices of market and media consumption (Rakhmani 2016, p. 2), and exhibiting it in public spaces (Schmidt 2014, p. 25). As a result, the character of the Indonesian Muslim public sphere in the post-Suharto period has changed dramatically. Islam (or precisely Islamic symbols, languages, and discourses) is not only increasingly jostled into the public life and space through sights, sounds, touches and other corporeal sensibilities, but is also becoming a popular idiom with which the state, religious authorities, and Muslim groups of different interests, identities and ideologies, compete with each other to define public morality, market economy, political authority, and law-making policies. The definition of being a good Muslim is therefore widely contested in public spaces.

In the case of visual media space for example, the last ten years has witnessed the rising popularity of "Islamic cinema", or "films that breathe Islam" in Indonesia, marked by the 2008 phenomenal release of *Ayat-ayat Cinta* [Verses of Love, Dir. Hanung Bramantyo]. It is a film about a "polygamous" love story between Indonesian Muslim students of Al-Azhar University in Cairo, that has attracted a new record audience. Its popularity has in turn triggered the increasing production of Islamic-themed films, along with the rise of street protests, Internet-based debates, and intellectual discussions, negotiating what a true representation of Islam and Muslim identity on screen should look like (Heryanto 2014). The influence of the rising popularity of Islamic cinema genre on the emerging cinematic *santri* cannot be overlooked. In order to explore this, I will shift the focus of my discussion into the cinematic practices of Sahal, my *santri* interlocutor who has led the spread of cinematic fever in the headquarters of NU.

The Cinematic Practices of Sahal: Contesting the Muslim Publics

A self-professed film enthusiast, Sahal was born in 1979 to a *santri* family in a vibrant and dense village near the town of Cirebon, West Java. As a schoolboy, he received his education at "general" (secular) public schools, *madrasah* and *pesantren*. Later in 2000, he attended a bachelor's programme at the Syariah Faculty of IAIN Yogyakarta (Institut Agama Islam Negeri, the State Institute of Islamic Studies), during which he was also active in LKiS (Lembaga Kajian Islam dan Sosial, the Institute of Islamic and Social Studies). In late 2006, he moved to work at the NU headquarters in Jakarta where his involvement started with the central Lakpesdam NU (Lembaga Kajian dan Pengembangan Sumberdaya Manusia, NU's Institute of Research and Human Resource Development). Both LKiS and Lakpesdam NU are among the first NU-affiliated non-government organizations (NGOs) to emerge in the late 1980s, seeking to promote civil society movements across NU communities (Bush 2009, p. 100).

When I first met him in early 2012, he was working in NU-Online, NU's online media centre located at the NU central building. My acquaintance with him, however, was triggered less by his work in his office than the passion and energy he has invested in his fellow *santri* at the NU headquarters to spread "cinematic fever" across the provision of *santri* communities in local regions. Since 2008, he has organized various forms of cinematic activities, ranging from film screening and mobile cinema practice, to film seminars and discussions, and film competition and (trainings in) filmmaking. He created an underground network of film exhibitions for NU audiences, and persuaded several of NU's elder cultural producers to become his patron. He has further developed connections with some of the country's more established filmmakers and has built communication with his *santri* compatriots at other centres of the NU community who share similar passion and activism in film. He has also benefitted from NU-Online and his personal social media accounts widen, as far as possible, the possible impact of his cinematic activism.

Sahal has no academic background in filmmaking, nor is he savvy with filmmaking technologies. His passion for cinematic practices has largely developed through his personal experiences and involvement in NU's civil society movements. He confessed to me, and apparently to anyone else, that his cinematic interest started at a young age when watching *"layar tancep"* performances, a mobile cinema practice that was popular in Indonesia's rural areas during the 1980s and 1990s. Yet it is his move to Yogyakarta that is crucial for the development of not only his religious knowledge, but also his cinematic activism. During our talks, he often recalled his experiences of watching and discussing a wide variety of films, covering/including American, France, Iranian and also local productions screened in *Jamaah Cinema*, a student cinema club at the Islamic university he had attended. It was obviously not about filmmaking (yet); but such experiences only harnessed Sahal's cinematic pursuit and desire to produce his own films in the years to come.[9] While his work in the NU headquarters has allowed him to meet other *santri* who have similar interest in cinematic practices, it is his political activism in NU's "civil society" movements that has in turn accorded his cinematic practices with a strong spirit of civic participation in the national debates of what counts as the "right" representation of Islam in the country's screen culture.

During our talks, Sahal often told me that his cinematic practices are primarily aimed at countering the rise of Islamic film genre that promotes the superficial symbols of Arabized Islam, clearly singling out the names of *Ayat-ayat Cinta*. It is common knowledge that *Ayat-ayat Cinta's* film director is affiliated with Muhammadiyah, and he has visited a Muhammadiyah religious leader to seek religious advice regarding the Islamic contents of his film. I have earlier cited that it was NU's conflicted relationship with the modernists that has signified its establishment in 1926, and ever since then, the rivalry has become the main driving factors of NU's socio-cultural and political behaviours in the public sphere (Bush 2009). Having this in mind, the *santri's* effort at countering the likes of *Ayat-ayat Cinta* reverberates the competition between the traditionalists and the modernist groups over the "right" interpretation of Islam is now extended into the realm of film. However, competitors do not come only from the modernist side.

In this regard, the novel version of the film is worth recalling. It is written by Habiburrahman el-Shirazy, a *santri* who was trained in a combination of Islamic institutions, *pesantren*, *madrasah* and Al-Azhar University. A member of FLP (*Forum Lingkar Pena*), a Muslim writers' network with a strong affiliation with PKS, el-Shirazy identifies himself in a different competing habitus from that of the NU *santri* in the NU headquarters and beyond. Significantly, identification with the PKS ideology is observable through the narratives, images and messages of *Ayat-ayat Cinta*, as they yield, according to Barker (2011, p. 224), a picture of Islamic piety that gives a commitment to social change and to the individual development of faith, a characteristic of the PKS's ideological emphasis on the "individualistic pattern of Islamization" (Machmudi 2008).

Here, one point is clear. The increasing production of Islamic-themed films in the post-Suharto Indonesia, particularly since the phenomenal success of *Ayat-ayat Cinta* in 2008, has incited the *santri* to return to the national cinematic battle after a long pause in the 1960s. Their (re)turn to the film arena resonates the relentless competition of authority regarding who has the legitimate right for "picturing Islam" (George 2010) on film screen. In the past, a similar motivation has forced the NU elders to establish their organization in 1926. Yet today, the situation is different. In the past the rivalry mainly came from the modernists, especially Muhammadiyah, now it also comes from the Islamists, especially the PKS-afilliated groups, who are similarly, with some overlapping interests, "not only comfortable with pop culture but also sees pop culture as a means by which *dakwah* can occur" (Barker 2011). Such differently armed rivalry has challenged the NU *santri* to once again respond to it with "a reform of their own" (Hefner 2009); that is by arming themselves with a similar weapon, and going back into the film arena. The cinematic *santri*, in short, is a figure that unfolds a struggle between the different political and religious orientations that come with being an Indonesian Muslim.

Exploratory Project Challenging the Traditional Authority

However, the rise of cinematic practices among the *santri* can be read as an effort to establish a new form of authority among the traditionalist Muslim Indonesia, one that is mediated through visual culture. To explain this, I will turn to the ways in which the rise of cinematic *santri* may pose a threat to the traditional structure of authority in the *santri* societies.

During our talks, Sahal often complained that his cinematic practices lack moral and financial support from the elite leaders and *kyais* of NU. When further asked to talk about the marginalization, he often blamed NU's political strategies, which apparently regard cultural programmes as less important than the political interests of the organization. While his argument has a point, my observation, however, reveals that the fear of film-related technologies and practices is still widespread especially among the older generations of *santri*, who, in my view, are generally conservative and ignorant about the use of these technologies. Their fear is fuelled by the technical affordances of film technologies for producing visual and communicative possibilities, that is, the technical ability of these technologies to show living images of other ideas, ideologies, life experiences, and worlds.

The fear of image-making technologies, however, should not be understood in relation with the prohibition of figural representation in Islamic tradition or with Muslims' iconoclastic practices throughout history. This is because, firstly, many Muslims throughout history have challenged the dominant interpretation of the legal prohibition of figural representation by celebrating the production of images (Ahmed 2015). And secondly, contemporary acts of Muslim iconoclasts have sought the logic of their iconoclasm within the roots of socio-economic and political realities of the global modernity (Barry-Flood 2002), or to say it differently, issues of iconoclasm may be perpetual in the history of Muslim societies, yet they are also historically situated.

I would instead pursue another path, in my view, the visual and communicative possibilities allowed by film technologies could be at odds with the *santri's* social structures and cultural values. As I have described earlier, the *pesantren* community recognizes the significance of social order, structure of authority, and standardized morality. The *kyais* are the main stronghold of religious authority, whose authoritative power and charisma are largely structured based on their knowledge of the *pesantren's* foundational texts, the interpretation of which has been solidly established for centuries. Obviously, texts are very different from images. Compared to written words, images are not only much more "vivid and indelible" (Daston and Galison 1992), but also much denser with meanings, and much more prone to be always in motion (Spyer and Steedly 2013). The movement of images, added Spyer and Steedly (2013, p. 8), is not only intransitive but also transitive, affecting their expected and unanticipated audiences in multifarious ways that are often unpredictable and uncontrollable, either by their producers or consumers. Images, in this regard, may contain an excess of "side effects" that are hard to control. Put in the context of the *santri* communities where social order is highly maintained by religious leaders whose authority is premised on their comprehensive knowledge on textual tradition, the omnipresence of images of Islam circulated on screens, with which these religious leaders are not familiar with, and are unable to control, can be deemed as threatening not only to the social order of the *santri* communities, but also to the traditional structure of their authorities.

Against the marginalization of cinematic practices by the elite NU authorities, the rise of cinematic *santri* finds its relevance with the project of exploratory discourses and practices. To explain this, Ahmed's notion of exploratory authority is worth recalling here. Exploratory authority, assigned to the business of searching the many possible ways of being Muslim, is especially concerned with the personal and social exploration of the possibilities of Muslim human condition (Ahmed 2015, p. 84). While the conservative majority of *santri* societies has kept on debating about the taboo of film-related technologies and practices, Sahal has went on to explore the possibilities of using film technologies for Islamic purposes. As he argues, the legal status of film technologies is an issue that has long been settled by a consensus of the NU leaders, as evidenced by the ability of NU cultural producers to make an Islamic-themed film in the 1960s through *Lesbumi*. For him, in the situation where vilification of Islam is omnipresent in public spaces, it is even imperative for the *santri* to participate in the efforts at producing alternative images of Islam that will articulate peaceful and moderate voices of the religion. Aware of the fact that his educational background has accorded him more authority to speak about Islam than to make a film, Sahal designates his cinematic practices as a collaborative project between several groups of *santri*, or between a group of *santri* and a third party, who could help him realize his film-related practices. In 2016, in collaboration with an NU-affiliated independent filmmaker, and funded by the Ministry of Religious Affairs, Sahal was able to produce a documentary *pesantren* film entitled, *Jalan Dakwah Pesantren* [Pesantren's Peaceful Jihad], which he screened across various *santri* communities. His cinematic practices, spreading the importance of establishing visual tradition in the *santri* societies, are an example of how Islamic authority in the traditionalist Muslim society may change in terms of its "mediatization" (Mandaville 2007), referring to the extension of textual forms of authority into visual ones, and of the personified figures of the *kyai* to *santri* filmmakers.

Conclusion

The remarkable rise of cinematic *santri* in present day Indonesia reflects the contestation and fragmentation of religious authority in the traditionalist Muslim Indonesia. While Islam continues to play a significant role in the country's Muslim public sphere, the cinematic *santri* represents a modern figure that struggles with the political and religious differences that come with being an Indonesian Muslim through the medium of cinematic expression. Additionally, the rising popularity of cinematic practices among the *santri* can be read as an effort to establish a new form of authority among the traditionalist Muslim Indonesia, one that is mediated through visual culture. Among the *santri* communities, the role of textuality, discursive methods and personified knowledge remain central; yet by using Ahmed's exploratory forms of authority, this chapter shows that a turn to visual images has allowed the cinematic *santri* to explore the possibilities of using film technologies for Islamic purposes. This challenges the traditional construction of authority in their communities, which have been solidly institutionalized and dominated over centuries by and through textual tradition.

NOTES

1. Asad (1986, p. 14), for example, writes that Islamic tradition "consists essentially of discourses that seek to instruct practitioners regarding the correct form and purpose of a given practice that, precisely because it is established, has a history".
2. I use this term to refer to the loyal followers of the four schools of *ulama* of the classical era of Islam, and devout observers of culturally-contextualized practices of Islamic rituals.
3. It assigns to those who solely adhere to the Quran and Hadith as their religious guidance, and strongly advocate for "purifying" Islam from local customs.

4. I use this term to refer to the many ways by which Muslims aligned the resurgent Islam with political ideology. An example of this is the establishment of Partai Keadilan Sejahtera (Prosperous Justice Party, PKS) in the early 2000s, which aims at "Islamizing Indonesia" through party-political activism leading to the establishment of an Islamic state (Machmudi 2008).
5. The number of *kitab kuning* taught in *pesantren* varies, but can be classified into the following categories: Islamic jurisprudence and its principles, doctrine of Islam, traditional Arabic grammar, hadith collections, Quranic exegesis, mysticism and morality, collection of prayers, invocations and Islamic magic, and texts in praise of the prophets and saints (Dhofier 1982; van Bruinessen 1990).
6. Despite being funded by foreign donors, and caters to global audiences of international film festivals, the film was commercially screened in the country's major cinema chains, in addition to its sold DVDs.
7. It is a coming-of-age film describing the pupils from three *pesantren* (called *santri*), who, after suffering from painful losses of their beloved ones, struggled to grapple with the difficulties in their everyday life by using the *pesantren's* Islamic teachings as their ethical guidance.
8. The suspension of *Lesbumi*, according to Jones (2013, p. 108), was partly because of "the decreasing importance of (and increasing state and social antipathy towards) political association" of the organization.
9. In 2016, in collaboration with an NU-affiliated independent filmmaker, and funded by the Ministry of Religious Affairs, Sahal was able to produce a documentary *pesantren* film, entitled *Jalan Dakwah Pesantren*.

REFERENCES

Ahmed, Shahab. 2015. *What is Islam? The Importance of Being Islamic*. Princeton and Oxford: Princeton University Press.

Arnez, Monika. 2009. "Dakwah by the Pen". *Indonesia and the Malay World* 37, no. 117: 45–64.

Asad, Talal. 1986. *The Idea of an Anthropology of Islam*. Washington: Center for Contemporary Arab Studies, Georgetown University.

Barendregt, Bart. 2006. "Cyber-*nashid*, Transnational Soundscapes in Muslim Southeast Asia". In *Medi@sia, Global Media/tion In and Out of Context*, edited by Todd Joseph Miles Holden and Timothy J. Scrase, pp. 170–87. Oxon: Routledge.

Barker, Thomas A.C. 2011. "A Cultural Economy of the Contemporary Indonesian Film Industry". PhD dissertation, Department of Sociology, National University of Singapore.

Barry-Flood, Finbarr. 2002. "Between Cult and Culture: Bamiyan, Islamic Iconoclasm, and the Museum". *Art Bulletin* 84, no. 4: 641–59.
Berkey, Jonathan P. 2010. "Audience and Authority in Medieval Islam: The Case of Popular Preacher". In *Charisma and Religious Authority: Jewish, Christian and Muslim Preaching, 1200–1500*, edited by Katherine L. Jansen and Miri Rubin, pp. 105–20. Belgium: Brepols Publishers.
Bush, Robin. 2009. *Nahdlatul Ulama and the Struggle for Power within Islam and Politics in Indonesia*. Singapore: Institute of Southeast Asian Studies.
Crone, Patricia and Martin Hinds. 1986. *God's Caliph: Religious Authority in the First Centuries of Islam*. Cambridge: Cambridge University Press.
Daston, Lorraine and Peter Galison. 1992. "The Image of Objectivity". *Representations* 40 (Special Issue, Seeing Science): 81–128.
Devji, Faisal. 2005. *Landscapes of the Jihad: Militancy, Morality and Modernity*. London: Hurst & Company.
Dhofier, Zamakhsyari. 2011 [1982]. *Tradisi Pesantren: Studi Pandangan Hidup Kyai dan Visinya Mengenai Masa Depan Indonesia*. Revised ed. Jakarta: LP3S.
Eickelman, Dale F. and Jon W. Anderson. 1999. "Redefining Muslim Publics". In *New Media in the Muslim World: The Emerging Public Sphere*, edited by Dale F. Eickelman and Jon W. Anderson, pp. 1–19. Bloomington and Indianapolis: Indiana University Press.
Feillard, Andrée. 1997. "Traditionalist Islam and the State in Indonesia: The Road to Legitimacy and Renewal". In *Islam in an Era of Nation-States*, edited by Robert W. Hefner and Patricia Horvatich, pp. 128–56. Honolulu: University of Hawai'i Press.
Geertz, Clifford. 1976 [1960]. *The Religion of Java*. Chicago and London: The University of Chicago Press.
George, Kenneth M. 2010. *Picturing Islam: Art and Ethics in a Muslim Lifeworld*. West Sussex, United Kingdom: Willey-Blackwell.
Hefner, Robert W. 2000. *Civil Islam: Muslims and Democratization in Indonesia*. Princeton and Oxford: Princeton University Press.
———. 2009. "Islamic School, Social Movement and Democracy in Indonesia". In *Making Modern Muslim: The Politics of Islamic Education in Southeast Asia*, edited by Robert W. Hefner, pp. 55–105. Honolulu: University of Hawai'i Press.
Heryanto, Ariel. 2008. "Pop Culture and Competing Identities". In *Popular Culture in Indonesia: Fluid Identities in Post-Authoritarian Politics*, edited by Ariel Heryanto, pp. 1–36. London and New York: Routledge.
———. 2014. *Identity and Pleasure: The Politics of Indonesian Screen Culture*. Singapore and Japan: NUS Press and Kyoto University Press.
Hoesterey, James B. 2008. "Marketing Morality: The Rise, Fall and Rebranding of Aa Gym". In *Expressing Islam: Religious Life and Politics in Indonesia*,

edited by Greg Fealy and Sally White, pp. 95–112. Singapore: Institute of Southeast Asian Studies.

Hosen, Nadirsyah. 2008. "Online Fatwa in Indonesia: From Fatwa Shoppping to Googling Kiai". In *Expressing Islam: Religious Life and Politics in Indonesia*, edited by Greg Fealy and Sally White, pp. 159–73. Singapore: Institute of Southeast Asian Studies.

Jones, Carla. 2010. "Images of Desire: Creating Virtue and Value in an Indonesian Islamic Lifestyle Magazine". *Journal of Middle East Women's Studies* 6, no. 3: 91–117.

Jones, Tod. 2013. *Culture, Power, and Authoritarianism in the Indonesian State: Cultural Policy across the Twentieth Century to the Reform Era*. Leiden and Boston: Brill and KITLV.

Kramer, Gudrun and Sabine Schmidtke. 2006. *Speaking for Islam: Religious Authorities in Muslim Societies*. Leiden: Brill.

Lukens-Bull, Ronald. 2005. *A Peaceful Jihad: Negotiating Identity and Modernity in Muslim Java*. New York: Palgrave McMillan.

Machmudi, Yon. 2008 (2006). "Islamising Indonesia: The Rise of Jamaah Tarbiyah and the Prosperous Justice Party (PKS)". PhD dissertation, ANU E Press.

Mandaville, Peter. 2007. "Globalization and the Politics of Religious Knowledge: Pluralizing Authority in the Muslim World". *Theory Culture & Society* 24, no. 2: 101–15.

Marvin, Carolyn. 1988. *When Old Technologies Were New: Thinking About Electric Communication in the Late Nineteenth Century*. New York and Oxford: Oxford University Press.

Rakhmani, Inaya. 2016. *Mainstreaming Islam in Indonesia: Television, Identity and the Middle Class*. New York: Palgrave MacMillan.

Robinson, Richard and David S.G. Goodman. 1996. "The New Rich in Asia: Economic Development, Social Status, and Political Consciousness". In *The New Rich in Asia: Mobile Phones, McDonald's and Middle-Class Revolution*, edited by Richard Robinson and David S.G. Goodman, pp. 1–18. London and New York: Routledge.

Salim, Arskal. 2008. *Challenging the Secular State: The Islamization of Law in Modern Indonesia*. Honolulu: University of Hawai'i Press.

Schmidt, Leonie K. 2014. "Visions of the Future: Imagining Islamic Modernities in Indonesian Islamic-themed Post-Suharto Popular and Visual Culture". PhD dissertation, University of Amsterdam.

Sen, Krishna. 1994. *Indonesian Cinema: Framing the New Order*. London and New Jersey: Zed Books Ltd.

Sen, Krishna and David T. Hill. 2007. *Media, Culture and Politics in Indonesia*. Jakarta: Equinox Publishing Indonesia. First published by Oxford University Press in 2000.

Spyer, Patricia and Mary Margaret Steedly. 2013. "Introduction: Images that Move". In *Images that Move*, edited by Patricia Spyer and Mary Margaret Steedly, pp. 3–39. Santa Fe, New Mexico: School for Advanced Reseach Press.

Srimulyani, Eka. 2012. *Women from Traditional Islamic Educational Institutions in Indonesia: Negotiating Public Spaces.* Amsterdam: Amsterdam University Press.

van Bruinessen, Martin. 1990. "Kitab Kuning: Books in Arabic Script used in the Pesantren Milieu; Comments on a New Collection in the KITLV Library". *Bijdragen tot de Taal-, Land- en Colkenkunde* 146, no. 2/3: 226–69.

———, ed. 2013. *Contemporary Development in Indonesian Islam: Explaining the Conservative Turn.* Singapore: Institute of Southeast Asian Studies.

van-Heeren, Katinka. 2012. *Contemporary Indonesian Film: Spirits of Reform and Ghost from the Past.* Leiden: KITLV Press.

16

THE POLITICS OF RELIGIOUS AND CULTURAL AUTHORITY: CONTESTATION AND CO-EXISTENCE OF SULTANATE AND ISLAMIC MOVEMENTS IN THE POST-SUHARTO YOGYAKARTA AND TERNATE

M. Najib Azca and Moh Zaki Arrobi

Introduction

This chapter attempts to delineate the politicization of religious and cultural authority in Ternate and Yogyakarta. It narrates the contestation and co-existence of two religious and cultural authorities in these cities, namely the Islamic Sultanate on the one hand, and Islamic movements on the other. The sultanate institution in both Ternate and Yogyakarta dated back to the pre-colonial era. Meanwhile, the rise of Islamism has been a key feature in both cities after the fall of the New Order in 1998. The two royal institutions have played a crucial role during the democratic transition in 1998 and beyond. The Keraton of Yogyakarta played a pivotal role in promoting the *reformasi* movement while at the same time preventing violence and riots during the critical power transition period. On the other hand, the Keraton of Ternate had been one of the warring parties during the communal conflict in North Moluccas in 1999–2001.

Within the existing scholarly debates, the re-emergence of the Sultanate and Islamism is widely portrayed as a representation of identity politics that emerged from the democratization process in post-authoritarian Indonesia (Assyaukanie 2009; Hilmy 2010; Klinken 2007b; Machmudi 2008; Mujani 2007; Platzdasch 2009; Salim 2008). This is reflected in the studies of the Sultanate both in Ternate and Yogyakarta. In Ternate, major studies explain how the decentralization process brought the resurgence of "tradition" in the political arena of Ternate and North Moluccas (Bubandt 2004; Klinken 2007a; Duncan 2009; Smith 2009).

In this wave of "politics of tradition", the Sultanate and Islamism are located as conflicting forces. This conclusion was drawn based on the rivalry between the Sultanate of Ternate and Islamist forces during the communal conflict, as well as during the power struggle for resources in the early years after the country underwent decentralization (Duncan 2005, p. 68; Klinken 2007a, pp. 109–23). Meanwhile, the Keraton of Yogyakarta is associated with cultural authority that represents Javanese high culture—"Javanese Islam"—and the symbol of pluralism (Woodward 2010). Gerry van Klinken (2007b) rightly pointed out that the re-emergence of Sultanate across the country after the collapse of Suharto's New Order regime in 1998 has become a model of neo-traditionalist leadership and a symbol of cultural pluralism.

This chapter aims to enrich the ongoing scholarly debate by narrating the contestation and cooperation between the Sultanate and Islamism in Ternate and Yogyakarta. In doing so, it will trace how the different trajectory experience by the Ternate and Yogyakarta Sultanates in reclaiming political authority has resulted in the different efficacy of their authority in the realm of religion, culture, and politics. In Ternate, the failure of the Sultanate to restore its political authority during the communal conflict, and the power struggle in the North Moluccas province, has limited its geographical (sphere of influence) and cultural authority. Meanwhile, the Yogyakarta Sultanate's success during the critical *reformasi* period and the victory of pro-Sultanate's camp during the struggle for the special law of Yogyakarta, has extended its traditional authority. Its authority is dominant politically, hegemonic culturally, and resourceful economically.

In proposing such an argument, this chapter will start by providing a brief historical background about the Sultanates in Ternate and Yogyakarta. Then it discusses the resurgence of political identities manifested in "tradition" and "Islamism" in both cities during and after the *reformasi* movement of 1998. This will be followed by: (1) narrating different trajectory of the two Sultanates in reclaiming political authority in the post-Suharto era; and (2) understanding the recent contestation and cooperation between the Sultanate and Islamism in the realm of politics, religion, and culture. Methodologically, this research employs a qualitative method based on fieldwork during 2014–16 in Yogyakarta and 2016 in Ternate. The data was collected through in-depth interviews, participant observations, and document analysis. In-depth interviews were conducted with the religious leaders, Islamic leaders, social activists, local state officials, as well as the royal family of the Sultanates.

Sultanates in the Modern Indonesia

Ternate and Yogyakarta were two of the most important Islamic Sultanates that have ever existed in Indonesia. Ternate was the biggest Islamic kingdom that had existed in Eastern Indonesia since the sixteenth century (Amal 2009), while Yogyakarta along with Surakarta was the most influential kingdom in Java since the eighteenth century (Woodward 2010). However, the fate of these two Sultanates in the modern era is different. Yogyakarta remains the only surviving traditional kingdom in the country, and even expands its role. Meanwhile, Ternate, like the other Sultanates in the archipelago, has declined in influence since the coming of the new republic in 1945.

The different fate of both kingdoms has much to do with their historical trajectory during the revolutionary struggle. After Dutch colonialism ended in the mid-twentieth century, Ternate, as with the other kingdoms in Nusantara, joined the new Republic of Indonesia. Its authority and centrality in public life began to decline with the emergence of the new nation-state of Indonesia. Within this new republic, Ternate along with the other kingdoms in the region was no more than a cultural and historical symbol. In this regard, this decline of influence was due to its absence during several determining moments of the nation, such as during the national awakening movement in the 1920s, independence struggle in 1945, and revolutionary struggle to resist the Dutch recolonization of Indonesia (Hanna and Alwi 1990, pp. 248–50). The role of Ternate in these political struggles was relatively less visible than the other Sultanates in Java, especially Yogyakarta. Let alone, the Sultanate of Ternate was on the side of the Dutch during the national revolution in the 1940s. Therefore, its existence came into disestablishment in the 1950–60s in the hands of the nationalists (Klinken 2007b, p. 153).

On the other hand, Yogyakarta took a divergent path during the revolutionary struggle and in Indonesia's postcolonial politics. Sultan Hamengkubuwono IX (HB IX) was a republican and a close friend of nationalist leaders Sukarno and Hatta. Under his leadership, Kasultanan of Yogyakarta in the 1940s fully supported the national revolution led by nationalist elites. It issued the so-called September 5th Mandate Letters, which stated that the Yogyakarta Kingdom is an integral part of the Republic of Indonesia (Woodward 2011, p. 1). He also demonstrated strong and distinct leadership by financing the salary of officers for four consecutive months and allowing Yogyakarta to be the temporary capital city for Indonesia after Jakarta was captured by the Dutch. In addition, he was also said to be the mastermind behind the "6 hours military operation" in Yogyakarta that demonstrated to the international community that the Republic continued to exist (Roem et al. 2011, pp. 76–77). Given all of his contributions, Sultan HB IX became a national elite that survived not only during the national revolution, but also during Suharto's New Order. He became the minister of defence during the Sukarno era; then, he served as vice-president between 1973 and 1978 during the Suharto era.

The Resurgence of Identity Politics in the *Reformasi* Era

In the post-Suharto era, both cities experienced a resurgence of ethnic and religious politics. Suharto's resignation impacted local politics across the country, with some arguing that the local level politics remains dominated by oligarchs inherited from the New Order (Hadiz and Robison 2004; Hadiz 2010). However, how these local elites deal with their denizens have profoundly changed (Berenschot, Nordholt, and Bakker 2017). The rise of identity politics at the local level since *reformasi* can be found in two areas: the first being local regulation and the second in public discourse. In the first area, there is widespread local ordinance inspired by religious teaching and morality. Robin Bush (2008) notes that in 2008, there were seventy-eight religion-influenced regional regulations in fifty-seven districts and municipalities throughout Indonesia. In these regulations, there were discrimination towards religious minorities and restrictions towards women. Meanwhile, the second area refers to the development of religious discourse towards conservatism and fundamentalism. Van Bruinessen (2013) reveals that in the post-Suharto era there is a "conservative turn" within the Islamic discourse in Indonesia, that the public presence of new Islamic transnational movements, the issuance of *fatwa* (religious opinion) by Indonesia's *ulama* council that declared secularism, liberalism, and pluralism to be incompatible with Islam, and frequent attacks on religious minorities are the exemplars of what he described as this conservative turn.

Identity politics also feature strongly in Ternate and Yogyakarta today. In Ternate, decentralization has not only meant the transfer of power from the central government to the local government, but it also meant the revival of identity politics manifested in the language of "tradition", "ethnic", or "religious" identities. According to Klinken (2007b), Ternate along with North Moluccas has been one of the key sites where communitarian politics has rejuvenated in the name of reviving the sultanate and tradition. During the communal conflict in 1999–2001, the symbol associated with the Sultanate was popularized. This was best reflected during the clashes between *"Pasukan Kuning"* (Yellow Troops) formed by the Sultanate of Ternate, and *"Pasukan Putih"* (White Troops) formed by the Islamist and supported by the Sultanate of Tidore. These troops strengthened existing Ternate's Sultanate youth militia *Gerakan Muda Sultan Babullah* (Gemusba), which was closely connected with the military and Golkar during the New Order (Klinken 2007a, p. 117). The extensive utilization of *adat* and traditions gained prominence in North Moluccas. In this wave of the "revival of Sultanate", Tidore which had no Sultan for a long time, reinstalled a ruler to balance Ternate, while the Sultanate of Jailolo and Bacan also reinstalled their new sultans, though their roles were limited (Klinken 2007b, p. 154).

After the communal conflict ended, and the province of North Moluccas was established, ethnic politics emerged during the direct regional election (*Pilkada*). This phenomenon appeared during the North Moluccas gubernatorial election in 2013. All candidates were perceived to be representing the dominant ethnicities in North Moluccas. For instance, KH Ahmad Ghani Kazuba, Sahrin Hamid, and Hein Namotemo represented the Tobelo-Galela; Syamsir Andili, Malik Sofyan, Nashir Thaib, and Hasan Doa represented the Tidore; Muhajir Albar and Ismail Arifin represented the Makean; and Hidayat Mus represented the Sanana and Buton.[1] The ethnic attribution on local political contest also appeared in the 2007 gubernatorial election where Thayib Armain represented the Makean ethnic group, while his rival, Abdul Ghafur, represented the Tidore. In addition, the post-Suharto Ternate has been signified by the emergence of religion-influenced regional regulations, or "shariatization" of the local regulation. There are two products of "sharia"-oriented laws in Ternate, namely the local regulation for teaching the Quran to children and regional regulation to entirely prohibit the circulation and consumption of liquor.

Meanwhile, the emergence of identity politics coincided with the rise of new Islamist movements. Several Islamist movements emerged after the *reformasi* era in Yogyakarta, such as Laskar Jihad/Jihad Troops and Majelis Mujahidin Indonesia (MMI)/Indonesian Mujahedeen Council. These organizations were actively involved in campaigning for sharia law and Islamization. Laskar Jihad was the largest and most well-organized group that sent voluntary jihad fighters to the Moluccas (Hassan 2006). It was part of Forum Komunikasi Ahlussunnah Wal Jama'ah that was established during religious mass gathering (*tabligh akbar*) in Yogyakarta in 2000 (Mubarak 2002, p. 122). Meanwhile, MMI was also among the most influential Islamist movements in post-Suharto Yogyakarta. It was established in Yogyakarta through an Islamic congress that aspired to uphold sharia law in Indonesia (Mubarak 2002, pp. 124–26). Apart from Laskar Jihad and MMI, Yogyakarta's post-Suharto has been signified by the growing presence and influence of Islamist vigilante groups, most of which were loosely connected to the political parties in Yogyakarta. Among the groups are Gerakan Pemuda Ka'bah/Kaaba Youth Movement, Gerakan Anti Maksiat/Anti-Vice Movement, Front Jihad Islam/Islamic Jihad Front, and Laskar Hizbullah/Hizbullah's troop. They were not formally connected to the Partai Persatuan Pembangunan (PPP)/United Development Party, but had strong emotional and historical relations with the party (Arrobi 2018).

In addition, growing intolerance in Yogyakarta in recent times also demonstrates the rise of identity politics. Although Yogyakarta has been prominently known as "the city of tolerance" in which diverse religions, cultures, and ethnicities can co-exist, there is growing intolerance in this city in the last five years. The Wahid Institute launched a report on religious freedom that located Yogyakarta as the "runner up" as the most intolerant province in Indonesia just behind West Java. The Wahid Institute (2014) noted 21 incidents from 154 total incidents in Indonesia that took place in Yogyakarta. The acts of intolerance manifested in various forms, from banning and threatening public discussions, closing the churches, and organizing public rallies to persecuting certain groups such as Shia, Ahmadiyya and the communists. These intolerant acts manifest in multiple forms, underpinning factors that can change in different occasions and times: they range from ideological, instrumental, and symbolic forms depending on the local political context (Azca, Ikhwan, and Arrobi 2019). Unsurprisingly, one of the leading proponents behind such actions is the Islamist vigilante groups. According to Infid (2016), the two major players behind the increasing intolerance in Yogyakarta are Islamic Jihad Front (FJI) and Indonesian Muslim Forum (FUI).

Reclaiming Political Authority

While both cities have been experiencing growing identity politics in the public sphere and discourse, the role and fate of both Sultanates are starkly different. The role of the Sultanate of Ternate has been limited to cultural and religious matters only. Its sphere of influence is also limited to the northern areas. Meanwhile, the Sultanate of Yogyakarta has successfully expanded its role in the realm of politics, culture, economics, and to some degree religion. What accounts for this difference is the divergent paths both Sultanates took to reclaim political authority in the post-authoritarian period. The Sultanate of Ternate failed to restore its political authority during the heated communal conflict in 1999–2001 and its aftermath, while the Sultanate of Yogyakarta was successful in reclaiming its political authority via the issuance of Special Law No. 13/2012 that granted Yogyakarta a special region status, in which the Sultan of Yogyakarta assumed the role of Governor of Yogyakarta province.

The Sultanate of Ternate attempted to restore its political authority during the transition from Suharto's authoritarian regime to *reformasi* era, but met with three failures: (1) the failure to name the new province as "Maluku Kie Raha"; (2) the rejection to Ternate's proposed location of the capital for the new province; (3) the defeat of Sultan Mudaffar Shah of Ternate in the North Moluccas gubernatorial election. These are elaborated in the three narratives below.

At the beginning of the *reformasi* era, the aspiration to form a new province called "North Moluccas" which is separate from "South Moluccas" gained momentum. On 4 October 1999, and after some political lobbying, student and mass demonstrations, President Habibie declared North Maluku a new province by signing Law No. 46/1999 (Klinken 2007a, pp. 110–12). It was the beginning of the real battle. After that, the power struggle began to the contest for the name, capital, and more importantly the position of the governor of this new region. In all these political battles, the Sultanate of Ternate was at the forefront but was later defeated. His first move to reclaim its political authority was a campaign to use "Maluku Kie Raha" as the name of the new province of North Moluccas. Maluku Kie Raha is originally from the traditional name of Ternate's Sultanate. It symbolized not only the new name of the province but also signalled the attempt to revive the Sultanate's values and customs into the new province institution. His manoeuvre triggered fierce resistance from other ethnic communities and Sultanates that worried about growing power and domination of Ternate.[2] As a result, instead of "Maluku Kie Raha" as proposed by the Sultan of Ternate, the new province was named as "North Moluccas" that had been approved by a majority of political actors in the region.

The Sultan's proposal to locate the new capital in Ternate or later Sidangoli was strongly rejected by Ternate's political opponents such as other ethnic elites in North Moluccas. According to the former secretary of Sultan Mudaffar Shah, Adam Mahrus, the Sultan at the beginning proposed Sidangoli to be the capital of the new province and Ternate as the transitional city of North Moluccas province.[3] One of the reasons for choosing Sidangoli was because of its strategic and central location and closeness to Ternate city. Mudaffar's proposal was immediately rejected by the other Sultanates in the region such as Tidore, Bacan, and Jailolo, and the Sultanate's opponents. Unsurprisingly, their rejection was caused by anxiety over rising power and dominance of the Ternate Sultanate. As a compromise, a relatively unknown city, Sofifi, was chosen by all competing parties as the capital of North Moluccas province.

Moreover, the Sultan of Ternate failed in the race for the North Moluccas governorship. This first race was between Mudaffar Shah and Bahar Andili that took place during the beginning of the communal conflict. The latter was an influential bureaucrat supported by anti-Sultan forces such as the United Development Party (PPP), HMI-elites, and Makian ethnic community (Klinken 2007a, pp. 115–16). However, neither the Sultan nor Bahar Andili secured the governor position. After two years of political factionalism and the cancellation of Abdul Ghafur as the elected governor, it was Thayib Armain who became the governor of North Moluccas in 2002. He was a senior bureaucrat and a Makian ethnic. Sultan Mudaffar Shah tried again in the 2007 regional election; he was supported by several small parties including Partai Persatuan Demokrasi Kebangsaan (PPDK). His coalition failed to meet the 15 per cent threshold votes or seats in the regional legislative body, thus Sultan Mudaffar's candidacy did not pass the administrative selection by the Election Committee/*Komisi Pemilihan Umum* (KPU). KPU's decision sparked a furious reaction from the Sultan's supporters, and they occupied the office of KPU for three days, and they even attacked security forces and destroyed public facilities in the northern area of Ternate (Husen 2016).

In these three cases, the Sultanate's defeats led to the failure in reclaiming its political authority. The failure diminished its political, economic, and cultural roles in this region. Although Sultan Mudaffar Shah and his wife were successful in securing legislative seats for the national parliament and regional representative body from 2004 to 2014, it was these three political struggles—the race for the name, capital, and the governorship—that determined the fate of the Sultanate of Ternate in the post-Suharto era. The failure of Sultan Mudaffar Shah to reclaim political authority during the critical time of power transition limited his role in cultural matters, and his sphere of influence is restricted to the northern area of Ternate. This unsuccessful story is starkly different compared to Yogyakarta's success story in the post-Suharto era.

Contrary to Ternate's fate, the Sultanate of Yogyakarta managed to reclaim its political authority in the post-Suharto era. Its success can be attributed to two significant moments: (1) the growing role of Sultan HB X and his pivotal role in directing *reformasi* movement and in maintaining peace and order during the turbulent times; (2) the political victory of pro-Sultanate's camp during the battle for special law in parliament and outside parliament. In these two occasions, Sultan HB X and his supporters obtained a significant political victory over his adversaries. This led to the strengthening role of the Sultanate's institution in the realm of politics, economics, culture, and to certain degree, religion.

In the first moment, Sultan HB X had been successful in directing the *reformasi* movement and maintaining peace in Yogyakarta. While other big cities like Jakarta and Surakarta were chaotic, the condition in Yogyakarta remained peaceful during the critical times of 1998. This peacefulness of Yogyakarta was even evidently reflected during a mass rally against Suharto on 20 May 1998 that mobilized more than half a million people when not a single shop window was broken, and not a single person was injured (Mas'oed, Panggabean, and Azca 2001, p. 120). This peaceful condition of Yogyakarta during the *reformasi* era cannot be separated from the role of Sultan HB X. According to Woodward (2010, p. 230), Sultan HB X had drawn a mix of cultural, religious, and nationalist legitimacy from the charisma of Yogyakarta as the "mother city" of Indonesia's revolution that enabled him to consolidate his power, and more importantly, to secure peace and order in Yogyakarta in 1998.

By exploiting his legitimacy as the cultural, religious, and nationalist leader, Sultan HB X had been successful in uniting *kejawen* and *santri* Muslims in a common struggle against the Suharto regime in the same way that they did in the struggle against the Dutch during the revolution (Woodward 2010). Furthermore, a positive role played by the Sultan both as a cultural and political leader of Yogyakarta that maintained close relations with different groups including the Chinese and the security forces enabled Yogyakarta to remain peaceful and safe (Panggabean and Smith 2011, p. 240). In the past, the heroic narrative of Sultan HB IX during the struggle against the Dutch and national revolution in the 1940s had been a distinct point that helped the Sultanate to survive, and fifty years later the exceptional leadership of Sultan HB X in the struggle for peaceful *reformasi* in Yogyakarta enabled him to remain in power.

While the positive role of Sultan HB X in *reformasi* strengthened his power as a governor and sultan, the political victory in the battle for *Keistimewaan Yogyakarta* (Yogyakarta's specialness) has been the most decisive moment that has successfully reclaimed political authority of the Sultanate. This pro-Sultanate's victory led to the issuance of Special Law No. 13/2012. According to that law, Yogyakarta is granted special region status along with special rights in the election system to choose the governor, local governance and institution, land, culture, and space regulation (UUK No. 12/2013). This special status strengthened the capacity of the Sultanate of Yogyakarta to control land as an essential power resource (Dardias 2019). Before that, although the special status of Yogyakarta was granted through Law No. 3/1950, in fact, there was no difference regarding power sharing, revenue sharing, and resources allocation between Yogyakarta and other provinces in Indonesia as reflected in Law No. 32/1956, Law No. 18/1965, and Law No. 5/1974. Yogyakarta was no different from other provinces except in one matter, namely the position of governor and vice governor that must be automatically filled by the Sultan of Yogyakarta and Pakualaman (Dardias 2009, p. 198). Thus, the issuance of Law No. 13/2012 marked a significant turning point that shapes the trajectory of the Sultanate of Yogyakarta.

The Sultanate for Yogyakarta's victory could not be achieved without political mobilization of grassroot, cultural, and indigenous organizations. Numerous indigenous organizations were formed, and they utilized local ethnic and cultural resources to build their legitimacy for mobilizing protest and participation that support the privileged status of Yogyakarta Special Region (Effendi 2012). Among them were Gerakan Rakyat Yogyakarta (Yogyakarta's People Movement), Genta Raja (United Yogyakarta Movement), Sekber Gamawan (Association for the Special Status of Yogyakarta), and Posko Referendum (Post Command Referendum); they were formed during 2007–10, and some of them continue to exist today. According to Dardias (2009), at the time the most prominent reason behind the demand of specialness of Yogyakarta had much to do with its history during Indonesia's struggle for independence. The supporters based their demands on the assumption that Sultan HB IX and the people of Yogyakarta have sacrificed for the existence of Indonesia, thus, the central government must value that contribution by granting special region status to Yogyakarta (Dardias 2009, p. 200). On the other hand, there was a group of civil society that preferred a democratic election to choose the governor of Yogyakarta; they consisted of non-government organizations, academics, activists, political parties, and students. Nevertheless, the pro-Sultanate forces had been relatively more successful in mobilizing support for the specialness. The issuance of Special Law No. 13/2012 signifies the political victory of pro-Sultanate's forces in the struggle for *Keistimewaan*.

Contestation over Authority

Two exemplars are taken here to elucidate how different efficacy of authority possessed by both Sultanates shaped the nature, extent, and actors of contestation between the Sultanates, Islamist movements, and other social forces at the local landscape. They are: (1) the issue of succession of the Sultanate; and (2) the electoral competition in Ternate and Yogyakarta. The issue of succession demonstrates how the two Sultanates have different efficacy of authority. In Ternate, the issue around succession emerged after the death of Sultan Mudaffar Shah in 2015. Before he died, he issued *Jaib Kolano*—a Sultanate decree that claimed to come from God—stating that he appointed the twin babies of Boki Nita—his last wife as well as his queen of Ternate—as the crown prince who will inherit his kingdom. This decision sparked fierce resistance within the Sultan's family. It was the sons of Sultan Mudaffar Shah from his three other wives who were at the forefront in resisting the Sultan's decision. They aligned with officers from other kingdom to challenge the decision of the Sultan through various means, including through a legal struggle. They questioned the validity of the twin babies of Boki, suspecting that Boki manipulated the identity and the origin of the twins. In short, they brought the case to the court; then the court ordered a DNA test for the twins. The result of the DNA test was surprising, revealing that the twins' DNA does not match with that of the Sultan and Boki Nita. Then, the court sentenced Boki Nita to eighteen months in prison due to misappropriation of the twins' origins.

Nevertheless, the royal family drama did not end with the court's decision. The conflict extended beyond the royal family. After the imprisonment of Boki Nita, the traditional supporters of the Sultanate from northern Ternate protested the court's decision and demanded the release of Boki Nita. They even clashed with security officers after their request to suspend the detention of Boki Nita was rejected by the Ternate's District Court.[4] This demonstrated that the loyalty of traditional supporters of the Sultanate in northern Ternate remains unshakable although the DNA test revealed the twin babies are not the Sultan's children. For them, the support for Boki Nita's twins to become the crown prince of Ternate symbolizes their loyalty to keep the Sultan's testament before he died.[5] While the battle for a new Sultan of Ternate among the royal family, especially between the sons of Sultan Mudaffar Shah and the Boki Nita's supporters continues, the local government, political parties, and Islamic organizations remained silent. The regional government of North Moluccas did not want to get involved in this royal family conflict. The similar stand was also taken by various Islamic organizations such as Nahdlatul Ulama (NU), Muhammadiyah, al-Khairat, and Hidayatullah. All of them argued that this battle for a new Sultan is an internal family matter, and they do not want to interfere by any means.

Ternate's succession narrative demonstrated the nature, extent, and actors of conflict and contestation within the kingdom. The issue around the succession of the Sultanate of Ternate remains an internal matter of the royal family. Therefore, the actors involved in the power struggle were only those family members either the sons of the Sultan from his three wives or Boki Nita and her supporters. External actors such as the local government, political parties, and Islamic organizations remained passive and did not demonstrate any interest. We argue that this is because the authority of the Sultanate is weak and limited to the cultural arena. As we have described earlier, the Sultanate of Ternate had failed to restore its political authority during the communal conflict and the struggle for the name, capital, and governorship of North Moluccas province. Accordingly, the efficacy of the Sultanate's authority was limited within the royal family and in the northern area, the stronghold of a traditional supporter of the Sultanate. When the battle for a new Sultan emerged, the conflicting parties are the family members and the northern royalists. Other parties did not have any interest to involve in such scramble. This is starkly different from Yogyakarta's succession experience that will be narrated below.

Unlike the Ternate's succession story, the battle for the new leadership of Yogyakarta's Sultanate involves more diverse actors and broader issues. The story began with the fact that Sultan HB X did not have any son to be appointed as crown prince. To remedy this problem, the Sultan had systematically attempted to prepare his elder daughter Gusti Pembayun as his successor. To realize his plan, the Sultan of Yogyakarta issued various decrees such as two *Sabdatama*, one *Sabdaraja* (proclamation) and two *Dawuh* (order) from 2012 to 2015. The contents of these decrees vary. The first *Sabdatama* on the declaration that Yogyakarta is an independent kingdom that deserves a "special status" from the central government was issued on May 2012. Among the four Sultanate decrees, it might be *Sabdaraja* that was the most controversial. This decree changed the title of the Sultanate from "*Buwono*" to "*Bawono*", and it abolished the title of "*Sayyidin Panatagama Khalifatullah*" which was considered by Muslims as the symbolism of the Sultanate's leadership in the Muslim society of Mataram—the genuine name for the Yogyakarta Sultanate. Then, in *Dawuh Raja*, Sultan HB X changed the title of his elder daughter from "*Gusti Kanjeng Ratu Pembayun*" to "*Gusti Kanjeng Ratu Mangkubumi*"; it symbolized that GKR Mangkubumi is now officially the successor of the Sultanate of Yogyakarta. Finally, in *Jejering Raja*, Sultan HB X declared that all members of the royal family should follow his orders and those who disobey them will be expelled from the Mataram kingdom.

Unsurprisingly, the response towards these Sultanate decrees have been divided and contested. Only *Sabdatama I* that aimed to support *Keistimewaan* struggle was unchallenged. It was supported by all members of the royal family, and it was effective in accelerating the issuance of Special Law No. 13/2012 on "Specialness of Yogyakarta" (Dardias 2016, p. 39). However, that was not the case for the other four Sultanate decrees. Dardias (2016) notes that in the four Sultanate decrees—*Sabdatama II, Sabdaraja, Dawuh Raja,* and *Jejering Raja*—that were issued in 2015, the reactions from both the internal and external Sultanates were divided, and the effectiveness of these decrees was challenged and contested by various actors. Sultan HB X faced serious challenges from the internal royal family—especially from his younger brother—and from external forces. The most serious challenge to the Sultanate decrees came from the Sultan's brother. This resistance was led by the trio brothers of Sultan HB X namely GBPH Prabukusumo, GBPH Yudhaningrat and KGPH Hadiwinoto. They consolidated the royal family to oppose the Sultanate decree and to defend the so-called "*Paugeran*" (custom) of Keraton. Their resistance was openly expressed in public events. For instance, in a sermon at the Universitas Gadjah Mada during the month of Ramadan in 2015, GBPH openly criticized and rejected the issuance of the Sultanate decree and insisted that the Sultan of Yogyakarta should be a male.

Opposition to the Sultanate decree did not only come from the royal family of the kingdom but also from various Islamic organizations in Yogyakarta. The Nahdlatul Ulama (NU) of Yogyakarta was amongst the most vocal in opposing the *Sabdaraja*. In the view of the NU branch of Yogyakarta, the *Sabdaraja* was erroneous and indeed inflaming religious tensions between the Islamists and the Catholics. For some NU leaders, the abolishment of the title of *Sayyidin Panatagama Khalifatullah* was designed by some Catholic elites who were in the circle of the Sultan. A young activist from NU said that: "the Catholics stab in the back" in the issuance of *Sabdaraja*.[6] Some NU and Muhammadiyah activists were also openly mobilizing banners to fight against the *Sabdaraja* through organizations such as Jamaah Nahdliyin Mataram and Laskar Surya Mataram. Meanwhile, some Islamist organizations were approached by the brother of the Sultan, GBPH Prabukusomo, to reject the Sultanate decree on the basis that the Sultan should be a male. Moreover, there was a banner that urged Yogyakartanese to reject the *Sabdaraja* organized by what they declared as *"Pejuang Khalifatullah"* (Khalifatullah Struggler). These banners were widespread in Kauman village.[7] What is surprising is that opposition to the Sultanate decree also came from former supporters of the Sultan during the *Keistimewaan* struggle, local-based organizations such as Paguyuban Seksi Pengamanan Keraton (Paksi Keraton) and Paguyuban Dukuh DIY Semar Sembogo openly rejected the Sultanate decree (Dardias 2016, p. 45).

It is evident that the succession of Yogyakarta's Sultanate has involved many actors and issues. In terms of conflicting parties, the battle for a new Sultan does not only involve the royal family members, but also various social and political forces, from Islamic organizations to local and indigenous organizations. Meanwhile, the succession has sparked heated public debates over the issues of "female Sultan"/*Sultanah*, women leadership, the Sultanate's custom, and so on. This demonstrates that the authority of Yogyakarta's Sultanate is broad, yet it remains contested. The success stories of raising the Sultanate's profile during *reformasi* and *Keistimewaan* struggle have located the Sultanate as the centrum of political, cultural, and religious authorities in Yogyakarta. Consequently, various actors have engaged in a scramble for a new Sultan in Yogyakarta. This is somewhat logical because the Sultanate possessed multiple authorities, ranging from politics, culture, and to some extent, religious authority. Furthermore, the Sultanate's family also owned various economics resources, such as land, hotels, and companies. Particularly in the case of land ownership, the Sultanate's ability to control it is pivotal, making Yogyakarta a powerful Sultanate in the country (Dardias 2019). This makes the Sultanate of Yogyakarta a battleground for political struggles.

Another example that demonstrates how different efficacy of the Sultanate's authority has been a determinant factor in shaping the nature of contestation and conflict in Ternate and Yogyakarta is electoral competition. In regional and local electoral competitions, both Sultanates supported their candidates through different means yet the outcome was starkly different. In Ternate, the direct intervention of Sultan Mudaffar Shah in electoral elections resulted in many political defeats and only few victories. Meanwhile, in Yogyakarta indirect intervention of the Sultanate's family helped the victory of their candidates in most elections.

In Ternate, Sultan Mudaffar Shah had been known as a politician in the region. He had issued *Idzin Kolano*, a Sultanate order, to support certain political candidates in several regional elections. For instance, during the local election to vote for the mayor of Ternate in 2010 and 2015, Sultan Mudaffar Shah issued *Idzin Kolano* to support his candidates in Ternate's electoral competition. In the 2010 election, *Idzin Kolano* was granted to Burhan Abdurrahman-Arifin Jafar, while in the 2015 election *Idzin Kolano* was issued to Sidik Dero Siokona-Djasman Abubakar. In the gubernatorial election of North Moluccas province, Sultan Mudaffar Shah also issued *Idzin Kolano* to Abdul Ghafur-Abdurrahim Fabanyo in the 2007 election and to Ahmad Hidayat Mus-Hassan Doa in the 2013 election. However, the Sultan's decree was only effective and successful in the case of Burhan Abdurrahman-Arifin Jafar, who was elected as the city mayor and vice mayor of Ternate for 2010–15. Except for this candidate, the other Sultan's candidates were defeated. This is because, as what happened during communal conflict and the Sultanate's struggle for the governorship, the Sultan's intervention on electoral competition was not unchallenged. Political parties and social forces opposing the Sultan's recommendation mobilized their resources to defeat the Sultan's candidates. For instance, during the 2013 gubernatorial election, the Sultan's support for Ahmad Hidayat Mus was challenged by Al-Khairat organization that seemingly supported its main cadre, Abdul Ghani Kazuba, who finally become the elected governor.[8]

Meanwhile, the Yogyakarta Sultan's intervention in electoral competition seems to be more effective. Taking the case of Yogyakarta's city mayor election in 2011, there were two strong candidates namely Haryadi Suyuthi-Imam Priyono supported by PDI-P and Golkar; and Hanafi Rais-Tri Harjun Ismail supported by the Democrat's party, PAN, PPP, Gerindra, and a coalition of smaller parties. Haryadi was an incumbent vice mayor, while Hanafi Rais was a respected Universitas Gadjah Mada (UGM) lecturer and the son of Amien Rais, the founder of PAN and a national figure. At the time of the election, there was a sharp polarization in society between pro-Sultan camp and pro-election camp in the debate around *Keistimewaan* or specialness. The pro-Sultan camp was obviously behind the Haryadi-Imam pair, with several members of the royal family such as GBPH Prabukusumo joining their *"Tim Sukses"* or campaign committee (Ula 2013, pp. 92–93). On the other hand, Hanafi-Tri Harjun's candidate was supported by the parties regarded as contra-Sultan's side. The Democrat's party was on the top list, his founder, as well as the president at the time, Susilo Bambang Yudhoyono (SBY), made a public statement that regarded the Sultanate of Yogyakarta as an example of absolutist monarchy. This statement was widely perceived as humiliating Sultan HB X and the people of Yogyakarta. In short, the battle between Hanafi Rais versus Haryadi Suyuthi was portrayed as the duel between contra-Sultanate's camp versus pro-Sultanate's camp. At the end of the day, the pro-Sultanate Haryadi Suyuthi won the election.

Conclusion

The narratives from Ternate and Yogyakarta demonstrate that contestation and cooperation between Sultanates and Islamic movements should be located within the broader context of authority. The different efficacy of authority possessed by the sultans of Ternate and Yogyakarta engendered the nature, extent, and variety of actors involved in the conflict, contestation and cooperation between Sultanates and Islamic movements. In this regard, the efficacy of authority is the product of trajectory of political struggle of both Sultanates in the post-Suharto era. In Ternate, the repeated failure of the Sultan of Ternate in reclaiming political authority during communal conflict as well as during power struggle in the making of North Moluccas province has led to the collapse of its authority. Its authority has been limited in cultural matters, while its sphere of influence is restricted to the traditional supporters in northern Ternate. On the other hand, the

Sultan of Yogyakarta has successfully reclaimed his political authority by demonstrating exceptional leadership during *reformasi*, including in maintaining peace and order, and more importantly, in gaining victory in the political struggle on the issue of *Keistimewaan* Yogyakarta in 2012. The Yogyakarta's trajectory has located its Sultanate at the centre of political, cultural, and religious stage at the local level. Accordingly, these two cities have revealed how the political trajectory of each Sultanate in the post-authoritarian era has shaped the nature, extent, and actors of contestation and cooperation between Sultanates and Islamic movements respectively.

NOTES

1. Interview with Salim Taib, Chairman of Gerakan Pemuda Ansor/Ansor Youth Movement in North Moluccas, 16 July 2016.
2. Ibid.
3. Interview with Adam Mahrus, former Secretary of Sultan Mudaffar Shah, 14 July 2016.
4. Fatimah Yamin, "Pendukung Istri Sultan Ternate Bentrok dengan Polisi, Wakapolres Terluka", *Kompas*, 21 April 2016, https://regional.kompas.com/read/2016/04/21/17331051/Pendukung.Istri.Sultan.Ternate.Bentrok.dengan.Polisi.Wakapolres.Terluka (accessed 25 May 2016).
5. Interview with Hidayat Shah, son of Sultan Mudaffar Shah, 15 July 2016.
6. Interview with Beni Setiawan, a young NU activist and coordinator of Masyarakat Anti-Kekerasan Yogyakarta/Anti-Violence Yogyakarta's Community, 13 July 2015.
7. Interview with Fuad Andreago, a young leader of Gerakan Pemuda Ka'bah, 18 July 2015.
8. Interview with Hasbi Yusuf, a young activist of Al-Khairat, 18 July 2016.

REFERENCES

Amal, Adnan. 2009. *Kepulauan Rempah-Rempah: Perjalanan Sejarah Maluku Utara 1250–1950*. Jakarta: Gora Pustaka Indonesia.

Andreago, Fuad. Interview by author, Yogyakarta, 18 July 2015.

Arrobi, Moh Zaki. 2018. "Vigilantism as 'Twilight Institution': Islamic Vigilante Groups and the State in Post-Suharto Yogyakarta". *PCD Journal* VI, no. 2: 214–37.

Assyaukanie, Luthfi. 2009. *Islam and the Secular State in Indonesia*. Singapore: Institute of Southeast Asian Studies.

Azca, Muhammad Najib, Hakimul Ikhwan, and Moh Zaki Arrobi. 2019. "A Tale of Two Royal Cities: The Narratives of Islamists' Intolerance in Yogyakarta and Solo". *Al Jamiah Journal of Islamic Studies* 57, no. 1: 25–50.

Berenschot, Ward, Henk Schulte Nordholt, and Laurens Bakker. 2017. "Introduction: Citizenship and Democratization in Postcolonial Southeast Asia". In *Citizenship and Democratization in Southeast Asia*. Leiden and Boston: Brill.

Bubandt, Nils. 2004. "Towards a New Politics of Tradition? Decentralisation, Conflict, and Adat in Eastern Indonesia". *Antropologi Indonesia* (Special Volume).

Bush, Robin. 2008. "Regional 'Sharia' Regulations in Indonesia: Anomaly or Symptom?" In *Expressing Islam: Religious Life and Politics in Indonesia*, edited by Greg Fealy and Sally White. Singapore: Institute of Southeast Asian Studies.

Dardias, Bayu. 2009. "Yogyakarta in Decentralized Indonesia: Integrating Traditional Institution in Democratic Transitions". *Jurnal Ilmu Sosial Dan Ilmu Politik* 13, no. 2: 190–203.

———. 2016. "Menyiapkan Sultan Perempuan: Legitimasi Langit Dan Efektivitas Rezim Sultan Hamengkubuwono X". *Masyarakat Indonesia* 4, no. 1: 31–49.

———. 2019. "Defending the Sultanate's Land: Yogyakarta, Control over Land and Aristocratic Power in Indonesia". Australian National University. https://bayudardias.staff.ugm.ac.id/wp-content/uploads/2019/11/Bayu-D-Kurniadi-Defending-the-Sultanate.pdf.

Duncan, Christopher. 2005. "The Other Maluku: Chronologies of Conflict in North Maluku". *Indonesia* 80: 53–80.

———. 2009. "Reconciliation and Reinvention: The Resurgence of Tradition in Postconflict Tobelo, North Maluku, Eastern Indonesia". *Journal of Asian Studies* 68, no. 4: 1077–104.

Effendi, David. 2012. "Local Politics and Local Identity: Resistance to 'Liberal Democracy' in Yogyakarta Special Regions of Indonesia". Thesis, University of Hawai'i.

Hadiz, Vedi R. 2010. *Localising Power in Post-Authoritarian Indonesia: A Southeast Asia Perspective*. California: Standford University Press.

Hadiz, Vedi R. and Richard Robison. 2004. *Reorganising Power in Indonesia: The Politics of Oligarchy in an Age of Markets*. Hong Kong: Routledge.

Hanna, Willard A. and Des Alwi. 1990. *Turbulent Times Past in Ternate and Tidore*. Jakarta: Pustaka Sinar Harapan.

Hassan, Noorhaidi. 2006. *Laskar Jihad*. ISIM Disse. Singapore: SEAP Publications.

Hilmy, Masdar. 2010. *Islamism and Democracy in Indonesia: Piety and Pragmatism*. Singapore: Institute of Southeast Asian Studies.

Husen, Muhammad Rahmi. 2016. "Konflik Elit Politik Dalam Pemilihan Umum Gubernur Dan Wakil Gubernur Provinsi Maluku Utara Tahun 2007". *Jurnal Holistik* IX, no. 17.

Infid. 2016. "Studi Tentang Toleransi Dan Radikalisme Di Indonesia: Pembelajaran Dari 4 Daerah Tasikmalaya, Jogjakarta, Bojonegoro Dan Kupang". Jakarta: Infid.

Klinken, Gerry van. 2007a. *Communal Violence and Democratization in Indonesia: Small Town Wars*. New York: Routledge.

———. 2007b. "The Return of the Sultans: The Communitarian Turn in Local Politics". In *The Revival of Tradition in Indonesian Politics: The Deployment of Adat from Colonialism to Indigenism*, edited by Jamies S. Davison and David Henley. London and New York: Routledge.

Machmudi, Yon. 2008. *Islamising Indonesia: The Rise of Jemaah Tarbiyah and the Prosperous Justice Party (PKS)*. Canberra: ANU E Press.

Mahrus, Adam. Interview by author, Ternate, 14 July 2016.

Mas'oed, Mohtar, S. Rizal Panggabean, and Muhammad Najib Azca. 2001. "Social Resources for Civility and Participation: The Case of Yogyakarta, Indonesia". In *The Politics of Multiculturalism: Pluralism and Citizenship in Malaysia, Singapore, and Indonesia*, edited by Robert W. Hefner. Honolulu: University of Hawai'i Press.

Mubarak, Zaki. 2002. *Genealogi Islam Radikal Di Indonesia: Gerakan, Pemikiran Dan Prospek Demokrasi*. Jakarta: LP3ES.

Mujani, Saiful. 2007. *Muslim demokrat: Islam, budaya demokrasi, dan partisipasi politik di Indonesia pasca Orde Baru*. Jakarta: Gramedia Pustaka Utama.

Panggabean, Samsu Rizal and Benjamin Smith. 2011. "Explaining Anti-Chinese Riots in Late 20th Century Indonesia". *World Development* 39, no. 2: 231–42.

Platzdasch, Bernhard. 2009. *Islamism in Indonesia: Politics in the Emerging Democracy*. Singapore: Institute of Southeast Asian Studies.

Roem, Mohammad, Muhtar Lubis, Kustiniyati Mochtar, and S. Maimoen. 2011. *Tahta Untuk Rakyat: Celah-Celah Kehidupan Sultan Hamengkubuwono IX*. Jakarta: Kompas Gramedia.

Salim, Arskal. 2008. *Challenging the Secular State: The Islamization of Law in Modern Indonesia*. Honolulu: University of Hawai'i Press.

Setiawan, Beni. Interview by researcher team, Yogyakarta, 13 July 2015.

Shah, Hidayat. Interview by author, Ternate, 15 July 2016.

Smith, Claire Querida. 2009. "The Return of the Sultan? Power, Patronage, and Political Machines in 'Post'-Conflict North Maluku". In *Deepening Democracy in Indonesia? Direct Elections for Local Leaders*, edited by Maribeth Erb and Priambudi Sulistiyanto. Singapore: Institute of Southeast Asian Studies.

Taib, Salim. Interview by author, Ternate, 16 July 2016.

Ula, Rizkal. 2013. "Strategi Pemenangan Haryadi Suyuti Dan Imam Priyono Dalam Pilwali Kota Yogyakarta Tahun 2011". Universitas Airlangga.

van Bruinessen, Martin. 2013. *Contemporary Developments in Indonesian Islam: Explaining the "Conservative Turn"*. Singapore: Institute of Southeast Asian Studies.

Wahid Institute, The. 2014. "Laporan Tahunan Kebebasan Beragama Dan Berkeyakinan Dan Intoleransi 2014: 'Utang' Warisan Pemerintah Baru". Jakarta: The Wahid Institute. https://drive.google.com/file/d/0B91i4HE8Ta2meTNFTlVfanlnbU0/view.

Woodward, Mark. 2010. *Java, Indonesia and Islam*. Tempe, USA: Springer.

Yamin, Fatimah. "Pendukung Istri Sultan Ternate Bentrok dengan Polisi, Wakapolres Terluka". *Kompas*, 21 April 2016. https://regional.kompas.com/read/2016/04/21/17331051/Pendukung.Istri.Sultan.Ternate.Bentrok.dengan.Polisi.Wakapolres.Terluka (accessed 25 May 2016).

Yusuf, Hasbi. Interview by author, Ternate, 18 July 2016.

17

JIHAD AGAINST THE *GHAZWUL FIKRI*: ACTORS AND MOBILIZATION STRATEGIES OF THE ISLAMIC UNDERGROUND MOVEMENT[1]

Hikmawan Saefullah

Introduction

Born from the processes of neoliberal globalization and the strengthening opposition to the New Order regime in the late 1990s, the underground rock music movement (*gerakan musik rock bawah tanah*) in Indonesia emerged as a bastion of progressive politics (Wallach 2005) and the radical Left (Pickles 2001 and 2007; Saefullah 2017a). The movement participants, called "underground youths" (*pemuda underground*), protested against social and cultural orthodoxies, capitalist economic system, and state authoritarianism. After taking part in toppling General Suharto through democratic mobilizations in the late 1990s, their activism went through a period of decline. This was followed by the emergence of a new subcultural movement that, unlike their predecessors who tended to regard religiosity as a private matter, displays religious piety as necessity and uses right-wing Islamism as a political ideology. The founders called their movement the "Islamic underground" (*Underground Islam*), the name was chosen to distinguish themselves from the existing underground movement which they considered "too secular" and "too liberal". Overlooked by scholars of Indonesian Islam, this stream of underground movement played an important role in disseminating conservative and even "radical" narratives of Islam to marginalized youths through ways that were never carried out by mainstream Islamic organizations.

This chapter discusses the Islamic underground movement by examining its key actors and mobilization strategies. It firstly discusses a brief history of the Indonesian underground movement, followed by an examination of the social, political, and economic conditions that have advanced the emergence of the Islamic underground movement. Subsequently, the key actors and mobilization strategies that have supported the growth of the movement will be discussed.

The Leftist Beginnings of the Underground Movement in Indonesia

Underground music only began to be popular amongst Indonesian youths in the mid-1990s. This was due to the rapid globalization that allowed the influx of western popular culture to the country (Sen and Hill 2007; Pickles 2007; Baulch 2007). The word "underground" was used by local youths as an umbrella term for a "variety of imported rock music genres on the loud side of the spectrum" (Wallach 2003), such as punk rock, rap, hardcore, heavy metal, oi, and grindcore. The word itself refers to an alternative space for social and cultural practices, as Dunn asserts, which are beyond the "formal domain of commercial life" (Dunn 2016, p. 90). True underground rock musicians rarely seek popularity or commercial success and instead, emphasize music authenticity and its potential for individual and collective empowerment. Furthermore, some musicians develop an anti-capitalism stance and reject capitalist sponsorship of their events.

The popularity of underground music among Indonesian youths was situated within the context of social, political, and cultural opposition to the country's authoritarian New Order in the 1990s (Sen and Hill

2007; Baulch 2007; Wallach 2005; Bodden 2005; Pickles 2007). As Sen and Hill assert: "Musical performances and texts were important sites for signifying opposition to the New Order discourse of 'order' and stability" (Sen and Hill 2007, p. 164). Similarly, Hadiz argues that "youth culture provides an outlet for normally blocked aspirations, and a channel to convey social criticism" and provides a space for "non-conformity" (cited in Baulch 2002, p. 221).

For over thirty years, the New Order silenced criticisms through direct repression and also policies that contributed to the depoliticization of the younger generation (Aspinall 1995; Pickles 2007). The rise of student activism in the late 1980s (Heryanto 1996) gradually drew many Indonesian youths into political movements. By the late 1990s, Indonesian underground music scene had become a site for the anti-establishment political struggle against the authoritarian state, thanks largely to university students who were also involved in the left-wing student movement (Pickles 2007; Martin-Iverson 2012; Donaghey and Xiao 2018). In big cities like Bandung, Jakarta, and Surabaya, punk rockers formed left-wing groups, such as the Anti-Fascist Front or Front Anti Fasis (FAF), Anti-Fascism, Anti-Racism Action (AFRA), and the Anti-Oppression Front (BAP) (Pickles 2001, 2007; Saefullah 2017a, 2017b).[2] These groups then set up an umbrella organization called the Nusantara Anti-Fascist Network (JAF-Nus or ANTIFARA), which consolidated their opposition to militarism, state repression, discrimination (sexism, racism, homophobia), and capitalism, as well as calling for individual sovereignty, environmental protection, and internationalism (Pickles 2001 and 2007; Saefullah 2017a; Donaghey and Xiao 2018). Another characteristic of these groups was the blurring of class and occupational differences (Pickles 2000 and 2007; Dunn 2008; Wallach 2008; Martin-Iverson 2012). As Pickles notes: "university students, unemployed youths, school students, workers and street kids 'hang out' together as punks, unbound by religious, ethnic, or class distinctions" (Pickles 2007, p. 226). It is unsurprising then that many underground youths saw their community as a model for a democratic, egalitarian society, and distinguish themselves from the mainstream society that tends to be structured, elitist, and hierarchical.

FIGURE 17.1
Bandung's hardcore punk band Powerpunk performing in a DIY underground rock show *Kekesed Fest 2019* at the Institut Francaise d'Indonesie (IFI), Bandung

Source: Hikmawan Saefullah, 31 March 2019.

The Post-Authoritarian Indonesia and the Rise of the Religious Right

Following the fall of Suharto in the late 1990s, many Indonesians expected post-Suharto leaders to deliver the political reform agenda needed for democratic change. Despite their attempts to fulfil the agenda, post-Suharto leaders and the new political environment failed to meet the people's expectations. As Heryanto (2014, p. 1) describes, the country "enjoyed a brief period of euphoric optimism", but this is followed by "disillusionment, disorientation, and despair". The post-Suharto leaders are reluctant to address past human rights issues, particularly the suppressions of the leftist since the communist purge in the mid-1960s. The capitalist development in this period has also failed to meet the expectation of young people from the working class and middle-class background as it has maintained existing social and economic inequalities. Furthermore, post-Suharto governments have continued to suppress the Left-wing activism. Since the late 1990s and early 2000s, the government has arrested many Left activists, on allegations of sedition and attempts to revive the Indonesian Communist Party (PKI). The Indonesian government has also been consistently monitoring and shutting down intellectual discussions and seminars which had featured left-wing politics. As a consequence, many left-wing activists stayed away from leftist politics, joined the ruling elites, or shifted their political allegiance. The absence of leftist activists/figures within the underground scene contributed to the weakening leftist political narratives within the scene, and the participants' declining interest in political activism (Pickles 2007; Saefullah 2017a and 2017b; Donaghey and Xiao 2018).

Meanwhile, right-wing Islamism has gained wider ground. This is marked by the ideological and organizational prominence of right-wing Islamist organizations that used both formal and informal political channels to achieve their objectives, including transforming Indonesia into an Islamic state, and amending the state's constitution to follow the Islamic law (Hosen 2005; Aspinall 2010). Amongst them are Islamist political parties like Prosperous Justice Party (PKS, formerly known as Justice Party/PK), mass organizations such as the Islamic Defenders Front (FPI), the Indonesian Mujahedeen Council (MMI), the Communication Forum for Ahlu Sunnah Wal Jama'ah (FKASWJ)/ Laskar Jihad (LJ), and Hizbut Tahrir Indonesia (HTI). The resurgence of right-wing Islamist organizations played a significant role in turning Indonesian Islam in a conservative direction (van Bruinessen 2013b). To oppose the right-wing Islamist forces, some Muslim intellectuals created a "moderate" version of the Islamic movement, such as the Liberal Islam Network (JIL) and the Muhammadiyah Youth Intellectuals Network (JIMM).

The conservative direction of Indonesian Islam is also due in part to the importation, adoption, and promotion of Islamist political thoughts (i.e. Sayyid Qutb, Al-Maududi, Al-Qaradawi, etc.) by some scholars and preachers that have received study grants, scholarships, and donations from Gulf countries (Hefner 1997 and 2000; Hasan 2005 and 2007; Machmudi 2008; Bubalo and Fealy 2005, pp. viii–ix;

van Bruinessen 2013b, p. 5; van Bruinessen 2015, pp. 66–67; Chaplin 2018, p. 6). One idea which has been adopted from Egypt's Muslim Brotherhood (Ikhwanul Muslimin) is *ghazwul fikri* (van Bruinessen 2018, p. 4). *Ghazwul fikri* refers to the "invasions of ideas" or the "cultural invasions", that is "deliberately imposed on the Muslim's world by the West, as a part of the new Crusade to weaken and defeat Islam" (van Bruinessen 2018, p. 4). It uses a non-military approach to subvert Islamic cultures and values using western popular culture (i.e. movies, music, books, lifestyles) as well as religious and political ideologies (secularism, liberalism, pluralism, democracy, etc.) (van Bruinessen 2015, 2018).[3] Ustadz Bachtiar Nasir,[4] the former Secretary General of Intellectual Assembly of Young Ulama Indonesia, argues that liberalism is a part of *ghazwul fikri* that corrupts Muslims' lives in three key aspects: economy, politics, and Islamic creed (*aqidah Islam*), and thus poses as the "most dangerous enemy for the Islamic ummah" (*Republika* 2015). In the following section, I discuss how the Islamist idea of *ghazwul fikri* inspired the formation of Islamic underground movement.

The Rise of the Islamic Underground Movement

The Islamic underground movement started as a cultural project of several underground Muslim musicians and fans, who were disillusioned with the state of underground music scene in post-authoritarian Indonesia. They viewed the scene as stagnant, lacking ideological foundations particularly with the absence of coherent political Left, and incapable of responding to new social and political challenges. They found that Islam provided answers to their disillusionment and a viable ideological foundation to deal with the new social and political challenges that mainly generated from the contradictions of the capitalist development in the country.

The term "Islamic underground movement" itself was first used in the early 2000s by underground scene participants or activists that had informal affiliation with the HTI. It was also introduced by a Muslim rapper Thufail Al Ghifari during an interview with Islamic magazine *Sabili* (Satria 2008, p. 43). Thufail defined the Islamic underground as a countercultural movement that was formed to oppose the Indonesian underground movement which he considered as predominantly "agnostic and secular" (Satria 2008, p. 43).

Unlike the 1990s' underground movement which was predominantly pro-democracy and supportive of progressive social change (Wallach 2005, pp. 19–20),[5] the Islamic underground movement endorses conservative right-wing Islamism, despises western ideologies (i.e. liberalism, anarchism, communism), and adopts sectarian position particularly towards the *Ahmadiyya* and *Shia*. The growth of the Islamic underground movement has been facilitated by several key actors, mobilization strategies, and some political aspirations that bind its participants. I will elaborate them in the following section.

Key actors and collaborations

Most of the key actors that played their part in the growth of the Islamic underground movement did not have any formal Islamic education. Instead they learnt about Islam by reading translated Islamic literature, joining public religious learning events (*majlis taklim*) or sermons and campus-based religious learning groups (*liqo'*). Most of them also had religious mentors (*murabbi*) who guided their learning process. Through these informal religious learnings, they were introduced to and became inspired by the intellectual thoughts of modern Islamist thinkers, such as Hizb ut-Tahrir's Taqi al-Din al-Nabhani, and Muslim Brotherhood's (Ikhwanul Muslimin) Hassan al-Banna, Sayyid Qutb, and Yusuf al-Qaradawi. The desire to share not only what they had learnt, but also to seek an alternative political vision and activism, led them to create an "Islamic" version of the underground movement.

Four key individuals are worthy of discussion in this chapter as they have, either individually or collectively, formed religious youth communities which have defined the Islamic underground movement. The first key actor is a Muslim rapper and underground rock musician Muhammad Thufail Al Ghifari. Thufail was born in the early 1980s in Makassar, South Sulawesi to a Christian missionary family. Because of his involvement in the underground music community in Bekasi and Bandung, Thufail became familiar with American hip hop band Public Enemy, and rock band with a left-leaning political view, Rage

Against the Machine. Through these bands, Thufail was introduced to the struggle of Afro-American Muslim figure Malcolm-X which later inspired him to convert to Islam.

During the *reformasi*, Thufail sympathized with the progressive leftist movement and claimed to be part of leftist student organization, People's Democratic Party (PRD) (*Republika* 2009).[6] However, like many other underground youths, Thufail became disillusioned with the movement, particularly following the arrests of left-wing activists and sympathizers including the ones from the local underground music scene around 2000–1 (*Republika* 2009). As he said to the Islamic daily newspaper *Republika*, "PRD's prominent figures were missing, some were kidnapped and some went into hiding. This is the beginning of my disappointment with, so-called, individual revolution" (*Republika* 2009). Due to his disillusionment, Thufail became engaged with transnational Islamist ideas including its religious and political cause.[7]

To express his Islamist vision and stance against Indonesian hip hop music which he considered as predominantly "agnostic and secular" (Satria 2008, pp. 42–43),[8] Thufail created a sub-genre of rap called "Microjihad" (from "Microphone Jihad") (Al Ghifari 2008). Thufail's music and lyrics contain Islamic messages, including the promotion of anti-Zionism, jihad, and death (Martyrdom). In the mid-2000s, Thufail was praised by Muslim activists for verbally attacking (*diss*) Indonesia's left-wing hip hop band Homicide whom he alleged was "blasphemous" for equating Islam with fascism in their song "Puritan" (Brys 2012, p. 73).[9] Despite the external praise, Thufail's Microjihad was not welcomed within the Indonesian hip hop community and the support for the sub-genre waned. Thufail then created a metal/rock band The Roots of Madinah (2008–11) and its fan base *Berandalan Puritan* (means "Puritan Delinquents") (Brys 2012, pp. 70–81). Whilst he was in this band, Thufail collaborated with a lawyer and the vocalist of Jakarta-based grindcore band Muhammad Hariadi "Ombat" Nasution to create a countercultural underground movement known as One Finger Movement (*Komunitas Salam Satu Jari*/OFM).

FIGURE 17.2
Lead vocal of Jakarta's grindcore band Tengkorak,
Muhammad Hariadi "Ombat" Nasution, the founder of the
One Finger Underground Movement (*Komunitas Salam Satu Jari*)
at Jakcloth Festival 2016 in Jakarta

Source: Hikmawan Saefullah, 6 May 2016.

Ombat himself is considered here as another key actor that played a significant role in the growth of the Islamic underground movement, particularly in building alliances with conservative, right-wing Islamist organizations such as the Indonesian Muslim Forum (FUI), MMI, and FPI. Before forming OFM with Thufail, Ombat felt disillusioned with the underground music scene, which he thought was moving toward nihilism (i.e. drugs abuse, sex outside marriage, alcoholism). Ombat became religious in the early 2000s when he started to be concerned about the future of his family. During this time period he became interested in jihadi discourse, particularly in relation to the U.S. global war on terrorism across the Muslim world. Citing RAND Corporation's (2007) report, Ombat believes that the American war on terrorism has created conflicts within the Indonesian Muslim community by juxtaposing "moderate" and "radical" Muslims (*Panjimas*, 6 May 2017). In his opposition to this war on terror, Ombat used his capacity as a lawyer to defend Muhammad Jibril Abdul Rahman, a terror suspect of the 2009 Jakarta bombings.

Ombat's sympathy for the jihadi discourse was linked to *ghazwul fikri* as he believes that underground music is part of a Zionist/Western conspiracy to corrupt Indonesia's Muslim youths (Mubarak 2011; Saefullah 2017a, p. 270).[10] In relation to this, Ombat asserted: "war manifests in different forms. This country [Indonesia] can be colonised easily through cultural means" (Satria 2010, pp. 40–41). He continued: "to destroy Muslim lands, particularly in Indonesia, you don't need physical war, weapons, or nuclear bombs. It's enough by injecting [the young people] with drugs (narcotics), alcohol, porn films, gossip media, and also music" (Satria 2010, p. 41).

Given that Ombat was the leader of OFM, a brief discussion of the OFM is warranted. Ombat, along with Thufail, created OFM as he wanted to make underground community free from nihilistic behaviours and counter what he saw as a form of cultural imperialism. According to Ombat, the term "one finger" (*Satu Jari*) was chosen because of its symbolic opposition to the global metal salute. Ombat believes that the metal salute, a "three-finger-salute", symbolizes an adoration of Satan and rejection of God (Mubarak 2011). The one finger salute, a hand gesture with the index finger pointing at the sky, symbolizes an appraisal for the oneness of God (*tauhid*), a profession of Islamic monotheism (Mubarak 2011).[11]

Ombat, working together with Thufail and other like-minded underground musicians, launched the OFM on 27 March 2010 during a religiously-themed underground music event called Urban Garage Festival I. The event was a collaborative project between Ombat and religious underground groups, such as Berandalan Puritan and Mogerz Infantry (*Mogerz Infantry* 2010).[12] Although the theme of the event was "metal", a diverse range of underground music, including punk and rap, was included. A correspondent from the Islamic magazine *Sabili* credited the OFM bands and musicians as "unorthodox preachers" (*da'i*) who conducted *ijtihad* by using underground rock music for Islamic proselytization (*dakwah*) (Satria 2010).¹³

This collaborative *dakwah*, however, did not last very long. In the same year as OFM was announced, Thufail left the movement. In an interview with Surabaya-based fanzine *Sub Chaos*, Thufail said that as an Islamic movement, OFM did not have a clear mentoring or a membership platform (*Sub Chaos* n.d., p. 12). Thufail stated: "One Finger is only a Facebook group. In the real world, they are truly a myth of euphoria" (*Sub Chaos* n.d., p. 12). Not long after he left OFM, Thufail collaborated with a punk veteran and former anarchist from Surabaya Aditya Abdurrahman (a.k.a. Aik) to create another Islamic underground group called the Ghurabba (Militant Tawheed).

Aik is the third key figure that played a significant role in the advancement of the Indonesian Islamic underground movement. Before his engagement with the movement, Aik was a member of Surabaya-based hardcore punk band, The Fourty's Accident and Human Corruption. He was also the founder of the Anti-Oppression Front (*Barisan Anti Penindasan*/BAP), an anarcho-punk group that was part of JAF-Nus. Aik maintained his activism in the leftist group as he thought that it was important to spread the political awareness amongst underground youths in Surabaya through means of discussions and street actions to articulate their anti-capitalist stance and state-sponsored social injustices (Abdurrahman, interview, 17 September 2017). His activism at the BAP stopped when he found underground scene participants in Surabaya had become less interested in politics. Following BAP's decline, Aik and other anarchist punks in Surabaya created another group called the Flower Collective (*Kolektif Bunga*), which was very active in promoting leftist propaganda through Do-It-Yourself (DIY) fanzines and newsletters (Yani 2017, pp. 34–35). Amongst the fanzines was *Sub Chaos*, a DIY fanzine which was created by Aik and his brother Jack in 1999.¹⁴ Through the production and distribution of *Sub Chaos*, Aik's name became well-known amongst punk scene members across Indonesia's big cities. The publication of *Sub Chaos*, however, was halted when Aik became disillusioned with his involvement in the punk/underground scene. As Aik described: "Collective discussions became less actual, and only focused on impractical philosophical issues. Meanwhile, punk bands that used to be known for their militancy, is now nothing but [militant] in their lyrics" (Yani 2017, p. 37).

Prior to his decision to withdraw from his punk/underground scene, Aik was searching for answers to his life problems and began to attend religious sermons and read Islamic literature. He was firstly inspired by the sermons of Ustadz Abdullah Gymnastiar (Aa Gym), a celebrity preacher from Daarut Tauhid, a popular Islamic boarding school (*pesantren*) in Bandung. Learning Islam became more relevant for him particularly after the passing of his brother Jack in 2007 and he started thinking about raising a family (Abdurrahman, interview, 20 July 2016). After learning about Islam, Aik concluded that both Islamic sacred guidance of Quran and Sunnah provided him with the complete answers to life's problems (Yani 2017, p. 43). In the following years, Aik became more involved in Islamic missionary activities (*dakwah*), such as joining MIUMI (East Java branch) and publishing religious propagation through his DIY publications.

After a few years of engaging in *dakwah* activities, Aik was invited by Thufail to join the collaborative *dakwah* group called Ghurabba (Militant Tawheed)/GMT. This group was later rebranded as Underground Tauhid (UGT). Although the new *dakwah* group shared the idea of *ghazwul fikri* with the OFM, it stated that it could not align with OFM because of the allegation that some OFM members were linked to "*Shia* ideology" (*Sub Chaos* n.d., pp. 12–15; Saefullah 2017a, p. 271).[15] As Thufail asserted: "GHURABBA cannot tolerate the infiltration of Shi'ite sect (*aliran Syi'ah*) within the One Finger Movement. GHURABBA is strongly anti- Shia, especially because the sect is insulting the companions of the Prophet [Muhammad]" (*Sub Chaos* n.d., p. 12). Despite UGT's vibrant activism between 2011 and 2013, Aik had a falling out with Thufail that led both to leave the group in 2014. Not long after leaving the group, Aik started a collaboration with Ahmad Zaki, the last key figure of the Islamic underground movement that I would like to discuss here.

Zaki works for an Islamic philanthropy organization *Dompet Dhuafa* (Wallet of the Poor/DD) and became a mentor (*pembina*) of the Jakarta-based working class punk community "Punk Muslim" after the death of its founder, Budi Chaeroni (a.k.a. Buce).[16] The collaboration between Zaki and Aik resulted in the formation of a new chapter of Punk Muslim in Surabaya (Saefullah 2017a, p. 273).[17] Punk Muslim Surabaya (PMS) expanded the community's memberships from predominantly working-class (street punks) to middle-class punks. Although PMS claimed to be self-funded, Zaki's connection to DD helped the community to fund new programmes, such as the production of an annual DIY bulletin,

"Ramadan with Punk Muslim" (Abdurrahman, interview, 16 July 2016). With Zaki's assistance, the bulletin was printed over 900 times and distributed across punk/underground scenes in Indonesia (Saefullah 2017a, p. 273).[18] Furthermore, as a mentor of Punk Muslim, Zaki said that he wanted to help street punks to be accepted in the society by teaching them practical skills and empowering them through Islamic piety.

The Punk Muslim's main vision is to incorporate punk's resistance with Islamic piety. As Zaki posited: "Indeed, we want to maintain resistance within a special framework. How to make it in accordance to the Islamic values [:] [punk] must resist ignorance, laziness, tyranny, and deception [...][but] you don't want to resist God. Life has its rules" (Jamil 2017). Since its formation in 2007, Zaki often encourage Punk Muslim members to get involved in DD's humanitarian works, including helping the poor. In 2017, Zaki also formed an independent philanthropy organization called *Gerak Bareng Community*, a community that focuses on humanitarian work with DD, including providing assistance to marginalized people.

FIGURE 17.3
Gathering of Punk Muslim members (Jakarta, Surabaya, and Bogor) in an event *Ngobrol Bareng Punk Muslim* at Kebon Jeruk, Jakarta

Source: Hikmawan Saefullah, 14 January 2017.

Apart from Thufail, Ombat, Aik, and Zaki, there are of course many others who also played an important role in the growth of the Islamic underground movement. Amongst them were activists of the Indonesian chapter of the transnational Islamist group HTI that, according to my research, were the first that initiated the formation of the underground movement using Islamism as its political ideology.

DIY Mobilization Strategies

Since many underground music scene participants in Indonesia are Muslims (Wallach 2008; Martin-Iverson 2014, p. 188; Donaghey 2015, p. 30; Donaghey and Xiao 2018, p. 158), members of the Islamic underground movement see them as potential recruits. Interestingly, they have been largely overlooked by mainstream "official" Islamic organizations such as Nahdlatul Ulama (NU) and Muhammadiyah. Islamic underground youths are one step ahead of mainstream organizations in using modern means to seek younger recruits. I will discuss their mobilization strategies in the following section.

Youth collectives and communities

The first mobilization strategy is forming "independent" youth collectives and communities. The HTI student activists were amongst the earliest Islamist movements to come up with the strategy. The youth collectives and communities were used as a site to convert and recruit underground youths to join, or at least support, HTI's political cause (Martin-Iverson, conversation, 2015). These HTI's informal organizations have been overlooked by the existing studies of HTI's mobilization strategies (see for example, Ward 2009; Ahnaf 2009; Osman 2010a and 2010b; Nugroho 2017).

According to the former HTI leader from Bangka Belitung, Ayik Heriansyah, university students who were previously trained in HTI's learning circle (*halaqah*) created these collectives as "cover organizations" (*organisasi mantel*) to recruit young people outside their campus to join HTI (Heriansyah, interview, 23 May 2018).[19] As illustrated in an excerpt of my interview with Ayik:

> Author: So, you're saying that these organizations [youth collectives] were intended to attract [underground] youths to join HTI? That's why they adjust their strategy of recruitment based on the market?

Ayik: That's true. The only HTI's extra-campus student organization was the Students' Liberation Movement (*Gerakan Mahasiswa Pembebasan* or *GEMA Pembebasan*). Apart from that, there were only unofficial cover organizations created by HTI students.

Author: I see. So, these cover organizations were still accepted by and benefitted HTI even though it was not part of the formal structure of the HTI? Is that correct?

Ayik: That's correct. These cover organizations were [made] to recruit potential cadres before they become prospective members by joining the official *halaqah* from the local HTI structure.

Among HTI's known cover organizations were Liberation Youth (LY), which was created in Bandung by former underground scene participants who had sympathized with the left-wing political cause. Established in early 2000s, LY was probably the earliest youth collective in Indonesia to use underground youth subcultures to promote HTI's political ideas, particularly the anti-capitalist rhetoric and the re-enaction of the Islamic caliphate. Although it claimed to be an "independent subcultural movement" (Liberation Youth 2007a),[20] the founders or the group members had a direct and indirect affiliation with HTI's formal student organization, *GEMA Pembebasan* (Osman 2010a, p. 605; Osman 2010b, p. 742; Nugroho 2017, pp. 128–29). In their recruitment, LY targeted a special segment of urban youths, mainly university students who were also consumers of popular culture, including underground music, and sympathized with leftist anti-establishment ideologies (Liberation Youth 2007a).

There were other HTI's informal organizations, including Sons of Liberation (Makassar), Fikr Community (Banjarmasin), Menara Revolusi (Makassar), Hambos Community (Jakarta, Bogor, Tangerang, Bekasi), Kolektif Jembatan Harokah (Jakarta/Bekasi), Commanders Society, and the Pyrates Army.[21] To make their organization's outlook familiar to potential recruits, the activists appropriated jargon, symbols, images, and mobilization strategies that were identical with the leftists. For instance, they rarely call themselves "Muslim activist" (*aktivis Muslim*) or "Aktivis Dakwah" (*Dakwah Activist*), but instead "Revolters" or "Islamic revolutionaries". Whilst the groups were widespread across Indonesia, they shared similar activism; holding online and offline discussions, conducting rallies and public orations, and producing DIY publications.

DIY publications

The second mobilization strategy that contributes to the surge of the Islamic underground movement is the production of DIY publications. The low budget, self-publishing strategy was inspired from the punk's DIY practice of producing alternative media such as fanzine and newsletters (Dunn 2008 and 2016; Triggs 2006). Fanzine is a low budget magazine that usually contains the personal views of the zine makers and the contributors on art, music, culture, and sometimes, politics. As Triggs (2006, p. 70) asserts, fanzine is a form of subcultural communication which played a significant role in constructing punk identity and a political community. In Indonesia, the productions of fanzine began in the mid-1990s, and contained news and articles mainly about underground rock music. Only after the social and political crisis in the late 1990s do the zines' contents become more political.

During the decline of the left-wing movements in the early post-Suharto years, some HTI activists, who were also participants of the local underground music scene, re-appropriated the DIY publication as a tool to disseminate propaganda. They produced several fanzines, including *Revolt 'n' Rise* (Hambos Community), *Rebel* (Fighters Malang), *One Liberation* (Fikr Community), *No Compromise* (Liberation Youth), and *Unforgiven Beat Zine* (Liberation Youth, Solo). The zines called for readers to oppose western political products of democracy, capitalism, liberalism, nationalism, socialism, and instead, support an "Islamic revolution" (*Revolusi Islam*) or "white revolution" (*Revolusi Putih*) by reviving the Islamic caliphate (*khilafah*).

The production of DIY publications is also used by non-HTI-linked actors. Aik of the Fourty's Accident/PMS, for instance, used this strategy for his personal *dakwah*. He published his first Islamic fanzine called *SA'I zine* in June 2008, which covered his personal religious thoughts, such as about Muslim unity (*Ukhuwah Islamiyyah*), literacy (*Iqra'*), and the Palestinian cause. In emphasizing the importance of literacy, Aik called Muslim youth to "proselytise with pen" (*dakwah bil qolam*) (Abdurrahman 2009a, pp. 3–6; Abdurrahman 2009b, pp. 4–6):

> Through writing, we can counteract our enemy's thoughts and their hegemony. Through writing, we can fortify our Islamic creed (*aqidah*). Through writing, we can influence the Islamic ummah to participate in real actions of defending Islam. Through writing, we can make the hearts of the enemies of Islam trembled. Through writing, we can spread the

essential truth. Through writing, we can move the Islamic ummah to help those who are vulnerable to Christianisation (*kristenisasi*). Through writing, we can educate the Islamic ummah. Through writing, we can counter orientalist thoughts that often make comments about Islam without thinking its negative consequences (Abdurrahman 2009a, p. 6).

The first edition of *SA'I zine* was printed over 500 times and distributed bimonthly at Aik's campus mosque and his networks outside Surabaya (Yani 2017, p. 53). Not long after the first edition was published, Aik received financial support from his readers, which he used to cover production costs and donate to the Palestinian cause. Through *SA'I zine*, Aik's name became well-known amongst members of the local Campus Proselytising Network (*Lembaga Dakwah Kampus*/LDK), where he sometimes was invited to give sermons or join discussions with university students (Yani 2017, p. 53).

Aik then continued doing *dakwah bil qolam* through his old fanzine *Sub Chaos*, which had been put on hold whilst he was undertaking *hijrah*. He replaced its contents, which used to be left-leaning, with

FIGURE 17.4
Islamic DIY publications circulated within the circles of the Islamic Underground Movement

Source: Hikmawan Saefullah, 24 January 2018.

Islamic propaganda (Saefullah 2017a, p. 272). Through this publication, he attacked western political ideologies, including anarchism, marxism, and feminism. Around the same time with his activism in GMT, Aik created an online media platform called the Underground Tauhid (UGT) which extended his ability to disseminate religious and political propaganda (Fiscella 2012, p. 267; Saefullah 2017a, pp. 272–73; Yani 2017, p. 58).[22]

DIY clothing and merchandises

The third mobilization strategy is the production of DIY clothing and merchandises. Islamic DIY-clothing companies and distros emerged alongside the growth of consumerism amongst Indonesian middle-class in post-New Order Indonesia (Rakhmani 2016). Their products are mostly sold through informal channels, from *lapak*, distros, clothing exhibitions and music festivals, to social media. The producers of Islamic DIY clothing often use religious reasons and grievances to justify their business. As the founder of Sa'i distro Aik asserted:

> Making your own shop, no matter how small or big it is, as long as it has an orientation towards dakwah, can give a significant impact to the ummah's lifestyle. The more ummah use Muslims' products, the less they rely on the products produced by infidels (*orang-orang kuffar*) (Abdurrahman 2009a, p. 5).

The punk's DIY ethos, in this sense, is used by the members of the Islamic underground to enhance Muslims' autonomy in the realm of cultural production and improve the economic status of young Muslims particularly with regards to competition with non-Muslim businesses. As Aik posited:

> If the mentality of the [Islamic] ummah is only limited to becoming an employee, then you can't expect to see the ummah's economy in the future. The capitals will be dominated by infidels[;] whilst the bosses will be Christians, Muslims will only be their security guards, cleaning service, car drivers, etc. I don't mean to discredit their profession, but we must see things objectively here, that the Islamic ummah must be strong […] (Abdurrahman 2009a, p. 5).

The producers used the term "visual *dakwah*" to refer to their clothing and merchandises which contain *dakwah* messages. This includes texts and graphics that remind their consumers, or anyone who see their products, about the obligations of Islamic worships (*ibadah*), such as remembering Allah (*dzikir*) and religious emigration (*hijrah*). Some Islamic clothing brands, particularly those that share political orientation with HTI, glorify the notion of Islamic struggle (*jihad*) and caliphate (*khilafah*) on their t-shirts.

The Islamic Clothing United (ICU), a collaboration of Islamic clothing producers, was formed to counter *ghazwul fikri* through popular youth apparels. Iraz, one of the ICU founders, said that the collaboration was meant to build a consciousness amongst consumers, particularly those who are ignorant about the messages sent by the clothes they wear (VOA-Islam, 4 January 2016). For instance, the use of visual conspiracy symbols such as Freemasonry and Illuminati that have been popularized in youth apparels. Ombat of Tengkorak/OFM, who is also part of the ICU, posits: "When the liberals and the Jews' illuminati instigate war of ideas and cultures through creative industry, there will be resistance from the young people that work in the field, one of the resistances is through [the production of] dakwah t-shirt" (Suara-Islam 2016).[23]

DIY music productions and performances

The fourth strategy is DIY music productions and performances. The use of music for Islamic proselytization is not new to Indonesia. The history can be traced back to the fourteenth century when Islam began to grow significantly in Java due to Sufi saints (i.e. *wali songo*) such as Sunan Giri and Sunan Kalijaga who used music as a medium for *dakwah*. This strategy can also be seen in the 1970s, when a *dangdut* rockstar Rhoma Irama formed a band called the Soneta group that incorporated *dakwah* and entertainment (Weintraub 2011; Irama 2011). Rhoma's messages in his songs are surprisingly similar to the ones echoed by straight edge punks in the 1980s: to refrain oneself from drugs and alcohol consumption, and illicit sex conducts on straight edge punk movement (Haenfler 2006; Kuhn 2010; Martin-Iverson 2017).

Islamic underground rock musicians also transmit similar messages to their audience of a positive and healthy lifestyle based on Islamic values. Aik of the Surabaya-based punk band the Fourty's Accident said that positive acts and healthy lifestyle should be guided by a religious intention (*niat*), or otherwise, they would go to waste in the afterlife (*akhirat*) (Yani 2016, pp. 61–63). He adds that whilst straight edge lifestyle would bring positive outcomes for its adherents on earth (*duniawi*), Islamic lifestyle, which necessitates *niat* in all acts, would bring positive outcomes for both the lives on earth and afterlife (Yani 2016, p. 63). Here, Aik implies that being a committed Muslim is more superior than being a straight edge punk.[24]

The transmission of Islamic messages through underground rock music is conducted mainly through anti-commercial, DIY music production and distribution. This is different from Rhoma's Soneta group which relied on the commercial music industry or corporate music distribution to transmit his Islamic messages (Irama 2011, p. 188). Despite his claim of broadening influence, Rhoma's reliance on the commercial music industry actually limited his *dakwah*, particularly in reaching out to segments of the urban population, such as the underground community that generally have less interest in commercial music.

Like *dakwah* through Islamic clothing, *dakwah* through DIY music production is often justified by Islamic underground musicians as part of their resistances against *ghazwul fikri* through Western underground rock music. Their belief in *ghazwul fikri* is often mixed with a belief in conspiracy theories. As a *Sabili* correspondent and observer of Islamic underground movement posited:

> It's no longer secret. The fact that various loud music has now flourished [to Indonesia] significantly, it always transforms [one's life] mission, there's a hidden agenda to corrupt the morality of the young generation. The anti-establishment ideology, anti-state, anti- capitalism, [and] anti-religion are the themes that had been promoted by various music styles (*aliran*), such as metal, punk, hardcore, and rap (Satria 2010, p. 41).[25]

To counter this, underground musicians like Thufail and Ombat, both once affiliated with the OFM, created an "Islamic" version of underground music which not only functions as a medium for expressing Islamic faith, but also as a tool for resistance (*jihad*) against *ghazwul fikri*.[26] The "consciousness" of *ghazwul fikri* or conspiracy theory played a significant part in justifying the formation of OFM. As Thufail once posited:

> The current war is the war without weapons. As Muslim, the highest religious obligation (*ibadah*) is *jihad qital* [physical war]. However, *jihad qital* is not yet possible to be applied in Indonesia. Thus, what we must do, is to counter idea with idea, technology with technology, economy

with economy, lifestyle with lifestyle. This is the manoeuvre that we call war without weapons (Satria 2010, p. 45).

In resisting *ghazwul fikri*, DIY music production benefitted Islamic underground musicians as it provided them freedom to articulate their transgressive messages, especially when compared to producing music through the corporate industry. During his productive years as a rapper (2005–7), Thufail produced Islamist transgressive messages in his songs such as "Sehelai Tirai Demokrasi", "Syair Perang Panjang", and "Puritan" (Homicide is Dead). Similarly, Tengkorak wrote songs with transgressive messages such as "Capitalism Agenda", "Destroy Zionism", "Jihad", and "Boycott Israel". The similar anti-Zionist messages are also expressed by Bandung's death metal band Saffar in their debut album *Mandatory El Arshy* (2013) (James 2018).[27]

Social media

The final strategy that contributes to the rise of the Islamic underground movement is the use of social media. Internet-based communication media comprises tools and mobile apps, such as blogs and blogging platforms (i.e. BlogSpot, WordPress), social networking sites and apps (i.e. Friendster, MySpace, Facebook), content sharing sites and apps (i.e. YouTube and Instagram), and online forums and communities (i.e. Yahoo Groups, Kaskus, WhatsApp Groups). The global range of social media enabled Muslims around the world, including Indonesia, to create an imagined global Muslim community—*ummah*, where local users can engage with transnational Muslim discourses (Lim 2012). Social media provides a platform for the Islamic underground movement participants to communicate with their audience and potential followers and influence them with their propaganda.

Amongst Indonesian Islamist forces, HTI activists were some of the earliest actors that made use of social media to promote their movement activities, extend their propaganda, and increase followers and networks. Interactions through social media are usually followed by offline meetings where collaboration amongst the activists/participants can be organized. An example of this collaboration is their first gathering and mass rally *Senayan Keras Kepala '07* (meaning "Hard-headed Senayan '07"), which was organized to enliven HTI's International Caliphate Conference (*Konferensi Khilafah Internasional*) on 12 August 2007 in Gelora Bung Karno, Jakarta. Amongst those who joined this event were members of Liberation Youth, Hambos Community, Menara Revolusi, Sons of Liberation, Brigade Lawan Arus, and Kolektif Jembatan Harokah. In this collaboration, the participants blended and called themselves "Islamic Revolutionaries!" (RISE!) (Liberation Youth 2007b).[28]

Conclusion

In this chapter, I have discussed the Islamic underground movement, a self-claimed countercultural movement with many variants that emerged as a result of contradictions of capitalist development in post-authoritarian Indonesia. This environment that created the contradictions has paved the way for ideological prominence of right-wing Islamism in some underground music scenes in Indonesia and is manifested in the formation of religious youth collectives and communities associated with the Islamic underground movement such as Liberation Youth, Punk Muslim, Underground Tauhid and One Finger Movement. They have emerged as viable alternative vehicles for disillusioned underground youths to deal with the post-authoritarian social, political, and economic challenges. Furthermore, through these collectives and communities, young people can channel their anger and articulate their resentment towards the social structure that have marginalized and alienated them.

I have discussed the key actors that played an important role in developing the Islamic underground movement. They employed DIY mobilization strategies to reach out to the marginalized youth audience who have been neglected by mainstream Islamic organizations. Despite its growth and appearance in some parts of Indonesia, the Islamic underground movement has never been a solid, unified entity. Over the years, collectives and communities of the Islamic underground movement have been riddled with internal ruptures, fragmentations, and disorganization. Because of this, some of their actors have moved to or created different organizations whilst some others have chosen to leave the movement completely. When I came to do my fieldwork in Indonesia between 2015 and 2016, HTI-linked underground youth collectives such as LY were either dissolved or in hiatus.[29] It was a similar case with OFM and GMT/UGT.[30] Only Punk Muslim survived as they formed new collaborations and regenerated. The reasons for this are varied: from boredom, saturation, and the lack of direction in the movement, to sectarianism (particularly anti-Shia sentiment) and different political orientations. Despite the decline of some of its collectives and communities, the Islamic underground movement has continued to grow with the coming of new actors and thus require further research.

NOTES

1. This chapter forms part of my PhD dissertation. It is an extended version of the draft presented at the ISEAS – Yusof Ishak Institute-Indonesian Institute of Sciences (LIPI)'s Conference on "Religious Authority in Indonesian Islam: Contestation, Pluralization, and New Actors", Singapore, 3–4 July 2018.
2. Sharing the same hostility towards the New Order, FAF collaborated with PRD until the latter transformed into a formal political party in 1996, changing its name from "People's Democratic Union" (Persatuan Rakyat Demokratik) to "People's Democratic Party" (Partai Rakyat Demokratik) (see Lane 2008 and Beittinger-Lee 2009 about this left-leaning student organization/political party). Herry Sutresna aka Morgue Vanguard or "Ucok Homicide", said that FAF members, many of them punks, soon decided to leave PRD by making signatures on a long mural to state their protest against the PRD's transformation into a political party (Sutresna, conversation 14 January 2012).
3. Similarly, in the late 1950s, Indonesia's anti-imperial Sukarno once made a speech against the consumption of western rock 'n' roll music which he described as "mixed-up noises" (*ngak-ngik-ngek*) and part of western cultural imperialism (Sen and Hill 2007, pp. 165–66).
4. Nasir is a Saudi university graduate and played a significant role in the National Movement to Uphold the Fatwa of the Indonesian Council of Ulama (GNPF-MUI), an organization behind the mass mobilizations in the "Action of Defending Islam" (*Aksi Bela Islam*) to oust Jakarta's Christian governor Basuki Tjahaja Purnama (Ahok) on the allegation of blasphemy (Chaplin 2017, 2018; Burhani 2018). Nasir is also the chairman of the Love Family Alliance (ALIA), a non-governmental organization that filed a judicial review at the constitutional court to criminalize LGBT communities in Indonesia.
5. American ethnomusicologist Jeremy Wallach credited Indonesian underground movement as an "important component in an emerging culture of democracy in Indonesia" (Wallach 2005, p. 20).
6. His claim to be part of PRD, however, was refuted by a former PRD member who was also part of Bandung underground scene (TD (pseudonym), interview, 16 December 2016).

7. Thufail once claimed to be part of the Tarbiyah movement (Al Ghifari 2008). However, it appears that he was also active in other Islamic movements (*harokah*), including organizations that had informal affiliation with HTI.
8. He made a concept of his resistance called "Microjihad", as an opposition to what he called as the "secular and agnostic" Indonesian hip-hop scene (referred to the "HipHopIndo" community). The "Microjihad" is designed for those who like hip hop but in line with the Islamic credo to "command the good and forbid the bad" (*amar makruf nahyi munkar*) (Al Ghifari 2008). Based on her conversation with Thufail, Brys (2012, p. 73) said that Thufail was excluded from the HipHopIndo.net because of his Islamist stance.
9. According to Homicide members, their song "Puritan" does not mean to attack Islam as alleged by Thufail. Instead, they criticize the political articulations of Islam by right-wing Islamist groups (i.e. FPI) which use violence and tend to attack others who disagree with them (Saefullah 2017b). Check out Homicide's "Puritan" song here: https://www.youtube.com/watch?v=j51IKd-WfC0, and Thufail's cover of the song: https://www.youtube.com/watch?v=Y8ZpmfiOLlk.
10. The similar conspiracy theory is also shared by the proponents of "Neo-Nazi music" or "White power music" in the West, where the corruption of "white culture" is perceived to be the result of Jewish conspiracy that promotes multiculturalism through MTV programmes (Corte and Edwards 2008, pp. 10–11).
11. Rita Katz of the SITE Intelligence Group asserts that the "one finger salute" has a political meaning: it expresses one's rejection of any form of government that is "not under the Shariah law" which explains the use of the salute by Islamists worldwide, including Osama bin Laden and Islamic State militants (Crowcroft 2015). Notably, the "one finger salute" was also used by right-wing Indonesian nationalists in the Red and White Coalition (*Koalisi Merah Putih*) as a symbol of political allegiance or support for General Prabowo's candidacy in the 2014 presidential election. Interestingly, Indonesian Islamists that previously claimed to be "anti-secularism" and "anti-democracy", aligned with Prabowo's coalition during the election, which suggests that both parties shared the same desire for authoritarianism (Wilson 2014).
12. Urban Garage Festival I was part of the OFM's charity programmes. Twenty per cent of the ticket price (Rp5,000 out of Rp25,000, or 50 cents out of AUD 2.50) were said to be donated for the Palestinian cause. OFM organized a similar event, called the Urban Garage Festival II, several months later in Bekasi. How and through which institution this donation was made, however, is unknown.

13. Postcolonial Islamic thinkers defined *ijtihad* as a "shorthand for intellectual and social reform, and as a break from *taqlid* or blind imitation of past legal rulings" (Fareed 2004, p. 345). In other words, *ijtihad* is an attempt to reform the meanings of the sacred texts (Quran and Hadith) based on the urgencies of a modern context.
14. *Sub Chaos Zine* was inspired by *Tigabelas Zine*, a Bandung-based DIY fanzine that was published by the lead singer of Bandung's hardcore punk band Puppen Arian Arifin (a.k.a. Arian 13) (Abdurrahman, interview, 18 July 2016; Yani 2017, p. 23).
15. Nevertheless, Ombat, who is also the head of the Centre for Islamic Human Rights (PUSHAMI), opposes Shi'ism. As he asserted, "It becomes obvious that the Shi'ites do not have any knowledge [of Islam], that's why their acts are foolhardy and misguided" (cited in Muttaqin 2015). He continued, "Pushami will sue Shia with both penal [*pidana*] and civil code [*perdata*], if necessary, with the international law" (Muttaqin 2015).
16. Buce was a street busker in Jakarta and a graduate of Pesantren Al-Hikmah Islamic Boarding School in Central Java. Upon his return, Buce lived on the streets around Pulo Gadung bus station in Jakarta and provided assistance to street kids and the homeless. He built a street side shelter in a ditch for them, and called it "Sanggar Warung Udix" (literally means "Udix Stalls Studio") whereby people from the streets, including buskers, beggars, stand-up vendors (*pedagang asongan*), and street punks, can hang out, rest, and interact with one another. Buce shared his experience of living in the shack with the kids: "I slept there too. When it rains, we all get wet. When it's hot, we all suffer from the heat. If we get up for *shubuh* [early morning] prayer, our body surrounded by flies. It's because our shack was close to a trash depot" (Ummi, 26 April 2016). Buce also felt that he had an obligation to protect the faith of the street kids who lived in extreme poverty. As he said: ""[They supposed to] maintain their faith. Even though they're starving[,] don't let their faith replaced with *supermi* [instant noodles]" (Ummi, 26 April 2016). The friendship between Buce and Zaki began as Zaki often invited Punk Muslim members to perform at his music events. Through Zaki's connection, Dompet Dhuafa provided a building for Punk Muslim members to conduct their activities, so the members would not have to fear being arrested or evicted by Satpol PP. Before this, Satpol PP often came and destroy their shack and arrested the street kids for hanging around at the public place. Buce often came to release the kids and rebuild the shack. Buce kept helping the kids until his death (the same story about Buce and Punk Muslim is also shared by Hidayatullah 2014).
17. Right after his decision to leave GMT/UGT in 2014, Aik created another online media that covers news and gossips surrounding subcultural music, called "konterkultur.com".

18. The bulletin contains articles and Q&A's about the basic practices of Islamic devotion (*ibadah*) in the Muslim holy month of Ramadhan, featuring Aditya Abdurrahman (Aik) as the author and popular clerics (*ustadz*) such as Ustadz Bachtiar Nasir (MIUMI and GNPF-MUI/Ulama) and Ustadz Ammi Nur Baits as the reference for the Q&A section. The bulletin was made to help nominal young Muslims particularly those from the local punk/underground music scene who had problems or are hesitant to access religious learnings.
19. In an interview on 23 May 2018, Ayik said that he was raised in the Nahdlatul Ulama's (NU) Islamic tradition, which emphasized the Sufistic approach to Islam. He was interested in political Islam and joined HTI when he was studying at the University of Indonesia (UI) in Depok, West Java (2001–3). Over the years, Ayik became the head of HTI in Bangka-Belitung province (2004–10) and was active in recruiting people to join HTI. After having a rupture with some HTI's central board members, he resigned from the organization in 2011. Ayik returned to NU and became a strong adherent of NU's religious and political tradition. His story is similar to that of a former British member of HT, Ed Husain, who returned to Sufistic Islam after feeling disillusioned with the transnational Islamist movement (see Husain 2007; Aidi 2014, p. 73).
20. Their use of Islamist symbols and jargons as part of their propaganda, however, shows their connection to HTI. They were using symbols, like *ar-Royah* (black flag) and *al-Liwa* (white flag) that were used in their propaganda arts and graphic designs. Amongst the Islamists, both flags with the *tauhid* calligraphs are believed to be the "flags of Rasulullah" (*bendera Rasulullah*) which were used by the Prophet during battles. However, this is rejected by Nadirsyah Hosen, an Islamic scholar from Wollongong University, Australia, who argues that the hadith is "weak" (*dhaif*) in telling the origins of the flags and thus, cannot be trusted (Hosen 2017). Apart from the flags, HTI activists used Islamist jargons in their propaganda, such as the term "Liberation" (which is *Tahrir* in Arabic), "Khilafah Islamiyyah" or "Daulah Islamiyah" and phrases like "democracy as *kufr* system".
21. Notably, the activists used English instead of Indonesian or Arabic to name their groups. This is a part of their strategy to connect with underground youths that favours the use of English, particularly in their cultural productions. For a discussion about the use of English within the Indonesian underground cultural production, particularly music, see Wallach (2003), pp. 53–86.
22. Underground Tauhid (UGT) is an online media project of Ghuraba Militant Tauhid (GMT). Within two years of intensive publication of articles through this online platform, readers become more familiar with the name of the

online media platform (IUGT) than the group's real name. Thus, since 2012, GMT changed its name to UGT (Yani 2017, p. 58).
23. In an interview scene within the *Global Metal* (2007) documentary, Ombat was asked about his controversial statement against the Jews and he replied: "It is not the Jewish people that we are against, only their system [Zionism]" (Dunn and McFadyen 2008).
24. Aik suggests that straight edge lifestyle, which encompasses vegetarianism and veganism, is in conflict with Islam since the latter suggests meat consumption (i.e. the religious practice of *qurban*, or livestock sacrifice on Idul Adha) (Yani 2016, p. 62).
25. See also Artawijaya, "Jejak Freemasonry dalam Aliran Musik" [The Traces of Freemasonry in Music Streams], *Sabili* 12, 27 December 2007, pp. 6–9.
26. Music is only one of many forms of aesthetic expressions of jihad, see Hegghammer (2017) and Swedenburg (2010), pp. 291–307.
27. Despite Saffar's claim that as a secular band, they are only a "band of Muslims rather than a Muslim band" (James 2018), the songs in their debut album contain a mixture of conspiracy theory and Islamist views. This can be found in the songs "Novus Ordo Seclorum", "Atmospheric Intifadha", and "Mandatory El Arshy". Their music video which is published on YouTube, featured scenes with the band members playing music interspersed by scenes where they imagined themselves as jihadi fighters. In the latter scenes, the band members wearing *kuffiya* and military outfit, picked up and held (fake) rifles such as AK-47, whilst also listening to a *tausiyah* about tauhid as an antidote to false ideologies that corrupt people's mind. See their video here: https://www.youtube.com/watch?v=O_BVwHRJ7qQ.
28. As a member of RISE! describe their collaborative movement:
    RISE! is not a group. Nor its ist a community. Rather, RISE! is a cup that unites all movement. RISE! is a flintstone for all types of rebellion that had had a long sleep on a bed of desperation and had begun to freeze in a refrigerator called stagnation. RISE! is born to pump back the spirit of those who had lost their spirit when struggling in the underground to create a revolution. Revolution is only a matter of time, and we are the pedal drivers of the revolution (Liberation Youth 2007a).
29. This is even more of the case when President Joko Widodo issued a decree to disband HTI in mid-2017 based on the allegation that the organization opposed Pancasila (see Burhani 2017 for an analysis of the disbandment of HTI). Over the years, some of the activists left HTI and joined the Islamic State in Iraq and Syria (ISIS), a militant Islamist organiszation that justifies violence to establish an Islamic caliphate (Taufiqurrohman and Prasetya 2016).

30. On 15 January 2016, OFM was in the spotlight due to *Tempo* magazine's allegation that the community had links with Bahrun Naim, the terror suspect of the Sarinah terror attack which happened a day earlier. This allegation was soon refuted by Ombat through his Facebook page (Lazuardi 2016; Florentin 2016).

REFERENCES

Abdurrahman, Aditya. 2009a. "Gerakan-gerakan yang Mengkonstruksi Peradaban" [Movements That Build Civilization]. *SA'I zine #4*, February–March 2009.

———. 2009b. "Urgensi Dakwah Bil Qolam" [The Urgency to Proselytize with Pen] and "Berperang Lewat Tulisan" [To Fight with Writing]. *SA'I zine #5*, 4–6 April–May 2009.

———. 2016. Interview. Surabaya, 16 July 2016.

———. 2016. Interview. Surabaya, 18 July 2016.

———. 2016. Interview. Surabaya, 20 July 2016.

———. 2016. Interview. Messenger, 23 August 2016.

———. 2017. Interview. WhatsApp Voice Call, 17 September 2017.

Ahnaf, Mohammad Iqbal. 2009. "Between Revolution and Reform: The Future of Hizbut Tahrir Indonesia". *Dynamics of Asymmetric Conflict* 2, no. 2: 69–85.

Aidi, Hisham. 2014. *Rebel Music: Race, Empire, and the New Muslim Youth Culture*. New York: Pantheon Books.

Al Ghifari, Thufail. 2008. "Rap Itu Budaya Perlawanan". Interview by Mia Yunita, 22 August 2008. https://diarypuan.wordpress.com/2008/08/22/thufail-al-ghifari-rap-itu-budaya-perlawanan/ (accessed 6 January 2018).

Artawijaya. 2007. "Jejak Freemasonry dalam Aliran Musik". *Sabili* 12, 27 December 2007, pp. 6–9.

Aspinall, Edward. 1995. "Students and the Military: Regime Friction and Civilian Dissent in the late Suharto Period". *Indonesia* 59 (April): 21–44. https://www.jstor.org/stable/3351126 (accessed 23 August 2018).

———. 2010. "The Irony of Success". *Journal of Democracy* 21, no. 2: 20–34.

Baulch, Emma. 2002. "Alternative Music and Meditation in late New Order Indonesia". *Inter-Asia Cultural Studies* 3, no. 2: 219–34.

———. 2007. *Making Scenes: Reggae, Punk, and Death Metal in 1990s Bali*. Durham: Duke University Press.

Beittinger-Lee, Verena. 2009. *(Un)Civil Society and Political Change in Indonesia: A Contested Arena*. London: Routledge.

Bodden, Michael. 2005. "Rap in Indonesian Youth Music of the 1990s: 'Globalization,' 'Outlaw Genres,' and Social Protest". *Asian Music* 36, no. 2: 1–26. http://www.jstor.org/stable/4098514 (accessed 29 August 2017).

Brys, Jitte Amanah. 2012. "We Rock Your Life Without Drugs, Alcohol, and Zina: de locale interpretaties van een globale cultuur in een snel veranderende samenleving: islamitische hiphop en rap in Indonesie". Master thesis, Universiteit Leiden, Leiden.

Bubalo, Anthony and Greg Fealy. 2005. "Joining the Caravan? The Middle East, Islamism and Indonesia". Lowy Institute Paper No. 5, Lowy Institute for International Policy, Sydney.

Burhani, Ahmad Najib. 2017. "The Banning of Hizbut Tahrir and the Consolidation of Democracy in Indonesia". *ISEAS Perspective*, no. 2017/71, 19 September 2017. https://www.iseas.edu.sg/images/pdf/ISEAS_Perspective_2017_71.pdf (accessed 25 September 2017).

———. 2018. "Plural Islam and Contestation of Religious Authority in Indonesia". In *Islam in Indonesia: Negotiating Modernity*, edited by Norshahril Saat, pp. 140–63. Singapore: ISEAS – Yusof Ishak Institute.

Chaplin, Chris. 2017. "The Alliance between Indonesia's Islamic Conservatives and Politicians Cannot Last". *Policy Forum*, 16 May 2017. https://www.policyforum.net/alliance-indonesias-islamic-conservatives-politicians-cannot-last/ (accessed 30 August 2018).

———. 2018. "Salafi Activism and the Promotion of a Modern Muslim Identity: Evolving Mediums of *Da'wa* amongst Yogyakartan University Students". *South East Asia Research* 26, no. 1: 3–20.

Corte, Ugo and Bob Edwards. 2008. "The Mobilization of Racist Social Movements". *Music and Arts in Action* 1, no. 1: 4–20.

Crowcroft, Orlando. 2015. "Isis: What is the Story behind the Islamic State One-Fingered Salute?" *International Business Times*, 16 June 2015. https://www.ibtimes.co.uk/isis-what-story-behind-islamic-state-one-fingered-salute-1506249 (accessed 28 November 2016).

Donaghey, Jim. 2015. "'Shariah Don't Like It…?' Punk and Religion in Indonesia". *Punk & Post-Punk* 4, no. 1: 29–52.

Donaghey, Jim and Jian Xiao. 2018. "A Comparison Between Indonesian and Chinese Punks: Resistance, Hangouts, and DIY". In *Punk Culture in Contemporary China*, by Jian Xiao, pp. 155–76. Singapore: Palgrave Macmillan.

Dunn, Kevin C. 2008. "Never Mind the Bollocks: Punk Rock Politics of Global Communication". *Review of International Studies* 34, Special Issue: 193–210.

———. 2016. *Global Punk: Resistance and Rebellion in Everyday Life*. New York: Bloomsbury.

Dunn, Sam and Scott McFadyen. 2008. *Global Metal*, directed by Sam Dunn and Scott McFadyen. DVD, Banger Films, Canada.

Fareed, Muneer Goolam. 2004. "Ijtihad". In *Encyclopedia of Islam and the Muslim World*, vols. 1 and 2, edited by Richard Martin, pp. 344–45. New York: Macmillan Reference USA.

Fiscella, Anthony T. 2012. "From Muslim Punks to Taqwacore: An Incomplete History of Punk Islam". *Contemporary Islam* 6, no. 3: 255–81.

Florentin, Vindry. 2016. "Bahrun Naim Bukan Penggagas Komunitas Salam Satu Jari" [Bahrun Naim is not the Founder of the One Finger Movement]. *Tempo.co*, 16 January 2016. https://nasional.tempo.co/read/736746/bahrun-naim-bukan-penggagas-komunitas-salam-satu-jari (accessed 15 February 2017).

Haenfler, Ross. 2006. *Straight Edge: Clean-Living Youth, Hardcore Punk, and Social Change*. London: Rutgers University Press.

Hasan, Noorhaidi. 2005. "Laskar Jihad: Islam, Militancy, and the Quest for Identity in Post-New Order Indonesia". PhD dissertation, University of Utrecht, Utrecht.

———. 2007. "The Salafi Movement in Indonesia: Transnational Dynamics and Local Development". *Comparative Studies of South Asia, Africa, and the Middle East* 27, no. 1: 83–94. https://muse.jhu.edu/article/215898.

Hefner, Robert W. 1997. "Print Islam: Mass Media and Ideological Rivalries among Indonesian Muslims". *Indonesia* 64 (October): 77–103. https://www.jstor.org/stable/3351436.

———. 2000. *Civil Islam: Muslims and Democratization in Indonesia*. Princeton: Princeton University Press.

Hegghammer, Thomas, ed. 2017. *Jihadi Culture: The Art and Social Practices of Militant Islamists*. Cambridge: Cambridge University Press.

Heriansyah, Ayik. 2018. Interview. WhatsApp Chat, 23 May 2018.

Herrera, Linda and Asef Bayat, eds. 2010. *Being Young and Muslim: New Cultural Politics in the Global South and North*. New York: Oxford University Press.

Heryanto, Ariel. 1996. "The Student Movement". *Inside Indonesia* 48 (October–December).

———. 2014. *Identity and Pleasure: The Politics of Indonesian Screen Culture*. Singapore: NUS Press.

Hidayatullah, Rahmat. 2014. "Punk Muslim: Ekspresi Identitas Keagamaan Subkultur Muslim Urban". *Kawalu: Journal of Local Culture* 1, no. 2: 145–64.

Hosen, Nadirsyah. 2005. "Religion and the Indonesian Constitution: A Recent Debate". *Journal of Southeast Asian Studies* 36, no. 3: 419–40.

———. 2017. "Soal Bendera Rasulullah, Gus Nadir: Jangan Mau Dibohongi ISIS dan HTI" [About the Messenger's Flag, Gus Nadir: Do No Let ISIS and HTI Manipulates You]. *Nadirhosen.net*, 29 July 2017, https://nadirhosen.net/berita/soal-bendera-rasulullah-gus-nadir-jangan-mau-dibohongi-isis-dan-hti (accessed 11 August 2018).

Husain, Ed. 2007. *The Islamist: Why I Joined Radical Islam in Britain, What I Saw Inside and Why I Left*. London: Penguin Books.

Irama, Rhoma. 2011. "Music as a Medium for Communication, Unity, Education, and *Dakwah*", translated by Andrew Weintraub. In *Islam and Popular Culture in Indonesia and Malaysia*, edited by Andrew Weintraub, pp. 185–92. London: Routledge.

James, Kieran. 2018. "Islamic Religion and Death Metal Music in Indonesia". *Journal of Popular Music Studies* 30, no. 3: 129–52.

Jamil, Eeng Reni Nuraisyah. 2017. "Mendaur Ulang Punk dalam 'Punk Muslim'". *Ayobandung.com*, 21 April 2017. http://ayobandung.com/read/2017/04/21/18991/ (accessed 12 August 2018).

Kuhn, Gabriel, ed. 2010. *Sober Living for the Revolution: Hardcore Punk, Straight Edge, and Radical Politics*. Oakland: PM Press.

Lane, Max. 2008. *Unfinished Nation: Indonesia Before and After Suharto*. London: Verso.

Lazuardi, Iqbal. 2016. "Bahrun Naim Disebut Gagas Komunitas Underground Satu Jari" [Bahrun Naim is said to be the Founder of the One Finger Underground Movement]. *Tempo.co*, 15 January 2016. https://nasional.tempo.co/read/736564/bahrun-naim-disebut-gagas-komunitas-underground-satu-jari (accessed 6 April 2018).

Liberation Youth. 2007a. "Kisah Seorang Punker" [A Story of a Punk]. *Liberation Youth*. https://lymovementkaltim.wordpress.com/anti-copyright/ (accessed 10 June 2018).

———. 2007b. "Scene Report: Senayan Keras Kepala '07". *Liberation Youth*, 28 August 2007. https://lymovementkaltim.wordpress.com/2007/08/ (accessed 1 June 2016).

Lim, Merlyna. 2012. "Life is Local in the Imagined Community: Islam and Politics in the Blogosphere". *Journal of Media and Religion* 11, no. 3: 127–40.

Machmudi, Yon. 2008. *Islamising Indonesia: The Rise of Jemaah Tarbiyah and the Prosperous Justice Party (PKS)*. Canberra: ANU E-Press.

Martin-Iverson, Sean. 2012. "Autonomous Youth? Independence and Precariousness in the Indonesian Underground Music Scene". *The Asia Pacific Journal of Anthropology* 13, no. 4: 382–97.

———. 2014. "Running in Circles: Performing Values in the Bandung 'Do It Yourself' Hardcore Scene". *Ethnomusicology Forum* 23, no. 2: 184–207.

———. 2015. Conversation. University of Western Australia, Perth, 21 December 2015.

———. 2017. "'Life in the Positive Way': Indonesian Straight Edge and the Limits of Lifestyle Politics". *Punk & Post-Punk* 6, no. 2: 233–61.

Martin, Richard, ed. 2004. *Encyclopedia of Islam and the Muslim World*, vols. 1 and 2. New York: Macmillan Reference USA.

Mogerz Infantry. 2010. "Approach Deen Avoid Sins – Part 1", 23 February 2010. http://mogerz-infantry.blogspot.com/2010/02/approach-deen-avoid-sins-part-1.html (accessed 18 July 2018).

Mubarak, Zulham. 2011. "Berjihad lewat Musik Underground, Ubah Salam Metal jadi Satu Jari Tauhid" [Jihad through Underground Music, Changing

Metal Salute with Tauhid's One Finger Gesture]. JPNN.com, 9 March 2011. https://www.jpnn.com/news/berjihad-lewat-musik-underground-ubah-salam-metal-jadi-satu-jari-tauhid (accessed 26 April 2016).

Muttaqin, A.Z. 2015. "Menodai Islam, Pushami akan menggugat Syiah" [Desecrating Islam, Pushami Will Sue the Shi'ites]. *Arrahmah*, 23 February 2015. https://www.arrahmah.com/2015/02/23/menodai-islam-pushami-akan-menggugat-syiah/ (accessed 28 April 2017).

Norshahril Saat, ed. 2018. *Islam in Indonesia: Negotiating Modernity*. Singapore: ISEAS – Yusof Ishak Institute.

Nugroho, Dimas Oky. 2017. "The Indigenisation of a Transnational Islamic Movement in Contemporary Indonesia: A Study of Hizbut Tahrir Indonesia". PhD thesis, University of New South Wales, Australia.

Osman, Mohamed Nawab M. 2010a. "The Transnational Network of Hizbut Tahrir Indonesia". *South East Asia Research* 18, no. 4: 735–55.

———. 2010b. "Reviving the Caliphate in the Nusantara: Hizbut Tahrir Indonesia's Mobilization Strategy and Its Impact in Indonesia". *Terrorism and Political Violence* 22, no. 4: 601–22.

Panjimas. 2017. "PUSHAMI: Awas Umat Islam Jangan Masuk Jebakan RAND Corporation" [PUSHAMI: Watch Out Don't Let Islam Sucked into RAND Corporation's Trap]. Panjimas.com, 6 May 2017. https://www.panjimas.com/news/2017/05/06/pushami-awas-umat-islam-jangan-masuk-jebakaan-rand-corporation/ (accessed 12 May 2017).

Pickles, Joanna. 2000. "Punks for Peace: Underground Music Gives Young People Back Their Voice". *Inside Indonesia* 64 (October–December). http://www.insideindonesia.org/punks-for-peace (accessed 20 May 2018).

———. 2001. "Of Purple and Protest: Beyond Spectacular Style, Bandung's Punks in Collective Action". Honours Thesis, Australian National University.

———. 2007. "Punk, Pop, and Protest: The Birth and Decline of Political Punk in Bandung". *Review of Indonesian and Malaysian Affairs* 41, no. 2: 223–46.

Rakhmani, Inaya. 2016. *Mainstreaming Islam in Indonesia: Television, Identity, and the Middle Class*. New York: Palgrave Macmillan.

Republika. 2009. "Mengenal Islam Melalui Musik Underground" [Knowing Islam Through the Underground Musik]. *Republika* 16 (March). https://www.republika.co.id/berita/shortlink/41167 (accessed 14 December 2016).

———. 2015. "MIUMI: Liberalisme Musuh yang Paling Berbahaya bagi Umat Islam" [MIUMI: Liberalism is the Most Dangerous Threat to the Islamic Ummah]. *Republika*, 5 February 2015. https://www.republika.co.id/berita/nasional/umum/15/02/05/njab3l-miumi-liberalisme-musuh-yang-paling-berbahaya-bagi-umat-islam (accessed 28 February 2017).

Saefullah, Hikmawan. 2017a. "Nevermind the *Jahiliyyah*, Here's the *Hijrahs*: Punk and the Religious Turn in the Contemporary Indonesian Underground Scene". *Punk & Post-Punk* 6, no. 2: 263–89.

———. 2017b. "Skena Musik Underground, Agama, dan Politik Islam di Indonesia" [Underground Music Scene, Religion, and Islamic Politics in Indonesia]. In *Trialektika: Agama-Budaya-Politik*, edited by Alfathri Adlin, pp. 333–52. Bandung: Studia Humanika – YPM Salman ITB.
Satria, Adhes. 2008. "Underground: Musik Doktrin dan Pemikiran" [Underground: Doctrinal Music and Thought]. *Sabili* 24, no. xv (12 June): 84–74.
———. 2010. "Underground pun Menggempur Zionis" [Underground Also Pounds Zionist]. *Sabili* 13, no. xvii (21 January): 40–45.
Sen, Krishna and David Hill. 2007. *Media, Culture and Politics in Indonesia*. Jakarta: Equinox Publishing Indonesia.
Suara-Islam. 2016. "Dakwah lewat T-Shirt di Acara JakCloth". *Suara-Islam.com*, January 2016. http://suara-islam.com/read/index/16630/Dakwah-Lewat-T-Shirt-di-Acara-JakCloth-2015?fbclid=IwAR0ONHVLa-reHybzgdhTBaIi57vew sXvV1nR2XZ1MfNNfYdyMnIUg2Z-sBM (accessed 20 July 2018).
Sub Chaos. n.d. "Interview with Ghurabba (Militant Tawheed)". *Sub Chaos* #9, pp. 12–15.
Sutresna, Herry. 2012. Conversation. WhatsApp, 14 January 2012.
Swedenburg, Ted. 2010. "Fun^Da^Mental's 'Jihad Rap'". In *Being Young and Muslim: New Cultural Politics in the Global South and North*, edited by Linda Herrera and Asef Bayat, pp. 291–307. New York: Oxford University Press.
Taufiqurrohman, Muhammad and Ardi Putra Prasetya. 2016. "A Rising Indonesian Jihadist Plotter Bahrun Naim". *Counter Terrorist Trends and Analysis* 8, no. 11: 8–10. http://www.jstor.org/stable/26351466.
TD (pseudonym). 2016. Interview, 16 December 2016.
Triggs, Teal. 2006. "Scissors and Glue: Punk Fanzines and the Creation of a DIY Aesthetic". *Jurnal of Design History* 19, no. 1: 69–83.
Ummi. 2016. "Sanggar Warung Udix, Jembatan Kehidupan Anak Jalanan". *Ummi Online*, 26 April 2016. https://www.ummi-online.com/sanggar-warung-udix-jembatan-kehidupan-anak-jalanan-simak-selengkapnya/ (accessed 16 August 2018).
van Bruinessen, Martin, ed. 2013a. *Contemporary Developments in Indonesian Islam: Explaining the "Conservative Turn"*. Singapore: Institute of Southeast Asian Studies.
———. 2013b. "Introduction: Contemporary Development in Indonesian Islam and the 'Conservative Turn' of the Early Twenty-First Century". In *Contemporary Developments in Indonesian Islam: Explaining the "Conservative Turn"*, edited by Martin van Bruinessen, pp. 1–20. Singapore: Institute of Southeast Asian Studies.
———. 2015. "*Ghazwul Fikri* or Arabization? Indonesian Muslim Responses to Globalization". In *Southeast Asian Muslims in the Era of Globalization*, edited by Ken Miichi and Omar Farouk, pp. 61–85. New York: Palgrave Macmillan.

———. 2018. "Indonesian Muslims in a Globalising World: Westernisation, Arabisation, and Indigenising Responses". RSIS Working Paper No. 311, Rajaratnam School of International Studies, Nanyang Technological University, Singapore, 3 May 2018. https://www.rsis.edu.sg/wp-content/uploads/2018/05/WP311.pdf (accessed 5 May 2018).

VOA-Islam. 2016. "Ada Kampanye Anti-Syiah di JakCloth 2015", 4 January 2016. https://www.voa-islam.com/read/syariahbiz/2016/01/04/41465/ada-kampanye-antisyiah-di-jakcloth-2015/ (accessed 4 January 2016).

Wallach, Jeremy. 2003. "'Goodbye My Blind Majesty': Music, Language, and Politics in the Indonesian Underground". In *Global Pop, Local Language*, edited by Harris M. Berger and Thomas Carroll, pp. 53–86. Mississippi: University Press of Mississippi.

———. 2005. "Underground Rock Music: And Democratization in Indonesia". *World Literature Today* 79, no. 3/4: 16–20.

———. 2008. "Living the Punk Lifestyle in Jakarta". *Ethnomusicology* 52, no. 1: 98–116. http://www.jstor.org/stable/20174568 (accessed 14 August 2014).

Ward, Ken. 2009. "Non-Violent Extremists? Hizbut Tahrir Indonesia". *Australian Journal of International Affairs* 63, no. 2: 149–64.

Weintraub, Andrew N., ed. 2011. *Islam and Popular Culture in Indonesia and Malaysia*. New York: Routledge.

Wilson, Ian. 2014. "Resisting Democracy: Front Pembela Islam and Indonesia's 2014 Elections". *ISEAS Perspective*, no. 2014/10, 24 February 2014, pp. 1–8. https://www.iseas.edu.sg/images/pdf/ISEAS_Perspective_2014_10.pdf (accessed 3 November 2016).

Yani, Aditya Rahman. 2016. *Melawan Arus: Membedah Pemikiran Subkultur Punk Islam di Indonesia* [Against the Stream: Examining the Subcultural Thoughts of Punk Islam in Indonesia]. Waru-Sidoarjo: Kanzun Books.

———. 2017. *Aku (Pernah) Punk: Sebuah Cerita Perjalanan Seorang Punk Menuju Hidayah* [I Once a Punk: A Story of a Punk's Journey Towards Islamic Guidance]. Waru-Sidoarjo: Kanzun Books.

INDEX

Note: Page numbers followed by "n" refer to endnotes.

A
abangan, 3, 4, 24
Abbas, Syahrizal, 69, 79
Abdul Ghafur, 301, 304
Abdul Ghani Kazuba, 311
Abdullah Gymnastiar (Aa Gym), 90, 251, 258, 328
Abdullah, M. Amin, 6, 41
Abdullah, Zaini, 69
Abdul Qadir Jawas. *See* Yazid bin Abdul Qadir Jawas
Abdurrahman Wahid, 32, 38, 41, 42, 50, 52–53, 77, 232
Abidin, Firanda Andirja, 163, 172
Abidin, Zainal, 163, 172
Abou El Fadl, Khaled, 23, 24, 39
'Abubakar, Alyasa, 68, 69, 78
Abu-Rabi', Ibrahim M., 14, 22, 23
Abu Zayd, Nasr Hamid, 49
acceptance of authority, 71
  components of, 65
Aceh
  Department of Islamic Shariah. *See* Department of Islamic Shariah (DSI)
  "development of religion" plan, 66
  female leadership, 85
  five-year development plan, 66
  Grand Design for Shariah Islam, 69–70
  Islamic development, 65
  Nanggroe Aceh Darussalam, 66
  province, 68, 71
  shariah implementation in, 64, 65, 73, 76
  Strategic Plan of the Special Province of Aceh 2001–2005, 66
Aceh Besar regent, 78–79
Aceh Government (UUPA), 68–69
Aceh Shariah Development Index, 70
Adi Hidayat, 57
Agung Mosque, 250
ahl sunna wa al-jama'a, 152, 153, 168
ahlul bid'ah (the people of religious innovations), 265
ahlussunnah (the people of the Prophet's Sunnah), 265
"*Ahlussunnah wal jama'ah an-nahdliyah*" faction, 264
Ahmad Hasan, 243
Ahmad Hidayat Mus, 311
Ahmadiyah movement, 117
Ahmadiyya, 54, 60, 323

Ahmad, Mirza Ghulam, 117
Ahmad Subagyo, 185, 186, 192n5
    statistics from, 181
Ahmad Syafii Maarif, 32, 41, 42, 269
Ahmad, Ziauddin, 74
Ahok. *See* Basuki Tjahaja Purnama
Ahok controversy, 268
Aik (Aditya Abdurrahman), 327, 328,
    330, 332, 334, 341n17, 342n19,
    343n24
Aksi Bela Islam, 5, 251
Aktuil (magazine), 242
Alatas, Syed Hussein, 30
Al-Azhar University, 262
al-Albani, Muhammad Nasir al-Din,
    131–32
al-Albani, Syeikh Muhammad
    Nasiruddin, 172
Al-Furqon Mosque, 254n2
Al-Ghazali, Imam, 264
Aliansi Cinta Keluarga (AILA), 106,
    112, 121
aliran, 229, 336
aliran sesat, 53
Al-Khairat organization, 311
Al-Latief Mosque, 241, 245, 249, 250
al-Qaeda-linked Jamaah Islamiyah
    (JI), 134
amar ma'ruf nahi munkar (enjoining
    good and forbidding evil), 267
Amien Rais, 32
amil (village official in charge of
    collecting *zakat*), 228
anarcho-punk group, 327
Antara Jihad dan Terorisme [Between
    Jihad and Terrorism], 144
anti-Ahmadiyah regulations, 117–21
    implementation, 120
    and party affiliations, 120
    of public order and social harmony,
        119
    since 2008, 118–19
    violence against, 117
anti-Islam Liberal rhetoric, 43
Anti-Oppression Front, 327
anti-pornography bill, 114–15
anti-Sultan forces, 304
anti-Wahhabi preachers, 158
anti-Wahhabism, 154–56
anti-Zionist messages, 337
aqidah Islamiyah, 75
Arabized Islam, 287
Arifin Ilham, 90, 94, 250, 251
Arkoun, Mohammed, 49
al-Ash'ari, Abu Hasan, 145
asrama, 197, 202, 204, 208
asrama Turki, 202
Association for the Special Status of
    Yogyakarta, 306
Association of Syam Alumni of
    Indonesia (Alsyami), 271
aswaja an-nahdliyah, 264
aswaja dakwah, 152, 154–57, 161, 166
aswaja defenders, 157–63, 166, 169,
    173
    Habib Noval b. Muhammad
        Alaydrus, 157–59
    Muhammad Idrus Ramli, 159–60
    Sarkub, 160–63
aswaja group, 152, 153, 156–57, 163,
    164, 167–72
    and opposing "deviancy", 163–67
authoritarian New Order, 318
authoritarian regime, 14
authoritative, 36–38
authority, 1, 36–38
    challenged, 38–40
    contestation over, 307–12
    fragmentation of, 141–45, 268
    kinds of, 35
    understanding, 35–36
Ayat-ayat Cinta, 285, 287, 288
Azhar Basyir, Ahmad, 49
Azra, Azyumardi, 7, 41, 271

Index

B
Ba'abduh, Lukman, 141–44
Ba'asyir, Abu Bakar, 134
Banda Aceh, 78
Bandung,
  cosmopolitan outlook of, 243
  paradoxes of, 242–44
bangsa abangan, 3
bangsa putihan, 3
Banten, 228–29
Bappeda, 72–73
Barisan Anti Penindasan (BAP), 327
Basuki Tjahaja Purnama (Ahok), 5, 6, 18, 19, 58, 78, 105, 227, 251
Basyariyah, 264
bayan (explanation), 59, 186
Berandalan Puritan, 324, 326
Bhinneka Tunggal Ika, 115
bid'ah, 168, 169, 215, 225
Bina Peradilan (Strengthening the Shariah Court), 66
BMX bicycle society, 243
Boki Nita, 307–8
Bonny, Handy, 244
Border *Da'i* programme, 73–76
"Brigez Berzikir untuk Indonesia" event, 250
Budi Chaeroni (Buce), 328, 341n16
bureaucracy, 80
bureaucracy reform, 77

C
Cak Nur. *See* Nurcholish Madjid
cendekiawan Muslim, 32
Center for the Study of Islam and Society, 248
Central Bureau of Statistics (BPS), 72
charismatic authority (Weber), 191, 197
cinematic *santri*, 291
civil court, 84, 99n1
Civilized Indonesia Movement, 121
Civil Society Network for Shariah Concerns (JMSPSI), 69
classical doctrine *vs.* state law, 94–95
combating national moral degradation, 110
communal piety, strengthening of, 220–23
conservative institutions, 85
conservative Islamic movements, 106, 107
  activism, 110
  anti-Ahmadiyah regulations, 117–21
  anti-pornography bill, 114–15
  against extra-marital affairs, 121–22
  forefront of, 112
  ideational factors, 109
  in Indonesia, 112
  influence policy, 107–10
  institutionalized movements, 109
  issues raised by, 114
  LGBT acts, 121–22
  local sharia laws, 116–17
  main contribution of, 114
  organizations, 110
  in policy-making, 108, 109, 113
  political influence by, 107
  political parties, 107–10, 113–14
  research on, 107
  saliency of, 122
  strategy of, 107
conservative Muslim groups, 105
contemporary Indonesian Islam, 33
contemporary Indonesia, urban middle-class Muslims in, 216–20
contemporary Islamic scholarship, 29
contemporary urban Muslims, 218, 222
conventional religious discourse, 44
Convention on the Elimination of All Forms of Discrimination Against Women (CEDAW), 88, 100n5

Convention on the Rights of the
    Child (CRC), 88, 100n6
Council of Indonesian Ulama, 50, 115
cultural Islam, 230
cultural pluralism, 297
cyberspace, 13, 37

D
Da'i Performance Assessment (report), 74
da'is'
  mission and approach, 74
  number of, 75
  performance, 75
  recruited, 74
dakwah, 32, 35, 59, 75, 131, 132, 136,
    137, 151, 152, 155, 156, 162, 164,
    165, 167, 184, 205, 241, 246, 253,
    254n2, 260, 272, 288, 327, 328,
    332, 334, 335
  expansion of Salafism, 157
  experience of, 188
dakwah activities, 86
  democratization of, 90, 97, 98
  female preachers involvement in, 89–91
  programmes, 98
  social media in, 90
dakwah bil qolam, 332, 333
dakwah hijrah, 254n3
dakwah hizbiyya, 139
dakwah salafiyya, 139
dakwahtaintment, 84, 90
dangdut music performance, 335
dauras, 147
Dawuh Raja, 309
defending national morality, 112
democratization, 17
  of *dakwah*, 90, 97, 98
  and economic liberalization, 107
  of Indonesia, 2, 106, 111–13
  and Islam, 111

of Islamic knowledge, 279
of religious authority, 5
Department of Islamic Shariah (DSI),
    7, 65
  authority establishment, rationale
      for, 66–67
  budgeting consultation exercise, 73
  bureaucratic authority, 65
  competence of, 77
  current authority, 81
  da'i programme by, 73–74
  direct involvement, 79
  expertise, 76–79
  formation of, 66
  and GDSI design, 69
  insufficient managerial capabilities,
      76–79
  internal structure of, 72
  legal authority, 65
  limitations of, 68–69
  media spotlight on, 79
  office leaders' personal influence,
      79–80
  operational aspects of, 71
  organizational structure, 71
  and outreach, 68–69
  personnel, 78
  positions in, 71–80
  Regional Regulation No. 33 of 2001,
      66, 68
  research and development working
      unit, 71–73
  staff recruitment, 77
  strategic planning, 72
  working plan, 75
Dewan Perwakilan Rakyat Daerah
    (DPRD), 116
Dinas Syariat Islam. *See* Department
    of Islamic Shariah (DSI)
Do-It-Yourself (DIY), 243, 327
  clothing and merchandises, 334
  mobilization strategies, 330–38

music productions and
performances, 335–37
publications, 332–34
dormitory system, 201
Dutch colonialism, 298
Dutch recolonization of Indonesia, 299
dzikir (remembering Allah), 335
Dzulqarnain, M. Sanusi, 141, 142

E
economic liberalization, 107
education, women's involvement in, 84
Effendi, Evie, 244
Election Committee. See *Komisi Pemilihan Umum* (KPU)
elections
  issues during post-election period, 108
  political parties in, 108
el-Shirazy, Habiburrahman, 288

F
Fachruddin, A.R., 49
Faisal Ismail, 38
family law in Indonesia, 84
  Islamic, 86, 87, 92, 94, 95, 97
  legal reforms on, 84, 86–89
  on women issues, 86–89
Fani Krismandar. See Inong
fatwas, 5, 51, 53, 54, 143, 172, 190, 259, 267, 271
  compilation, 54
female leadership, 85
female preachers
  classical doctrine *vs.* state law, 94–95
  deal with familial legal rules, 85
  involvement in *dakwah* activities, 89–91
  and legal notions, 86, 91–95

media-using, 86
fiqh, 205, 225
Firanda Andirja, 55, 56
foreign Islam, 232
formal Islamic education, 323
Forum Kiai Muda, 160
Forum Komunikasi Ahlu Sunnah wal Jamaah (FKASWJ), 112
framing, 109
  issues as morality, 112
  as strategy of social protest, 109–11
Frankfurter Allgemeine Zeitung, 22
Friday prayer, 59
Front Pembela Islam (FPI), 106, 112
  massive protests by, 115
  massive violent protests, 115
  violence, 252

G
Gallipoli Mosque, 199
GEMA Pembebasan, 331
gender asymmetries in women, 92–93
Genta Raja (United Yogyakarta Movement), 306
Gerakan Indonesia Beradab (GIB), 121
Gerakan Keagamaan Transnasional, 192n1
Gerakan Muda Sultan Babullah (Gemusba), 300
Gerakan Nasional Pengawal Fatwa-MUI (GNPF-MUI), 58
Gerakan Rakyat Yogyakarta, 306
Gerak Bareng Community, 329
ghazwul fikri, 230, 322, 326, 328, 335–37
Ghuraba Militant Tauhid (GMT), 342n22
Ghurabba (Militant Tawheed), 327, 328
glocalization, 203
Golkar Party, 115, 117, 123n5

Grand Design for Shariah Islam (GDSI), 69–70
Gus Dur. *See* Abdurrahman Wahid
Gusti Pembayun, 308

H
habaib, 5, 7, 157, 158, 164–66, 169, 171–73
Habib Ahmad b. Zein Al-Kaff, 166
Habib Mahmud b. Umar Al-Hamid, 171
Habib Munzir, 169–70, 172
Habib Noval b. Muhammad Alaydrus. *See* Noval Alaydrus
Habib Rizieq. *See* Rizieq Shihab, Habib
hadith, 220
haji, 229
Haji Tjetjep Marzuki, 180, 182, 188
  religious movement, 189
  Tablighi Jamaat, 183
halqas, 147
Hamka, Buya, 49
haram practices, 21
hardline groups, 120
hardline Islamic groups, 115
al-Hawali, Safar, 144
Heriansyah, Ayik, 330
heterodox (*sesat*), 56
hijab, 220–22
hijrah, 246, 271, 333, 335
  communities, 57
  interpretation, 56–58
hizbiyya, 139–40
Hizbut Tahrir (HT), 2, 6, 112, 151, 164
Hizbut Tahrir Indonesia (HTI), 50, 60, 246, 262, 321, 322, 330–32, 335, 337, 340n7, 342n19, 342n20, 343n29
hizmet, 197, 199, 200, 202
hoca, 207
homosexuality, 121

HTI-linked underground youth collectives, 338
Humanist Legal Analysis Framework, 69
Huzaimah Tahido Yanggo, 91

I
ibadah, 336
iconoclasm, 289
identity politics, 51, 106
ideological approach, 14
Idrus Ramli, Muhammad, 159–60, 168
Idzin Kolano, 311
ijtihad, 49, 50, 101n12, 327, 341n13
ijtima', 185, 186
Ikatan Cendekiawan Muslim Indonesia (ICMI), 52
ikhwan, 199
Ikhwanul Muslimin, 243
illiberal politics, 52–53
Ilmu Sosial Profetik (Kuntowijoyo), 41
image-making technologies, fear of, 289
Indonesia, 2, 214
  anti-imperial Sukarno, 339n3
  Bureaucracy Reform agenda in, 71
  civil rights in, 117
  conservative Islamic movements in, 112
  "conservative turn" in, 20
  contemporary urban middle-class Muslims, 222
  court systems in, 99n1
  critical force in, 106
  culture of, 122
  dakwah activities in, 90
  declaration of independence in, 16
  democracy in, 53
  democratic and decentralized government, 13
  democratization of, 2, 106, 111–13
  Dutch recolonization of, 299

efflorescence of Salafism, 132–34
family law, 84
female judges, 89, 93
government of, 321
interpretations of Islam in, 49–52
Islamic discourse in, 35
Islamic education in, 201
Islamic family law in, 94
Islamic preaching scene in, 240
Islamic religious authority in, 36
knowledge production, 135–38
Ministry of Culture and Museum in Jakarta, 193n5
Muslim communities in, 191, 221
Muslim groups in, 54
Muslim-majority country, 14
Muslim women involvement in, 85
National Law Development Agency Director, 66
national motto of, 115
official Islam in, 24
oppositional Islam in, 19
oppositional Islam movement in, 18
policies in contemporary, 106
policy-making, 107
political parties in, 114
reform, 65
sacred national principles, 115
Salafi doctrine in, 155
Salafi group in, 7
Salafi influence in, 147
scholars on, 3
Shia groups in, 166
society classification in, 3
Sulaimaniyah in, 197–200
Sunnah groups in, 55
Sunni and traditional Islam in, 152–54
Turkish Muslim movements in, 196
ulama council, 300
underground movement in, 318–20

wide community, 86
Indonesian Communist Party (PKI), 321
Indonesian intellectual discourse, 29
Indonesian intellectual history, 29
Indonesian Islam, 4, 5, 10, 13, 14, 19, 24, 52, 57, 169, 191
  conservative direction of, 321
  development of, 34
  religious authority in, 6
  securing of, 20–24
Indonesian Islam discourse, 30, 32, 33
Indonesian Islamic Propagation Council, 111, 133
Indonesian Islamic underground movement, 327
Indonesian Islamist forces, 337
Indonesian Law of Children Protection, 88
Indonesian Muslim community, 326
Indonesian Muslim Forum (FUI), 325
Indonesian Muslim public sphere, 283–86
Indonesian Muslim religious intellectuals
  accomplishment of, 40–43
Indonesian Muslims, 24, 34, 131, 141, 190, 202, 226, 230, 259, 269
  threat to, 265
Indonesian political system, 273
Indonesian religious intellectuals, 28
  discursive themes and concerns, 33–35
  emergence of, 31–33
Indonesian Salafism, 133
Indonesian society, 220
Indonesian Sulaimaniyah movement, 200
Indonesian Sulaimaniyah organization, 202
Indonesian youths, 318
informal organizations, HTI's, 331

information and communication technology (ICT), 13
Inong, 245, 249, 253n1
Institute of Islamic and Arabic Sciences, 133
Institute of Malay Culture, 263
institutional access, 108
institutionalized organizations, 106, 107, 109, 113
International Caliphate Conference, 337
International Covenant on Civil and Political Rights (ICCPR), 88, 100n5
International Crisis Group, 155
Internet-based communication media, 337
interpretations of Islam. *See* Islamic interpretation
inter-religious marriage, 87
Iranian Revolution, 132, 139, 155
Isha prayer, 186, 190
Ishomuddin, Ahmad, 265–66
Islam
  authoritative body of, 5
  authoritative in, 2
  branch issues, 54
  defender of, 37
  democratization and, 111
  fundamental sources of, 141
  and identity politics, 106
  interpretation of, 17
  legal argument, 59
  narrow-minded interpretation of, 22
  non-believers of, 120
  political, 59–61
  political parties, 114–15
  in post-authoritarian Indonesia, 16
  principle of, 54
  traditionalist group of, 4
  traditionalist Sunni version of, 151
  understanding of, 14
Islam Berkemajuan, 20, 22, 191
Islamic activism, 131
Islamic authority, 106
  fragmentation in, 279
Islamic caliphate (*khilafah*), 332
"Islamic cinema", 285
Islamic civil society, 107, 111
Islamic Clothing United (ICU), 335
Islamic commercialism, 219
Islamic communal piety, 219
Islamic consumerism, 219
Islamic creed (*aqidah*), 332
Islamic Defenders Front, 112
Islamic discourse, in Indonesia, 35
Islamic doctrine, masters of, 189
Islamic education, 29, 145–47, 201
Islamic family law, 86, 87, 92, 94, 95, 97
  reforms on, 99
Islamic fundamentalism, 14
Islamic fundamentalist groups, 178
Islamic groups, 6, 111
  radical and moderate, 115
Islamic hardline groups, 244
Islamic identity, 244
Islamic intellectual discourse, 41
Islamic interpretation, 88
  deep approach, 49
  philosophical approach, 49
  PKS in, 59
  progressive and moderate type, 61
  right-leaning, 61
Islamic (re)interpretation texts, 48
  activity within Persis, 50
  Cak Nur's general model of, 51
  conservative, 53
  deep and philosophical approach in, 49
  desacralization approach, 51
  hijrah, 56–58
  illiberal politics and liberal, 52–53

inclusive and progressive, 51
in Indonesia, 49–52
method of, 57
model of, 54
MUI dominance, 53–54
Muslim scholars, 49
newly emerging contestants for, 54–59
political Islam, 59–61
political state system, 53
populist orientations of, 58–59
puritanical approach in, 50, 56
solid methodology of, 52
Sunnah groups, 55–56
and traditions, 49
Islamic Judicature Act (1989), 100n8
Islamic judiciary, 83, 89
legal transaction in, 85
women involvement in, 85, 99
Islamic jurisprudence, 267
Islamic knowledge, 83
Islamic law (shariah), 21, 55, 64, 65, 78, 88, 248, 321
emergence of, 17
of familial issues, 95
Islamic laws in Indonesia (KHI), 100n4
Islamic legal rules, 86
Islamic legal theory, 137
Islamic literature, 146
Islamic movements, 106–7, 121, 154
Islamic organization, 1, 7, 243, 248, 308, 318
Islamic orientation, 13
Islamic political parties, 59
Islamic political system, 60
Islamic pop preachers, 244
Islamic populism, 223–28
Islamic preaching, 8, 9
Islamic proselytization, 335
Islamic radicalization, 23
Islamic religious arena, 2

Islamic religious authority, 83, 278
in Indonesia, 36
traditional construction of, 279
"Islamic revolution" (*Revolusi Islam*), 332
Islamic scholarship, 30, 33
Islamic State of Iraq and Syria (ISIS), 14
Islamic teaching, 8, 14
Islamic-themed films, 285, 288
Islamic tradition, 258
in Serang, 233
Islamic transnational organizations, 196
Islamic ummah, 332, 333
Islamic underground movement, 318, 322, 333, 337–39
Islamic values, 4
Islamic worships (*ibadah*), 335
Islamism, 223–28
Islamist groups, 33
Islamist movements, 164, 246
Islamist party, 116
Islamist political parties, 321
Islamization, 169
Islam kaffah, 4
Islam KTP, 4
"Islam Liberal", 38, 39
Islam Nusantara, 20, 22, 191, 230
Islam Transformatif (Moeslim Abdurrahman), 41
istiqbal, 186
Isya prayer, 249
i'tidal (justice), 264
i'tikaf, 184, 186–88

J
jabariyah (fatalism), 264
al-Jabri, Muhammad Abed, 49
JAF-Nus. *See* Nusantara Anti-Fascist Network
jahiliyah, 266

jahiliyya, 57
Jakarta gubernatorial election (2017), 58
Jakarta Post, 112
Jalan Dakwah Pesantren (film), 290
Jamaah Nahdliyin Mataram, 310
Jamaat al-Salafi al-Muhtasiba (JSM), 142
jawara, 228
al-Jawi, Abu Turab, 141
Jefri al Buchori, 90
Jejering Raja, 309
jihad, 111, 134, 140, 335, 336
jihadists, 14, 17, 134, 138–41, 143, 147
jinayah, 69, 74
    law enforcement, 64
JMSPSI. *See* Civil Society Network for Shariah Concerns (JMSPSI)
Joko Widodo, 263, 343n29
Junaid Al-Baghdadi, Imam, 264

K
kajian, 249, 252
karguzari, 178
kaum adat, 4
kaum padri, 4
kebhinekaan (diversity), 273
Keistimewaan, 307, 309–10, 312, 313
Keistimewaan Yogyakarta, 305
kejawen Muslims, 305
Keluarga Sakinah (the pious family), 121
Keraton of Yogyakarta, 297
Kesatuan Aksi Mahasiswa Muslim Indonesia (KAMMI), 106, 111
Khalid Basalamah, 55–57
Khariji, 143
khatim, 206
khilafah, 60, 61, 266, 272, 335
khuruj, 7, 8, 178–79, 184
    activity, 187
    basic rationale for, 188
    breeding ground for, 182–85
    experiences in Indonesia, 188
    foreign Tablighis planning to, 185
    group of five people, 186–87
    Indonesia to, 181
    registration process, 184
kiais, 164–66, 173
Kitab al-Tawhid, 146
kitab kuning, 282, 292n5
Kolektif Bunga, 327
kolot-kolot (the elders), 228
Komisi Pemilihan Umum (KPU), 304
Komite Indonesia Untuk Solidaritas dengan Dunia Islam (KISDI), 111
Kompilasi Hukum Islam, 84, 87
Kongres Ulama Perempuan Indonesia (KUPI), 91
Kuntowijoyo, 41
kyai, 85, 93, 228–29, 281–83
    of NU, 289
    to *santri* filmmakers, 291

L
Laskar Jihad, 140, 301
Laskar Surya Mataram, 310
Law No. 3/1950, 306
Law No. 5/1974, 306
Law No. 13/2012, 306
Law No. 18/1965, 306
Law No. 32/1956, 306
Law No. 46/1999, 303
Law of Marriage, 84, 86, 87
Left-wing activism, 321
legal modernization, 95–98
legal opinions, 92–93
legal reforms, 84, 86–89
Lesbumi, 284, 290, 292n8
LGBT acts, 121–22
liberal Islamic interpretation, 52–53
liberalism, 267
liberal political system, 52
Liberation Youth (LY), 331, 338

liqo' (campus-based religious learning groups), 323
literacy (*Iqra'*), 332
local Islam, 232
local Muslim organizations, 197
Lulu Susanti, 91
Lutfiah Sungkar, 91

M

madhāhib, 49, 50, 60
   framework of, 50
al-Madkhali, Rabi' ibn Hadi, 137, 142
madrasahs, 131, 138, 147
madzahib, 168
madzhab, 181–82
Maghrib prayer, 186, 190, 249
Mahkamah Syar'iyah (Syariah court), 66
Maimun Zubair, 269
majelis, 158–59
majelis taklim, 158, 166, 167, 170, 218
Majelis Ulama Indonesia (MUI), 36, 48, 50–51, 115
   centralized Islamic interpretation, 53
   dominance, 53–54
   fatwa, 58
majlis taklim, 323
Mamah Dedeh, 91–93, 95–96, 251
   conservative legal opinion of, 98
   legal opinion of, 97
   preaching programmes, 97
manhajī, 50
Mansour Fakih, 40, 41
Masjid al-Haram, 132, 133
mass-based Muslim organizations, 106, 111, 113, 122
al-Maturidi, Abu Mansur, 145
Maulana Rahman, 180, 181
maulid, 153, 265
medium-sized regency (*kabupaten*), 219

Medium-Term Development Plan (RPJM), 72
Menebar Dusta Membela Teroris Khawarij (2007), 144
Mereka Adalah Teroris (2005), 143
Mesjid Kebon Jeruk, 177
   committee of, 183
   functions of, 186
   glimpse of, 179–82
   imam in, 182
   khuruj, breeding ground for, 182–85
   religious gatherings, limited services for, 181
   steering committee of, 182, 192n5
   Tablighis, point of assembly, 185–88
meunasah, 73
Microjihad, 324, 340n8
micro-*ustadz* celebrity, 248–51, 253
middle-class Muslim groups, 216
Middle East, Salafi centres of learning in, 132
Ministry of Religious Affairs, Indonesia, 203
moderate Islamic organizations, 105, 106, 111, 112, 123
modern Indonesia, Sultanates in, 298–99
modern Islamist thinkers, 323
modern Islam, religious authority in, 9
modernization, 218
modern Muslims, 214
Moeslim Abdurrahman, 41
Mogerz Infantry, 326
moral authority, 108
moral decadence, bandwagon against, 115
moral degradation, 110
muḥaddith, 55
muballigh, 179, 181, 190
muhallil, 95
Muhammad (Prophet), 55, 56, 58

Muhammadiyah, 4–7, 13–16, 19–24, 36, 49, 52–53, 60, 288, 330
   ijtihād by, 50
   Nahdlatul Ulama and, 105, 113
   puritanical approach of, 49
   reformist approach, 52
Muhammadiyah central leadership, 244
mukholli, 95
Mukti Ali, 41
Municipal Police Service. *See* Satpol PP
murabbi (religious mentors), 323
Muslim
   Islamization and re-Islamization in, 214
   purification of, 135
"Muslim activist" (*aktivis Muslim*), 331
Muslim activists, 107
Muslim community, 2, 14, 191, 221
Muslim female authorities, in Indonesia, 84
   dakwah activities, 89–91
   female preachers. *See* female preachers
   involvement. *See* women's involvement
   judiciary, legal transaction in, 85
   media-using, 86
   religious authority. *See* religious authority
   in religious preaching, 89
   wide community, 86
Muslim fundamentalists, 13
Muslim groups, 57, 89
Muslim iconoclasts, 289
Muslim mass organizations, 36
Muslim public sphere, 44, 272
Muslim religious education, 44
Muslim religious intellectuals, 36, 37, 39
Muslim scholars, 49, 51
Muslim societies, 279
Muslim Student Action Union, 106
Muslim traditionalists, 153
Muslim unity (*Ukhuwah Islamiyyah*), 332
Muslim vigilante organizations, 54
Muslim world, 260, 279
Mustofa Bisri, Ahmad, 5, 6, 269

N
al-Nabhani, Taqiyuddin, 60
Nahdlatul Ulama (NU), 3–7, 13–16, 19–24, 36, 48, 50, 152–54, 163, 178, 243, 310, 330
   ʿaqīdah system of, 56
   civil society movements, 287
   cultural producers, 290
   Islamic tradition, 342n19
   Lembaga Bahtsul Masail (LBM), 159
   members, 52
   and Muhammadiyah, 52–53, 105, 113
   organization, 265
   strict affiliation of, 50
   theological concept of, 56
   ulama, 56
nahdliyyin, 259, 265, 273
Nakşibendi Sufi order, 205
Nanggroe Aceh Darussalam, 66
Naqshabandi group, 208
Naqshbandi Sulaimaniyah, 197
Nasir, Bachtiar, 59
Nasution, Harun, 38, 41, 51
National Awakening Party (PKB), 20, 59, 113
National Counterterrorism Agency (BNPT), 23
National Mandate Party (PAN), 59, 113
national Muslim scholars, 50
National Survey Media, 264

neo-khawarij activists, 143
neoliberal globalization, 317
neo-Salafi groups, 111
new contestants for Islamic interpretation, 54–59
   Sunnah group, 55–56
New Order, 17, 32, 41, 214, 216, 296, 299, 319, 339n2
   administration, 213, 233
   in 1998, 216
New Order regime, 153, 317
   in 1998, 219
niat (religious intention), 335
non-believers of Islam, 120
non-Islamic state system, 53
non-mainstream groups, 48, 54
non-military approach, 322
non-practising Muslims, 4
non-revolutionary approach, 140
normative competence, 76
   of DSI personnel, 78
normative texts of Islam, 278
North Moluccas, 303, 304, 308, 312
Noval Alaydrus, 157–59, 165, 168–70
NU-affiliated non-government organizations, 286
NU community, 284, 286
"NU Garis Lurus", 265
NU-Online, 287
Nurcholish Madjid, 32, 38, 41, 42, 51
Nusantara Anti-Fascist Network (JAF-Nus or ANTIFARA), 319, 327
nyai, 85

O
official Islam, 14–16
   religious authority of, 24
official Islamic organizations, 24
Oki Setiana Dewi, 91, 94, 95
Ombat, 326, 330, 341n15

One Day One Just (ODOJ) movement, 90, 240
One Finger Movement (OFM), 324–26, 338, 344n30
one finger salute, 326
One Million Ummah, 240
"opportunity spaces", concept of, 196, 198, 200
oppositional Islam, 6, 14–21
oppositional Islamic organizations, 17, 21
organizational influence, 110
Osama bin Laden, 143, 144

P
Paguyuban Seksi Pengamanan Keraton (Paksi Keraton), 310
pahala, 221
Pancasila, 53, 134, 273
Pancasila-based parties, 114–16, 120
panghulu, 228
panjang mulud, 231, 232
Partai Demokrat, 115
Partai Keadilan Sejahtera (PKS), 59–60, 292n4
   issues, 59
   ulama, 59
Partai Persatuan Demokrasi Kebangsaan (PPDK), 304
Partai Persatuan Pembangunan (PPP), 301
partisan politics, 113
"*Pejuang Khalifatullah*" (Khalifatullah Struggler), 310
pembaharuan Islam (Islamic renewal), 51
pembangunanisme (the ideology of developmentalism), 52
Pemuda Hijrah, 8, 241
   Indonesian public sphere, 252
   map of, 247
   tagline and audiences, 246–48

Ustadz Hanan Attaki (UHA) and, 244–46
Pemuda Hijrah Bandung, 50
pengajian, 181, 214–15, 217, 220, 223, 227, 231, 233
People's Democratic Party (PRD), 324
Persatuan Islam (Persis), 50
Persatuan Pengusaha Muslim Indonesia (PPMI), 142
Persatuan Umat Islam (PUI), 50
pesantren, 37, 42, 85, 89, 113, 155, 158, 159, 197, 202, 204, 208, 223, 231, 241, 281–83, 289
  kitab kuning, 292n5
  Muslims in, 284
Pevi Permana, 249
Pilkada, 301
Playboy magazine, 115
pluralism, 42, 267
pluralized Islamic authority, 278
policy convergence, 114
policy-making, conservative Islamic movements in, 108, 109, 113
political authority, reclaiming, 302–7
political Islam, 53, 59–61, 154
political Islamic movements, 217
political opportunity, 108
political parties, 107–10, 113
  ideological consistency in, 117
  ideologies of, 114
  in Indonesia, 114
pondok pesantren, 200–203
pop Islam, 216, 220–23
populism, 18
populist-oppositional Islam, 17–20
pornography
  definition, 114
  production and distribution, 114
Posko Referendum (Post Command Referendum), 306
post-authoritarian era, 313

post-authoritarian Indonesia, 10, 216, 320–22
postcolonial Islamic thinkers, 340n13
post-independent Indonesia, 32
post-New Order era
  aswaja dakwah and anti-Wahhabism in, 154–56
  democratic administrations, 217
post-New Order Indonesia, 151, 220
post-Suharto era, 299, 300, 304, 321
post-Suharto Indonesia, 288
Prabowo Subianto, 263–64
preachers, religious authority and, 268–71
Pribumisasi Islam, 41
private television channels, proliferation and establishment of, 3
priyayi, 3
Prophetic Traditions (hadith), 141, 146
Prophet Muhammad, 167, 183, 189, 220, 265
Prosperous Justice Party (PKS), 116, 243
provincial DSI, 75
Provincial Legislation Programme in 2018, 70
public domain, 48
public religious authority, 84
public spaces, 18
public sphere, 13, 32, 154
"Punk Muslim", 328, 338
Punk Muslim Surabaya (PMS), 328
puritanical approach
  of Islam, 49
  of Muhammadiyah, 49

Q

qadariyah (free will), 264
qanun (law/bill), 69, 71
qawlī, 50

quietists, 134, 138–41
quietist Salafism, 133, 134
Quraish Shihab, 33, 51, 56, 269
Quran, 21, 22, 55, 132, 139, 141, 168
    interpretation of, 55
Quranic literacy, 72
Quran memorization, 199
    Ottoman method of, 199
Qurratu A'yun, 91

R
rabita (oath taking), 205, 206
Rabitat al-'Alam al-Islami (the Muslim World League), 155
radical groups, 115, 120
Rahardjo, M. Dawam, 40, 41
raka'at, 184, 231
Rakornis, 70, 71
"Ramadan with Punk Muslim" (bulletin), 329
Rapat Koordinasi Teknis (Technical Coordination Meeting). *See* Rakornis
rational authority, 35
realpolitik, 41
reformasi era, 2, 9, 36, 285, 324
    identity politics in, 299–302
    Suharto's authoritarian regime to, 303
    in Yogyakarta, 301
reformasi movement, 297
    of 1998, 297
reformation (*reformasi*) period, 17
reformist groups, 29
reformist thinkers, 90
Regional Development Planning Agency (Bappeda), 72
reinterpretation of Islamic texts, in Indonesia, 49–52
re-Islamization, 224
religious authority, 1, 2, 83, 251–52
    in contemporary Indonesia, 83
    contestation and fragmentation of, 9
    contestation phenomenon of, 5
    democratization of, 5
    making of, 228–33
    in modern Islam, 9
    Muslim women in public, 84
    of official Islam, 24
    politization of, 8
    and preachers, 268–71
religious commodification, 220–23
religious discourse, 43
religious intellectuals, 6, 28–30, 37, 38
    definition of, 30–31
religious knowledge, 9, 135, 138
religious leadership, 29
religiously motivated activists, 108
religiously-oriented programmes, 90
religious minority groups, 54
religious organizations, 2
religious preachers, 91
religious preaching, 89
religious right, rise of, 320–22
religious traditionalism, 29
Republika, 263, 324
Rhoma Irama, 335, 336
right-wing Islamism, 321
right-wing Islamist organizations, 321
Rizieq Shihab, Habib, 5, 59, 112, 165, 167, 267
RPJM. *See* Medium-Term Development Plan (RPJM)

S
Sabdaraja, 309–10
Sabdatama, 308
Sabdatama I, 309
Sabili, 322, 326, 336
sadaqah, 55
Sahal, cinematic practices of, 286–88
Said Aqil Siradj, 33, 160, 163–64, 166
SA'I zine, 332, 333

Salaf al-Salih, 146, 148
Salafi *dakwah*, 138
Salafi doctrine, in Indonesia, 155
Salafi expansion, 134
Salafi group, 7, 154, 163, 246
Salafi-inspired Muslim groups, 225, 232
Salafi interpretations, 53, 55, 57
Salafi Jihadists, 147
Salafi *madrasahs*, 137
Salafi media technology, proliferation of, 156
Salafi movement, 133, 156
Salafi-oriented foundations, 131
Salafi-oriented publishers, 132
Salafis, 157
  conflict within, 138–41
Salafism, 8, 131, 141, 148, 155, 216
  dakwah expansion of, 157
  efflorescence of, 132–34
  and Islamic education, 145–47
Salafist doctrines, 215
Salafi-Wahhabi group, 151, 164, 167
Salafi-Wahhabi movement, 152
Samudra, Imam, 143–45
sanad, 172
santri, 3, 4, 9, 24, 85
santri-abangan, 4
santri communities, 280–83
santri kolot, 4
santri moderen, 4
santri Muslims, 305
Sarjana Kuburan (Sarkub), 160–63
Satpol PP, 73–74, 79, 341n16
Saudi Arabia, collaborations with Indonesia, 133
Saudi campaign, 131–32
Saudi Salafism, 155
secularism, 267
Sekber Gamawan (Association for the Special Status of Yogyakarta), 306

Serang, Islamic tradition in, 233
sesat, 56
Shafi'i juristic doctrine, 89
sharia, 215
shariah enforcement, 65
shariah implementation in Aceh, 64, 65, 73
sharia law, 116–17, 217
Shia, 166, 323
  ideology, 328
Shi'ism, 166
shirk, 225
Siauw, Felix, 60, 241, 258, 269
sinetrons, 90
Sinta Nuriyah, 85, 91
Sjadzali, Munawir, 51
slametan (traditional feast), 264
social media, 39, 240, 337–38
  in *dakwah*, 90
  of movement organizations, 107
  prevalent use of, 51
social media platforms, 14, 241
social movement organizations, 107–10
social movement theories, 107, 108
Soneta group, 335, 336
Soroush, Abdol Karim, 30, 31, 34, 42
South Moluccas, 303
state Islamic law, 88, 92–93, 95, 98
Strategic Plan of the Special Province of Aceh 2001–2005, 66
Sub Chaos, 327, 333
Sub Chaos Zine, 341n14
Sufi leaders, 279
Sufi linkages, 207
Sufis, 168
Sufi saints, 335
Sufi wisdom, 258
Suharto, 52, 53, 317
  administration, 220
  ideology of national development, 52

illiberal politics, 52
New Order, 6, 297, 299
regimist *fatwa*-maker in, 51
Suharto era (1966–98), 49
Sukarno presidency, 253
Sulaimaniyah, 8
  case study of, 196–97
  curriculum and level of education, 204–5
  high-quality free Islamic boarding schools, 200–204
  in Indonesia, 197–200
  Sufi brotherhood among, 205–7
Süleyman Hilmi Tunahan, 197, 198, 200, 201
Sultanate for Yogyakarta, 306
Sultanate of Ternate, 302, 303
  succession of, 308
Sultanate of Tidore, 300
Sultanate of Yogyakarta, 9, 311
sultanates, in modern Indonesia, 298–99
Sultan Hamengkubuwono IX (HB IX), 299, 305, 306
Sultan HB X, 304–5, 308
Sultan Mudaffar Shah, 304, 307, 308, 311
Sultan of Ternate, 308, 312
Sultan of Yogyakarta, 302, 313
Sungkar, Abdullah, 134
Sunnah, 132, 139, 168, 225
Sunnah groups, 55–56
  and NU members, 56
Sunni authority, 167–71
Sunni, in Indonesia, 152–54
Sunni Islam, 1, 2, 152, 153
Sunni Muslims, 36, 167
Sunnism, 164, 167, 172
Sunni theology, 264
Susilo Bambang Yudhoyono (SBY), 312
Syafiq Riza Basalamah, 55, 57

Syrian civil war, 267

T
Tablighi Jamaat/Tablighis, 6, 178
  activities, 179, 180
  doctrines of, 183
  host institution for, 185
  Muslims in Indonesia, 190
  nurturing religious authority among, 188–90
  point of assembly, 185–88
  Syuro council of, 180, 189
  Ushulus Sittah, 182–83
Tadabur Al-Quran, 245
Tadrib al-Du'at (training for preachers), 138
tadzkirah (warning), 59
tafsir (Quranic exegesis), 51, 244
Tafsir al-Furqan, 50
taghut, 134
tahfidz, 197
tahlil (death ritual), 264, 265
tahlilan, 225, 231, 232
tajdīd, 50
tajwid, 205
Tarbiyah groups, 20
Tarbiyah movement, 246
Tarbiyat al-Nisa (education for women), 138
tarbiyya (education), 132
tarikat Sufism, 207
tasamuh (tolerance), 264
tasawwuf, 205, 206
tasfiyya (purification), 132
tashkil. See *khuruj*
tauhid, 135, 136
tawasuth (moderatism), 264
tawazun (balance), 264
tawhid, 145
Tawhid 3, 145–46, 148
Teologi Kiri (Mulkhan), 41
Thalib, Ja'far Umar, 140, 143

Thayib Armain, 301, 304
Thobary Syadzily, 161–63
Thufail Al Ghifari, 322–24, 327, 330, 337, 340n7
traditional authority, 260
  exploratory project challenging, 288–91
traditional Islam, 172, 173
  in Indonesia, 152–54
traditional Islamic authority, 171–72
traditional Islamic jurisprudence, 58
traditionalist group of Islam, 4
traditionalist Islam, 151
traditionalist Islamic organization, 113
traditionalist Muslim Indonesia, 291
traditionalist Muslim scholars, 48
traditionalist Muslim society, Islamic authority in, 291
traditional Muslim authorities, 260
traditional structure of Islamic authority, 190
traditional *ulama*, 31
transnational Islamic movements, 2, 7, 198
transnational Islamist groups, 17
triple divorce (*talak ba'in*), 92
"true" Islam, 223
Turkish Muslim movements, 199
  in Indonesia, 196
Turkish organizations, 197, 201
Turkish piety movements, 197
Turkish revivalist movements, 197
Turkish Sufi movement, 197

U
Ucok Homicide, 252, 339n2
UIN Jakarta, 51
ukhuwah (unity/fraternity), 264, 273
  ukhuwah Insaniyah (unity in humanity), 264

ukhuwah Islamiyah (Islamic unity), 264
ukhuwah wathaniyah (national unity), 264
ulama, 1, 3–6, 29, 32, 35, 37, 39, 83, 97, 144, 153, 162, 166, 168, 172, 190, 269–71
  council, 300
  and religious preachers, 91
Ulama Perempuan Indonesia, 91
Ulil Abshar Abdalla, 160
ummah, 216, 223, 225, 233
umrah, 216, 220, 267
underground movement, in Indonesia, 318–20
Underground Tauhid (UGT), 328, 334, 338, 342n22
underground youths, 10, 317
United Development Party (PPP), 20, 301
United Islamic Cultural Centre of Indonesia (UICCI), 199, 205
United Yogyakarta Movement, 306
UNKL 247, 245–46
Urban Garage Festival I, 326, 340n12
Urban Garage Festival II, 340n12
urban middle-class Muslims, 213
  in contemporary Indonesia, 216–20
ustadhs, 137–38
ustadz (religious teacher), 1, 37, 55, 177, 215, 229, 231
Ustadz Abdul Somad (UAS), 9, 58, 61, 259, 260
  "Datuk Seri Ulama Setia Negara", 263
  ideology of, 264–68
  new media, era of, 272
  profile of, 261–64
Ustadz Hanan Attaki (UHA), 8, 57, 239, 246, 248
  and *Pemuda Hijrah*, 244–51

al-Uthaimin, Muhammad Salih, 131–32, 136, 137, 141

V
visual media space, case of, 285

W
Wahhabi doctrine, 138
Wahhabi interpretations, 53, 55, 57
Wahhabism, 7, 164, 167, 168, 170, 173
Wahid Institute (2014), 302
wasatiyya Islam, 141
wayang (puppet), 264
"We Build This City", 245
western feminism movements, 121
Western scholarships, 4
WhatsApp, 240
"white revolution" (*Revolusi Putih*), 332
Wilayatul Hisbah (WH), 66, 73
  roles and noble mission, 73
  and Satpol PP, 73–74, 79
women(s)
  education, 84
  empowerment of, 85, 91
  gender asymmetries in, 92–93
  in Indonesia, 89
  in Islamic judiciary, 85
  legal awareness, 88
  legal rights, 93
  litigants, 84
  rights, 84
women's involvement
  in education, 84
  in Islamic education, 85
  in Islamic judiciary, 83
  in leadership, 83
  in religious authority, 83

Y
Yazid bin Abdul Qadir Jawas, 55, 147
yasinan, 225
Yogyakarta, *reformasi* era in, 301
youth community, 249
YouTube, 56
Yusuf, Abu Hamza, 143
Yusuf Mansur, 90, 251
Yusuf, Muhamad Fahrudin, 91, 96

Z
al-Zabidi, al-Imam al-Murtada, 168
Zainuddin MZ, 240
zakat, 55
Zaki, Ahmad, 328, 330, 341n16
Zakiyah Darajat, 91
ziarah, 232
ziarah kubur, 265
zikir, 206
Zulkarnain, Tengku, 59

www.ingramcontent.com/pod-product-compliance
Lightning Source LLC
Chambersburg PA
CBHW070009010526
44117CB00011B/1483